D0978123

SO MANY VERSIONS?

Twentieth-century English
Versions of the Bible

Revised and Enlarged Edition

Sakae Kubo & Walter F. Specht

Academie
Books Grand Rapids,
Michigan
Zondervan Publishing House

So Many Versions?
Copyright © 1975, 1983 by The Zondervan Corporation
Grand Rapids, Michigan

ACADEMIE BOOKS are published by Zondervan
Publishing House, 1415 Lake Drive, S.E.,
Grand Rapids, Michigan 49506

Library of Congress Cataloging in Publication Data

Kubo, Sakae, 1926–
 So many versions?

  1. Bible. English—Versions. I. Specht, Walter F.
(Walter Frederick) II. Title.

BS455.K8   1983   220.5′2   82-21965
ISBN 0-310-45691-6

All rights reserved. No part of this publication may be reproduced, stored in a
retrieval system, or transmitted in any form by any means—electronic,
mechanical, photocopy, recording, or any other—except for brief quotations in
printed reviews, without the prior permission of the publisher.

Edited by Mark Hunt
Designed by Mark Hunt

Printed in the United States of America

86   87   88   89   90 / 15   14   13   12   11   10   9

Contents

Preface to Revised Edition

The appearance of several important new Bibles since the first publication of this volume in 1975, and the revisions of older ones, have made imperative a revision of *So Many Versions?* We have been encouraged to undertake this updating by the wide use and favorable reviews given the first edition. A new edition has also afforded an opportunity of making corrections here and there.

The major changes in this edition include the following:

1. A revision and updating of chapter 2, "The Revised Standard Version," to take note of an ecumenical edition, and to provide some information regarding changes to be incorporated in the forthcoming second edition of the RSV. We are indebted to Professor Bruce M. Metzger, the current chairman of the RSV Committee, for our knowledge of this new edition and the changes it will contain.

2. A significant expansion of chapter 7, "The New Jewish Version," to include a discussion and evaluation of The Prophets, published in 1978, and The Writings, published in 1982, by the Jewish Publication Society of America. The completion of the New Jewish Version must be regarded as a very significant addition to recent versions of the Old Testament.

3. A thorough revision and expansion of chapter 11, "Today's English Version," made necessary by the publication of the entire Good News Bible (GNB) in 1976. For the first time the entire Old Testament of that version became available, calling for a careful examination and evaluation of that portion of the TEV. Not only so, but the New Testament portion of the Good News Bible contains the fourth edition of the New Testament. The extensive changes made in it as compared with the third edition made some of the comments we offered obsolete. Hence chapter 11 has been thoroughly updated, and much new material has been added.

We are indebted to Professor Keith R. Crim, one of the translators of the GNB Old Testament, for helpful information regarding the goals and methods of the OT committee of translators. We are also indebted to Dr. Erroll F. Rhodes of the American Bible Society for providing us with copies of the British usage edition of the version.

4. An expansion and revision of chapter 16, "The New International Version," called for by the publication of the entire NIV in 1978 that included the entire OT as well as revisions in the NT.

5. The addition of a new chapter dealing with the New King James Version, the NT of which was published in 1979, and the entire Bible in the summer of 1982.

We are indebted to Robert L. Sanford, of the Bible Editorial Department of Thomas Nelson, Inc., for supplying us with information regarding the history of this new version, and for allowing us to examine galley proofs of major portions of the OT. We are also indebted to Dr. Arthur L. Farstad for helpful information.

6. The addition of a chapter dealing with several colorful, free versions such as Wuest's Expanded Translation of the Greek New Testament, Jordan's Cotton Patch Version, Burke's God Is For Real, Man, Edington's The Word Made Fresh, Williams's and Shaw's The Gospels in Scouse.

7. The addition of a chapter on The Reader's Digest Bible, a

condensation of the Revised Standard Version, published in September 1982.

8. In the back of the volume the addition of a glossary dealing with some thirty-three technical terms that may be unfamiliar to some readers.

9. Finally, an attempt has been made to update the "Annotated List of Twentieth-century English Translations" in the Appendix, as well as the Bibliography. As an aid to the lay reader who is not familiar with the technical terms biblical scholars use, a glossary of thirty-three terms found in the volume has been added.

We trust that this revised edition of *So Many Versions?* may continue to serve as a guide to those who wish to know about English Bibles of the twentieth century.

Sakae Kubo
Walter F. Specht

Acknowledgments

Appreciation is expressed to the following publishers for permission to use selections from the Bible translations for which they hold copyright:

THE AMERICAN BIBLE SOCIETY. *Good News Bible*, the Bible in Today's English Version. Copyright © American Bible Society, 1976. Good News for Modern Man, The New Testament in Today's English Version. Copyright © American Bible Society, 1966, 1971.

WILLIAM COLLINS SONS AND COMPANY, LTD. *Barclay's New Testament* by William Barclay. Copyright © 1968, 1970 by William Collins Sons and Company, Ltd. Quoted by permission of William Collins & World Publishing Co., Inc., Cleveland, Ohio.

CONFRATERNITY OF CHRISTIAN DOCTRINE. *The New American Bible*. Copyright © Confraternity of Christian Doctrine, 1970.

DARTON, LONGMAN & TODD, LTD. and DOUBLEDAY & COMPANY, INC. *The Jerusalem Bible*. Copyright © 1966 by Darton, Longman & Todd, Ltd.

DIVISION OF CHRISTIAN EDUCATION, NATIONAL COUNCIL OF CHURCHES OF CHRIST IN THE UNITED STATES OF AMERICA. *The Revised Standard Version of the Bible*, copyright 1946, 1952, © 1971,

1973; and the *Revised Standard Version Common Bible,* copyright © 1973 by The Division of Christian Education, National Council of the Churches of Christ in the United States of America.

DUKE DIVINITY SCHOOL REVIEW. Excerpts from Edward Harwood's New Testament translation (1768) and Rodolphus Dickinson's *A New and Corrected Version of the New Testament* (1833) are reprinted from Bruce M. Metzger, "The Revised Standard Version," *Duke Divinity School Review* 44 (1979): 71–72, by permission of the publisher.

ANDREW EDINGTON. *The Word Made Fresh.* 3 vols. Copyright © 1975–1976.

WM. B. EERDMANS PUBLISHING CO. *Expanded Translation of the Greek New Testament* by Kenneth Wuest. 3 vols. Copyright © 1956–1959. Used by permission of Wm. B. Eerdmans Publishing Co.

HARPER AND ROW PUBLISHERS, INC. and HODDER AND STOUGHTON, LTD, *The New Testament,* A New Translation by James Moffatt. Copyright © 1964 by James Moffatt. Used by permission of Harper and Row, Inc. and Hodder and Stoughton, Ltd.

HARPER AND ROW PUBLISHERS, INC. and JAMES CLARKE AND COMPANY, LTD. *Weymouth's New Testament in Modern Speech* by Richard Francis Weymouth, as revised by J. A. Robertson. By permission of Harper and Row Publishers, Inc. and James Clarke and Company, Ltd.

THE JEWISH PUBLICATION SOCIETY OF AMERICA. A New Translation of the Holy Scriptures according to the Masoretic Text. First Section, *Torah: The Five Books of Moses.* Copyright © 1962, 1973, The Jewish Publication Society of America. Second Section, *The Prophets Nevi'im.* Copyright © 1978, The Jewish Publication Society of America. Third Section, *The Writings, Kethubim.* Copyright © 1982, The Jewish Publication Society of America.

THE LOCKMAN FOUNDATION. *The New American Standard Bible.* Copyright © 1960, 1962, 1963, 1968, 1971 by the Lockman Foundation.

THE MACMILLAN COMPANY and COLLINS PUBLISHERS. *The New Testament in Modern English.* Copyright © 1958, 1959, 1960 by

J. B. Phillips. *The Gospels* © 1952, 1957 by The Macmillan Company; *The Young Church in Action* © 1955 by The Macmillan Company; *Letters to Young Churches* © 1947, 1957 by The Macmillan Company; *The Book of Revelation* © 1957 by The Macmillan Company; *The Four Prophets* © 1963 by The Macmillan Company.

MOODY PRESS. *The Twentieth Century New Testament.*

THOMAS NELSON AND SONS. *The New King James Version.* Copyright © 1979, 1980, 1982, Thomas Nelson, Inc., Publishers.

NEW CENTURY PUBLISHERS, INC. *The Cotton Patch Version of Matthew and John* by Clarence Jordon © 1970. By permission of New Century Publishers, Inc., Piscataway, N.J. 08854. *God Is For Real, Man* by Carl F. Burke © 1969. By permission of New Century Publishers, Inc., Piscataway, N.J. 08854.

OXFORD UNIVERSITY PRESS and CAMBRIDGE UNIVERSITY PRESS. *The New English Bible.* Copyright © The Delegates of the Oxford University Press and The Syndics of the Cambridge University Press 1961, 1970.

READER'S DIGEST ASSOCIATION. *The Reader's Digest Bible* © 1982 by The Reader's Digest Association, Inc. Used by permission.

THE RELIGIOUS EDUCATION ASSOCIATION OF THE UNITED STATES AND CANADA. *Dig This: The Revealing of Jesus Christ* by Jeffrey N. Stinehelfer. Reprinted from the November–December 1969 issue of the journal, *Religious Education,* by permission of the publisher. The Religious Education Association, 409 Prospect St., New Haven, Conn. 06510. Membership or subscription available for $25.00 per year.

SEVERN HOUSE. *The Gospels in Scouse* by Dick Williams and Frank Shaw.

SHEED AND WARD, INC. and BURNS AND OATES, LTD. *The New Testament in the Translation of Monsignor Ronald Knox.* Copyright © 1944, 1948, and 1950 by Sheed and Ward, Inc., New York, with the kind permission of His Eminence, the Cardinal Archbishop of Westminster and Burns and Oates, Ltd.

TYNDALE HOUSE PUBLISHERS, *The Living Bible* by Kenneth N. Taylor, Copyright © 1971 by Tyndale House Publishers.

THE UNIVERSITY OF CHICAGO PRESS. *The New Testament: An American Translation* by Edgar J. Goodspeed, copyright © 1923, 1948 by the University of Chicago.

WATCHTOWER BIBLE AND TRACT SOCIETY. *New World Translation of the Holy Scriptures.* Copyright © 1950, 1953, 1955, 1957, 1958, 1960. *The Bible in Living English.* Copyright © 1972. The Watchtower Bible and Tract Society.

ZONDERVAN PUBLISHING HOUSE. *The Amplified Bible.* Copyright © 1954, 1958 by The Lockman Foundation. Copyright © 1962, 1964, 1965 by Zondervan Publishing House.

ZONDERVAN PUBLISHING HOUSE. *The Holy Bible, The Berkeley Version in Modern English* by Gerrit Verkuyl. Copyright © 1945, 1959, 1969 by Zondervan Publishing House.

ZONDERVAN PUBLISHING HOUSE. *The New International Version of the New Testament.* Copyright © 1973 by New York Bible Society International.

Abbreviations

AB	Amplified Bible
ASV	American Standard Version
BLE	Bible in Living English
GNB	Good News Bible
JB	Jerusalem Bible
KJV	King James Version
LB	Living Bible
LXX	Septuagint
MLB	Modern Language Bible (Berkeley)
MS(S)	manuscript, manuscripts
NAB	New American Bible
NASB	New American Standard Bible
NEB	New English Bible
NIV	New International Version
NJV	New Jewish Version
NKJV	New King James Version
NT	New Testament
NWT	New World Translation
OT	Old Testament
RDB	Reader's Digest Bible
RSV	Revised Standard Version
TEV	Today's English Version

Introduction

There is a need for a comprehensive evaluation of current versions of the Bible. Although there are good treatments of the history of the English Bible, they cannot give detailed treatment of every translation, especially recent ones. Moreover, new translations are constantly appearing and such books need updating from time to time. This book is an attempt to fill this gap. It is not possible to discuss every version, but we have selected what we consider to be the most important ones on the basis of their use today. However, we have included in the appendix as complete a list of twentieth-century English Bibles with annotations as we could compile.

There are several significant trends that we notice in twentieth-century Bible translations. One of the most significant is the abandonment of the King James Version tradition in the "official" Bibles—the Protestant New English Bible and the Jewish Publication Society Bible. Catholic Bibles likewise no longer follow the Rheims-Challoner tradition. Future "official" Bibles will undoubtedly follow this trend.

Another significant change is the almost complete dominance of one form or another of a critical Greek text in the NT, especially in recent translations. The major exception is the New King James Version, which retains the defective Textus Receptus on which the classic King James of 1611 was based. In the OT, the Masoretic text is still basic but is challenged by ancient versions and the biblical MSS of the Dead Sea Scrolls.

Among Catholic translations, the significant change has been in the use of the original languages rather than the Vulgate as the base for translation. In this respect, Ronald Knox's translation came a bit too soon. In Catholic Bibles also there is a noticeable reduction of specifically Catholic notes and explanations.

The incorporation of the principles of linguistics is a new trend that probably will influence future translations as it has already the GNB. The translation of Bibles for those with limited English background is influenced by the dominance of English in the Western as well as the Third World. A trend that is advanced especially in France is developing in this country with the adoption of the Common Bible. In the future, Catholics and Protestants will move beyond the adoption of a mutually acceptable RSV and will work together in the translation of a completely new Common Bible, although even now Protestants and Catholics use each other's Bibles freely, without official objection, since their most recent translations are quite similar.

In the evaluation of these versions, it is well to keep in mind the reasons for the continual publication of new translations. No translation of the Bible can ever be considered final. Translations must keep pace with the growth in biblical scholarship and the changes in language. It may be helpful to list the three main reasons for new versions of the sacred text.

The first reason is that the discovery of older and better manuscripts for both Testaments enables the scholar of today to have a sounder text of the original to translate. Several outstanding Greek MSS of the NT have come to light in this century. The oldest of these were written on papyrus. One of the most important collections of biblical papyrus MSS was acquired in 1930/31 by Chester Beatty and is now in the Beatty museum in a suburb of Dublin. Three of these were NT codices. One contained portions of 30 leaves of an estimated original 220 of the four Gospels and Acts dated in the first half of the third century. Another, dated around 200, has 86 leaves of an original

104 of 10 of Paul's Epistles. The third comprises 10 of an estimated original 32 leaves of the Book of Revelation from the middle or latter part of the third century.

More recently, about 1956, another collection of papyrus MSS of the NT came into the hands of M. Martin Bodmer, a Genevan bibliophile and humanist. They are now in the Bodmer Library of World Literature at Cologny, a suburb of Geneva. Among them was a papyrus codex MS known as Bodmer Papyrus II, containing most of the Gospel of John, and dated by the editor, Victor Martin, Professor of Classical Philology at Geneva, about A.D. 200. Another MS in the group contains the earliest-known copies of Jude and 1 and 2 Peter. The editor, Michel Testuz, dates it in the third century. A third codex contains the oldest-known copy of Luke and one of the earliest of John. The editors, Victor Martin and Rodolphe Kasser, date it between A.D. 175 and 225. It would be difficult to overestimate the textual importance of these newly acquired witnesses for the wording of the NT. Besides these, the most important early MSS known before the twentieth century were not fully utilized by the major translations.

For the OT there are the world famous Dead Sea Scrolls discovered in 1947 and since. The biblical scrolls among them are so sensationally significant because they have carried our knowledge of the Hebrew Bible back a thousand years. Before their discovery, apart from a few scraps, the oldest Hebrew MSS known were dated toward the end of the ninth century A.D. But now there are MSS to be dated as early as the first century B.C. These discoveries have their bearing on the conclusion of scholars regarding the original wording of the sacred Scriptures.

In the second place, along with the discovery of these earlier MSS, there has developed a better understanding of the meaning of these original languages. This is largely due to the wonderful archaeological discoveries of the past century. As an illustration of this significant point, there are the discoveries of nonliterary papyri that have shown what many of the Greek words used by NT writers meant in daily life. For the study of the OT languages there is an abundance of written documents such as the Amarna Tablets, the Lachish Letters, the Jewish-

Aramaic papyri, and the Canaanite tablets found at Ugarit, to name but a few. All of these have given scholars a better understanding of what the languages of the Bible really mean. Such knowledge must be reflected in better translations.

Earlier translations such as the KJV did not have the advantage of these tremendous discoveries. The KJV was dependent on late MSS of the Middle Ages, which had been corrupted as they were copied and recopied by hand through the ages. Translators today have access to MSS that are in some cases less than a century removed from the autographs. As a result, today we have translations that are more in harmony with what the apostles actually wrote. New understandings of the original languages through archaeological discoveries have helped to shed light on obscure passages and have aided us in understanding some passages better than they were understood before.

Finally, one of the major reasons for the revisions of the English Bible is the tremendous change constantly taking place in the English language. Languages are living and constantly changing. Many words become obsolete. Others change their meaning with the passing of time. Even in the Revised Versions, both English and American, words are used that are foreign to modern readers.

These are good and compelling reasons for producing new translations of the Bible. Perhaps, however, some will feel that there is a glut of translations on the market today. There are more than the people can digest. Some feel it is time to call a halt to the work of translation for a while until we absorb the flood of recent translations. At any rate, we hope that this volume will help in the evaluation of the many Bibles on the market today.

Perhaps something should be said about paraphrase and translation. As it is ordinarily used, the word "paraphrase" refers to a freely rendered restatement of a passage in a clearer form in the same language without altering its meaning. In using this word for Bible translation from one language to another, it has come to connote a rather free translation in which phrases are added or omitted and often fidelity to the meaning is thus sacrificed. Dr. Eugene Nida, in an article in the

Bible Translator (1 [July, 1950], 97–106), deplores the distinction between translation and paraphrase since it fails to take into consideration that in some instances the only way to translate is to paraphrase. He gives the example "bowels of mercies," which should be translated as "compassion" or "tender compassion." However, Nida admits that that type of paraphrasing is exceptional rather than usual. What Nida fails to consider in his article is that this term is not used for those translations that commonly "paraphrase" certain idioms or phrases. The usual meaning of "translation" is not opposed to using "paraphrase" in the kind of example Nida gives. What is meant by paraphrase is that the translator takes undue liberties throughout in adding, omitting, and altering the original in such a way that often the equivalence in meaning is not transferred. This does not mean that a mere slavish literalism to the form of the original is a good translation. Usually, in fact, such "faithful" translations are not translations at all. There is no quarrel with Nida's principles of translation from the point of view of dynamic equivalence but only with his attempt to identify "paraphrase" with "translation," not with respect to certain idioms alone but to the whole range of translation. There is a useful distinction that these words still make when used in this sense.

The word "paraphrase" also fittingly describes what Nida objects to—that which he calls "cultural translation" in distinction from "linguistic translation."[1] Beekman and Callow refer to Jordan's Cotton Patch Version, which substitutes contemporary Southern peoples, places, and parties for the biblical ones. For example, Corinth becomes Atlanta in 1 Corinthians 1:1 and Jews become "whites" and Gentiles, "Negroes."[2] They also refer to Captain J. Rogers's translation of the seaman's version of Psalm 23: "The Lord is my Pilot; I shall not drift," etc.[3] Such examples are dynamic equivalence with a vengeance. All responsible translators will avoid such renderings.

---

[1]Eugene Nida, *The Theory and Practice of Translation* (New York: Adler, 1969), p. 13.

[2]John Beekman and John Callow, *Translating the Word of God* (Grand Rapids: Zondervan, 1974), p. 35.

[3]Beekman and Callow, *Translating the Word*, p. 41.

Besides being opposed to lack of fidelity to historical references as in the above instances, Beekman and Callow are also against the same regarding didactic references. The latter refer to "commands, illustrations, parables, and similitudes." However, when wrong or zero meaning results from the maintenance of a word, fidelity to meaning "takes precedence over fidelity to the historical nature of the imagery," and thus a substitution may be justified.[4] Even here great care must be exercised.

Sometimes a translation becomes a mini-commentary, since explanations of words or expressions are placed in the text without indicating that these were not part of the original text. Some of these go beyond making explicit in the receptor language what was implicit in the original. Barclay does this type of thing in his translation. For instance, Matthew 9:17 reads, "Neither is new wine put into old wineskins" in the RSV, but Barclay has "No more do people pour new *fermenting* wine into old wineskins *that have lost their elasticity.*" Is this legitimate or not? Has Barclay placed in the text what should have been placed in the notes? How about his translation of Matthew 10:38: "Can you be submerged in the sea of troubles in which I must be submerged?" for "Are you able to drink the cup that I drink, or to be baptized with the baptism with which I am baptized?" Here the translator has taken over the role of a commentator and sets forth his commentary as a translation. This is the danger of paraphrases that are put forth as or considered translations. The free quality makes it easy for the translator to insert interpretations or other clarifying matters into the text. There is a place for such paraphrases as aids to the better understanding of Scripture if they are so identified. In this sense they stand between a true translation, which transfers the meaning of the original as accurately as possible, and a commentary, which gives a full-scale interpretation.

As much as possible, therefore, the translator must be faithful to his text while at the same time faithful to the receptor language. Historical and cultural references should not be altered. Notes can be used to explain what may not be clear to the reader

---

[4]Beekman and Callow, *Translating the Word*, pp. 36–37.

while at the same time the translation should be in the idiom and structures of the language into which the Scriptures are translated. This is not always an easy task, but we should not open the door to too free renderings through the general identification of translation with paraphrase. It is true that the basic distinction is whether a translation is faithful or not, for example, whether it

> transfers the meaning and the dynamics of the original text. . . . The expression, *transfers the meaning,* means that the translation conveys to the reader or hearer the information that the original conveyed to its readers or hearers. The message is not distorted or changed; it has neither unnecessarily gained nor lost information. The expression, *the dynamics,* means that (1) the translation makes a natural use of the linguistic structures of the RL [receptor language] and that (2) the recipients of the translation understand the message with ease.[5]

The key words in the above definition are "it has neither *unnecessarily* gained nor lost information." The crux of the problem is right at that point. Take Barclay's translation of Matthew 9:17 concerning new wine. He has actually clarified the meaning of the text. Is this legitimate translation or has he exceeded the bounds of translation? In our view, although the meaning has been clarified, he has not translated accurately. He has become a commentator. How much may a translator add and still be faithful? What may be added are only those things that are necessary to the accurate transference of the original into the linguistic structure of the receptor language. In his translation above, Barclay has exceeded this limitation. He has not merely made changes to suit the *linguistic* structure of the receptor language. What he has done, in fact, was to add content beyond that of the original. Such additions, if necessary, should be made in the notes.

Where we have differed with the translators, it has not been because they have used paraphrases, which may be necessary and legitimate, but because they have not been accurate in the transference of the meaning of the original into the structure of English.

---

[5]Beekman and Callow, *Translating the Word,* pp. 33–34.

1

Early Modern Speech Versions

The Reformers of the Protestant Reformation gave great impetus to the truth that the Bible belongs to common people. The Bible was not intended for scholars alone, but for common, ordinary men and women. It was this concept that led to translations in the vernacular. In the latter part of the fourteenth century, John Wycliffe, the first translator of the complete Bible into English, intended his version for ordinary people and put it in plain, pithy language. In the revised edition of this Bible, John Purvey wrote in the preface:

> Though covetous clerks are mad through Simony, heresy and many other sins, and despise and impede Holy Writ as much as they can, yet the unlearned cry after Holy Writ to know it, with great cost and peril to their lives. For these reasons and others a simple creature hath translated the Bible out of Latin into English.

In 1516 the first published Greek NT was edited by Erasmus. In the preface, this humanist wrote:

> I totally disagree with those who are unwilling that the Holy Scriptures, translated into the common tongue, should be read by unlearned. Christ desires His mysteries to be published abroad as widely as possible. I could wish that even all women should read the Gospel and St. Paul's Epistles, and I would that they might be read and known not merely by the Scots and the Irish but even by the

> Turks and the Saracens. I wish that the farm worker might sing parts of them at the plough, and that the weaver might hum them at the shuttle, and that the traveller might beguile the weariness of the way by reciting them.

In the sixteenth century William Tyndale risked his life to translate the Scriptures and died as a martyr in 1538. What was it that inspired him to undertake such a dangerous and daring work? In his note, "W. T. to the Reader," preceding his translation of the Pentateuch, he stated,

> Which thing only moved me to translate the New Testament. Because I had perceived by experience, how that it is impossible to stablish the lay people in any truth, except the scripture were plainly laid before their eyes in their mother tongue, that they might see the process, order, and the meaning of the text.

The KJV of 1611 contained a lengthy preface entitled "The Translators to the Readers," which reveals the guiding purposes, attitudes, and methods of the translators of that great version. It states that the task of translating is one

> which helpeth forward to the saving of soules. Now what can be more available thereto, than to deliver God's booke unto God's people in a tongue which they can understand? . . . How shall men meditate in that which they cannot understand? How shall they understand that which is kept close in an unknown tongue? . . . Translation it is that openeth the window, to let in the light; that breaketh the shell, that we may eat the kernel; that putteth aside the curtains, that we may looke into the Most Holy Place; that removeth the cover of the well, that we may come by the water. . . . Indeede without translation into the vulgar tongue, the unlearned are but children at Jacob's well (which was deepe) without a bucket or something to draw with. . . .

Unfortunately, the very version prefaced by these noble words is no longer speaking the language of the common man. To the average man of today the language of the KJV seems strange and foreign. There is therefore danger that the Bible may seem to modern man to be something out of date and irrelevant. This has been recognized now for nearly a century. Hence, toward the end of the nineteenth and the beginning of the twentieth century a movement arose calling for translations of the Bible in modern English.

This movement was strengthened by the discoveries of large quantities of papyri in Egypt particularly at about the turn of the century and later. These papyri have illuminated every aspect of the life of the Greek-speaking people of the ancient world in which the NT was written. They have revolutionized the study of NT Greek, for they have shown that in the main the NT was written in the vernacular Greek of common people. The NT documents are written in a plain, simple style to meet the needs of ordinary men and women. Should it not then be translated in the same kind of English? This is the argument of the translators of the modern-speech versions.

Four of the modern-speech versions of the early twentieth century are of special significance and must be considered here because of their merit and because of the influence they exerted on the Revised Standard Version. They are: The Twentieth Century New Testament, Weymouth's The New Testament in Modern Speech, Moffatt's A New Translation of the Bible, and Smith and Goodspeed's The Bible, An American Translation.

THE TWENTIETH CENTURY NEW TESTAMENT

One of the pioneer modern speech versions, The Twentieth Century New Testament, was reprinted in 1961 in a new paper cover edition by Moody Press of Chicago. The preface of the new edition states:

> *The Twentieth Century New Testament* is a smooth-flowing, accurate, easy to read translation that captivates its readers from start to finish. Born out of a desire to make the Bible readable and understandable, it is the product of the labors of a committee of twenty men and women who worked together over a period of many years to construct, we believe under divine surveillance, this beautifully simple rendition of the Word of God.

In 1933 the records of the secretary of this group of translators were deposited for safe-keeping in the John Rylands Library in Manchester by perhaps the last survivor of the committee. Without these papers we would probably never have known the story of the courageous people who put in fourteen years of difficult labor to produce this version. Prof. Edward Robinson, the Rylands librarian, kindly gave Prof. Kenneth W. Clark of Duke University access to these records. From them he reconstructed the story of the version, which he published as an article entitled, "The Making of the Twentieth Century New Testament," in the *Bulletin of the John Rylands Library* of September 1955.

The story begins in 1891 when the editor of the *Review of Reviews,* W. T. Stead, received two letters from writers unknown to each other, expressing the desire to have a translation that would make the meaning of the Bible plain to youth and uneducated people. One of these was Mrs. Mary Ann Kingsland Higgs of Greenacres, Oldham (near Manchester), the wife of a Congregational minister. Besides training four children of her own, she was a leader and teacher of youth groups in the churches where her husband pastored. She had become disturbed when she discovered that youth did not understand the traditional idiom of the KJV nor that of the Revised Version, and wrote to Mr. Stead regarding her problem. She also made an attempt to solve the problem by beginning her own idiomatic translation of the Gospel of Mark.

The writer of the other letter was Ernest de Mérundol Malan, a signal and telegraph engineer of Newland, Hull, and a grandson of the famous Swiss Reformed clergyman, César Malan. Mr. Malan also had four children and followed the custom of reading the Bible to them. In this bilingual family it became evident to the father that the modern French version of Lassere was better understood by his children than the traditional English Bible. So he, too, wrote about his problem to the editor of the *Review of Reviews.* Mr. Stead put Mr. Malan and Mrs. Higgs in touch with each other, and they began to collaborate on the translation of the Gospel of Mark. As their work progressed, they expanded their plan to include the other Gospels and Acts and solicited the help of other translators.

Stead printed a notice calling for "co-workers in the task of translating the Gospels and Acts of the Apostles into our everyday speech." As a result, a number of like-minded people responded, and the group of translators grew to twenty. Since they never met together as a group, it was necessary for them to collaborate by mail. Malan, just thirty-three years of age, was the driving spirit behind the project and acted as the secretary of the committee. He requested that each member send an autobiographical sketch that would serve as an introduction to the others. Fifteen of these sketches were preserved in the records, and they give us a vivid picture of the kind of people engaged in this task. Ranging in age from nineteen to sixty-three, they lived in various parts of the British Isles. They represented a wide range in education, in occupation, and in religious affiliation. About half were ministers or ex-ministers, and the rest included housewives, businessmen, and school-teachers. Denominationally, they included Anglicans, Methodists, Presbyterians, Congregationalists, and Baptists. The one thing they all seemed to have had in common was poor health. Most of them, too, represented large families. They were also caught up in the social and intellectual ferment that shook Victorian Britain in the late nineteenth century.

Malan took the main responsibility in organizing the translation work, financing the project, and publishing the finished product. His plan for the work was so well thought out and organized that it may be regarded as standard procedure for group translating. The original committee of twenty was divided into five groups, each with an assigned portion of the NT to translate. Within each group, individuals were given certain sections to render. Each translation was circulated among the group members for criticism and suggestions. Then each group was to interchange and criticize the translation of every other group. Each group assigned one of its members to serve on the revision committee. The revisers made changes only on the basis of a two-thirds vote. There was then an English Committee selected to review and improve the English idiom of the translation. Finally, the translation was published in three parts. It was a tentative edition to allow for further criticism and changes before the final edition was published.

As the work progressed, twelve more translators were added to the committee, but unfortunately we know nothing about them, as their autobiographies were not requested. Three scholars of note were also brought in as advisors: G. G. Findlay of Headingley College, Leeds; James Rendel Harris, of Cambridge; and Richard F. Weymouth, retired Headmaster of Mill Hill School.

The "tentative edition" was published in three parts between 1898 and 1900. After careful revision work, the permanent edition was published anonymously in 1904 in London and New York. It contained an anonymous preface written by Edward Deacon Girdlestone, the oldest member of the group. Girdlestone had also suggested the title The Twentieth Century New Testament. He gives as the purpose of the translation "to enable Englishmen to read the most important part of their Bible in that form of their own language which they themselves use." He expressed the fear that the retention of the Scriptures in a form of English no longer in common use "is liable to give the impression that the contents of the Bible have little to do with the life of today."

In the printing of the new translation some modification in the order of the books in the NT was made in the direction of chronological arrangement. The NT begins with Mark, regarded as the oldest of the Gospels. Between Acts and Paul's Letters is the Epistle of James. Paul's Letters are printed in the following order: 1 and 2 Thessalonians, Galatians, 1 and 2 Corinthians, Romans, Colossians, Philemon, Ephesians, Philippians, 1 and 2 Timothy, Titus, and Hebrews. The rest of the books follow in this order: 1 and 2 Peter; Jude; 1, 2, and 3 John; and Revelation. Each document is preceded by a brief introduction.

The Moody reprint of 1961 restores the traditional order of the books and leaves out the introductions. Unfortunately, the splendid preface by Girdlestone gives way to a new short one. In the text of the translation itself around seventy-five changes are made. Some of these are apparently intended to benefit American readers. Substitutions are given for "shillings," "pounds," "farthings," "quarters," "barrister," and "The Governor of the Gaol." The 1904 edition consistently rendered the Greek word "gehenna" as "the Pit." All but two of these are changed to "Hell" in the Moody reprint. Perhaps Matthew 5:22 and 18:9 simply escaped the eye of the editor. The 1904 edition consistently rendered the Greek "hades" as "Place of Death." With the exception of Revelation 6:8 and 20:13, 14, these are all changed in the reprint to "Hades," which is not in keeping with the aim of the original translators "to exclude all words and phrases not in current English." In describing Jesus' death on the cross in Mark 15:37, 39 and Luke 23:46, the translators say simply that He "expired." This is an exact rendering of the Greek, and there is no warrant for changing it, as the reprint does, to "dismissed His spirit." Nor is the reprint's "dismissed His spirit" in Matthew 27:50 an improvement over the translator's "gave up his spirit." A similar Greek phrase is found in the Septuagint of Genesis 35:18 for Rachel's death.

Nevertheless Moody Press has done a real service in making available this fine pioneer in modern speech English. With Weymouth, it shares the honor of inaugurating the era of Modern speech versions. The following examples will illustrate the simplicity and clarity of the translation:

Matthew 11:27–30

Everything has been committed to me by my Father; nor does any one fully know the Son, except the Father, or fully know the Father, except the Son and those to whom the Son may choose to reveal him. Come to me, all you who toil and are burdened, and I will give you rest! Take my yoke upon you, and learn from me, for I am gentle and lowly-minded, and "you shall find rest for your souls"; for my yoke is easy, and my burden is light.

John 1:4–5

That which came into being in him was Life;
And the Life was the Light of Man;
And the Light shines in the darkness,
And the darkness never overpowered it.

Philippians 3:20–21

But the State of which we are citizens is in Heaven; and it is from Heaven that we are eagerly looking for a Saviour, the Lord Jesus Christ, who, by the exercise of his power to bring everything into subjection to himself, will make this body that we have in our humiliation like to that body which he has in his Glory.

WEYMOUTH'S NEW TESTAMENT

Richard Francis Weymouth (1822–1902) was a distinguished classical scholar who in 1868 received the first Doctor of Literature degree offered by the University of London. From 1869 to 1886 he was headmaster of Mill Hill School, London, operated by nonconformists. He was a Baptist layman who was profoundly interested in the NT. In 1862 he published an edition of the Greek NT, presenting the text on which the majority of nineteenth-century editors agreed. In footnotes he indicated where the Received Text (Textus Receptus) or more recent editors disagreed with the text he established on the basis of the majority consensus. He called his edition *The Resultant Greek Testament*.

Evidently his work with the boys in the Mill Hill School impressed upon his mind the need for a modern speech version of the NT. When he retired at Brentwood, a town in Essex some twenty miles northeast of London, he proceeded to make such a translation of his *Resultant Greek Testament*. Although he completed the manuscript, ill health and finally his death in 1902, prevented him from seeing it through the press. This task he entrusted to his friend, Ernest Hampden-Cook, a Congregational minister, who served as resident secretary for the Mill Hill School from 1891 to 1896. Hampden-Cook also revised the translation, inserted the paragraph headings, and wrote some of the notes. He had been one of the translators of The Twentieth Century New Testament, and it was doubtless through his influence that Weymouth served as an advisor to that group of translators.

Weymouth called his translation "The New Testament in Modern Speech, an Idiomatic Translation into Every-day English. . . ." In the preface he outlines his aims and methods as a translator. He had no desire, he wrote, to supplant the standard English versions, and no wish that his version be used for public reading in church. Rather he hoped to supplement the other versions by furnishing, as he put it, "a succinct and compressed running commentary." He tried to the best of his ability to ascertain the meaning of every passage, and then to state that meaning as accurately and naturally as he could in present-day English. He also dreamed that his version might make some contribution to the new standard English Bible.

In his English he sought to avoid the use of colloquialisms on the one hand, and the language of English "society" on the other. He sought to clothe the thoughts of the NT in language that was modern, but at the same time dignified and reverent. As a Greek scholar he gave careful attention to points of grammatical accuracy. He tried, for example, to reproduce in translation the various nuances of the Greek tenses.

The text of the translation is arranged in paragraphs, with chapter and verse divisions given in the margin. Quotation marks are used extensively. However, quotations from the OT are printed in capital letters. The footnotes are extensive. For the most part, they seek to justify or explain the renderings given, though some deal with the readings MSS followed.

Several editions of this translation have been published. The first appeared in 1903. The second, appearing in 1907, corrected misprints and removed "a few infelicities in the English of the translation." The editor sought for improvements with the note: "Criticisms of this translation, and suggestions with regard to future editions, will be welcomed. . . ." Further corrections and changes were made in the third edition. But the first major overhaul was made in the fourth edition, published in 1924, the work of "several well-known New Testament scholars." In the fifth edition the editor, James Alexander Robertson of Aberdeen, supplied numerous notes, some "illustrating the text," some "being of a geographical or historical character, and others aiming at expounding the teaching of the New Testament, and at the explanation of difficulties." This edition was published in 1929, with a number of reprints since. It was printed in the United States by the Pilgrim Press in Boston, and later by Harpers.

Among the "infelicities" in the English of Weymouth was the rendering of the Greek phrase meaning eternal life by "the life of the ages." Apparently Weymouth failed to appreciate the Semitic background of the phrase. It is really an eschatological conception meaning the life of the coming age, which, however, according to John, is made available to believers here and now. The revisers of the translation in the fourth edition changed "the life of the ages" to "eternal life."

The rendering of the Lord's Prayer will give some idea of the nature of this translation:

Matthew 6:9–13

Our Father in heaven, may Thy name be kept holy; let Thy Kingdom come; let Thy will be done, as in heaven so on earth; give us to-day our bread for the day; and forgive us our shortcomings, as we also have forgiven those who have failed in their duty towards us; and bring us not into temptation, but rescue us from the Evil one.

A comparison of 1 Thessalonians 4:13–17 as given in the second and fifth editions will also exhibit some of the more striking changes made by later revisers:

Now, concerning those who from time to time pass away, we would not have you to be ignorant, brethren, lest you should mourn as others do who have no hope. For if we believe that Jesus has died and risen again, we also believe that through Jesus God will bring with Him those who shall have passed away. For this we declare to you on the Lord's own authority—that we who are alive and continue on earth until the Coming of the Lord, shall certainly not forestall those who shall have previously passed away. For the Lord Himself will come down from heaven with a loud word of command, and with an archangel's voice and the trumpet of God, and the dead in Christ will rise first. Afterwards we who are alive and are still on earth will be caught up in their company amid clouds to meet the Lord in the air.

—Second edition

Now, concerning those who fall asleep we would not have you ignorant, brethren, lest you should mourn, as do the rest who have no hope. For if we believe that Jesus died and rose again, in the same way also through Jesus God will bring with Him those who have fallen asleep. And this we declare to you on the Lord's own word—that we who are alive and survive until the Coming of the Lord will have no advantage over those who have fallen asleep. For the Lord Himself will come down from heaven with a loud summons, with the voice of an archangel, and with the trumpet of God, and the dead in Christ will rise first. Afterwards we who are alive and survive will be caught up along with them in the clouds to meet the Lord in the air.

—Fifth edition

THE MOFFATT BIBLE

James Moffatt (1870–1944) was a brilliant Scottish scholar who was born and educated at Glasgow. He received a Master of Arts degree with honors in classics from Glasgow University in 1890 and took his theological degree from the Free Church College of Glasgow. Following his ordination, he served as a minister of the United Free Church for some fifteen years. During this time he continued his scholarly pursuits. In 1901 he published The Historical New Testament, an original translation of the New Testament documents arranged in their chronological order according to the critical literary theories of his time. This won for him a Doctor of Divinity degree from St. Andrews University, which had never previously conferred the degree on so young a man. He was professor of Greek and NT Exegesis at Mansfield College, Oxford, from 1911 to 1915, and on his departure Oxford conferred the Doctor of Divinity degree on him. He was professor of Church History at the United Free College of Glasgow from 1915 to 1927, and at Union Theological Seminary in New York from 1927 to 1939.

In 1913 he published his first edition of The New Testament: A New Translation. As the name implies, it was an entirely fresh rendering and not a revision of The Historical New Testament. In the preface he stated his aim "to translate the New Testament exactly as one would render any piece of contemporary Hellenistic prose." He endeavored to divorce himself from all previous versions and produced a strikingly independent modern speech translation, brilliant and stimulating. Unfortunately, he used as his base the Greek text of Hermann von Soden, in which textual critics see many defects. For example he translates Matthew 1:16 as: ". . . Joseph (to whom the virgin Mary was betrothed) the father of Jesus, who is called 'Christ.'" This rendering is, of course, flatly contradicted by the story of the virgin birth in verses 18 to 25. In some 130 instances he departed from von Soden's Greek text. In quite a number of these instances such modern Greek editions as Westcott-Hort, Nestle-Aland, and the United Bible Societies would agree with his conclusions. One striking reading in which some recent translations have followed him gives the name of the notorious prisoner released in place of Jesus Christ as "Jesus Bar-Abbas" (Matt. 27:17).

Moffatt at times accepted readings of the so-called "Western" type, which most modern editors have not adopted as original. In Matthew 25:1, for example, on the basis of a few Greek and Latin MSS, he has the ten maidens with their lamps go out to meet the bridegroom *and the bride.* At Jesus' baptism, according to Luke 3:22, a voice from heaven exclaims, according to Moffatt: "Thou art my son, the Beloved, *to-day have I become thy father.*" The last clause is probably an early adaptation of the baptismal endorsement to Psalm 2:7. In Acts 16:30 a "Western" reading is adopted that adds a vivid touch to the story of Paul and Silas's release from prison. It was only "after securing the other prisoners" that the Philippian jailer took the missionaries out of prison and asked, "Sirs, what must I do to be saved?" At Ephesus, Paul, according to the reading accepted in Acts 19:9, taught "every day from eleven to four in the lecture-room of Tyrannus."

Moffatt often adopts readings that have little MS support. But beyond that, he has accepted around thirty conjectural emendations, without MS support. The reading in John 19:29, "so they put a sponge full of vinegar on a spear," rather than "on hyssop," rests on a conjectural emendation, though one medieval MS has that reading. There is no MS evidence for dropping from the text the words of 1 Timothy 5:23, "Give up being a total abstainer; take a little wine for the sake of your stomach and your frequent attacks of illness." Moffatt says they are "either a marginal gloss or misplaced." In James 4:2 he accepts Erasmus's conjecture and reads "you covet," rather than "you kill." But one of the most striking was the suggestion of J. Rendel Harris that "Enoch" had dropped out of 1 Peter 3:19, which Moffatt renders, "It was in the Spirit that Enoch also went and preached to the imprisoned spirits. . . ."

Moffatt also felt at liberty to rearrange the materials in the NT. He frequently changes the order of verses, supposedly restoring them to their "original position." The Gospel of John has suffered more than any other book in the NT from this attempted "restoration." John 3:22–30 is transposed to its supposedly "true position" between 2:12 and 2:13. John 7:15–24 is placed in "its original position" after John 5:47. John 11:5 is placed between verses 30 and 31. John 12:45–50 is placed in the middle of verse 36. Chapters 15 and 16 are "restored to their original positions in the middle of 13:31." Finally, in chapter 18, verses 19 to 24 are placed between verses 14 and 15.

In 1924 Moffatt startled the English-speaking world with the publication of his The Old Testament: A New Translation, in two volumes. He states that this fresh translation was designed "to present the books of the Old Testament in effective and intelligible English." Moffatt regarded the traditional text as "often desperately corrupt." Hence "nearly every page" of his translation, he tells us, "contains some emendation of the text." At times he felt that the text was too defective to be restored, and he simply omitted such words and inserted ellipses (. . .). Except in such compound titles as "the Lord of hosts" he, like the French, translated YHWH, the sacred name of God, as "The Eternal."

Moffatt did even more rearranging of the materials within the documents of the OT than he had in the New. One is startled to read as the first words of Genesis a sort of subtitle derived from Genesis 2:4a: "This is the story of how the universe was formed." Both the transfer of these words from chapter 2 and their translations are open to question. The expression "these are the generations (or descendants of)" occurs ten times in Genesis, dividing the book into ten sections. Furthermore, the Hebrew title of many of the Hebrew books is derived from the beginning words. The Hebrew title for "Genesis" means "in the beginning," clearly indicating that the book began as our standard translations have it. This unwarranted re-editing of the documents, together with the all-too-free use of emendations is the greatest weakness in Moffatt's translation.

The complete Moffatt Bible was published as a single volume in 1926. Many editions of it came from the press in subsequent years. Moffatt then put out his "Revised and Final Edition" in 1935. He asserted in the preface that almost every sentence of his translation had been restudied. He wrote, "It is a revision as thorough as I can make it; and I mean it to be final."

The Moffatt Bible certainly makes for interesting reading. The language is fresh and colorful. A few examples will serve to illustrate this.

Among other things, a bishop must not be "addicted to pilfering" (Titus 1:7). On the cross Jesus was offered "a drink of wine mixed with bitters" (Matt. 27:34). Concerning the town of Meroz, which refused to take part in the battle against the Northern Canaanites, Moffatt translated, "Curse Meroz, the Eternal's angel cries, blast her burghers with a curse!" (Judg. 5:23). Mourners are to be given "coronals for coronachs" (Isa. 61:3). Moses' mother put him in "a creel made of papyrus reeds, daubed . . . over with bitumen and pitch" (Exod. 2:3). Amos accuses the "careless citizens" of Samaria of "lolling on their irovy divans, sprawling on their couches, dining off fresh lamb and fatted veal, crooning to the music of the lute . . . lapping wine by the bowlful . . . with never a single thought for the bleeding wounds of the nation" (Amos 6:4–6). Rezin and Pekah are called "two fag-ends of flickering torches" (Isa. 7:4). Paul speaks of the danger of young widows "gadding about from one house to another—and not merely idle but gossips and busybodies, repeating things they have no right to mention" (1 Tim. 5:13). Christ was slain "by hanging on a gibbet" (Acts 5:30; 10:40). The righteous man finds his joy in God's law, "poring over it day and night" (Ps. 1:2). Jesus said, "Do not pray by idle rote like pagans, for they suppose they will be heard the more thay say; you must not copy them" (Matt. 6:7–8). Again He declared, "Till heaven and earth pass away, not an iota, not a comma, will pass from the Law until it is all in force" (Matt. 5:18).

The exotic sound (to American ears) of some of Moffatt's vocabulary is to be attributed, at least in part, to his Scottish background. He lists *bagpipes* as among the musical instruments played at the dedication of Nebuchadnezzar's image (Dan. 3:10, 15). In Jesus' parable of the vineyard, the master summons his *bailiff* to pay the workers (Matt. 20:8). The Tertullus who represented the Jews in accusing Paul was a *barrister* (Acts 24:1). *Cairn* is used several times for a monument of stones (Gen. 31:48, et al.). "There was a rich man who had a *factor"* who mismanaged his property (Luke 16:1). Joseph's master put him in *gaol* (Gen. 39:20). Jerusalem's leaders "are like *harts* that find no pasture" (Lam. 1:6). The lover of Canticles says, "I will *hie* me to your scented slopes" (Song of Sol. 4:6). Isaiah predicts, "Then there shall be a *highroad* between Egypt and Assyria" (19:23; cf. 11:16). When David danced he wore "a linen *kilt* round his middle" (2 Sam. 6:14; 1 Chron. 15:27). Micah accused his compatriots of "crushing *yeomen* and their homes, *smallholders* and their livings" (2:2).

The Moffatt Bible achieved great popularity, and was used as the basic text for *The Moffatt Commentary*. Moffatt achieved his goal of making the Bible "more interesting" and "less obscure."

AN AMERICAN TRANSLATION

One of the most eloquent advocates of modern speech versions was Edgar Johnson Goodspeed (1871–1962) of the University of Chicago as the following sample paragraph indicates:

> If the purpose of New Testament translation is to bring what the New Testament writers meant to convey directly and vividly before the modern American reader, then it should not be necessary for him to detour through a course in sixteenth century English, such as is necessary for the understanding of even the simpler parts of the New Testament (*New Chapters in New Testament Study,* p. 113).

On February 24, 1920, Goodspeed presented a paper on translation to the New Testament Club of the University of Chicago. He discussed and freely criticized the three leading modern speech versions of the time: The Twentieth Century New Testament, Weymouth, and Moffatt. There followed a discussion period in which one of Goodspeed's colleagues, Dr. Shirley Jackson Case, drily remarked that if the NT professor saw so many flaws in these earlier versions, perhaps he should produce one of his own. Amid the laughter that followed at Goodspeed's expense, there was one young man present who took the suggestion seriously—Guy M. Crippen of the University of Chicago Press. After a sleepless night, Crippen presented the idea to the editor of the Press, Gordon G. Laing, who wrote the professor, inviting him to make the translation.

Goodspeed was at first disposed to brush the request aside. "Every translation of a masterpiece is a failure," he mused. "Why add another?" At lunch, however, he read Laing's letter to his wife, who encouraged him to consider the request seriously. He therefore tried his hand at rendering Mark and eventually accepted the invitation. No man in America was better equipped by background and training for such a task.

Goodspeed soon learned that he could do only fifteen or sixteen verses a day. Concerning his experience, he said:

> The most difficult thing, I found, was to forget the old translations, King James and especially the Revised Versions, English and American, which I found I knew better than I did King James. The familiarity we all have with the English Bible was my greatest obstacle. For of course I did not wish merely to reproduce that but to give my version something of the force and freshness that reside in the original Greek. I wanted my translation to make on the modern reader something of the impression the New Testament must have made on its earliest readers, and to invite the continuous reading of the whole book at a time. That was what I was striving for (*As I Remember*, p. 162).

From the very beginning the professor kept in mind not merely the use of his NT in private reading and study but also its reading in public. "It is difficult for me," he said, "to conceive a translation of the New Testament designed only for private meditation and study since every part of it so unmistakably addresses not the solitary Christian but the Christian public, religiously a most significant feature of the book. Religion is a social experience!" (*As I Remember*, p. 160). He proceeded to try out his translation in public. When called on to speak in the Divinity School Chapel, he would read a few pages from his new version, and he found the students listening with rapt attention. In his own home before the evening sing on Sundays, he would read the Scripture lesson from his own translation. It was therefore geared to public reading from the very first.

Goodspeed felt "that the most appropriate English form for the New Testament is the simple, straightforward English of everyday expression." He wanted to produce "a version with something of the ease, boldness, and unpretending vigor which mark the original Greek." He conceived of his task as, first, to grasp what the several NT writers meant to say, and then to cast that thought in simple, clear, present-day English (Preface, p. iii).

He avoided the use of "thee" and "thou" even when Deity was addressed. He called his new version An American Translation. It was to be an American translation by an American scholar for American readers in their own vernacular. "For American readers, especially, who have had to depend so long upon versions made in Great Britain," he declared, "there is room for a New Testament free from expressions which, however familiar in England and Scotland, are strange to American ears" (*As I Remember*).

Goodspeed based his translation on the Greek text of Westcott and Hort. In a half dozen places he departed from this text. Three of these are conspicuous: the reading "on a pike" for "upon hyssop" in John 19:29; "Lybians" for "Libertines" (i.e., freedmen) in Acts 6:9; and the insertion of "Enoch" in 1 Peter 3:19.

This new translation was published by the University of Chicago Press in 1923. It also appeared in serial form in the Chicago *Evening Post* and in twenty-four other newspapers throughout the United States and Canada. For a time there was considerable opposition from many quarters to this modern speech version, but it was also widely acclaimed. America has not produced a better modern-speech version.

The following are a few samples of its renderings:

Matthew 5:3

Blessed are those who feel their spiritual need, for the Kingdom of Heaven belongs to them!

Matthew 5:17–18

Do not suppose that I have come to do away with the Law or the Prophets. I have not come to do away with them but to enforce them. For I tell you, as long as heaven and earth endure, not one dotting of an *i* or crossing of a *t* will be dropped from the Law until it is all observed.

1 Corinthians 1:17–25

For Christ did not send me to baptize, but to preach the good news—but not with fine language, or the cross of Christ might seem an empty thing. For to those who are on the way to destruction, the story of the cross is nonsense, but to us who are to be saved, it means all the power of God. For the Scripture says "I will destroy the wisdom of the wise, I will thwart the shrewdness of the shrewd!" Where now is your philosopher? Your scribe? Your reasoner of today? Has not God made a fool of the world's wisdom? For since in God's providence the world with all its wisdom did not come to know God, God chose, through the folly of the gospel message, to save those who had faith in him. For Jews insist upon miracles, and Greeks demand philosophy, but we proclaim a Christ who was crucified—an idea that is revolting to Jews and absurd to the heathen, but to those whom God has called, whether they are Jews or Greeks, a Christ who is God's power and God's wisdom. For God's folly is beyond the wisdom of men, and God's weakness is beyond their strength.

Philippians 2:5–11

Have the same attitude that Christ Jesus had. Though he possessed the nature of God, he did not grasp at equality with God, but laid it aside to take on the nature of a slave and become like other men. When he had assumed human form, he still further humbled himself and carried his obedience so far as to die, and to die upon the cross. That is why God has so greatly exalted him, and given him the name above all others, so that in the name of Jesus everyone should kneel, in heaven and on earth and in the underworld, and everyone should acknowledge Jesus Christ as Lord, and thus glorify God the Father.

Within a matter of weeks following the publication of Goodspeed's NT, the University Press approached him regarding a similar treatment of the OT. Doctor Goodspeed referred the Press to Professor J. M. Powis Smith of the OT department. In the OT translation, Professor Smith associated with him three graduates of Chicago who were competent and highly trained experts in Hebrew and related languages. They were Theophile J. Meek of the University of Toronto, Alexander R. Gordon of McGill University, and Leroy Waterman of the University of Michigan. Smith acted as the editor.

This translation was based on the traditional Hebrew text. The editor wrote, "Our guiding principle has been that the official Masoretic text must be adhered to as long as it made satisfactory sense. We have not tried to create a new text; but rather to translate the received text wherever translation was possible" (Preface, p. xii). The passages where changes in the text were made on the basis of ancient versions, or what they called "scientific emendation," were listed in the appendix of the separate printing of the OT in 1927. The extent of these changes is quite disturbing.

Special attention was given to the poetic portions of the OT. The translation sought to bring "into clear light many of the hidden beauties of Hebrew poetry." Poetic form was given to these passages.

The language is modern, though in the OT "thou," "thee," and "thy" have been retained where the second personal pronoun occurs in words addressed to God. The editor set forth this guiding principle:

> The translator to do his best work must be in sympathy with his subject matter and be able to put himself into mental and spiritual contact with its authors. . . . On the other hand, a translation should read well. It should be in a vocabulary and style appropriate to the thought which it is designed to express. If the original be dignified, impressive, and eloquent, those qualities must not be lacking in the translation; if it be trivial, commonplace, and prosaic, the translation must take on the same character. The content of the Old Testament is, with little exception, upon a high literary plane. The language of the translation, therefore, cannot be allowed to fall to the level of the street. . . . (Ibid., p. xiv)

In 1931 Goodspeed's NT and Smith's OT were combined to form The Bible—An American Translation. Though a few changes were made, the translations were essentially the same as when published as separate volumes. In 1938 Goodspeed also made a translation of the Apocrypha. In 1939 this translation was included with the OT and NT to form The Complete Bible: An American Translation.

The four versions discussed in this chapter are important as inaugurators of the era of modern speech versions in the twentieth century. They helped to accustom the English-reading public to the sacred Scriptures in modern English. In addition, each of these translations has an intrinsic merit of its own and is still being used. They are all noteworthy also because of the contribution they made to the RSV. Two of the translators, Goodspeed and Moffatt, served on the NT committee for the RSV while Leroy Waterman was on the OT committee. James Moffatt acted as secretary for both committees until his death in 1944.

2

The Revised Standard Version

THE OT AND NT

Translations Behind the RSV

For more than two centuries the King James Version (KJV) dominated the Protestant churches of the English-speaking world. During the nineteenth century, however, the demands for revision became increasingly strong. Finally, on 10 February 1870, Bishop Wilberforce (of Winchester) submitted a resolution to the Upper House of the Convocation of Canterbury that a committee be appointed to study the advisability of a revision of the Bible. The following May, a Revision Committee of fifty-four members was formed, representing not only the Church of England, but nearly all the evangelical bodies as well: Baptist, Congregational, Methodist, and Presbyterian. An American Committee of thirty men was selected in 1871 to go over the work of the English revisers and to offer suggestions. In 1881 The Revised Version of the New Testament was published, and the publication of The Revised Old Testament followed in 1885.

The recommendations of the American Committee were carefully considered by the English revisers, but only those that were approved by a two-thirds vote by the British Committee were incorporated in the text. The remaining readings and renderings preferred by the American Committee were published in an appendix. The Americans, on their part, agreed to give their support to the Revised Version, and not to issue an edition of their own for a period of fourteen years.

This agreement expired in 1901, and the American Committee in the meanwhile had had adequate time to prepare its edition. This was published in August, 1901, and bore the subtitle "Being the Version Set Forth A.D. 1611 Compared with the Most Ancient Authorities and Revised A.D. 1881–1885." Then followed this significant addition: "Newly Edited by the American Revision Committee, A.D. 1901. Standard Edition." From this title page is derived its name: The American Standard Version (ASV). This version represented the best biblical learning of its time.

Nevertheless, the English Revised Version and its American counterpart had serious defects. The principles laid down for the guidance of the revision committees were too conservative. The committees were instructed, for example, to make as few changes as possible in the text of the KJV, consistent with faithfulness to the original. A two-thirds vote was required before a change could be made. And the wording of such changes was to be limited as far as possible to the language of the KJV and earlier versions. This meant that the language was not really modernized.

Furthermore, the Revised Versions strove for consistency in rendering. They sought to render a given word in the original by the same English word consistently, regardless of its context. In their view, faithfulness to the original demanded a meticulous word-by-word rendering. They attempted a precise rendering of the tenses and the article. Often in the NT they even followed the order of the Greek words rather than the word order that is natural to English. The result is that the Revised Versions are stiff, pedantic, and unidiomatic. They lack the free literary charm of the KJV. Hence, there soon arose demands for another, more thorough revision.

The italicized words in the following statements from the ASV will illustrate its use of antiquated words, foreign to the modern reader, or an archaic usage of common words.

"And they shall be an *abhorring* unto all flesh" (Isa. 66:24).

"The Holy Spirit testifieth . . . that bonds and afflictions *abide* me" (Acts 20:23).

"The day of Jehovah is great and very terrible, and who can *abide* it" (Joel 2:11).

"The *abjects* gathered themselves together against me" (Ps. 35:15).

"He had thirty sons; and thirty daughters he sent *abroad,* and thirty daughters he brought in from *abroad* for his sons" (Judg. 12:9).

"It was nothing *accounted* of in the days of Solomon" (1 Kings 10:21).

"Come, and I will *advertise* thee what this people shall do to thy people in the latter days" (Num. 24:14).

"Being *affectionately desirous* of you" (1 Thess. 2:8).

"Solomon made *affinity with* Pharaoh" (1 Kings 3:1).

"*Opening* and *alleging* that it behooved the Christ to suffer" (Acts 17:3).

"He sendeth an *ambassage,* and asketh conditions of peace" (Luke 14:32).

"And all they that cast *angle* into the Nile shall mourn" (Isa. 19:8).

"In everything ye *approved* yourselves to be pure in the matter" (2 Cor. 7:11).

"He *assayed* to join himself to the disciples" (Acts 9:26).

"Their own doings *beset* them about" (Hosea 7:2).

"Though thou shouldest *bray* a fool in a mortar with a pestle" (Prov. 27:22).

"*Cause* that it be read also in the church of the Laodiceans" (Col. 4:16).

"Not in *chambering* and wantonness" (Rom. 13:13).

"Jacob was *wroth,* and *chode* with Laban" (Gen. 31:36).

"And *consorted* with Paul and Silas" (Acts 17:4).

"And *contemned* the counsel of the Most High" (Ps. 107:11).

"And Pilate, wishing to *content* the multitude, released unto them Barabbas" (Mark 15:15).

"But Martha was *cumbered* about much serving" (Luke 10:40).

"And the *dam* sitting upon the young" (Deut. 22:6).

"But *doting* about questionings and disputes of words" (1 Tim. 6:4).

"And he would *fain* have filled his belly with the husks" (Luke 15:16).

"As many as desire to make a *fair show* in the. flesh" (Gal. 6:12).

"And in covetousness shall they with *feigned* words make merchandise of you" (2 Peter 2:3).

"As though they would lay out anchors from the *foreship*" (Acts 27:30).

"Not only to the good and gentle, but also to the *froward*" (1 Peter 2:18).

"So as no *fuller* on earth can whiten them" (Mark 9:3).

"It is good for thee to enter into life *maimed* or *halt*" (Matt. 18:8).

"His strength shall be *hunger-bitten*" (Job 18:12).

"Not only of the *lading* and the ship, but also of our lives" (Acts 27:10).

"They *left* the horsemen to go with him" (Acts 23:32).

"They had no *leisure* so much as to eat" (Mark 6:31).

"Every *lusty* man and every man of valor" (Judg. 3:29).

"They *mar* my path" (Job 30:13).

"A man that beareth false witness . . . is a *maul* and a sword" (Prov. 25:18).

"He shall not stand before *mean* men" (Prov. 22:29).

"Look ye out the best and *meetest* of your master's sons" (2 Kings 10:3).

"Lest haply your hearts be *overcharged* with surfeiting, and drunkenness, and cares of this life" (Luke 21:34).

"For with me thou shalt be in *safeguard*" (1 Sam. 22:23).

"And *scrabbled* on the doors of the gate" (1 Sam. 21:13).

"Delicate living is not *seemly* for a fool" (Prov. 19:10).

"Better is a dinner of herbs . . . than a *stalled* ox" (Prov. 15:17).

"Your words have been *stout* against me" (Mal. 3:13).

"Or having a *wen*" (Lev. 22:22).

"If they bind me with seven green *withes* . . . then shall I become weak" (Judg. 16:7).

In 1928 the copyright of the ASV, which had been held by Thomas Nelson and Sons, was transferred to the International Council of Religious Education. This body is an association of the educational boards of forty major Protestant denominations of the U.S. and Canada. This council renewed the copyright and established an American Standard Bible Committee of scholars to be the custodian of the text of the ASV with authority to undertake further revisions as deemed advisable. In 1937 the International Council of Religious Education voted to authorize a new revision. The action stated:

There is need for a version which embodies the best results of modern scholarship as to the meaning of the Scriptures, and expresses this meaning in English diction which is designed for use in public and private worship and preserves those qualities which have given to the King James Version a supreme place in English literature. We therefore define the task of the American Standard Bible Committee to be that of the revision of the present American Standard Bible in the light of the results of modern scholarship, this revision to be designed for use in public and private worship, and to be in the direction of the simple, classic English style of the King James Version.

Principles of Translation

Thirty-two scholars served on the committee charged with making the revision. Dean Luther Weigle of Yale Divinity School acted as chairman, and James Moffatt of Union Theological Seminary was the secretary until his death in 1944. He was succeeded by Fleming James, dean emeritus of the School of Theology, the University of the South (Tennessee). In addition to the committee, there was an advisory board of fifty representatives of cooperating denominations. The committee was divided into two sections, one dealing with the OT, the other with the NT. The details of the principles and the procedures followed are given in two pamphlets, with chapters written by various members of the committee: *An Introduction to the Revised Standard Version of the New Testament* (1946), and *An Introduction to the Revised Standard Version of the Old Testament* (1952).

The RSV NT was published in February 1946. The preface does not undertake to set forth the lines along which the revision was made. But it does again emphasize the need for the revision in these words:

Let it be said here simply that all the reasons which led to the demand for revision of the King James Version one hundred years ago are still valid, and are even more cogent now than then. And we cannot be content with the Versions of 1881 and 1901 for two main reasons. One is that these are mechanically exact, literal word-for-word translations, which follow the order of the Greek words, so far as this is possible, rather than the order which is natural to English; they are more accurate than the King James Version, but have lost some of its beauty and power as English literature. The second reason is that the discovery of a few more ancient manuscripts of the New Testament and of a great body of Greek papyri dealing with the everyday affairs of life in the early centuries of the Christian era, has furnished scholars with new resources, both for seeking to recover the original text of the Greek New Testament and for understanding its language (pp. v–vi).

Regarding the Greek text underlying the NT, one of the translators, F. C. Grant, has written:

With the best will in the world, the New Testament translator or reviser of today is forced to adopt the eclectic principle: each variant reading must be studied on its merits, and cannot be adopted or rejected by some rule of thumb, or by adherence to such a theory as that of the "Neutral Text." It is this eclectic principle that has guided us in the present Revision. The Greek text of this Revision is not that of Westcott-Hort, or Nestle, or Souter; though the readings we have adopted will as a rule, be found either in the text or the margin of the new (17th) edition of Nestle (Stuttgart, 1941) (*An Introduction to the Revised Standard Version of the New Testament*, p. 41).

The RSV OT is based on the consonants of the traditional Masoretic Hebrew and Aramaic text. In the main, the vowels supplied by the Masoretes between the sixth and ninth centuries A.D. were also followed. Occasionally, however, different vowels were used when the translators were convinced that a more probable reading would be obtained. The revisers were also convinced that the consonantal text had frequently suffered in transmission. Hence, use was made of ancient versions and the available material from the Qumran MSS in an endeavor to restore the original reading. In thirteen passages in Isaiah readings were adopted from the Isaiah scroll of the Qumran library. In seven of the thirteen instances the reading has the support of one or more of the ancient versions (Isa. 14:30; 15:19; 45:2; 49:24; 51:19; 56:12; 60:19), such as the Greek, Syriac, Latin, and Aramaic Targums. Numerous other readings supported by one or more of these versions or, for the Pentateuch, the Samaritan recension, were also accepted. Several substantial additions to the text in various places were thus made. For example, "Let us go out to the field" is inserted in Genesis 4:8, and "Why have you stolen my silver cup?" in Genesis 44:4. In

Judges 16:13–14 the revisers restored some fifteen words from the Greek that they felt had dropped out of the Hebrew text. Substantial material was also added to the traditional text of 1 Samuel 10:1 and 14:41. Psalm 145 is an alphabetical acrostic psalm, but the Hebrew text lacks the lines beginning with the letter *nun*. The RSV has added these two lines from the Greek at the end of verse 13 (For other additions, see 2 Sam. 17:3; 1 Kings 8:12; Song of Sol. 3:1).

But there still remained passages in which the revisers felt that neither the traditional Hebrew text nor the ancient versions had preserved the original reading. In such instances they resorted to a conjectural reconstruction. Footnotes indicate these by the abbreviation *Cn,* followed by a translation of the traditional Hebrew text. Conservative scholars feel that the RSV has been too free in resorting to these supposed corrections, as well as in too frequently following the ancient versions.

Features of the RSV

The year 1977 marked the twenty-fifth anniversary of the publication of the complete RSV. During the nearly three decades in which this version has been available it has perhaps become the most widely used of recent translations, and has been officially adopted for use in worship by a large number of Christian denominations. It seems, therefore, unnecessary to quote samples from it. However, it may be helpful to call attention to some of its main features. To begin with, it is not a new translation, but a revision of earlier standard English versions. As such it seeks to preserve the best of the earlier versions while at the same time substituting modern English for antiquated language. Nevertheless, it still conforms to the general pattern and often the exact wording of Tyndale's version of the sixteenth century. The revisers strove for simplicity yet dignity in rendering. The goal of the translators of the KJV in 1611 was the goal of the RSV committee: "Truly (good Christian Reader) we never thought from the beginning, that we should need to make a new translation, nor yet to make a bad one a good one . . . but to make a good one better."

The text of prose passages in the RSV is arranged in sense

paragraphs as in the ASV, instead of being broken up into separate verses as in the KJV. The system used in the KJV tends to destroy all sense of connection between the verses and gives the impression that each is a separate unit standing by itself. The first complete English Bible to use verse divisions was the Geneva Bible of 1560. Rabbi Nathan is credited with devising the present verse numbers for the OT in 1448. The verse divisions for the NT were made by the scholar-printer, Robert Stephanus, for his Greek-Latin NT of 1551. They constitute a useful reference tool and are essential for a concordance. The verse numbers are printed throughout the paragraphs of the RSV in smaller type at the top of the line.

The RSV has continued and extended the practice of the ASV in printing poetic passages in poetic form. The metrical nature of ancient Semitic poetry is better understood today than it was when the KJV was produced. One of its characteristics is accentual meter. This means that each line contains a certain number of accents or beats. A more striking characteristic is its parallelism of members. The basic unit of Hebrew poetry is a line followed by a second (or, at times, by a third), which complements it by restating it (synonymous parallelism), contrasting with it (antithetic parallelism), or further developing or completing it (synthetic or step parallelism). The RSV has sought to reproduce the accentual meter in its renderings and has arranged the lines in couplets or triplets. But it has gone further and sought to arrange the poetic passages in stanzas. Approximately forty percent of the OT is in poetic form. This includes not only the poetic books—Job, Psalms, Proverbs, parts of Ecclesiastes, the Song of Solomon, and Lamentations—but major portions of many of the prophetic books as well. In addition, there are poetic passages in the Pentateuch and the historical books.

In contrast to the OT, the RSV does not arrange much of the NT in poetic form. In the Gospels it seems to be limited to quotations from poetic portions of the OT and a very few sayings of Jesus. But it is generally recognized today that much of Jesus' teaching was cast into the mold of Semitic poetry and could well be printed as poetry. The hymns or poetic passages of the first two chapters of Luke are in poetic form. Some of the songs of the Apocalypse are also printed as poetry.

With regard to the Tetragrammaton, the ineffable divine name, rendered "Jehovah" in the ASV OT, the revisers returned to the practice of the KJV in rendering it LORD (or, under certain circumstances, GOD). This harmonizes with the long-established synagogue practice of reading the letters YHWH as *Adonai*, meaning "Lord," as well as the Septuagint Greek rendering *Kyrios* (Lord), and the Vulgate *Dominus*.

THE RSV APOCRYPHA

In October 1952, the General Convention of the Protestant Episcopal Church requested that the Division of Christian Education of the N.C.C.C., U.S.A. organize a committee to revise the English translation of the Apocrypha. Accordingly, the General Board of the N.C.C.C. authorized the appointment of a group of scholars to make and publish The Revised Standard Version of the Apocrypha.

The Apocrypha were included in all the sixteenth-century English versions, including the KJV of 1611. The English Revised Version of the document was published in 1894. As is well known, there is a wide difference of opinion regarding the status of these books among Christian bodies.

Roman Catholics regard them, with the exception of 1 and 2 Esdras and the Prayer of Manasseh, as inspired and canonical Scripture, and call them "Deuteroncanonical." The Fourth Session of the Council of Trent on 8 April 1546, decreed that these books "entire and with all their parts" are "sacred and canonical" and pronounced an anathema on anyone who "knowingly or deliberately" rejects them. Though denied canonicity and authority, 1 and 2 Esdras and the Prayer of Manasseh are included in Latin MSS of the Vulgate, and are printed as an appendix to the Bible in later editions.

The Church of England, the Lutheran churches, and the Zurich Reformed churches hold that these books are useful, but not canonical. In Luther's German translation of the Bible, these books are segregated between the OT and NT, with the title: "Apocrypha, that is, books which are not held equal to the sacred Scriptures, and nevertheless are useful and good to read." The Swiss Reformer Oecolampadius stated in 1530: "We do not depise Judith, Tobit, Ecclesiasticus, Baruch, the last two books of Esdras, the three books of Maccabees, the additions to Daniel; but we do not allow them divine authority with the other." Article Six of the famous Thirty-nine Articles of the Church of England (1562) states that these books are read "for example of life and instruction of manners," but the Church does not use them "to establish any doctrine."

The position of the Calvinistic and other Reformed churches is clearly stated in the Westminster Confession of Faith (1647): "The books commonly called Apocrypha, not being of divine inspiration, are no part of the Canon of the Scripture; and therefore are of no authority in the Church of God, nor to be any otherwise approved, or made use of, than any other human writings." However, even the Protestants who take this last position have come to realize these documents have an immense historical value. They serve to bridge the four hundred-year gap between the Testaments, and aid the reader in understanding the social, political, and religious background of the NT. They are intensely interesting and significant literary documents of an important period in religious history.

The publication of The Apocrypha of the Old Testament, Revised Standard Version, on 30 September 1957, was therefore welcomed by Christians of many faiths. The appearance of these books constituted an important step in the direction of finding a version acceptable to both Catholics and Protestants.

RSV CATHOLIC EDITION

In 1965 a Catholic edition of the RSV NT, prepared by the Catholic Biblical Association of Great Britain with the approval of the Standard Bible Committee, was published. A "List of Changes" made in the text for this edition is given in Appendix Two. The minimal number of changes made consist of two kinds: those having to do with the underlying Greek text and those giving a different translation of the Greek. The first consisted in restoring the sixteen passages found in the Received Text that the RSV had placed in footnotes. This included such passages as the long ending of Mark (16:9–20), the story of the woman taken in adultery (John 7:52–8:11), and the Lucan account of Peter running to the tomb (Luke 24:12). In each instance, the RSV has a footnote stating, "Other ancient authorities add. . . ." The Catholic edition restores the passage and has in the footnote, "Other ancient authorities omit. . . ." The second type of change consists in giving a different translation. Joseph in Matthew 1:19 does not resolve to "divorce" Mary quietly but "to send her away quietly." The "brothers" of Jesus (Matt. 12:48f.; Mark 3:31ff.; Luke 8:19ff.; John 7:34) are "brethren," based on the belief that they were not real brothers—"the Greek word or its Semitic equivalent is used for varying degrees of blood relationship." The angel Gabriel's greeting to Mary is "Hail, full of grace," instead of "Hail, O favored one" (Luke 1:28). "Who," rather than "which," is used in referring to the Holy Spirit (Rom. 5:5; 8:11; Eph. 1:14). The marginal translation is preferred in Romans 9:5, "Christ, who is God over all, blessed for ever." Appendix One consists of "Explanatory Notes" of various passages as required by Canon Law. The large majority of these notes are acceptable to Protestants and are helpful. Of course, Protestants would take exception, in part at least, to the interpretation of Matthew 16:18–19.

The Catholic edition of the entire Bible was published in 1966. No changes were made in the RSV text of the OT. All of what Protestants call the Apocryphal books, except 1 and 2 Esdras and the Prayer of Manasseh, are included as integral parts of the canon. The order of the books follows that found in the Latin Vulgate, except that the additions to Esther are incorporated in that book. There are twenty-three pages of "Explanatory Notes."

The publication of the RSV Catholic Edition marks a new day in ecumenical relations. The RSV, with a few modifications, provides a translation of the Word of God that all English-speaking Christians can share. Although the problem of the OT canon remains, Protestants and Catholics have largely come to an agreement on the translation of accepted books. This means that in theological discussions both can appeal to the same authoritative text. Dialogue between them is therefore greatly facilitated. It is worthy of note also that the Oxford Annotated RSV Bible with the Apocrypha received the *Imprimatur* of Cardinal Cushing, Archbishop of Boston, in 1965.

The RSV Bible Committee is a continuing committee, with authority to make revisions in the text of the RSV when it is deemed advisable.

A few changes were made in the New Testament at the time of the publication of the entire Bible in 1952. The most significant was the restoration of the words "sanctify" and "sanctification," which had been replaced by "consecrate" and "consecration." For the sake of euphony, the wording of Acts 17:28, "In him we live and move and are" was replaced by the familiar KJV rendering, "In him we live and move and have our being." A number of changes were made in the text in 1959 as the result of criticisms and suggestions from various readers. These include changing the rendering "married only once" (1 Tim. 3:2, 12; 5:9) to "the husband of one wife." In Job 19:26 "without my flesh I shall see God." "Loaf" in Matthew 7:9 and 1 Corinthians 10:17 is changed to "bread." The Roman centurion's exclamation is now given as in the KJV: "Truly this was the Son of God!" not "a son of God" as previously (Matt. 27:54; Mark 15:39). The translation of 1 Corinthians 15:19 and John 16:23 is also improved.

The second edition of the RSV NT was copyrighted in 1971. Again suggestions and criticisms from individuals and from two denominational committees were carefully studied. Attention was also given to textual and linguistic studies that had been made since 1946. As the result, a few changes in the underlying Greek text were made. The most conspicuous of these was the restoration to the text of two notable passages previously given only in footnotes: the longer ending of Mark (16:9–20) and the story of the woman taken in adultery (John 7:53–8:11). The blank space separating them from the rest of the text calls attention to them, and footnotes give information regarding the textual problems involved. Two passages in Luke are also restored to the text (Luke 22:19b–20; 24:51b) while another (Luke 22:43–44) is removed and placed as a footnote. New notes calling attention to significant textual variations in

MSS are added in a few places (e.g., Matt. 9:34; Mark 3:16; 7:4; Luke 24:32, 51).

A number of changes in the wording of the translation were also made, resulting in greater clarity. In 2 Corinthians 3:5–6, "competent" and "competence" are substituted for "sufficient" and "sufficiency": "Not that we are competent of ourselves to claim anything as coming from us; our competence is from God, who has made us competent to be ministers of a new covenant. . . ." In Matthew 12:1 "heads of grain" is more American than "ears of grain." "Move from here to there" (Matt. 17:20) sounds more up-to-date than "Move hence to yonder place." In 2 Corinthians 5:19 instead of "God was in Christ reconciling the world to himself" the second edition reads: "In Christ God was reconciling the world to himself." In Luke 22:29, "I assign to you, as my Father assigned to me, a kingdom" is given in place of "As my Father appointed a kingdom for me, so do I appoint for you." These examples illustrate the kinds of changes made.

THE COMMON BIBLE

Not only is the RSV Committee a continuing committee, but it has been internationalized by the inclusion of members from Great Britain and Canada, as well as from the U.S.A. Herbert Gordon May was elected as chairman of the committee in 1966. Following May's death in 1977, Bruce M. Metzger of Princeton Theological Seminary became the chairman. In 1969 the membership of the committee was extended to include six Roman Catholic scholars, two of whom were from Great Britain, and one from Canada. A member of the Greek Orthodox Church was also added in 1972. In the interest of ecumenism the committee in 1973 published the RSV Common Bible with the Apocrypha/Deuterocanonical Books. It appeared during the "Week of Prayer for Christian Unity" in England in February, and during Lent in the U.S.A. It has international endorsement by Roman Catholics, Greek Orthodox, and Protestants.

To facilitate the use of the RSV as a common Bible this edition arranged the apocryphal books in an order familiar to Roman Catholics and divided them into two groups, separated by a blank page: (1) the Deuterocanonical books, accepted by them as Scripture, and (2) the three books, 1 and 2 Esdras and the Prayer of Manasseh, which are not regarded as authoritative, but are included in the Greek canon of Scriptures. In the preface the position of the various Christian bodies with respect to the Apocrypha is clearly explained (pp. viii–xi).

Significant as the publication of The Common Bible was, it failed in one respect of being completely ecumenical: it did not include 3 Maccabees, which is recognized by such Eastern Orthodox churches as the Greek, Russian, Ukranian, Bulgarian, and Armenian. It also did not contain Psalm 151 at the close of the Psalter and 4 Maccabees as an appendix to the Old Testament, both of which are included in the Greek Bible. In 1972 a subcommittee of the RSV Bible Committee was commissioned to prepare a translation of these three documents. On the completion of this work in 1976, the translation was made available to the five publishers authorized to print the RSV. In May, 1977, the Oxford Press published the Expanded Edition of the New Oxford Annotated Bible, edited by Herbert G. May and Bruce M. Metzger, which included the translation of the three documents.

The publication of this truly ecumenical edition of the RSV is indeed a significant event in the history of the English Bible. It is a new day when Catholic, Eastern Orthodox, and Protestant Christians can all use the same translation, without compromising their respective canonical positions. This ecumenical version marks the end of controversy regarding an authoritative English Bible to be used in interdenominational dialogue.

A NEW EDITION

A new second edition of the RSV Bible is in the making. In 1977 the second edition of the RSV New Testament was published. The major changes made in it were described above, but further changes made in it will be published along with the second edition of the Old Testament. The Old Testament is in process of being carefully reviewed by the Committee and revised in the light of the best information available and set forth in present-day English. It is anticipated that this work will be completed in the middle of the 1980s.

Professor Bruce M. Metzger, the current chairman of the RSV Committee, has revealed some of the changes that are being made in this edition ("The Revised Standard Version," *The Duke Divinity School Review*, Spring, 1979, pp. 79–84). A noteworthy change in the English of both Testaments will be the elimination of the archaic second personal pronoun "thou" with its correlative forms "thee," "thy," and "thine," together with the corresponding verbal ending -est (-edst, -st, -t). The first edition had retained these archaic forms in language addressed to God. The trend today is toward the use of the same grammatical forms in prayers and liturgies as one uses in speaking to human persons. The abandonment of these archaic forms will in reality make the RSV more accurately reflect the Hebrew, Aramaic, and Greek, originals, for in these languages there is no linguistic differentiation made between language addressed to God and that used in conversation with human beings. The first edition had already eliminated the archaic nominative plural pronoun "ye," as well as the old endings -eth, -th for the third person singular. With the abandonment of "thou," "thee," "thy," and "thine," the modernization of the grammatical forms in the RSV will be complete. Naturally the change will be most noticeable in the Psalms.

Professor Metzger also discloses that the RSV Committee has become sensitive to what is called "masculine-oriented" language, and in the second edition is planning to use more "inclusive" English where this can be done without doing violence to the original texts. The generic use of the word "man" as a general term for people of both sexes has become offensive to some segments of modern society. Substitutions are being proposed for "man" in a number of passages, especially when there is no equivalent for it in the original. Thus in passages where the KJV has such phrases as "any man," "no man," "every man," or "he who," the new edition will use "anyone," "no one," "everyone," and "the one who" respectively. Other substitutions for "man" in a generic sense will include "people," "mankind," "humanity," "human beings."

We are assured, however, that the masculine designations for God, Jesus Christ, and the Holy Spirit will be retained. The committee is determined that the text of the new edition shall remain faithful to the Hebrew, Aramaic, and Greek manuscripts.

In the light of the changes in the forthcoming second edition, the closing paragraph of the preface of the first edition takes on new significance:

The Bible is more than a historical document to be preserved. And it is more than a classic of English literature to be cherished and admired. It is a record of God's dealing with men, of God's revelation of Himself and His will. It records the life and work of Him in whom the Word of God became flesh and dwelt among men. The Bible carries its full message, not to those who regard it simply as a heritage of the past or praise its literary style, but to those who read it that they may discern and understand God's word to men. The Word must not be disguised in phrases that are no longer clear, or hidden under words that have changed or lost their meaning. It must stand forth in language that is direct and plain and meaningful to people today. It is our hope and our earnest prayer that this Revised Standard Version of the Bible may be used by God to speak to men in these momentous times, and to help them to understand and believe and obey His Word.

3

The Knox Translation

THE HISTORY OF CATHOLIC TRANSLATIONS

It is difficult, almost impossible, for permissive, flabby, twentieth-century Christians to understand Christians of the sixteenth century who were willing not only to die for their faith but, what is stranger still, to kill for their faith. It was in that climate that William Tyndale translated the Bible into English for the Protestants. For this he ultimately paid with his life. Since the Bible was of central importance to the Christian faith, how it was translated could determine to a certain extent the direction of that faith. Should the Greek verb *metanoeō* be translated "repent" or "do penance"? The theological implications were weighty. Semantics, therefore, was tremendously important. Not only were battles fought over the words in the translation but also over the notes appended to the translation. What could not be written into the translation was written in the footnotes. This was usually an attack against the Catholics or the Protestants, depending on who did the translation.

The Catholics in England were placed at great disadvantage when the Protestant Bible was translated. Armed with the Bible in English, the Protestants could quickly turn to it in a dispute and simply read the passage. The unfortunate Catholic had no English Bible and had to translate on the spot. Even in teaching their own parishioners, the Catholic priests were handicapped. William Allen, a leading Catholic of the time who also assisted Gregory Martin in producing the Rheims-Douai translation, sensed this predicament when he wrote:

> Catholics educated in the academies and schools have hardly any knowledge of the Scriptures except in Latin. When they are preaching to the unlearned and are obliged on the spur of the moment to translate some passage into the vernacular they often do it inaccurately and with unpleasant hesitation because either there is no vernacular version of the words, or it does not occur to them at the moment. Our adversaries however, have at their finger tips from some heretical version all those passages of Scripture which seem to make for them, and by a certain deceptive adaptation and alteration of the sacred words produce the effect of appearing to say nothing but what comes from the Bible. This evil might be remedied if we too had some Catholic version of the Bible, for all the English versions are most corrupt. . . . If His Holiness shall judge it expedient, we ourselves will endeavor to have the Bible faithfully, purely, and genuinely translated according to the edition approved by the Church, for we already have men most fitted for the work. (*Letters and Memorials of Cardinal Allen,* pp. 64, 65, as quoted in Hugh Pope, *English Versions of the Bible,* p. 250.)

The NT (called the Rheims NT) was published in 1582 and the OT (called the Douai OT) was published in 1609/10, even though it was translated before the NT. Unlike the Protestant Bible, which was based on the Greek and Hebrew, this Catholic version was based on the Latin Vulgate. However, like the KJV, the Rheims-Douai version possessed a strange fascination and continued to be the Bible for Catholics through the years (in revised form, primarily that of Bishop Challoner). The King James tradition also continued on into the RSV. Not until the publication of the NEB (1961, 1970) did we have a fresh, *official* translation of the Protestant Bible. However, there have been many fresh translations that were privately produced.

The revised form of the Rheims-Douai version was the only Catholic Bible to have official approval until the translation of Monsignor Knox's NT in 1945. The latter did not displace the former, but they were both approved versions for Great Britain.

The OT was published in 1948 but, unlike the NT, was not approved as an official version. Knox's translation was received with great acclaim when it appeared. It had broken the shackles of the tradition of the Rheims-Douai version, which was essentially a sixteenth-century translation in spite of its revisions. *Time* (Feb. 11, 1952, p. 41) called Ronald Knox "the man who made the great twentieth-century translation of the Bible." At the time it may have seemed so, but events since have shown that it was only the beginning of freer translations and his use of the Vulgate even for a Catholic translation has been unfortunate. He translated too soon.

ITS CHARACTERISTICS

Ronald Knox was born into the home of an Anglican priest, educated at Eton and Oxford, was a brilliant student of classics, and a writer of vigorous prose and detective novels. At the age of twenty-nine, he became a convert to Catholicism. In 1939 he began his work of translating the Bible into English. One can appreciate his writing ability, with its witticisms and forceful illustrations, by reading *Trials of a Translator*, a collection of several of his articles dealing with his translation. He follows Belloc's principle of translation in asking himself, not "How shall I make this foreigner talk English?" but "What would an Englishman have said to express the same?" He criticizes the KJV as "essentially a word-for-word translation, no less than the Septuagint, no less than the Vulgate. 'For the Pharisees and all the Jews, except they wash their hands, eat not, holding the tradition of the elders'; is that English idiom? 'For the Nazis, and all the Germans, except they say Heil Hitler! meet not in the street, holding their lives valuable'; is that English idiom?" (pp. 75–76).

Knox's forte is his literary ability. After one reads *Trials of a Translator*, however, one feels that he is somewhat restricted in translation. His translation for his day was new and fresh but there are very few memorable translations in the NT. Take for example his translation of Romans 12:1–2:

> And now, brethren, I appeal to you by God's mercies to offer up your bodies as a living sacrifice, consecrated to God and worthy of his acceptance; this is the worship due from you as rational crea-

tures. And you must not fall in with the manners of this world; there must be an inward change, a remaking of your minds, so that you can satisfy yourselves what is God's will, the good thing, the desirable thing, the perfect thing.

Nevertheless, one feels the vigor of his prose in certain portions of the OT by his inversion of subject and verbs and by his elimination of conjunctions and articles. Notice these features in this passage from Nahum 2:3–4:

Bright flash that enemy's shields, warriors of his go clad in scarlet; dart like flame his chariots as he goes to the attack, dizzily sways charioteer. How jostle they in the streets, those chariots, hurtle they in the open market-place; dazzle they like flame of torches, like the lightning that comes and goes!

One is surprised, therefore, that Knox with his taste for literature did not translate the poetic parts of the Bible according to Hebrew parallelism. He gives as one reason the need to be practical. He means by this two things. He felt the need to conserve paper because of the paper shortage at the time. Prose would take less space than poetry, so this would mean quite a saving of paper. He also means that by saving space it would make it easier for people to carry the Bible around with them. It would not be so cumbersome. But his real reason is that his translation might read like an original writing, not a translation. He says, "What the reader wants, I insist, is to get the illusion that he is reading, not a translation but an original work written in his own language. And to our notions of poetic composition, these remorseless repetitions are wholly foreign when you have read a page or two on end, they begin to cloy" (p. 40).

One is further surprised to find that when Knox has dispensed with Hebrew parallelism, he nevertheless maintains the use of acrostics. This is found in Psalms 24, 33, 110, 111, 118, 144; Proverbs 3:10–31; and Lamentations 1–4. There are different types of acrostics. In Psalm 24, each of the verses begins with a consecutive letter of the alphabet. In Psalms 110 and 111, the acrostic pattern is in the form of two letters in the verse, the first beginning the verse in capital and the second in the second half of the verse in lowercase. Thus A and b are found in verse 1 and C and d in verse 2, etc. The letters are always printed in boldface so they stand out. In Psalm 118, the first letter of each sentence in the first paragraph begins with A, the first letter of each sentence of the second paragraph begins with B, etc. These devices must have taxed the ingenuity of the translator. A few examples of acrostic types follow:

Psalm 24:1–3

All my heart goes out to thee, O Lord my God. Belie thou never the trust I have in thee, let not my enemies boast of my downfall. Can any that trust in thee be disappointed, as they are disappointed, who wantonly forsake the right?

Psalm 110:1–3

All my heart goes out to thee, Lord, in thanksgiving, before the assembly where the just are gathered. Chant we the Lord's wondrous doings, decreed to fulfill all his purposes. Ever his deeds are high and glorious, faithful he abides to all eternity.

Psalm 118:1–3

Ah, blessed they, who pass through life's journey unstained, who follow the law of the Lord! Ah, blessed they who study his decrees, make him the whole quest of their hearts! As for the wrong-doers, they leave his ways untrodden.

As we have mentioned earlier, the text of Knox's translation is the Vulgate, but it was the edition authorized by Pope Clement VIII in 1592. He felt bound to this particular edition even when he knew it could very well be wrong. For example, Acts 17:6 reads, "These that have turned the world upside down are come hither also." This was the way it originally read even in the Vulgate. But the Latin word for "world," *orbem,* later was changed to "city," *urbem,* a change easy to make, as anyone can see. But, stubbornly, Knox translates it as "state," since "that is how the thing stands in every Vulgate in the world nowadays, and it is no part of the translator's business to alter, on however good grounds, his original" (*Trials of a Translator,* p. 2). For the same reason he has included 1 John 5:7, 8 which are not found even in the best Latin MSS. Because it is a secondary version, as F. F. Bruce says, "No one will go to his version for help in determining the precise sense of the original." (*The English Bible: A History of Translations* [New York: Oxford University Press, 1961], p. 204.)

The use of the Vulgate has led also to the Latin form of the names of the books—a usage the Jerusalem Bible has abandoned. This is somewhat confusing to Protestants. Such names as Paralipomena, Osee, Abdias, Sophonias, and Aggaeus may not be decipherable. The Apocrypha are also included, scattered throughout, since they are a part of the Catholic Bible.

In a contemporary translation it is strange that quotation marks are not used to set off direct speech and that "thou" and "thee" are retained throughout as the second-person pronouns. John Reumann also points out certain Latinisms, such as "perdition" for "destruction" in Matthew 7:13 and "charity" for "love" in 1 Corinthians 13. Reumann decries an "amalgamation of the antique and the modern," such as "swaddling clothes"; "all must give in their names"; "his espoused wife"; and "in her pregnancy" in the Christmas story. (*The Romance of Bible Scripts and Scholars* [Englewood Cliffs, N.J.: Prentice-Hall, Inc., 1965], pp. 207, 210.)

The footnotes are generally of the explanatory type, but some go further to emphasize Catholic doctrine. For example, in connection with Matthew 1:25 ("he had not known her when she bore a son") we find this note: "The text here is more literally rendered 'He knew her not till she bore a son'; but the Hebrew word represented by 'till' does not imply that the event which might have been expected *did* take place afterwards. . . . So that this phrase does not impugn the perpetual virginity of our Lady." In connection with Matthew 12:46–50, where Jesus' brothers are mentioned, Knox adds, "Since it is impossible for anyone who holds the Catholic tradition to suppose that our Lord had brothers by blood, the most common opinion is that these 'brethren' were his cousins; a relationship for which the Jews had no separate name." In explanation of 1 Corinthians 3:10–15, he adds this note: "At the same time, we are to recognize that many whose actions in this world have had little value, will themselves escape condemnation, though only by passing through the fires of Purgatory." No connection, however, is made with the Virgin Mary in Genesis 3:15 and Revelation 12.

In checking the text of Knox, we find, generally speaking, that it is very similar to the KJV, which is to say it is not of good quality. Some differences are its omission of "for thine is the kingdom and the power and the glory forever. Amen" in Matthew 6:13; "nor the Son" in Matthew 24:36; and "even as Elias did" in Luke 8:54. Concerning Mark 16:9–20, which Knox includes in the text, he appends this note: "And in a few of our existing manuscripts these last twelve verses are wanting, which fact (together with the abruptness of their style) has made some critics think that they were added from another source. But they are evidently a primitive account, and there is no reason why we should not ascribe their inclusion here to St. Mark." Knox's practice in dealing with the text and his persistence in using the poor text of Vulgate manuscripts do not recommend him as a text critic. Patrick Skehan, a Catholic OT scholar, after careful examination of Knox's practice in textual matters, says concerning the OT translation that "the use made of the Septuagint is thoroughly disappointing and inadequate" and that "in his judgment such reference to MT has in fact served very little purpose" (*Theological Studies* X [1949], 326). He is referring to Knox's claim of making "constant reference to the Masoretic text." Skehan further adds that Knox's treatment of the Vulgate itself "as a text is uncritical to a remarkable extent."

Knox has been freer in the OT than in the New. Notice the following translations:

Genesis 1:1–5

God, at the beginning of time, created heaven and earth. Earth was still an empty waste, and darkness hung over the deep; but already, over its waters, brooded the Spirit of God. Then God said, Let there be light; and the light began. God saw the light, and found it good, and he divided the spheres of light and darkness; the light he called Day, and the darkness Night. So evening came, and morning, and one day passed.

Exodus 20:3–7

Thou shalt not defy me by making other gods thy own. Thou shalt not carve images, or fashion the likeness of anything in heaven above, or on earth beneath, or in the waters at the roots of earth, to bow down and worship it. I, thy God, the Lord Almighty, am jealous in my love; be my enemy, and thy children, to the third and fourth generation, shall make amends; love me, keep my commandments, and mercy shall be thine a thousandfold. Thou shalt not take the name of the Lord thy God lightly on thy lips; if a man uses that name lightly, the Lord will not acquit him of sin.

Psalm 23 [24]

The Lord owns earth, and all earth's fulness, the round world, and all its inhabitants. Who else has built it out from the sea, poised it on the hidden streams?

Who dares climb the mountain of the Lord, and appear in his sanctuary? The guiltless in acts, the pure in heart; one who never played fast and loose with his soul, by swearing treacherously to his neighbour. His to receive a blessing from the Lord, mercy from God, his sure defender; his the true breed that still looks, still longs for the presence of the God of Jacob.

Swing back the doors, captains of the guard; swing back, immemorial gates, to let the King enter in triumph! Who is this great King? Who but the Lord, mighty and strong, the Lord mighty in battle? Swing back the doors, captains of the guard; swing back, immemorial gates, to let the King enter in triumph! Who is this great King? It is the Lord of Armies that comes here on his way triumphant.

Hebrew parallelism is abandoned. The familiar "For three transgressions . . . and for four" of Amos has become "Thrice forfeit . . . and forfeit once again."

Knox did break new ground by a fresh translation instead of revising Douai-Rheims. His NT was officially approved along with that of Rheims, and this was quite a progressive step. However, the optimistic claims for his translation from our vantage point are not as valid today. For since Knox, we now have Catholic Bibles consistently based on the original languages and using contemporary speech. The Jerusalem Bible and The New American Bible will eclipse Knox, since they have most of his virtues without his weaknesses and disadvantages.

4

Phillips's Translation

PHILLIPS'S FIRST EDITION

Its Background

What started out as one pastor's attempt to make the NT understandable to a London youth group eventually turned out to be Phillips's translation of the NT. It was because the young people "couldn't make head or tail" of the Authorized Version that J. B. Phillips felt led to the work of translation. And it was because he happened to send his first translation (Colossians) to C. S. Lewis, who encouraged him to go on, that Phillips's *Letters to Young Churches* (1947) was published. C. S. Lewis's reaction to Phillips's first attempt was "It's like seeing an old picture that's been cleaned. Why don't you go on and do the lot?" When he had completed the Pauline Epistles, Phillips was encouraged by people from various parts of the world to go on to the Gospels. He was reluctant to do this, since people might object to his paraphrasing the actual words of Jesus. He completed the Gospels in 1952, the Acts (The Young Church in Action) in 1955, and the Book of Revelation in 1957. The entire NT was published in 1958, Four Prophets in 1963, and the revised NT in 1973.

The great popularity of this version lies in its freshness of style and its readability. The NT reads as if it were originally written in twentieth-century English. It does not read like a translation at all. True, there are places where Phillips has not succeeded as well as in the major part of his work and where Britishisms hinder some understanding, but these are few and far between. As a whole, he succeeds admirably. This success is due to the care he took in avoiding "translator's English" and in trying out his translations with his friends.

But Phillips was concerned not only about his readers, he was also concerned about his authors. He wanted to write as if he were in their shoes. He says, "For myself I have taken the bold step of trying to imagine myself as the original writer, whether he be the careful and precise Matthew, the sturdy, blunt Mark, the sympathetic, understanding Luke, or the more profound and mystically-inclined John" (*Bible Translator,* IV [1953], 55).

Any translation that attempts to translate not merely words but ideas and seeks to bridge the gap between the ancient past and the present faces many problems. How far should one go? Amounts of money, measures, and weights may be relatively easy to translate, but does one modernize "Greet . . . with a holy kiss" with "Shake hands," or "sandals" with "shoes," or "girding one's loins" with "tighten one's belt"? What about ideas that are foreign to our modern culture? One can see how translation might imperceptibly merge into interpretation. Perhaps Phillips has chosen the better part by avoiding both the literalism that cannot be considered a translation at all and a radical modernization that would require the complete rewriting of a book like Hebrews or Revelation. Nevertheless, Phillips tends to overmodernize and is sometimes inconsistent. In his revised edition (1973) Phillips has corrected some of these weaknesses. His major improvement is the use of a better Greek text and more precision and accuracy in the translation of the text. The revised translation is placed in brackets when quoted with that of the first edition. Where no indication is given, the translation is the same in both editions. A more detailed account of the 1973 edition will follow later.

Its Features

There are some excellent features in this translation. The paragraph form with section headings is excellent for reading and understanding, though for those who want to check any specific verse, it presents a difficulty, since only the first verse of each section is numbered. In the new edition no verse numbers appear at all, making it even more dificult to check. The best feature, of course, is the translation itself.

William Smalley (*Bible Translator*, XVI [1965], 165–70) has made a comparative study of PHILLIPS and the NEB on Romans 12. He finds PHILLIPS superior in verses 1–3, 9, 10, 17–21. One unforgettable verse, which Smalley calls "one of the most powerful renderings in the whole New Testament," is Phillips's Romans 12:2: "Don't let the world around you squeeze you into its own mold, but let God remold your minds from within. . . ." [". . . but let God re-make you so that your whole attitude of mind is changed. . . ."] The KJV already had an excellent translation with "conform" and "transform" but lacks the vigor of PHILLIPS. One would appreciate PHILLIPS more if comparison were made throughout with the KJV. Some exceptionally good translations of PHILLIPS are the following:

Matthew 5:5

Happy are those who claim nothing, for the whole earth will belong to them!

Matthew 7:29

For his words had the ring of authority.

Romans 3:20

No man can justify himself before God by a perfect performance of the Law's demands—indeed it is the straight-edge of the Law that shows us how crooked we are.

Romans 5:20–21

Now we find that the Law keeps slipping into the picture to point the vast extent of sin. Yet, though sin is shown to be wide and deep, thank God his grace is wider and deeper still! The whole outlook changes—sin used to be the master of men and in the end handed them over to death; now grace is the ruling factor, with righteousness as its purpose [with its purpose making men right with God] and its end the bringing of men [them] to the eternal life of God [to eternal life] through Jesus Christ our Lord.

Romans 7:7–11

It now begins to look as if sin and the Law were very much the same thing [were the same thing]. Can this be a fact? Of course it cannot. But it must in fairness [om. in fairness] be admitted that I should never have had sin brought home to me but for the Law. For example, I should never have felt guilty of the sin of coveting if I had not heard the Law saying "Thou shalt not covet." But the sin in me, finding in the commandment an opportunity to express itself, stimulated all my covetous [om. covetous] desires. For sin, in the absence of the Law, has no chance to function technically as "sin" [has not life of its own]. As long, then, as I was without the Law I was, spiritually speaking [om. spiritually speaking], alive. But when the commandment arrived, sin sprang to life and I "died." The commandment, which was meant to be a direction to life, I found was a sentence to death. The commandment gave sin an [its] opportunity, and without my realizing what was happening [what it was doing], it "killed" me.

Romans 8:18–19

In my opinion whatever we may have to go through now is less than nothing compared with the magnificent future God has planned [has in store] for us. The whole creation is on tiptoe to see the wonderful sight of the sons of God coming into their own.

Romans 12:1–2

With eyes wide open to the mercies of God, I beg you, my brothers, as an act of intelligent worship, to give him your bodies, as a living sacrifice, consecrated to him and acceptable by him. Don't let the world around you squeeze you into its own mold, but let God re-mold your minds from within [re-make you so that your attitude of mind is changed], so that [thus] you may [will] prove in practice that the plan of God for you is good, meets all his demands and moves toward the goal of true maturity [the will of God's good, acceptable to him and perfect].

Romans 12:6–8

Through the grace of God we have different gifts. If our gift is preaching, let us preach to the limit of our vision. If it is serving others let us concentrate on our service; if it is teaching let us give all we have to our teaching; and if our gift be stimulating of the faith of others let us set ourselves to it. Let the man who is called to give,

give freely; let the man who wields authority think of his responsibility [man in authority work with enthusiasm]; and let the man who feels sympathy for his fellows act cheerfully [his fellows in distress help them cheerfully].

Romans 12:14–21

And as for those who try to make your life a misery, bless them. Don't curse, bless. Share the happiness of those who are happy, and the sorrow of those who are sad. Live in harmony with one another [each other]. Don't become snobbish but take a real interest in ordinary people. Don't become set in your own opinions. Don't pay back a bad turn by a bad turn, to anyone. Don't say, "It doesn't matter what people think," but [om. Don't . . . but] see that your public behavior is above criticism. As far as your responsibility goes, live at peace with everyone. Never take vengeance into your own hands, my dear friends: stand back and let God punish if he will. For it is written: "Vengeance belongeth unto me: I will recompense." [add, saith the Lord] And these are God's words [And it is also written]: "If thine enemy hunger, feed him; if he thirst, give him to drink: For in so doing thou shalt heap coals of fire upon his head." Don't allow yourself to be overpowered with [by] evil. Take the offensive—overpower evil by [with] good!"

Romans 15:1–2

We who have strong faith ought to shoulder the burden of the doubts and qualms of others and not just to go our own sweet way. Our actions should mean the good of others—should help them to build up their characters [We should consider the good of our neighbor and help to build up his character].

1 Corinthians 2:6

We do, of course, speak "wisdom" among those who are spiritually mature, but it is not what is called wisdom by this world, nor by the powers-that-be, who soon will be only the powers that have been.

Its Weaknesses

Lack of faithfulness to text. In spite of the excellence of this translation, some word of caution needs to be voiced. In an excellent article (*Bible Translator* [1959], 135–43) Robert Bratcher points out the vulnerability of this translation—its lack of faithfulness in translating the text. Phillips translates Matthew

6:2, "Don't hire a trumpeter" where the Greek simply says, "Sound no trumpet." The idea that someone else is to do the trumpeting for the one who gives alms is not stated and therefore it should not have been translated in the above manner. Perhaps the phrase "the bread we need" [add, "for the day"] in Matthew 6:11 is justifiable, since it translated the idea of the Greek word whose meaning is not altogether clear but is usually translated "daily" or "morrow."

"Brush your hair" was a bit too free for "anoint your head" (Matt. 6:17). Thus Phillips in the new edition has gone back to "anoint your head." The same is true for "This is the essence of all true religion" (Matt. 7:12), a translation for "For this is the law and the prophets." The new edition reads, "This is the meaning of the Law and the Prophets." "You have worked on the side of evil" (Matt. 7:23) is not exactly what Jesus said ("you evildoers"). Phillips adds "comfortably" in Matthew 15:35 but the Greek original does not have this word. In Matthew 16:18 Phillips adds "the rock" after Peter, an addition many will consider interpretive rather than a translation. The forcefulness of Jesus' expression "for your hardness of heart" is lost by Phillips's "It was because you knew so little of the meaning of love" (Matt. 19:8). "Mosquito" for "gnat" (Matt. 23:24) seems to take away from the comparison. "Where he can weep and wail over his stupidity [where there will be tears and bitter regret]" (Matt. 25:30) is too interpretive and loses the force of "gnashing their teeth." "Talitha cumi" and "Ephphatha" become "in Aramaic" followed by the translation (Mark 5:41; 7:34). "Utterly astounded" is not the same as Phillips' "scared out of their wits" (Mark 6:51). "Spoils your faith" for "causes you to sin" is too generalized (Mark 9:42). "Rubbish heap" (Mark 9:43) for "hell" (gehenna) is weak. "Don't bully people" is less forceful to an American than "Rob no one by violence" (Luke 3:14).

Phillips writes much more than the text says in Luke 7:33–34, "For John the Baptist came in the strictest austerity and you say he is crazy. Then the Son of Man came, enjoying life [food and drink], and you say, 'Look, a drunkard and a glutton, a bosom friend of the tax collector and the outsider!'" To avoid being explicit about the greeting by a kiss, Phillips in the first edition translated Luke 7:45, "There was no warmth in your greeting," but he has changed this to "You gave me no kiss of welcome." "He rejoiced in the Holy Spirit" (Luke 10:21) was distorted by Phillips to "Jesus himself was inspired with joy," but this too he later rendered more accurately as "Jesus' heart was filled with joy by the Holy Spirit." "How many of my father's hired servants" (Luke 15:17) is changed to "Why, dozens of my father's hired men."

"For God's sake" (Mark 5:7), "To hell with you and your money" (Acts 8:19), "May he be damned" and "be a damned soul" (Gal. 1:9) are unfortunate translations. "Practical and spiritually-minded" for "full of the Spirit and of wisdom" (Acts 6:3) is too free. "Speaking in foreign tongues" (Acts 10:46) is interpretive, as also is NEB's "speaking in tongues of ecstasy." "From cultured Greek to ignorant savage" (Rom. 1:14) is too strong for "to Greeks and non-Greeks, to the wise and to the foolish." "For Christ means the end of the struggle for righteousness-by-the-Law" (Rom. 10:4) is commentary rather than translation. "Greet one another with a holy kiss" (Rom. 16:16) is translated, "Give one another a hearty handshake all around for my sake [in Christian love]," but it is questionable if this is a proper modern equivalent.

Phillips recognizes many of his earlier translations as being too free and has made more accurate translations in his new edition. He had translated "when he appears" (1 John 3:2) as "if reality were to break in," but saw that this was indefensible and thus revised it to read as above. In earlier editions Ephesians 1:1 read, "to all faithful Christians at Ephesus (and other places where this letter is read)" but now the words in parentheses have been omitted. We see the same in 1 John 3:2 where he had translated, "Oh, dear children of mine (forgive the affection of an old man!), have you realized it?" Actually all this translated the one word, "Beloved." In the new edition, this sentence is omitted and "my dear friends" is substituted for it.

In a careful study of 1 Corinthians 1, the following deviations from the original were observed. We compare it with RSV, which in these verses is faithful to the original.

RSV	PHILLIPS
1:2 To those sanctified in Christ Jesus	to those whom Christ [add Jesus] has made holy
1:2 together with all those in every place who call on the name of our Lord Jesus Christ	to all true believers in Jesus Christ
1:4 because of the grace of God which was given you in Christ Jesus	for what the gift of grace in Jesus Christ [Christ Jesus] has meant to you
1:5 that in every way you were enriched in him with all speech and all knowledge	he has enriched your whole lives, from the words of your life to the understanding in your hearts
1:7 so that you are not lacking in any spiritual gift	And you have been eager to receive his gifts
1:8 who will sustain you to the end	He will keep you steadfast in the faith to the end
1:10 by the name of our Lord Jesus Christ	by all that Christ [our Lord Jesus Christ] means to you
1:12 each of you says	each making different claims
1:17 to baptize	to see how many I could baptize [primarily to baptize]
1:17 lest the cross of Christ be emptied	for I have no desire to rob the cross
1:18 to those who are perishing . . . who are being saved	to those who are involved in this dying world . . . who are being saved from that death
1:20 Where is the wise man? Where is the scribe? Where is the debater of this age?	For consider, what have the philosopher, the writer and the critic of this world to show for all their wisdom?
1:21 For since, in the wisdom of God, the world did not know God through wisdom, it pleased God through the folly of what we preach to save those who believe	For it was after the world in its wisdom had failed to know God, that he in his wisdom chose to save all who would believe by the "simple-mindness" of the gospel message
1:30 He is the source of your life in Christ Jesus	Yet from this same God you here received your standing in Jesus Christ

Style of language. There are certain of Phillips's translations that, although not wrong, seem incongruous in such a modern speech version. Some of these are too literary, whereas others are too colloquial. In the first group are the following: "the entail of sin and death" (Rom. 5:12), "magnificent denouement" [revelation] (Col. 3:4), "palpable frauds" (Titus 1:16), "express purpose of liquidating [undoing] the devil's activities [work]" (1 John 3:8), "invidious distinctions" (James 2:9), "inevitable disintegration" (2 Peter 1:4), "he is dilatory" (2 Peter 3:8), "slightest prevarication" (1 Peter 2:22), "serried ranks of witnesses" (Heb. 12:1). In the second group are these: "the whole assembly was at sixes and sevens" (Acts 19:32), "too high and mighty" (Rom. 1:26), "parting shot" (Acts 28:25).

There are also certain inconsistencies. In Matthew 5:40 "coat" and "overcoat" ["cloak"] are used, but for the same words "coat" and "shirt" are used in Luke 6:29. In Acts 12:8 and Matthew 10:10 "sandals" is used, but elsewhere "shoes." Monetary items are used rather loosely. In Matthew 25:14 a "talent" is $1,000 [one thousand pounds] but in Mark 6:37, 200 denarii is translated "ten dollars" ["twenty pounds"] and in Mark 14:5, 300 denarii is "thirty dollars" ["thirty pounds"].

In addition to the above unsuitable translations, there are others that could be improved. The expression "little faith" (Matt. 6:30, 14:31) is not proper English. "Cornfields" (Matt. 12:1 and "ears of corn" (Luke 6:1) are good English but the American needs to retranslate "corn" into "grain." In reference to Simon in Matthew 10:4, "the patriot" is a bit mild for "the Zealot." "Look of earth and sky" (Luke 12:56) is not the way that thought is expressed by Americans. For an American, the expression "foxes have earths" (Matt. 8:20) sounds peculiar. "Play actors" is more obscure than "hypocrites" (Matt. 23:13, 15). "Protest" does not seem to be the right word in Luke 9:5. "Thieves' kitchen" (Luke 19:45) is not an American expression. Perhaps Phillips should have studied English as used elsewhere as carefully as he studied British English if he expected his translation to be used in the entire English-speaking world. The common denominator has not been reached in the above instances.

In the first edition, after the Epistle he appended the name of the writer except for 2 Thessalonians, Hebrews, and 2 Peter. It should be understood, however, that these names are not found at this place after any of the letters in the original. He has now omitted these. Bratcher notes that "he curiously omits a translation of *ho presbuteros* 'the elder' in 2 John 1, but more than makes up for it in 3 John 1, where he translates the same *ho presbuteros* by 'John the Elder'!" Phillips has now corrected these by adding "the Elder" in 2 John 1 and omitting "John" in 3 John 1.

Greek text. Another weakness of Phillips was the Greek text he used. In his Letters to Young Churches he indicates that his Greek text was the same as that for the Revised Version of 1881. Unfortunately, this text is not the best by today's standards. He has now changed to the United Bible Societies' Greek text. But unfortunate still is his treatment of Mark 16:9–20 and John 7:53–8:11. The latter is kept in the traditional position without any differentiation, with only an asterisk referring to a note, and the former is differentiated only by the subject heading which reads "An ancient appendix" and the addition of an alternative reading. There is only a brief unsatisfactory note with the shorter ending: "An alternative ending found in certain manuscripts following verse 8." The UBS text has much fuller explanations at both places and omits the second passage from its traditional position, placing it at the end of the Gospel of John. The UBS text brackets, Luke 24:12, indicating words of dubious textual validity, but Phillips does not. The same is true for Luke 24:36cd. John 5:3b–4 is omitted by UBS but Phillips includes it in parentheses. UBS has "hyssop" in John 19:29 but Phillips continues to translate it as "spear." UBS double-brackets Luke 22:19b–20 showing this as a later addition to the text, but Phillips translates it without any signs. UBS single-brackets Matthew 12:47 but Phillips does not.

There are certain passages where the original is ambiguous and may be translated in different ways. We present a few of these. PHILLIPS is printed on the right:

Mark 15:39
The son of God (RSV)

a son of God

John 1:9
The true light that enlightens
*every man was coming into the
world* (RSV)

That was true light [,] which
shines upon every man *as he
comes* [, which was now com-
ing] *into the world*

John 1:11
he came to his *own home;* and his
own people (RSV)

He came into his *own creation*
[world], *and his own people* . . .

Romans 9:5
to them belong the patriarchs and
of their race, according to the
flesh, is the *Christ.* God who is
over all be blessed for ever (RSV)

The patriarchs are theirs, and so
too, as far as human descent
goes, is Christ himself, *Christ
who is God* over all [Christ who
is over all. May God be],
blessed for ever

1 Corinthians 7:36
But if any man think that he be-
haveth himself uncomely toward *his virgin* (KJV)

But if any man feels he is not behaving honorably toward the
woman he loves . . . (Compare
with NEB)

Hebrews 2:7
Thou didst make him for a *little
while lower* than the angels (RSV)

Thou madest him *a little lower*
than the angels

Hebrews 10:20
by the new, living way which he
has opened for us through the
curtain, *the way of his flesh* (NEB)

by a fresh and living Way, which
he has opened up for us by
himself passing through the
curtain, *that is, his own human
nature*

Revelation 12:17
which keep the commandments
of God and *have* the testimony
of Jesus Christ (KJV)

Those who keep the commandments of God and *bear* their
witness to Jesus

Revelation 19:10

For the testimony of Jesus is the spirit of prophecy (RSV) (Compare with NEB)	(This witness to Jesus inspires all prophecy.)

The second edition is the same as the first edition except for two significant changes. John 1:9 now reads, "That was the true light, which shines upon every man, which was now coming into the world"; and Romans 9:5 reads, "The patriarchs are theirs, and so too, as far as human descent goes, is Christ himself, Christ who is over all. May God be blessed for ever. Amen." There is one slight change in John 1:11 where "creation" has been changed to "world."

There is not much distinction in Phillips's translation of Hebrews and especially Revelation. This results no doubt from the difficulty of translating the ideas represented in these books, since they are foreign to this modern age.

Because of the tremendous popularity of this version, it deserves careful scrutiny. We have pointed out some of the weaknesses above so that the reader may be aware of these as he uses this version. Concerning its style, there is unanimity in favor of its excellence. Bratcher's evaluation here is typical: "Of its merits we can only add our voice to the chorus of praise. . . ."

This version was never intended to be used for scholarly and careful exegesis and should not be used for this purpose but for private use as a second Bible. Everyone can use it with great profit and like C. S. Lewis will sense over and over, "It's like seeing an old picture that's been cleaned!"

PHILLIPS'S REVISED EDITION (1972)

There are several reasons Phillips gives for undertaking a revised version. In his own words:

> The most important by far was the fact, which perhaps I had been slow to grasp, that "Phillips" was being used as an authoritative version by Bible Study Groups in various parts of the world. . . . This passion of mine for communication . . . has led me sometimes into paraphrase and sometimes to interpolate clarifying remarks which are certainly not in the Greek. But being now regarded as "an

authority," I felt I must curb my youthful enthusiasms and keep as close as I possibly could to the Greek text. Thus most of my conversationally-worded additions in the Letters of Paul had to go. Carried away sometimes by the intensity of his argument or by his passion for the welfare of his new converts I found I had inserted things like, "as I am sure you realise" or "you must know by now" and many extra words which do not occur in the Greek text at all. . . .

There was a further reason for making the translation not merely readable but as accurate as I could make it. It has been proposed that a Commentary on the Phillips translation should be undertaken. I felt it essential that the scholars who would contribute to such work should have before them the best translation of which I am capable. I certainly did not want them to waste time in pointing out errors which I had in fact by now corrected!

The last, but not least important, reason for making a fresh translation was to check the English itself. . . . Rather to my surprise only a few alterations were necessary, and this showed me that the ordinary English which we use in communication changes far more slowly than I had imagined (Introduction, pp. viii–ix).

Another reason for the new edition, though he does not give this as one, is the opportunity to use a better Greek text. He had based his translation on the Greek text used by the English Revised Version but for this edition he changed to the United Bible Societies' Greek text of 1966.

In his introduction, Phillips calls this new edition "a new translation" and "a wholly new book," although he admits that he retained "some considerable parts of the former translation." The jacket indicates that "more than two thousand improvements and corrections" were made. What do we really find in this new PHILLIPS?

First of all, there are a considerable number of minor changes: in matters of punctuation, some words formerly capitalized (e.g., "Gentiles") are now lowercase and vice versa; "toward" is changed to "towards"; "kneeled" becomes "knelt." Quotations from the OT are no longer italicized. Verse numbers are not indicated at all (not even for major divisions). English spellings of words are kept in the American edition. Words are more frequently hyphenated (e.g., "first born" is now "first-born").

Some books have been revised only slightly. In the first three chapters of Revelation, not counting the minor changes noted above, only the following alterations were noticed: "martyred" was changed to "killed" (2:13) and "purified" to "refined" (3:18).

Considerable changes were noted in Colossians, the first book translated by Phillips. Approximately 160 major and minor changes were noted. Not including changes due to the text, the majority of changes are the omission of expressions not in the Greek and the retranslation of those portions that appeared to be more interpretive than necessary. The following are examples of expressions that are omitted: "I want you to know by this letter that" (1:3); "very much" (1:7); "As a matter of fact" (1:8); "As you live this new life" (1:11); "we must never forget that" and "that is, in the kingdom of light" (1:13).

The following are modifications made to come closer to the Greek text: the addition of "we have heard that" (1:4); "boundless resources" changed to "glorious power" (1:11); "by his Son alone" changed to "by him" (1:14); "whether spiritual or material" changed to "whether heavenly or earthly" (1:16); "which is composed of all Christian people" changed to "which is the Church" (1:18); "Life from nothing began through him, and life from the dead began through him, and he is, therefore, justly called the Lord of all" changed to "He is the Beginning, the first to be born from the dead, which gives him pre-eminence over all things" (1:18); and "by virtue of the sacrifice of the cross" changed to "making peace by virtue of Christ's death on the cross" (1:20).

In checking the Gospel of Matthew, we noted fewer changes than in Romans or Colossians though more than in Revelation. Most were slight changes. Romans did not have as many changes as Colossians, but the same type of changes were noted. Complete retranslations were made in 7:22–23 and 8:11. Major changes were made in 3:29; 11:25, 36; 12:3; 14:4; 15:4, 16, 27.

Phillips claims that "this new edition is in fact a new translation from the latest and best Greek text published by the United Bible Societies in 1966." Our observations above do not indicate that it is a "new translation." We have not checked every instance of deviation between the former Greek text used and the present one. No doubt, there is real improvement here. However, in checking certain crucial passages, we have not found the changes significant.

Over all, one must say that the new PHILLIPS is an improvement over the old, especially in regard to the Greek text and greater accuracy in translation. However, it is basically the same PHILLIPS. In some verses, one will not find the spiciness of the old but in its place a more accurate translation, more faithful to the Greek. A moderately conservative introduction for each book has been added.

FOUR PROPHETS (1963)

At the urging of many, J. B. Phillips turned his translational skill to a portion of the OT (Amos, Hosea, Isaiah 1–35, and Micah, arranged in that order). He had made a popular and successful translation of the NT, but since his "knowledge of Hebrew was rather sketchy" and the problems of translating the Hebrew were great, he was reluctant to try it. He realized the difference between translating Greek and translating Hebrew. First of all, Hebrew expresses much in few words—"message after message is packed full of power, and expressed with a terrifying economy of words." Second, he rediscovered that while Greek had difficulties, Hebrew had greater difficulties, such as the untranslatable play on words and the defective text. Third, while he could translate the NT into ordinary English, Hebrew did not lend itself to this approach. As he expresses it, "It is wildly unsuitable for transferring into English of the dignified utterance or the passionate pleading of these ancient men of God. There is little hint in any of them of a conversational, let alone a colloquial, style. They were speaking in the name of the Lord and, like King James's translators 2,000 years later, both they and their later editors thought that only the highest language could do justice to the oracles of the Most High." Fourth, Hebrew idioms and thought are more distant to us than those of Greek.

Phillips chose these four prophets because they did their work at a crucial time in the history of God's people and because they "pierce through a great many falsities (including religious falsities)."

In addition to the translator's preface, a general historical background written by E. H. Robertson serves as introduction for all the prophets, and an introduction is provided by the translator for each of the books. In contrast to his usage in the NT, each verse is numbered, making it much easier for one to locate a particular verse. Subject headings are provided, as in the NT. Two maps are provided at the end, one of "the world surrounding the four prophets" and one of Palestine. Unlike Knox, Phillips has kept the Hebrew poetic form of parallelism.

The translation is rather free at times; at other times it is much like the RSV, which seems to have influenced Phillips quite heavily, although Phillips is fairly independent where textual difficulties appear. Because of the different original languages, it is difficult to compare this translation with that of his NT. In the latter he is quite free, especially in bridging the gap between the past and present in the translation of ideas instead of words. In the former he seems to have been somewhat restricted in this respect, although he translates Isaiah 5:27, "Not a belt is loose, not a shoe-string broken" for "Not a waistcloth is loose, not a sandal-thong broken."

Hebrew is concrete rather than abstract, but the concrete images of the Hebrew do not always communicate to a Western mind. Therefore we find Phillips usually translating by giving the meaning of the image, and this has the effect of making the picturesque prosaic. Sometimes he uses a Western figure for a simple description in Hebrew. Sometimes he substitutes a Western figure for a Hebrew figure.

Notice the following examples where the meaning of the image is given (the first is PHILLIPS, followed by the more literal translation of the RSV): "break the power" for "break the bow" (Hosea 1:5); "pass which is bright with promise" for "door of hope" (Hosea 2:15); "the land is withered" for "the land mourns" (Hosea 4:3); "like a bow which never shoots straight" for "like a treacherous bow" (Hosea 7:16); "I will destroy the power of the house of Hazael" for "I will send a fire upon the house of Hazael" (Amos 1:4); "made justice a bitter jest" for "turn justice to wormwood" (Amos 5:7); "the starry universe" for "Pleiades and Orion" (Amos 5:8); "cries of woe" for "alas! alas!" (Amos 5:16); "who only lives while he breathes" for "in whose nostrils is breath" (Isa. 2:22); "will never be able to shake themselves free" for "cannot remove your necks" (Micah 2:3). Some of the changes are not really necessary, however, since the Hebrew is not always obscure to the English reader.

The following examples show how Phillips has used a Western figure for a plain description in the Hebrew: "nursed the anger in his heart" for RSV's "his anger tore perpetually" (Amos 1:11); "wash the paint from her face" for "put away her harlotry from her face" (Hosea 2:2); "lick their lips" for "greedy" (Hosea 4:8); "rotten to the core" for "sinful" (Isa. 1:4); "hand in glove with thieves" for "companions of thieves" (Isa. 1:23); "raise their necks in pride" for "shall not walk haughtily" (Micah 2:3).

The following examples show how Phillips has used a Western figure for a Hebrew one: "grind the faces of the poor" for "trample the head of the poor" (Amos 2:7); "like a lonely watch-tower" for "like a besieged city" (Isa. 1:8); "turn my face away" for "hide my eyes" (Isa. 1:15); "Let them be led by the nose" for "babes shall rule over them" (Isa. 3:4); "noses in the air" for "outstretched necks" (Isa. 3:16); "green growth" for "branch" (Isa. 4:2).

Occasionally Phillips has added explanatory expansions that are sometimes helpful, sometimes unnecessary. In Amos 5:4 after "Bethel" he has added "House of God," which is the meaning of the word Bethel. Instead of the simple "I am like a moth to Ephraim" of the RSV, PHILLIPS has "I am the moth which rots the fabric of Ephraim" in Hosea 5:12. In Isaiah 2:12 "the Lord of hosts has a day" is expanded by Phillips to "the Lord of hosts has a day of reckoning."

Phillips's translation is very free at times. Usually the translation is acceptable but it is sometimes questionable. "The words of Amos . . . which he saw concerning Israel" becomes "These are the words of Amos when he saw the truth about Israel" (Amos 1:1). "For three transgressions . . . and for four" becomes "Because of outrage after outrage" (Amos 1:3). "When the Lord first spoke through Hosea" becomes "While Hosea was waiting" (Hosea 1:2). "As the Lord lives" becomes "My God" (Hosea 4:15). "New moon" becomes "any month" (Hosea 5:7). "Hear, O heavens" becomes "Let the heavens hear" (Isa. 1:2). "And the mountains will melt under him and the valleys will be cleft" becomes "Beneath him the mountains melt and flow into the valleys" (Micah 1:4). "For from the hire of a harlot she gathered them, and to the hire of a harlot they shall return" becomes simply "For the price of her unfaithfulness pays for her betrayal!" (Micah 1:7). Micah seems to have been translated most freely. Especially is this true of Micah 1:10–15 where there is a play on words in the Hebrew. To bring out this force Phillips has added quite a bit to the text. Compare PHILLIPS with the RSV which follows:

PHILLIPS

So then, in Gath where tales are told, breathe not a word!

In Acco, the town of Weeping, shed no tear!

In Aphrah, the house of Dust, grovel in the dust!

And you who lie in Shaphir, the Beauty-town, move on, for your shame lies naked!

You who live in Zaanan, the town of Marching, there is no marching for you now!

And Beth-ezel, standing on the hillside, can give no foothold in her sorrow,

The men of Maroth, that town of Bitterness, wait tremblingly for good,

But disaster has come down from the Lord, to the very gate of Jerusalem!

Now, you who live in Lachish, the town far-famed for horses,

Take your swiftest steeds, and hitch them to your chariots!

For the daughter of Zion's sin began with you,

And in you was found the source of Israel's rebellion.

So give your farewell dowry to Moresheth of Gath!

The houses of Achzib, that dried-up brook, have proved a delusion to the kings of Israel,

And once again I bring a conqueror upon you, men of Moresheth,

While the glory of Israel is hidden away in the cave of Adullam.

RSV

Tell it not in Gath,
  weep not at all;
in Beth-le-aphrah
  roll yourselves in the dust.
Pass on your way,
  inhabitants of Shaphir,
  in nakedness and shame;
Inhabitants of Zaanan
  do not come forth;
the wailing of Beth-ezel
  shall take away from you its standing place.
For the inhabitants of Maroth
  wait anxiously for good,
because evil has come down from the LORD
  to the gate of Jerusalem.
Harness the steeds to the chariots,
  inhabitants of Lachish;
you were the beginning of sin
  to the daughter of Zion,
for in you were found
  the transgressions of Israel.
Therefore you shall give parting gifts
  to Moresheth-gath;
the houses of Achzib shall be a deceitful thing
  to the kings of Israel.
I will again bring a conqueror upon you,
  inhabitants of Mareshah;
the glory of Israel
  shall come to Adullam.

Some of the differences are due to a defective text, but most of the changes are due to expansion on the part of Phillips to try to convey the play on words.

Phillips has some excellent translations. Among them are the following:

Hosea 2:9

Therefore when the corn is ripe I shall take it away, And when the wine is ready, I will take it back. And when the wool and flax are ready to clothe her, I will snatch them away.

Isaiah 1:15

Your hands are dripping with blood.

Isaiah 1:21

Once a home of righteousness, now a haunt of murderers.

Micah 3:11

Her leaders dispense justice—at a price, Her priests teach—what they are paid to teach, And her prophets see visions—according to the fees they receive.

Others have mentioned Amos 3:12b; 6:4; 7:2; Isaiah 5:26–30; 28:4; and 30:16 as superb examples of his work.

Scholars who are looking for an accurate translation will not be completely happy with Phillips's production. Neither was it intended to be used for study purposes. It takes too many liberties to be so used. Phillips, however, has given us a readable translation of these prophets and many will find new understandings of their messages through his work.

5

The Modern Language Bible

ITS HISTORY

The Modern Language Bible (MLB) is a new edition of the Berkeley Version, with an updating and improvement of the OT and a major revision of the NT by a group of scholars. It is therefore also known as The New Berkeley Version in Modern English. The Berkeley Version came into being as the result of the vision of a Dutch-born American, Gerrit Verkuyl. For many years he served with the Board of Christian Education of the Presbyterian Church, U.S.A. He had a growing conviction of the need for a translation of the Bible in modern English. He wrote, "As thought and action belong together so do religion and life. The language, therefore, that must serve to bring us God's thoughts and ways toward us needs to be the language in which we think and live rather than that of our ancestors who expressed themselves differently" (preface to Berkeley NT, p. iii).

Verkuyl was in many ways a remarkable man. Over twenty-one years of age when he came to America in March, 1894, he worked as a farm hand in California. He had yet to learn English and gain an education. At Park College, Missouri, where he received his Bachelor of Arts degree in 1901, his interest in Greek was aroused while he was a freshman. He received his

Bachelor of Divinity degree from Princeton Theological Seminary in 1904, with NT as his specialty. A NT fellowship enabled him to study in Europe, where he received his Doctor of Philosophy degree from the University of Leipzig in 1906. He did additional graduate work in Berlin.

His work with the Presbyterian Board of Christian Education brought him into contact with children and youth all over the United States, and the need for a translation in up-to-date language was impressed on his mind. He was kept so busy in writing, lecturing, and teaching, however, that for many years he did not find time to carry out his dream of producing such a version. But in 1936 he began working on his translation in earnest. In the following year he moved to Berkeley, California, and two years later resigned from the Board of Christian Education to devote his full time to the project. The finished product was published in 1945 as the Berkeley Version of the New Testament, its name coming from the city of Berkeley, California.

Four years later Zondervan Publishing House invited him to undertake the OT as well. A staff of twenty scholars under Verkuyl's chairmanship did the work, and in 1959 the complete Berkeley Version in Modern English was published. Then in 1969 the revised edition known as The Modern Language Bible came from the Zondervan Publishing House, which had obtained the rights of publication to the Berkeley Version.

ITS CHARACTERISTICS

Verkuyl "aimed at a translation less interpretive than Moffatt's, more cultured in language then Goodspeed's, more American than Weymouth's and freer from the King James Version than the Revised Standard." He based his NT translation on the eighth edition of the Greek text of Tischendorf, though he consulted other texts such as Nestle's. In deference to readers familiar with the KJV, he added to this text in parentheses such words, clauses, and passages as are found in the Received Text, but which, in the opinion of most textual critics, rest on insufficient manuscript evidence to be considered as an original part of the documents. He felt that to leave out such passages would be an offense to "these little ones," the designation he used for such devout Bible readers. In the revision of his NT in the MLB these passages are enclosed in brackets (see Matt. 6:13; 12:47; 17:21; 21:44; 23:14, et al.). In each instance there is a footnote usually worded thus: "The words enclosed in brackets are not found in the majority of the most reliable ancient manuscripts." The footnote for John 5:3b–4 reads, "The manuscript evidence for the words in vv. 3 and 4 that are enclosed in brackets is so slight that it is virtually certain that they were not in the original Greek text." Similarly, a footnote to Acts 8:37 states, "So many reliable ancient manuscripts omit v. 37, here enclosed in brackets, that it is practically certain that it was not part of the original text." The question then may well be raised: Should any words that we are reasonably certain were not in the original text be printed in the translated text, even in brackets?

The MLB, furthermore, is not entirely consistent in putting in all the additions found in the Received Text. The KJV of Matthew 19:9 after the words "Whosoever shall put away his wife, except it be for fornication, and shall marry another, committeth adultery" adds "and whoso marrieth her which is put away doth commit adultery." But this last clause is not in the MLB even in brackets. Likewise the last clause of the KJV of Mark 9:49, "and every sacrifice shall be salted with salt," is not given in the MLB. The same is true for "blessed art thou among women" in the KJV of Luke 1:28. Other phrases in the KJV of the Gospels not given in the MLB include "and they that were with him" (Luke 8:45); "even as Elias did" (Luke 9:54); "written . . . in letters of Greek, and Latin, and Hebrew" (Luke 23:38); "and of an honeycomb" (Luke 24:42).

For the most part, the translators of the OT endeavored to render the traditional Hebrew text just as it reads. However, when they were convinced the text had suffered in transmission, they did not hesitate to correct or emend it. But the instances of such corrections are far less numerous than in most recent English or American versions. In three passages in Isaiah they accepted the reading of the famous Isaiah Scroll of the Qumran Community (Isa. 14:4; 45:8; 56:12). There are footnotes to fifteen other passages, calling attention to other variant readings in the Isaiah Scroll that they did not adopt. In Genesis 44:4 they inserted the question "Why have you stolen my silver cup?" in parentheses with the footnote "The Septuagint translation contains this brief sentence which seems quite in place." In Song of Solomon 3:1 there is no footnote to indicate that the last line, "I called him, but he did not answer," is lacking in the Hebrew and was supplied from the Septuagint. In Exodus 8:23 the MLB, like the KJV and RSV, follows the Septuagint in translating, "I will make a distinction between My people and your people," rather than the Hebrew, which has "I will put redemption between my people and your people." No footnote, however, advises the reader that a change has been made. Likewise, there is no footnote to indicate that the reading "Edom" and "troops of Edom" in 2 Samuel 8:12, 13 comes from the Greek, whereas the Hebrew has "Syria" and "Syrians." Nor is there a footnote to 1 Samuel 6:18 to show that the translation "the great stone in the field of Joshua" does not correspond to the Hebrew. (See also Job 5:5; 32:9; 37:7; 1 Kings 19:3; Neh. 6:16; Zech. 3:15; Ps. 68:23; Mic. 6:16, et al.)

The MLB purports to be a completely new translation and not a revision of earlier versions. The translators sought, above all, to be faithful to the original Hebrew, Aramaic, and Greek. They were on guard against paraphrase, for, as Verkuyl puts it, "That leads so readily to the infusion of human thought with divine revelation, to the confusion of the reader" (Preface). This means that the MLB is fairly literal. Verkuyl states, "As far as possible this is a complete translation of every word in the Bible" (ibid.) At the same time, an effort was made to use English "according to its choicest current usage." In the earlier edition the language, particularly in the NT, was often unidiomatic and, at times, wooden. Fortunately, the NT has been thoroughly revised, resulting in marked improvement. In general, the present edition is accurate, clear, and simple.

Like the RSV, the text is divided into paragraphs. The verse numbers are given throughout in small superscript type. The Psalms, most of Proverbs, some of Ecclesiastes, Song of Solomon, Lamentations, most of Joel, and the third chapter of

Habakkuk are printed in poetic form. Surprisingly, the sublime poetry of Job is printed as prose. The same applies to the large poetic portions of Isaiah and other prophets.

Quotation marks are used throughout the Bible. The second personal pronouns—"Thou" in the nominative, "Thy" ("Thine") in the possessive, and "Thee" in the objective—are retained in language addressed to Deity (1 Kings 8:23–53; Ezra 9:6–15; Dan. 8:14–19; Matt. 6:9, 10, et al.). Otherwise the version follows modern usage in using "you" and "your" for the second personal pronoun.

One of the distinctive features of this version is the capitalization of pronouns referring to Deity, including references to Jesus, even when He was an infant (Matt. 2:11; Luke 2:21ff.).

In the OT there does not seem to be complete consistency in dealing with divine names. The Tetragrammaton, YHWH, is rendered "Jehovah" in Exodus 3:15 and Psalm 8:1, 9; YAHWEH, in Hosea 12:5; and "the Lord" in Amos 5:8.

This name came to be regarded by the Jews as too sacred to be pronounced. Hence in the synagogues down to the present day "Adonai," i.e., "Lord," is substituted for it. Scholars today generally regard the correct pronunciation as "Yahweh," but often the late medieval form "Jehovah" is still used for it. Usually in the MLB and the RSV, the name is rendered LORD, spelled with small capital letters. In Ezekiel 2:4 the Hebrew has the combination *Adonai Yahweh*, which the MLB gives as LORD God. One would expect, rather, LORD GOD. In Psalm 45:11 one finds LORD but one would expect Lord, as the original has *Adonai*.

There is no uniformity in dealing with place names involving the Tetragrammaton. In Genesis 22:14 occurs the transliteration "Jehovah-Jireh," with the footnote: "Meaning, The Lord will provide." In Exodus 17:15 the place name is translated, "The LORD my Banner," with the footnote: "Jehovah Nissi." In Judges 6:24 a similar name, "Jehovah-Shalom," is given as "Adonai-shalom," with the note "The Lord is peace." Finally, Ezekiel 48:35 states, "And the name of the city henceforth shall be THE LORD IS THERE," with the note giving the transliterated form: "YAHWEH SHAMMA."

Of interest also are the dates given, beginning with Genesis

12. This continues Dr. Verkuyl's work in the NT of which he says, "To the best of our ability we have tried to determine the dates of events, of sayings, and of writings." The dates given in the NT are certainly not far off. But the dates given for Abraham's call and other events in Genesis are, to say the least, debatable.

Another characteristic feature of the MLB is its explanatory footnotes, or as the title page puts it, "Informative Notes to Aid the Understanding of the Reader." From the very beginning of his work as a translator, Verkuyl felt the need for explanatory notes. "When I began my translating," he said, "I did not know that Weymouth had supplied footnotes; but I did know that there was need for them, if only to avoid interpreting within the text, as Moffatt so often does."

The footnotes are of various kinds. Some have to do with the text, as noted above. Others give explanation of proper names. For example, a note to Matthew 1:16 deals with four Marys in the NT. Notes to Matthew 2:1 advise us that "Bethlehem is situated five or six miles south of Jerusalem," that "Herod the Great, who ruled from 37–4 B.C., was the father or ancestor of other Herods," and that the wise men were "Magi, from *magus* meaning *great*, a Persian title that was used for teachers and wise men, in this instance astrologers." In succeeding notes there are explanations of the scribes, Pharisees, Sadducees, etc. Obviously this kind of information is helpful to the average Bible reader.

Occasionally there are also notes of a linguistic nature. Matthew 5:22 reads, "Whoever speaks abusively of his brother is liable before the Sanhedrin." A note states, "The Aramaic word *rhaka* used here in the original text means *empty, worthless*." A note to Matthew 5:48, "You then, are to be perfect," explains, "'Perfect' is from the Greek *teleios* meaning *complete, mature*." Matthew 13:27 has a note explaining, "The Greek word *doulos* means *slave* and is so translated here and in many places throughout the NT. . . ." On the same page a note to verse 8 states, "The Greek word here rendered 'world' *kosmos*, means primarily *orderly arrangement*. It also denotes *universe, world*, and inhabitants of the earth. . . ."

Still other notes are of an interpretive nature, often involving theology. Genesis 6:2 speaks of intermarriage between the "sons of God" and the "daughters of men." A note explains: "Some have it that this refers to fallen angels, but there is no Scripture evidence that they could become men with body and soul; nor, if they could, would wicked men be called 'sons of God.' We believe that the sons of Seth's family married daughters of Cain's family; that the home thus became ungodly and children grew up without relating life to God." A note to Isaiah 58:13 is also illustrative of this type: "The appointed Sabbath is holy ground. To observe the day cheerfully is a test of the people's fidelity to the Lord. The Sabbath is as a sanctuary, not to be trodden upon with irreverent feet." According to the footnote on 1 Peter 3:19, Christ's preaching to "the spirits in prison" means, "It was by the Holy Spirit that Christ preached through Noah to men of his day who are now in prison because they rejected the message." One other illustration must suffice: A note to Ephesians 4:22 explains "old nature" as "literally 'the old man,' all that the Christian is apart from Christ. In verse 24 it is 'the new man' (lit.), that is, what the believer is in his new birth through Christ." Generally speaking, Protestants have felt that the Bible should be allowed to speak for itself apart from interpretive notes.

There are other notes of a homiletic or devotional nature. Genesis 3:8 speaks of the sound of God walking in the garden in the cool of the day. A note suggests, "The hour of twilight remains a choice season for spiritual recreation—quiet communion." Concerning Adam's blaming Eve for giving him the forbidden fruit (v. 12), a footnote comments, "Blaming someone else is as old as humanity; it shows lack of repentance." Finally, the explanation of the rainbow in Genesis 9:15 is the basis for the covenant: "To the worshipper of God, the rainbow still says: 'God is faithful; trust Him.'"

The translators of the MLB approached their task from the stance of conservative evangelicals. This is reflected in their approach to messianic prophecies. In the preface Verkuyl has said, "We are in tune with the 'Authorized Version' of 1611 in fidelity to the Messianic Promise, first made as soon as man had sinned, renewed to Abraham, Isaac and Jacob, narrowed to Judah's offspring and later to David's descendants." A footnote to Genesis 3:15 declares that this verse contains the "first promise of the Redeemer, Victor over sin and Satan." In the verse the capitalization of the pronoun "He," referring to the offspring of the woman, makes this messianic interpretation evident: "*He* will crush your head and you will crush his heel." The failure to capitalize "his" is perhaps an oversight. Genesis 49:10 reads, "The scepter shall not depart from Judah, nor the leader's staff from between his feet until Shiloh comes and Him the peoples shall obey." A footnote states, "Pointing, we believe, to Messiah." Balaam's prediction, "A star shall come up out of Jacob, a Scepter shall rise out of Israel" (Num. 24:17), is interpreted in a note as, "The coming Messiah. The star has long been the symbol of royalty and imperial greatness."

Several psalms are interpreted messianically. Psalm 2 carries the title "The Lord and His Anointed Are Supreme," and a note points out that the Hebrew for "Anointed" is *Messiah*. The seventh verse is particularly significant (note the capitalization):

> I will tell the decree:
> The Lord said to Me, Thou art My Son;
> This day have I begotten Thee.
> (See also vv. 8–9, 12.)

Concerning Psalm 22, a note explains, "This is one of the striking Messianic psalms, depicting marked details of the sufferings of Christ." A note interprets "the angel of the Lord" in Psalm 34:7 as "The Redeemer, of the New Testament." In Psalm 45 we are informed, "The one addressed is, man plus, God among men, the Godman." Concerning the king who is to revere God "while the sun endures," a note tells us that "As this goes beyond human attainments, we consider it Messianic" (Ps. 72:5). Another note says, "How accurate a picture the poet draws of the Messiah's character! This King is more than human." A note to Psalm 89:27 states, "Neither David nor any other mortal could literally be God's first-born; but Christ, David's offspring could." Another note to verse 36 says, "In

Christ the covenant with David was amply fulfilled." Psalm 110 is also interpreted as messianic.

While the term "servant" in Isaiah is used "with elasticity," it refers especially to the Messiah, particularly in such passages as Isaiah 42:1–4 (note the capitalization of the third-person personal pronouns); 49:5–7; and, above all, 52:13–53:12, picturing the Servant's sufferings. A note also tells us that "The speaker in chaps. 61 and 62, is the Great Deliverer." A messianic interpretation is furthermore given to Daniel 9:24–27: "From the going forth of the message to restore and rebuild Jerusalem until the coming of the Prince, a Messiah, there are seven weeks and sixty-two weeks" (v. 25). "But after the sixty-two weeks Messiah shall be slain, although there is nothing against Him" (v. 26). The "He" of verse 27 is also the Messiah: "In a week He shall make the covenant to prevail for many, and in the middle of the week He will cause sacrifice and offering to cease."

The MLB is, in general, a simple, clear, and accurate rendering in contemporary English. The thorough revision given the work of Verkuyl has resulted in a far more satisfactory translation than the original Berkeley New Testament. Textually, one could wish that readings found in the KJV that have poor support in the Greek MSS had been placed in footnotes rather than included in the text in brackets. Other prominent variant readings that never found a place in the KJV could also have been included in footnotes, unless the evidence in their favor demands they be included in the text.

The Old Testament translation represents the work of twenty scholars who combined competence with reverence for the sacred text. These translators, however, apparently labored independently rather than as a committee. No doubt the rendering could have been further refined by more interchange and by direct confrontation among the translators in committee sessions.

Nevertheless, the MLB is a work of high quality and stands as a monument to evangelical scholarship. It is a useful tool to compare with other versions in the study of the Word of God.

6

The New World Translation and the Bible in Living English

THE NEW WORLD TRANSLATION

Its Doctrinal Bias

Denominational versions are fortunately rare. Such versions are generally usable only by the group that sponsored the translation. Some earlier Protestant and Catholic translations also fall into this group, especially with their biased and one-sided notes. The Common English Version of the American Bible Union (Baptist) of 1862 underlined its point of view by such translations as "John the Immerser" and "when he saw many of the Pharisees and Sadducees coming to his Immersion." The most biased of such is The New World Translation (1961) of the Jehovah's Witnesses.

Not only does the word "Jehovah" recur in the OT (as it did also in the ASV), but it is introduced 237 times into the text of the NT and 72 times in the footnotes. There is absolutely no basis for the translation of the Greek original by the word "Jehovah." By the way, the word "Jehovah" is an artificially created form resulting from the consonants of the name of God transliterated YHWH and the Hebrew vowels of the word for Lord, *Adonai*. This resulted from the fact that Jews refrained from uttering the name of God and usually substituted in its place the word *Adonai*. Thus the vowels of this latter word were placed with the consonants of YHWH so that the reader would know he should read *Adonai* instead. Most English Bibles follow the Jewish practice of translating YHWH as Lᴏʀᴅ, except when YHWH is preceded by the word *Adonai* in which case it is translated Gᴏᴅ, since *Adonai* itself is translated Lord.

The ɴᴡᴛ translators arbitrarily decide when the word "Lord" in the Greek should be rendered "Jehovah" and when it should be left as "Lord." While they sometimes use the title "Lord" with reference to Jesus—for example, in 1 Corinthians 12:3, "Nobody can say: 'Jesus is Lord!' except by the holy spirit," and 2 Corinthians 4:5, "For we are preaching, not ourselves, but Christ Jesus as Lord"—at other times they translate it as "Jehovah" even when the reference to Jesus is clear. This is the case in Acts 19:20 where the ɴᴡᴛ reads, "Thus in a mighty way the word of Jehovah kept growing and prevailing," even though they had earlier translated the parallel thought by the words "and the name of the Lord Jesus went on being magnified" (Acts 19:17). The expression "the Spirit of the Lord" is always translated "The spirit of Jehovah," and yet in the NT it sometimes refers to the Spirit of God and sometimes to the Spirit of Christ. Such a use even occurs within one verse, Romans 8:9: "But you are not in the flesh, you are in the Spirit, if the *Spirit of God* really dwells in you. Any one who does not have the *Spirit of Christ* does not belong to him" (ʀsᴠ, italics ours). Here the ɴᴡᴛ has "God's spirit" and "Christ's spirit."

Especially objectionable is the ɴᴡᴛ translation of John 1:1, "In [the] beginning the Word was, and the Word was with God, and the Word was a god." This is completely in harmony with the theology of Jehovah's Witnesses, since for them Christ is a created being. Therefore, He is to them not God but a god. It is true that the Greek does not have the article before "God" here. However, since in this verse in Greek *theos* (God) is a predicate noun and precedes the verb and subject, it is definite, since a definite predicate noun when it precedes the verb never takes an article in Greek. Some also see the anarthrous construction as emphasizing quality and translate *theos* as "divine." There is no justification for the Jehovah's Witnesses' translation.

There is no consistency in their translation of *theos* without the article. In the Gospel of John it is always written as "God"; that is, with a capital G (including, surprisingly, John 20:28), except in four instances. John 6:45 has a quotation from 54:13. The Greek has a form of *theos* but the Hebrew has *Yahweh* and this has led to the NWT's use of "Jehovah." "God" is not in these verses. This is understandable but not an accurate translation of the Greek. In the three other instances *theos* without the article is translated "a god." The first instance of this is John 1:1 about which we have already commented. But this same translation is found in the following verses:

John 1:18

No man has seen God at any time; the only begotten god who is in the bosom position with the Father is the one that has explained him.

John 10:33

The Jews answered him: "We are stoning you, not for a fine work, but for blasphemy, even because you, although being a man, make yourself a god."

What the NWT translators have done with John 1:18 is very interesting. They could have selected two other MS readings, "the only one" and "the only son of God," but they steadfastly kept the text they were following and translated it "the only begotten god." The word for "only begotten" probably should be translated "only" and there is absolutely no reason for not translating *theos* as "God." As we have already mentioned, there is no consistency except that of dogmatic consistency in their translation of *theos* as "a god." They have not even been consistent in their dogmatism in the translation of John 20:38 where we would have expected, "My lord and my god!"

There are several passages where the names "God" and "Jesus Christ" are joined by a conjunction, with one article before the first name. The rule is that usually two nouns in such a grammatical structure refer to the same person or thing. However, in every case of this kind where the nouns "God" and "Jesus Christ" are found together, they are translated so as to make God and Jesus Christ separate persons. Compare, for example, the following translations of Titus 2:13:

Looking for that blessed hope, and the glorious appearing of the great God and our Saviour Jesus Christ (KJV)

awaiting our blessed hope, the appearing of the glory of our great God and Savior Jesus Christ (RSV)

looking forward to the happy fulfilment of our hopes when the splendour of our great God and Saviour Christ Jesus will appear (NEB)

while we wait for the happy hope and glorious manifestation of the great God and of our Savior Christ Jesus (NWT)

The first three translations are similar and make God and Jesus Christ the same person, although it is ambiguous in the KJV. There is only a slight change in the NWT, but given the Witnesses' theological bias, it is sufficient to show that a clear distinction is made between the two by the repetition of the preposition "of." This same tendency shows up in the NWT translation of 2 Peter 1:1: ". . . the righteousness of our God and [the] Savior Jesus Christ." The article is not present before Savior in the Greek text, but before God only; the translators added it to make the distinction.

With the same theological bias the NWT translates Colossians 1:16–17 in the following way: ". . . because by means of him all [other] things were created. . . . All [other] things have been created through him. . . . Also, he is before all [other] things and by means of him all [other] things were made to exist." Needless to say, the words in the brackets are not in the original but are added to imply "other than Christ himself," that is to say, Christ Himself was created but He created all *other* things.

A more subtle translation with the same theological motivation is the NWT rendering of Philippians 2:6: ". . . who, although he was existing in God's form, gave no consideration to a seizure, namely, that he should be equal to God." Compare this with the translation of the JB: "His state was divine, yet he did not cling to his equality with God." Or the RSV: ". . . who, though he was in the form of God, did not count equality with God a thing to be grasped." The NWT implies simply that Jesus gave no consideration to being equal with God while the others assert that He did not cling to His equality with God but emptied Himself. There is a vast difference of meaning and an important theological implication in these translations.

Still another theologically motivated characteristic is the way "Holy Spirit" is printed. Since Witnesses do not believe in the deity of the Holy Spirit, these words are never capitalized. According to them, "The holy spirit is not a person or being, and no scripture authorizes the conclusion that it is. It is the active force of God with which he accomplishes his purpose. The Scriptures are crystal clear on the subject." (*Awake!* June 22, 1955, p. 261)

Even though Jehovah's Witnesses believe the Lord's Supper was only a memorial service, this does not justify their translation of 1 Corinthians 11:24–25: " 'This means my body which is in YOUR behalf. Keep doing this in remembrance of me! . . . This cup means the new covenant by virtue of my blood.' " The Greek verb used is "is" and should have been translated thus. Their concern for accuracy and literalism seems to be set aside whenever the literal text conflicts with their theological position.

Besides the examples noted above, there are other interpretive translations. Jehovah's Witnesses believe the dead have no conscious existence, but there is no justification for their translation of 1 Corinthians 15:29: "Otherwise, what will they do who are being baptized for the purpose of [being] dead ones? If the dead are not to be raised up at all, why are they also being baptized for the purpose of [being] such?" In the margin of their NT edition, there is a reference to Romans 6:4, which indicates they interpret this verse to mean that Paul is referring to the fact that the Christian dies with Christ at baptism. However one interprets this passage (and this interpretation is very unlikely), at least the passage should be translated accurately. The Greek word translated "for the purpose of" means more likely "in behalf of," "for," or "in place of." The addition of "being" is purely interpretive. The KJV translates the phrase as "for the dead"; the RSV and NEB as "on behalf of the dead."

Another interpretive translation, though without apparent theological bias, is made in 1 Corinthians 7:36: "But if anyone thinks he is behaving improperly toward his virginity, if that is past the bloom of youth, and this is the way it should take place, let him do what he wants; he does not sin. Let them marry." The first thing to be said about this verse is that no matter what translation one takes up, it will surely be an interpretation. It is almost impossible to translate this passage without interpreting it. Notice the words we have italicized in the following translations:

> But if any man think that he behaveth himself uncomely toward his *virgin, if she pass the flower of her age* (KJV)

> If any one thinks that he is not behaving properly toward his *betrothed, if his passions are strong* (RSV)

> But if a man has a *partner in celibacy* and feels that he is not behaving properly towards her, if, that is, his *instincts are too strong* for him (NEB)

However, it is difficult to justify "virginity" in NWT. The Greek word means "virgin" and the word for "virginity" is another word coming from the same root.

Its Translation

This special pleading in the NWT is its worst feature. Another weakness is the translation itself. The OT scholar, H. H. Rowley, writes—

> The jargon which they use is often scarcely English at all, and it reminds one of nothing so much as a schoolboy's first painful beginnings in translating Latin into English. The translation is marked by a wooden literalism which will only exasperate any intelligent reader—if such it finds—and instead of showing the reverence for the Bible which the translators profess, it is an insult to the Word of God. (*Expository Times* 65 [1953–54]: 41–42)

Examples of these poor renderings abound:

Genesis 18:20–21

Consequently Jehovah said: "The cry of complaint about Sodom and Gomorrah, yes, it is loud, and their sin, yes, it is very heavy. I am quite determined to go down that I may see whether they act altogether according to the outcry over it that has come to me, and, if not, I can get to know it."

Genesis 6:1–3

Now it came about that when men started to grow in numbers on the surface of the ground and daughters were born to them, then the sons of the [true] God began to notice the daughters of men, that they were goodlooking; and they went taking wives for themselves, namely, all whom they chose. After that Jehovah said: "My spirit shall not act toward man indefinitely in that he is also flesh."

Exodus 20:3

You must not have any other gods against my face.

Isaiah 1:13

Stop bringing in any more valueless grain offerings. Incense—it is something detestable to me. New moon and sabbath, the calling of a convention—I cannot put up with the [use of] uncanny power along with the solemn assembly.

Daniel 7:25

And he will speak words against the Most High, and he will harass continually the holy ones themselves of the Supreme One.

Matthew 5:18

For truly I say to YOU that sooner would heaven and earth pass away than for the smallest letter or one particle of a letter to pass away from the Law by any means and not all things take place.

1 Corinthians 5:1

Actually fornication is reported among YOU, and such fornication as is not even among the nations, that a wife a certain [man] has of [his] father.

1 Corinthians 10:11

Now these things went on befalling them as examples, and they were written for a warning to us upon whom the ends of the systems of things have arrived.

The above examples are in harmony with the Witnesses' attempt to be as literal as possible, but when literalism obscures the meaning of the verse it has gone too far. To this obscurity they add such a nonliterary style as to repulse the reader. We do not want to imply that the entire translation is of the same poor quality as the above examples. However, there are enough renderings of this kind that were we to judge it simply on this basis, it would score very low.

There are other peculiarities in translation that should be noted. The use of "torture stake" for the cross and "impale" for crucify are two of these unfortunate examples. It is based on the belief of the Jehovah's Witnesses that the cross on which Jesus was crucified was a single stake. John Mattingly marshals the evidence to show the fallacy of the Witnesses' contention:

> Another unusual translation our unidentified committee gives us is that of Mt 10:38, "whoever does not accept this torture stake and follow after me is not worthy of me." Again all sorts of authorities are marshaled, this time to back their contention that Christ was "impaled" (Mt. 27:38 and al.). First it should be noted that "impale" is used in a sense not acknowledged by Webster's New International Dictionary (Unabridged, 1949). They do not mean the Oriental custom of thrusting a body down on a pointed stake. Rather they give an illustration from Justus Lipsius' *De Cruce,* showing a man affixed by nails to a single upright pole but with the hands attached about a foot above his head on the one upright. It is not mentioned that Lipsius gives five different pictures in all and that he himself held in this same book for the traditional representation as true. They do lay great emphasis on the original meaning of "stauros" as a single upright pole. That this single upright pole was used for executions they prove by citing Roman literature. But there is a strange silence about the descriptions of the crucifixions of slaves at the beginning of the Christian era. Customarily the slaves were made to carry the *patibulum* or horizontal bar of their cross to the place of execution. So common was this form of crucifixion that the Roman authors use *patibulum* as synonymous with *crux* (Seneca, *De Vita Beata,* 19:3; *Epistola* 101:12. Tacitus, *Historiae,* IV, 3). To hold that Constantine introduced the traditional cross as a relic of his pagan worship of the sun god (p. 771) is unworthy of their evident scholarship. True the cross does not appear in the catacombs as a symbol of Christ before 312 A.D. Neither does their "torture stake"; nor later, for that matter. As for the Fathers, it is the traditional cross they describe. To cite only two witnesses; Irenaeus speaks of Christ's cross as having five ends, two longitudinal, two latitudinal, and a fifth on the support for

the body of the victim (*Adversus Haereses*, II, 24, 4). He wrote before 200 A.D. Still earlier is the witness of the *Epistle of Barnabas*, X, 8. Here the writer speaks of the cross as having the shape of a Greek *Tau*. (*Catholic Biblical Quarterly* XIII [1951], 441)

What is gained by this insistence on the use of "torture stake" for "cross" and of "impale" for "crucify" is difficult to see. Surely there is nothing gained for the Witnesses' doctrinal position to risk these idiosyncrasies in translation.

Other features that characterize this translation are the names the translators give to the OT and the NT, their use of capitals to indicate the plural of the second person, their attempt to translate more accurately the Greek verbs, their Greek text base, and their complete dropping of the archaic second person pronouns such as thou, thy, thine, thee, and ye.

The Witnesses do not call the first division of the Bible the Old Testament or the second division the New Testament. Instead, they designate these parts respectively as The Hebrew-Aramaic Scriptures and The Christian Greek Scriptures, thus making a distinction in the language and perhaps an unintentional implication that the OT is not Christian.

While their attempt to distinguish between the singular and plural of the second person is commmendable, it presents certain problems. The pronoun is capitalized in its entirety when it refers to the plural. This involves the verb when it is in the imperative. This makes for awkwardness in reading.

The attempt to indicate the force of the Greek verbs is good but is done at the expense of literary beauty. Note such translations as the following:

Matthew 5:25

Be about settling matters quickly with the one complaining against you at law.

Matthew 5:44

Continue to love YOUR enemies.

Matthew 6:19

Stop storing up for yourselves treasures upon the earth.

Matthew 6:33

Keep on, then, seeking first the kingdom and his righteousness.

One commendable feature of this translation is that it is based on a relatively good Greek text, mainly that of Westcott and Hort. This leads to the dropping of many late readings due to a tendency toward harmonization, especially in the Gospels. The spurious passages in 1 John 5:7–8 is also omitted, whereas John 7:53–8:11, concerning the adulterous woman, is placed in the lower margin in smaller print and Mark 16:8 is followed by the longer and shorter conclusion both in smaller print with an introductory explanation.

The dropping of the archaic second person pronouns puts NWT in line with more modern translations.

Certain other interesting and peculiar translations appear. One of these is the translation of the Greek word usually translated "age" or "world." The NWT consistently translates it as "system of things." Surely no improvement, this practice merely adds to the woodenness and awkwardness of the translation. For example, take the following:

Matthew 13:22

this is the one hearing the word, but the anxiety of this system of things and the deceptive power of riches choke the word.

Matthew 28:20

And, look! I am with YOU all the days until the conclusion of the system of things.

Hebrews 1:2

and through whom he made the systems of things.

Hebrews 11:3

By faith we perceive that the systems of things were put in order by God's word.

2 Timothy 4:10

For Demas has forsaken me because he loved the present system of things.

The translation of the word *petra* as "rock-mass" every time it is used is unnecessary and awkward. Thus Romans 9:33 reads, "Look! I am laying in Zion a stone of stumbling and a rock-mass of offense . . ." and 1 Corinthians 10:4 says, "For they used to drink from the spiritual rock-mass that followed them, and that rock-mass meant Christ." In this day when rock mass has quite a different meaning, "spiritual rock-mass" may conjure up an entirely different image than what the text calls for.

"Holy ones" for "saints" is not any improvement. For example, Ephesians 1:1 reads, "Paul, an apostle of Christ Jesus through God's will, to the holy ones who are in Ephesus. . . ." "Inspired expression" for "spirit" cannot be justified in 1 John 4:1–3, 6. The Greek word is translated as "spirit" in 3:24; 4:13; and 5:6, 8 in the Epistle. There is no valid reason for this change.

An ultra-consistency has led to the translation of the Greek word *parousia* in every instance as "presence." The word has this meaning but surely in the majority of the cases, especially where it refers to the second advent, it should be translated "coming." One English word cannot always translate a particular Greek word accurately. A particular Greek word, as well as a particular English word, does not always have the same meaning. The context must determine its meaning. Unfortunately, the translator(s) of the NWT did not have this flexibility.

There are certain peculiar translations in the NWT. Compare them with the RSV, which follows each passage:

Genesis 7:15

in which the *force of life was active*
in which there was the *breath of life*

Genesis 8:21

And Jehovah began to smell a *restful odor*
And when the Lord smelled the *pleasing odor*

Genesis 16:12

As for him, he will become a *zebra* of a man
He shall be a *wild ass* of a man

Genesis 17:4

As for me, look! my covenant is with you, and you will certainly become father of a *crowd of nations*

Behold, my covenant is with you, and you shall be the father of a *multitude of nations*

Genesis 21:9

And Sarah kept noticing the son of Hagar the Egyptian whom she had borne to Abraham, *poking fun*

But Sarah saw the son of Hagar the Egyptian, whom she had borne to Abraham, *playing with her son Isaac*

Psalms 1:2

But his delight is in the law of Jehovah, And in his law he *reads in an undertone* day and night

but his delight is in the law of the LORD, and on his law he *meditates* day and night.

Isaiah 58:1

Call out *full-throated;* do not hold back
Cry *aloud,* spare not

Malachi 3:8

Will *earthling man* rob God?
Will *man* rob God?

Matthew 6:17

"*grease* your head"
"*anoint* your head"

1 Corinthians 2:7

"*Sacred secret*"
"*mystery*"

Revelation 13:1

"*wild beast*"
"*beast*"

The text is arranged by sense paragraphs rather than individual verses like the KJV. This is a definite improvement. However, the use of ancient terms for weights, measures, money, and time is definitely a backward step.

Dr. Bruce M. Metzger's evaluation is that "on the whole one gains a tolerably good impression of the scholarly equipment of the translators." The translation at times is also good. However, the theological bias and the inconsistent quality of the translation neutralize the good elements within it.

THE BIBLE IN LIVING ENGLISH

When the Watchtower Bible and Tract Society published this new version, it was thought at first that it was a revised edition of its earlier New World Translation. However, this is not the case. It is an entirely new translation by one Steven T. Byington (1868–1957), who was not a Jehovah's Witness. He attended a Congregational church that later merged with another to form the United Church of Ballard Vale, Massachusetts. He obtained an A.B. in classics from the University of Vermont and later spent one year at Union Theological Seminary and a half year at Oberlin studying biblical languages. After his death, the Watchtower Bible and Tract Society of Pennsylvania received the publication rights for the translation and published it in 1972.

According to the translator, the purpose of this translation "is to put the Bible into living present-day English." His principles of translation can be seen from the following statements: "To say in my own words what I thought the prophet or apostle was driving at would not, to my mind, be real translation; nor yet to analyze into a string of separate words all the implications which the original may have carried in one word; the difference between conciseness and prolixity is one difference between the Bible and something else. So far as a translation does not keep to this standard, it is a commentary rather than a translation: a very legitimate and useful form of commentary, but it leaves the field of translation unfilled." He tends to be more literal than free, yet is not completely bound to the limitations of the translated language. "The test," he says "is generally whether the English translated into Hebrew or Greek would have had to give what the Hebrew or Greek writer wrote."

It will seem strange that in pronouns addressed to God the BLE has "thou" in the NT but "you" in the OT. Byington's justification for this is "that the New Testament men had nearly the same feelings as we have about addressing God, but the Old Testament men, those of them who had most to say to God, such as Abraham, Moses, Elijah, Jeremiah, had not such feelings as lead us to give God a special pronoun."

One feature, at least, that led the Witnesses to publish this translation is the rendering of the name of God as "Jehovah." The translator recognizes that this name is due to a blunder but does not feel that the spelling and pronunciation are important. "What is highly important is to keep it clear that this is a personal name."

The translation is set forth in one column with the verse numbers on the left-hand margin. There are no subject headings, notes, or references. Marginal notes are found at the end of each book. These consist of alternative translations, the literal rendering, or alternative readings for the verse indicated. The designations "Old Testament" and "New Testament" are not found before each section, although the translator refers to these in his preface. This lack of designation is probably due to the influence of the Witnesses who do not use these terms. Two charts and two maps are found at the end of the Bible.

Spellings of some of the names of the books of the Bible and of some persons in the Bible are different from those we have become accustomed to and that Catholic Bibles also now use. For instance, we find the following: Hambakuk, Hoshea', Malaki, Sephaniah, Zecariah, Enoc, and Lamec.

The translator refers to the fact that the "old version" (KJV) contains "forged texts." He is quite aware of textual criticism as his reference to the OT text also indicates. In checking the text of the NT, we found that Byington used considerable freedom in his selection. He probably used a text like that of Nestle but did not follow it slavishly. Mark 16:9–20 is set off with this heading: A WRITING SAID TO BE BY ELDER ARISTON: THE VERSES ARE NUMBERED AS PART OF THE SIXTEENTH CHAPTER OF MARK. John 7:53–8:11 is placed at the end of the Gospel of John instead of in the traditional location and is set off from the last of the Gospel with a heading. Especially interesting is the choice of "Jesus Barabbas" instead of "Barabbas" in

Matthew 27:16. He follows the NEB here. Also following the NEB, he has "on a pilum [javelin]" in John 19:29, instead of "hyssop," and omits Matthew 16:2b–3. Luke 22:43–44 and 23:34 are placed in brackets. In the "Explanation" at the beginning it is mentioned that "adjustments made by the Publishers are indicated by the use of square brackets." Does this mean that these verses were actually omitted by the translator but were added by the publishers? If that is the case, he has gone further than most translations, which keep these verses.

In checking a few of the "Marginal Notes to First Corinthians" the following observations were made. The note to 1:28 reads, "*Lit.* supersede the somethings." Actually the Greek text reads, "in order that he might bring to nothing things that are." The note on 2:4 reads, "*Var.* with persuasion by wisdom of words." Nestle lists six other readings besides the one the translator chose to follow, but none of them reads as he has given. Also it is difficult to know by what principles he is selecting the variants he lists. Most of the notes give the literal form of the text.

While this translation is completely independent from the NWT, we made a comparison of the two. Since it is published by the Jehovah's Witnesses, we were especially interested in those passages where the characteristic biases of the NWT were evident. In the BLE, "Jehovah" is used in the OT but is not found in the NT. The word "God" is capitalized when referring to Jesus Christ, e.g., in John 1:1; 1:18; 6:45; 10:33. Where the NWT added the article "the" in brackets in Titus 2:13 and 2 Peter 1:1 and "other" in Colossians 1:16, 17, this translation does not, so that Jesus Christ can be identified with God in these passages. Furthermore, by its punctuation in Romans 9:5 it has clearly identified Christ as God: "Whose are the fathers, and from whom in the way of flesh comes the Christ, he who is over everything, God blessed forever—Amen!"

The designation "Holy Spirit" is capitalized, contrary to the NWT, and the words "cross" and "crucify" are used instead of "torture stake" and "impale."

The only apparent reason for the Witnesses' publishing this translation is the translator's use of "Jehovah" for God's name in the OT, unless they also want to tone down the idiosyncrasies in their own translation.

The translation leans more to the literal side of the spectrum and is rather straightforward. We give two samples, one from the OT and one from the NT:

Genesis 3:1–5

And the snake was the shrewdest of all the wild beasts that God Jehovah had made; and it said to the woman, "A pity God said you were not to eat of all the trees in the garden." And the woman said to the snake, "Fruit from the trees in the garden we are to eat, but as to the fruit of this tree in the middle of the garden God said, 'You are not to eat any of it, nor touch it, or you will die.'" And the snake said to the woman, "Die you would not; but God knows that on the day you eat of it your eyes will be opened and you will be like gods, knowing good and bad."

Matthew 5:17–20

"Do not suppose that I came to tear down the law or the prophets; I did not come to tear down but to fill up. For I tell you verily, till the heavens and the earth pass away, not the dot of an i nor the cross of a t in the law shall pass away, till everything is done. So whoever breaks one of the pettiest of those commandments, and teaches men so, shall be called petty in the Reign of Heaven; but whoever does them and teaches them shall be called great in the Reign of Heaven. For I tell you that unless your righteousness outdoes the scribes and Pharisees you shall not get into the Reign of Heaven."

The above samples point our some of the weaknesses of this translation. It lacks literary beauty and in some places it tends toward the novel. It is no surprise to discover these weaknesses in a translation made by one man who has no real professional training for the task. We list below some of these peculiar translations. The translation from the BLE will be given first, followed by that of the RSV.

Genesis

1:28 "bear empire over the fishes"—"have dominion over the fish"
2:4 "line of the heavens"—"generations of the heavens"
2:13 "Negroes' country"—"land of Cush"
3:7 "pinned fig-leaves together and made themselves belts"—
"sewed fig leaves together and made themselves aprons"

3:15 "it bursting your head and you bursting its heel"—"he shall bruise your head, and you shall bruise his heel"

4:23 "For I have killed a man for my scratch, a child for my bruise"—"I have slain a man for wounding me, a young man for striking me"

6:14 "Make yourself a gopher-wood box"—"Make yourself an ark of gopher wood"

Exodus

20:3 "no other gods to face me down"—"no other gods before me"

In Leviticus new terms appear such as "sin-steer" for "sin offering," "lessons" for "testimony" (referring to the ark), "farina" for "fine flour," "welfare-sacrifice" for "peace offering," and "handsel-oblation" for "offering of first fruits."

Leviticus

2:4 "And when you present the oblation of a grain-offering baked in a baking crock, farina in ritual-matzoth shortened with oil and in sheet matzoth rubbed over with oil"—"When you bring a cereal offering baked in the oven as an offering, it shall be unleavened cakes of fine flour mixed with oil, or unleavened wafers spread with oil."

1 Samuel

17:38 "And Saul dressed David in his own brigandine"—"Then Saul clothed David with his armor"

17:40 "chose five pebbles out of the bed of the arroyo and put them in his shepherd's wallet, his yalkut"—"chose five smooth stones from the brook, and put them in his shepherd's bag or wallet"

2 Samuel

18:21 "the Negro"—"the Cushite"

Isaiah

1:18 "Come let us have it out"—"Come now, let us reason together"

8:6 "admire the hubbub of Rason"—"melt in fear before Rezin"

40:15 "a drop hanging on a bucket"—"drop from a bucket"

Daniel

12:4 "keep the things under a stopper and seal the book till an ultimate date"—"shut up the words, and seal the book, until the time of the end"

Matthew

4:21 "putting their nets to rights"—"mending their nets"

5:6 "because they shall have their meal"—"for they shall be satisfied"

5:11 "twit you and persecute you"—"revile you and persecute you"

5:37 "anything in excess of this is so much of bad"—"anything more than this comes from evil"

5:48 "be thorough as your heavenly Father is thorough"—"be perfect, as your heavenly Father is perfect"

9:29 "Have it as you have faith for"—"According to your faith be it done to you"

13:15 "for this people's wits are thickened"—"for this people's heart has grown dull"

13:57 "they were staggered at him"—"they took offense at him"

18:6 "ass-power millstone"—"a great millstone"

18:7 "Woe to the world for trippings-up! for the trippings-up have to come, yet woe to the man through whom the tripping-up comes"—"Woe to the world for temptations to sin! For it is necessary that temptations come but woe to the man by whom the temptation comes!"

John

1:12 "gave the chance to become children of God"—"gave power to become children of God"

1:16 "out of his fullness all of us have had portions"—"from his fulness have we all received"

Romans

2:13 "not the audience of the law"—"not the hearers of the law"

6:5 "if we have come to be twinned with the likeness of his death"—"if we have been united with him in a death like his"

8:11 "through his Spirit your inmate"—"through his Spirit which dwells in you"

11:5 "there are leavings in accordance with the choice made by grace"—"there is a remnant, chosen by grace"

Hebrews

1:14 "servient spirits"—"ministering spirits"

2:16 "take up angels, methinks"—"surely it is not with angels that he is concerned"

4:13 "thrown flat on its back for his eyes"—"laid bare to the eyes of him"

9:14 "from the corpses of our deeds"—"from dead works"
11:2 "old-timers"—"men of old"
12:9 "our bodily fathers"—"earthly fathers"

Revelation

1:15 "green gold"—"burnished bronze"
2:16 "mouth-sword"—"sword of my mouth"
4:3 "jaspid stone and a sard"—"jasper and carnelian"
7:11 "aged men"—"elders"

Some of these translations are not only peculiar but also misleading and wrong. Byington has also introduced certain words not usually found in the Bible such as "jubilate" (Rom. 15:10), "chaplain" (Rom. 15:16), "serving-man" (Matt. 20:26), "twitting" (Matt. 27:44), "lugubrious" (Matt. 6:16), "gormandizer" (Matt. 11:19), "gratis" (Matt. 10:8), "hectoring" (Isa. 3:5), besides those also included above. Awkward renderings were also found in Matthew 9:34; John 4:9; Romans 8:28; 14:1, 5, 20–21, 23; 15:1; Hebrews 5:11; 11:29; and Revelation 21:1.

It is interesting that in Matthew 16:18 after "Peter" these words are placed: "[in English, 'you are a Rock']." "Every text is inspired by God" (2 Tim. 3:16) is surprising for a literal translation.

This translation has some interesting renderings, but there are too many peculiarities and awkward translations for it to be acceptable, especially since there are so many more excellent versions today. No doubt it will have a wide circulation through the diligent and indefatigable efforts of the Witnesses.

7

The New Jewish Version

THE HISTORY OF JEWISH TRANSLATIONS

The Jewish translation of the Hebrew Scriptures into English began with the version of Abraham Benisch, published in England in 1851. In 1884 A Jewish Family Bible, edited by Michael Friedländer, was published for Anglo-Jewry. The first complete Jewish translation for American Jewry was produced in 1853 by Rabbi Isaac Leeser of Philadelphia. Although Leeser was not an expert in Hebrew philology, he did make use of various scholarly German translations by Jews of the nineteenth century. His version became the standard Bible for English-speaking Jews in America, and was also reproduced in England.

With the influx of Jews from western Europe to the American continent in the late nineteenth century, the need for an improved version in English for use in synagogue, school, and home was felt. In 1892, four years after its organization, the Jewish Publication Society of America took steps to prepare such a version. The original plan was to have Jewish scholars in Britain and America work independently on the several books, using Leeser's translation as a base. The resulting translation of each book was then to be submitted to the critical revision of an Editorial Committee under the chairmanship of Dr. Marcus Jastrow. Discussion regarding the translation was to be carried on by correspondence. By 1901 it became evident that this procedure was too slow. In 1903 Dr. Jastrow died, and a few years later a new plan was formulated. A Board of Editors, six in number, was created to work with the new Editor-in-Chief, Max L. Margolis of Dropsie College. Margolis prepared a draft of the version, which was then revised by the Board of Editors.

The version was published in 1917 under the title, The Holy Scriptures According to the Masoretic Text, A New Translation. According to the preface,

> It aims to combine the spirit of Jewish tradition with the results of biblical scholarship, ancient, medieval, and modern. It gives to the Jewish world a translation of the Scriptures done by men imbued with the Jewish consciousness, while the non-Jewish world, it is hoped, will welcome a translation that presents many passages from the Jewish traditional point of view.

Behind it, as behind other efforts by Jews at biblical translation, was the sentiment that "the Jew cannot afford to have his translation prepared for him by others. He cannot have it as a gift, even as he cannot borrow his soul from others."

Nevertheless, the 1917 version owed much to the non-Jewish English versions that preceded it. It was modeled after the classic style of the KJV, and was, in reality, only a mild revision of the RV of 1885. While it satisfied the needs of English-speaking Jewry for several decades, it became apparent that the time demanded a new version—one that would speak in a twentieth-century idiom to modern man and embody the latest discoveries in understanding the Bible. Protestants and Catholics had already begun producing new versions.

THE TORAH

Principles of Translation

In 1955 the Jewish Publication Society appointed a committee of seven scholars to prepare a new Jewish translation, beginning with the Torah. Three eminent Hebraists were selected to act as editors: Harry M. Orlinsky (editor-in-chief), H. L. Ginsberg, and Ephraim A. Speiser. Three learned rabbis—Max Arzt, Bernard J. Bamberger, and Harry Freedman—

representing, respectively, the Conservative, Reform, and Orthodox divisions of Judaism, were appointed as consultants. The representative of the Jewish Publication Society, Solomon Grayzel, served as the secretary of the committee.

The original draft of the translation, prepared by Orlinsky, was circulated among the members of the committee. The resulting comments, criticisms, and suggestions of each member were also sent to all seven. Periodic meetings were then held in which decisions were made regarding the wording of the text by a majority vote. The MS was then sent to the press and was published in 1962. Eleven years later a second edition was published, embodying a substantial number of improvements. Orlinsky also prepared a helpful companion volume based on the text of the second edition, entitled *Notes on the New Translation of the Torah*. This volume, published in 1969, contains a helpful introduction to the history of Jewish versions in English, in addition to the notes which explain significant departures of The New Jewish Version from the version of 1917.

Characteristics of the NJV

The NJV is not a revision of the Jewish version of 1917, nor of any other version, Jewish or Christian, but is a completely fresh translation of the traditional Hebrew text in living, up-to-date, and highly readable English. Although it is not a mechanical, word-by-word translation, as was the 1917 version, it is, on the whole, faithful to the original Hebrew text. The translators strove for the principle of equivalent effect, i.e., their goal was to produce a version that would carry the same message to modern man as the original did to the world of ancient times. They sought to determine as accurately as possible the meaning of the Hebrew and then to state that meaning in good, contemporary English. They broke away from the traditional biblical English of earlier standard versions.

They therefore endeavored to avoid the use of all obsolete words and phrases. The phrase "and it came to pass," familiar in traditional English versions, has disappeared (Gen. 6:1; 7:10; 8:6, 13; 24:52; 25:11, et al.). The use of "thou" and its various case forms has been abandoned, even in language addressed to

God. Surprisingly, the somewhat antiquated idiom "to take to wife" is used several times (Gen. 25:20; 29:28; Exod. 6:20, 23, 25; Lev. 21:14; Deut. 21:11). The translators were well aware of the fact that the Hebrew particle *wāw*, usually translated "and" in the traditional English versions, can be used in a number of senses: conjunctive, disjunctive, and adverbial, depending on the context. Consequently, they translated it not only as "and," but also as "but," "however," "when," "then," "so," "thus," "thereupon," and "although." On occasion it was left untranslated (e.g., Gen. 1:3, 6, 9, 14, 20, 24, 29). This has greatly improved the translation's readability. The sentence structure has in some instances been modified over the 1917 version. Occasionally, long sentences have been broken up into smaller units. At other times sentences have been combined into larger units.

The new version is a model of typographical art. Printed on excellent paper in large easy-to-read type, with a single column to the page, the text is arranged in paragraphs, though the verse numbers are given in small type.

The version is supplied with useful footnotes. These are of various kinds. Some call attention to significant variants in the ancient MSS and versions (e.g., Gen. 4:8; Exod. 5:5; 19:18; Num. 21:1; Deut. 31:1). Others give the Hebrew words, or indicate that there is a play on the Hebrew word. Others indicate that the Hebrew text is obscure and the translation is uncertain. Where a translation is somewhat free or an idiom is involved, a note calls attention to the literal meaning of the Hebrew (e.g., Gen. 29:1; 31:10). Alternate translations are suggested by the rubric "Or." The rubric "Others" introduces renderings given by previous versions or perhaps preferred by scholars outside the committee. There are also interpretive or explanatory notes (Lev. 13:13; Deut. 26:14).

There are a few instances in which the NJV has departed from the Masoretic Hebrew text. One is in Genesis 49:10 where Shiloh is understood as *shoi lo*, "tribute to him," with the resulting translation being "So that the tribute shall come to him." In Genesis 22:13 instead of "behind him a ram" the NJV with the RSV and others reads "a ram." In Genesis 10:5 the clause "These are the descendants of Japheth" is inserted in brackets (cf. RSV). Conjectural emendations are also made in Numbers 21:24; 25:1. But in comparison with most modern versions, the handling of the Hebrew text is very conservative indeed.

In its handling of the sacred ineffable name, YHWH, the NJV has followed the long-established synagogue custom of rendering it as LORD. In Exodus 6:3, however, this Tetragrammaton is printed in Hebrew letters and a footnote explains, "This divine name is traditionally not pronounced; instead Adonai '(the) LORD,' is regularly substituted for it." Deuteronomy 6:4 in this version reads, "The LORD is our God, the LORD alone." In Exodus 3:14, in answer to Moses' request for God's name, the answer is simply transliterated "Eyeh-Asher-Eyeh," for which a footnote provides various suggested translations. The divine name *El-Shaddai*, traditionally translated as "God Almighty," is transliterated (Gen. 17:1; 28:3; 35:11; 43:14, 48:3; Exod. 6:3, et al.). The same is true of *El-Roi* (Gen. 16:13). *El-Elyon*, however, is translated "God Most High" (Gen. 14:18–20, 22), and *El 'Olam* "The Everlasting God" (Gen. 21:33).

The NJV represents an honest, unbiased attempt by world-renowned Hebrew scholars to put into current English what they believe the Hebrew text says. Nevertheless, it is not to be expected that all of its renderings will find favorable acceptance even among Jews. The translation begins:

> When God began to create the heavens and the earth—the earth being unformed and void, with darkness over the surface of the deep and a wind from God sweeping over the water—God said, "Let there be light"; and there was light.

A complicated sentence of three verses has displaced the three simple sentences of the traditional version. The temporal clause with which the account begins is a possible rendering, but not the only possible one. Though found in other modern versions, such as the NEB, and advocated by competent scholars, it is still debatable. Even more debatable is the rendering "a wind from God sweeping over the water," rather than that of 1917: "the Spirit of God hovered over the face of the waters."

At this point, Christians, who will find this version of inestimable value, may be tempted to accuse the translators of religious bias, though An American Translation reads "a tempestuous wind raging over the surface of the waters." It must be granted that *ruach* can mean "wind" or "breath" as well as "spirit." It is so used, e.g., in Genesis 3:8, which the NJV renders "as the breezy time of day," literally "at the wind of the day." But it is doubtful that *ruach elohim* elsewhere in the Pentateuch means "a wind from God." Rather, the phrase means "spirit of God" (Gen. 41:38; Exod. 31:3; 35:31; Num. 24:2). Furthermore, the verb *rachaph* means to "hover" or "flutter" and is used in Deuteronomy 32:11 of an eagle that "hovereth over her young." The medieval Jewish commentator Rashi likened the Spirit of God in Genesis 1:2 to a dove.

In the first edition of the NJV Genesis 1:26 read, "And God said, 'I will make man in My image, after My likeness. . . .'" However, the second edition has returned to the rendering "Let us make man in our image, after our likeness" (cf. Gen. 3:22: "And the Lord said, 'Now that the man has become like one of us . . .'"). Likewise, the first edition's "Let me, then, go down and confound their speech there . . ." (Gen. 11:7) has been changed to "Let us . . ." in the second edition.

There is no note to explain why the singulars of the Hebrew are translated as plurals in Genesis 3:15b: "They shall strike at your head, and you shall strike at their heels." In Genesis 4:7 where the first edition read, "Sin is the demon at the door," the second has "Sin couches at the door." The traditional rendering "the sons of God" in Genesis 6:2 has become "the divine beings." In verse 3 the first edition's "My spirit shall not shield man forever" has been changed in the second edition to "My breath shall not abide in man forever." In Genesis 16:5 the NJV renders the Hebrew *tsedeq* (righteousness) as "merit." Thus the statement regarding Abraham's righteousness by faith, quoted by Paul in Romans 4:3, is translated, "And because he put his trust in the Lord, He reclaimed it to his merit."

Leviticus 24:10ff. contains the account of a quarrel between one of the "mixed multitude" (Exod. 12:38) and a full-blooded Israelite. During the quarrel the former, a son of an Egyptian father and a Hebrew mother, uttered a curse in which he desecrated the name of God. The NJV translates, "The son of the Israelite woman pronounced the Name in blasphemy" (v. 11). "The Name" evidently refers to the sacred, ineffable Tetragrammaton (YHWH). The blasphemer was placed in custody until it was determined that the Law against desecrating God's name applied to the half-breed as well as to the full-blooded Israelite. The general principle, as translated in the first edition of the NJV, was: "Anyone who blasphemes his God shall bear his guilt; but if he pronounces the name LORD (i.e., YHWH) he shall be put to death" (vv. 15–16). This rendering apparently reflects the rabbinic concept that it was wrong for the ordinary man to pronounce the sacred, ineffable name, but the meaning must be to say the name in blasphemy. The second clause is somewhat modified in the second edition: "If he also pronounces the name LORD; he shall be put to death."

With the exception of passages in Deuteronomy in which "heart and soul" are used in juxtaposition (4:29; 6:5; 10:12; 11:13; 26:16; 30:2, 6, 10), the NJV Torah has correctly abandoned "soul" as a translation for the Hebrew *nephesh*. In Genesis 2:7 it is rendered "being": "The Lord God formed man from the dust of the earth. He blew into his nostrils the breath of life, and man became a living being." *Nephesh* has also been rendered "creature" (Gen. 1:20), "person" (Gen. 46:15), "desire" (Exod. 15:9), "feeling" (Exod. 23:9), and even "corpse" (Num. 19:11). Sometimes it is also rendered by a form of the personal pronoun (Gen. 12:13; Deut. 4:9; 12:15, et al.).

In the first edition the term *mishpat*, particularly when used in conjunction with such legal terms as "statute" and "law," was frequently translated as "norm." In the second edition this was changed to "rule" (Deut. 4:1, 8, 14, 44, et al.). It is difficult to find a distinctive word for each Hebrew legal term, but certainly "rule" is better than "norm." In Numbers 12:6 the second edition reads, "When a prophet of the Lord arises among you." This is an improvement over the first edition's "When the Lord speaks through one of you." One could also wish the "spokesman" in Exodus 4:16 would have been rendered "prophet" (cf. Exod. 7:1).

The reader will need to adjust to a number of new religious terms, particularly some connected with the sanctuary and the sacrificial system. The Hebrew *'eduth* is regarded as a synonym with *berith*, "covenant," as a designation for the Decalogue, and, as such, is translated "pact." In Exodus 31:18 and 32:15 the tables of stone inscribed with the Decalogue are called "the two tables of the Pact." Moses was instructed to deposit them in the ark (Exod. 25:16), which was called "the ark of the Pact" (Exod. 25:22), and the entire Tabernacle is designated "the Tabernacle of the Pact" (Exod. 38:21). The "mercy-seat" in the NJV is "the cover." "Show-bread" has become "bread of display" (Exod. 25:30, et al.). Instead of "peace offerings," it has "sacrifice of well-being" (Lev. 3:1, 3, 6, 9). "Afflict your soul" has become "practice self-denial" (Lev. 16:29, 31; 23:27, 32). On the "Day of Atonement" (Lev. 16:30; 23:27) expiation is made on behalf of Israel (Lev. 16:6, 10, 17; 23:28). Should it not, then, rather be called the "Day of Expiation"?

There are other interesting renderings, such as "goat demons" for "satyrs" in Leviticus 17:7; "*seraph* serpents" for "fiery serpents" in Numbers 21:6–7; and "expanse" for "firmament" (Gen. 1:6f.). Not everyone will be happy with the substitution of "Sea of Reeds" for "Red Sea" (Exod. 10:19; 13:18, et al.). Granted that *Yam Suph* means "sea of reeds," the body of water the name describes evidently refers to what is now called the Red Sea. At any rate, the *Yam Suph* mentioned in connection with the later wilderness wanderings of the Hebrews must refer to the Gulf of Aqabah, for the Israelites touched at Ezion-Geber and Elath (Deut. 1:40; 2:8; Num. 21:4) on their way to Canaan.

THE FIVE MEGILLOTH AND JONAH

The same committee, with the exception of E. A. Speiser who died in 1965, proceeded with the translation of The Five Megilloth and Jonah, published in 1969. H. L. Ginsberg acted as the editor-in-chief. This volume has the Hebrew text and the NJV in parallel columns and is designed for both public and private reading. These six documents—Song of Songs, Ruth, Lamentations, Ecclesiastes, Esther, and Jonah—are all associated with commemorative festivals in the Jewish religious calendar.

The volume includes a brief introduction to the five Megilloth as well as introductory essays (by Ginsberg) to each of the documents included. Again, the translation makes use of the latest available resources for the meaning of the text. The translation is well done in good, contemporary English.

THE PROPHETS

In the translation of the Prophets, Dr. H. L. Ginsberg served as the editor-in-chief, with Dr. Harry Orlinsky as his associate. The basic draft rather than being the work of the editor, as was the case with the Torah, was prepared by individual members of the Committee who assumed the task of translating an entire book or part of a book. The draft of each book was in turn circulated among the other members for the criticisms and suggestions of each. These were considered in the periodic sessions of the Committee, chaired by Dr. Bamberger. Differences of opinion were ultimately settled by a majority vote. "When a book was completed, it was subjected to review and revision as many times as seemed necessary" (Preface to The Prophets, p. vii).

In 1973 the translation of the Book of Isaiah was published together with a rather extensive introductory essay by the editor-in-chief, H. L. Ginsberg. The same general principles and methods were used as in the translation of the Torah. This was followed in 1974 by the publication of the Book of Jeremiah. A revised and corrected form of these along with Jonah appeared in The Prophets, published in 1978. Readers should remember that the term "Prophets" as a division of the Hebrew Bible, includes Joshua, Judges, Samuel, Kings, Isaiah, Jeremiah, Ezekiel, and the Book of the Twelve, i.e., the so-called Minor Prophets.

The NJV, as its subtitle indicates, is "a new translation of the Holy Scriptures according to the traditional Hebrew text." A strict adherence to the Masoretic Text saved the translators from the task of having to choose between traditional Hebrew readings and variant readings found in ancient versions that differ from them—to say nothing about offering conjectural emendations where the original is not clear. Variant readings from the MT in such ancient versions as the Greek, Syriac, and Latin are frequently cited in footnotes. In cases where the Hebrew text is "obscure" and an alteration seems to provide "a marked clarification," a footnote beginning, "Emendation yields," provides a rendering of a suggested emendation.

The NJV adheres more closely to the Hebrew text than any other recent English version. The translators have shown that many of the emendations used in other versions are not essential, and the text can be satisfactorily translated without such changes. But even in this version there are a few minor changes made in the MT, or we must understand the term "traditional Hebrew text" as including readings in the Dead Sea Scrolls, the Targums, and the testimony of a small group of Hebrew MSS as against the majority.

In a few instances words enclosed in brackets have been inserted in the text. Some of these insertions were derived from parallel Scripture accounts often called "deuterographs." In 2 Samuel 23:8, the bracketed words "[he wielded his spear]" are derived from the parallel account in 1 Chronicles 11:11, but they are also found in some Septuagint MSS of 2 Samuel. Similarly, in 2 Samuel 23:17 the words "[I drink]" are derived from 1 Chronicles 11:19, plus the Septuagint of 2 Samuel. Similarly, the words "[are God]" in Isaiah 37:20 are supplied from the parallel account in 2 Kings 19:19. The same is true of the phrase "[That night]" in Isaiah 37:36, which was supplied from 2 Kings 19:35.

Rarely, bracketed words are inserted that are found only in one or more of the ancient versions. In 1 Samuel 16:7, the bracketed words in the clause, "For not as man sees [does the Lord see]" come from the Septuagint. In the KJV, RV, and ASV, the words "the LORD seeth not" are printed in italics as though supplied by the translators to complete the sentence. There is no note to indicate that they are found in the Septuagint. In Isaiah 48:11, the words "[My name]" are supplied from such ancient versions as the Septuagint and the Old Latin. The two insertions in brackets in Isaiah 66:18 rest on the authority of the medieval Bible commentator and grammarian, David Kimhi.

The insertion of the unbracketed "if" in 2 Samuel 19:8 rests on the authority of a substantial portion of Samuel found in Qumran cave #4 (4 Q Sam a), plus the Septuagint, a few other Hebrew MSS, "and an ancient Masoretic tradition." At the end of the first line of Jeremiah 10:23, "I know, O Lord, that man's road is not his," the bracketed words "[to choose]" are inserted, evidently to complete the meaning of the sentence as the translators understood it.

A couple of other minor changes in the usual Hebrew text can be mentioned. In 1 Kings 15:6 most Hebrew MSS read, "There was war between Rehoboam and Jeroboam all the days of his life." In place of "Rehoboam" the NJV reads "Abijam" which is found in several Hebrew MSS. In Isaiah 14:4 the translation reads, "How is oppression ended!" following the reading *Marhebah* of the complete Dead Sea Scroll of Isaiah (1Q1s a), which has the support of the Septuagint rather than the traditional Hebrew reading *Madhebah*. It is to be noted that two readings differ in just one letter. The former has an "r" (Hebrew, ר, resh), rather than a "d" (Hebrew, ד, daleth). Because of their similarity in appearance these two letters were frequently confused. See also Isaiah 37:27 and 60:19 and the footnotes. For other examples see Joshua 8:13; and Judges 5:5; 14:15.

While the version adheres closely to the traditional Hebrew text, different meanings are frequently assigned to Hebrew words than in most recent translations. Thus in Hosea 2:17, whereas most versions have "door" (or gate) "of hope," the NJV reads "plowland of hope." In Hosea 5:13; 10:6 for "King Jareb" (KJV, RV, NASB) or "the great king" (RSV, NAB, NIV) this version reads "a patron king" (see explanatory note). Instead of "gray hairs" in Hosea 7:9, (RSV et al.) it reads "mold." (For other illustrations in Hosea see 6:3; 7:14; 10:11.) In Isaiah 41:3 where most versions read, "by paths his feet have not trod," the NJV reads, "No shackle is placed on his feet," (see note). Instead of the usual "brings forth" in Isaiah 43:17 it reads "destroyed" (see note). A variety of renderings have been given to the last line of Isaiah 47:12, which this version renders "Perhaps you will find strength" (see note). (For other illustrations in Isaiah see 7:9; 41:22; 54:11; 57:19; 65:5; 66:3, 11.) To every reader who has studied Hebrew this version is a challenge to a renewed and deeper study. It is a challenge to consider new and different meanings for old words in their contextual relationships in the Hebrew Bible.

The NJV of the Prophets like that of the Torah uses English suitable for public reading. In general the language is contemporary, though a few archaisms are retained. As a term for a male slave, the term "manservant" never occurs, but for female slaves the terms "handmaid" or "maidservant" are used in a number of passages (Judg. 9:18; 19:19; 1 Sam. 1:11, 16, 18, etc). In passages where older versions use "manservant" and "maidservant" together, the language is modernized to "male and female slaves," (1 Sam. 8:16; Jer. 34:9–10). These terms are more meaningful today than the older ones, and it is unfortunate that they were not used consistently.

In the "major" prophets the term "daughter" is frequently used to personify the inhabitants of a city or a country. In translating this idiom the NJV leaves out the word "daughter." "Daughter of Zion," meaning, "daughter who is Zion," is rendered "Fair Zion" (Isa. 1:8; 10:32; Jer. 4:31; 6:2, 23). "The daughter of my people" is given as "my poor people" (Isa. 22:4; Jer. 4:11; 6:26; 8:11, 19, 22), "my hapless people" (Jer. 14:17), or simply "my people" (Jer. 8:21). "Daughter of Tarshish" becomes "Fair Tarshish" (Isa. 23:10) "virgin daughter of Sidon," "fair Maiden Sidon" (Isa. 23:12). Similarly, "virgin daughter of Babylon" and "daughter of the Chaldeans" are translated "Fair Maiden Babylon" and "Fair Chaldea" respectively (Isa. 47:1).

The Hebrew idiom rendered in older English versions, "to gird up the loins," is translated "to tie up the skirts" in the books of Kings. (1 Kings 18:46; 2 Kings 4:29; 9:1). In Jeremiah, however, "gird up your loins" is retained (1:17), and in Nahum 2:2 one finds "steady your loins." In Isaiah 45:1 for "to loose the loins of kings" this version has "ungirding the loins of kings," which suggests disarming them.

In Judges 15:8 the idiom "he smote them hip and thigh" is translated, "He gave them a sound and thorough thrashing." A footnote explains the metaphor of Isaiah 37:3, "the babes have reached the birthstool, but the strength to give birth is lacking" as signifying "the situation is desperate and we are at a loss."

As in other versions, the footnotes are of various kinds: textual, translational, and explanatory. These notes are a mine of information for the careful student.

In a few passages the translators sought to imitate puns in the original. Thus in Judges 10:4 the thirty sons of Jair the Gileadite "rode on thirty burros (i.e., donkeys) and owned thirty boroughs (i.e., towns) in the region of Gilead." Samson's riddle propounded to thirty young Philistines (Judg. 14:14) is rendered:

> "Out of the eater came something to eat,
> Out of the strong came something sweet."

After slaying a thousand Philistines with "a fresh jawbone" of an ass, Samson exclaimed, according to this translation,

> "With the jaw of an ass
> Mass upon mass!"   (Judg. 15:16)

The word-play on the proper names in Judges 3:8 is reproduced by transliterating them into English: the Lord delivered Israel into the hands of "King Cushan - rishathaim of Aram - naharaim."

The two word-plays of Isaiah 5:7 are rendered:

> "And He hoped for justice
> But behold, injustice,"
> For equity,
> But, behold, iniquity!"

For illustrations of the use of the type of cryptogram known as "Atbash," in which letters of the alphabet are substituted in reverse order, see the notes on "Sheshach," a cipher for "Babylonia" (Jer. 25:26; 51:41); "Leb-kamai," a cipher for "Kasidim" (= Chaldea) (Jer. 51:1); and "land of Cabul," possibly meaning "worthless land" in 1 Kings 9:13.

THE KETHUBIM

The third section of the NJV consists of a translation of the Kethubim ("Writings" or Hagiographa) of the Hebrew Bible, which include the books of Psalms, Proverbs, Job, the Five

Megilloth, Daniel, Ezra, Nehemiah, and 1 and 2 Chronicles. Mention was made above of the publication of the Five Megilloth (Songs of Songs, Ruth, Lamentations, Ecclesiastes, and Esther) in 1969. A separate committee of translators for the remainder of the "Writings" was set up in 1966. It consisted of three world-renowned scholars: Moshe Greenberg, Jonas C. Greenfield (both now of the Hebrew University), and Nahum M. Sarna (of Brandeis University), together with three learned rabbis: Saul Leeman, Martin Rozenburg, and David Shapiro, who represented "the three sections of organized Jewish religious life in America." Chaim Potok, editor of the Jewish Publication Society, served as secretary of the committee. The first product of this committee was The Book of Psalms which came from the press in 1972. This was followed in 1980 by The Book of Job, and finally, by all The Writings in 1982.

Its Text

The Preface affirms that the translation published in The Writings, like that in The Law and The Prophets "is based on the traditional Masoretic Hebrew text—its consonants, vowels, and syntactical divisions—although on occasion the traditional accentuation has been disregarded for an alternative construction of a verse that appeared to yield a better sense" (p. v). Very few deviations from the MT are apparent, and these few are slight in nature. Although there are more than thirty-five notes beginning with the words, "Emendation yields . . ." none of the suggested possible emendations has been adopted.

Occasionally, however, the reading of some Hebrew MSS is accepted in preference to that of most MSS. Ruth 3:15, for example, begins, "When she [i.e. Ruth] got back to town . . ." although most Hebrew MSS read, "When he [i.e. Boaz] got back to town. . . ." Similarly in 4:4 while most Hebrew MSS read, "But if he will not redeem," this version has, "But if you will not redeem," the reading of a number of Hebrew MSS, the Septuagint, and Targum. The Jewish version of 1917, in agreement with several Christian versions (KJV, ASV, NASB, MLB, NIV) translated the Hebrew text of Ecclesiastes 11:5 into three major clauses:

As thou knowest not what is the way of the wind,
Nor how the bones do grow in the womb of her that is with child;
Even so thou knowest not the work of God who doeth all things.

The translators of the NJV combined the first two clauses into one, used the alternative "lifebreath," as a rendering of *ruach*, "wind," and adopted the variant reading "into" of many Hebrew MSS and Targum in place of "with" read by most Hebrew MSS with the resulting translation of the verse:

Just as you do not know how the lifebreath passes into
the limbs within the womb of the pregnant woman,
so you cannot foresee the actions of God, who causes
all things to happen.

But such instances are few in number.

In the study of the Hebrew Bible a distinction is drawn between the traditional consonantal text, the *kethib*, "what is written," and the vocalization and minor corrections provided by the Masoretes, indicating the *qere*, what is "to be read." The *kethib* of Psalm 100:3, for example, says of God, "He made us and not we ourselves." The Masoretes indicated that the *qere* of the last clause, that is, what is to be read, is "and we are his," hence the rendering of the NJV, found also in a number of other recent versions, "He made us and we are His." A footnote calls attention to this Masoretic reading. In reality the difference between *lo'* ("not") and *lō* ("His") in the Hebrew, is very slight, consisting in the addition of the letter aleph (transliterated ') in the spelling of "not." The *qere* is followed in Proverbs 26:2, which cites the *kethib* in a footnote, and in Job 33:28, where the *kethib* is cited as an alternative translation.

Occasionally the NJV of The Writings follows the *kethib* in preference to the *qere*. In Job 6:21 the choice is again between following *lo'* ("not"; *kethib*), or *lō* ("his," or "to him"; *qere*). The translators opted for the *kethib* supported by Targum and translated, "so you are nothing." Like the RSV they also followed the *kethib* in Job 13:15, "He will slay me; I have no hope." Many will regard it as a pity that the magnificent declaration of Job's faith found in the *qere* has been relegated to a footnote. But it must be admitted that the *kethib* seems to suit Job's mood better at this juncture of the drama. Another example is found in 2 Chronicles 34:8–9 which concerns the commissioning of three men by King Josiah to deliver to the high priest, Hilkiah, the silver for the repair of the Temple in Jerusalem that the Levites had collected "from Manasseh and Ephraim and from all the remnant of Israel and from all Judah and Benjamin, and [according to the *qere*] returned to Jerusalem." But again like the RSV, the NJV follows the *kethib* in ending the sentence with the clause, "and the inhabitants of Jerusalem."

In rare instances a rendering involving a slight change in the consonantal text, which is found in one or more of the ancient versions, has been followed because it seemed to make better sense in the context. A case in point is the substitution of "their voice" for "their line" in Psalm 19:5,[1] following the Septuagint, the Greek version of Symmachus, and the Latin Vulgate. This change, which is followed by most recent English versions, fits the context, particularly the parallelism of the verse:

> Their voice carries throughout the earth,
> Their words to the end of the world.

The substitution of "their grave" for "their inward thought" in Psalm 49:12 does not involve any change in the consonants of a Hebrew word, but does involve a change in the order of two of them. By transposing the order of the "r" and "b" in *qirbam*, "their inward thought" (KJV), one gets *qirbam*, "their grave," which fits the parallelism, and is followed by most recent English versions:

> Their grave is their eternal home,
> The dwellings-place for all generations
> of those once famous on earth.

A note to this text in the NJV indicates that the MT reading *qirbam* is "taken with ancient versions and medieval commentaries as the equivalent of *qibram*."

---

[1]The NJV like the Hebrew treats the titles to the Psalms where they occur as part of the sacred text of the Psalm. Hence the numbering of the verses in a Psalm often varies from that given in Christian Bibles. The numbering followed here is that of the NJV.

"He departed unpraised" is the NJV's rendering of the depre-
catory evaluation of the life of King Jehoram of Judah"
(2 Chron. 21:20). The Hebrew has, "to no one's regret," also
very uncomplimentary to the king. A note to "unpraised" explains: "Following the Septuagint; cf. Arabic *hamada*, 'praise.'"
Readings from the Septuagint are also cited in the notes to
Songs of Songs 2:17; 5:13; Ecclesiastes 2:10; 5:16. The Syriac
Peshitta is cited along with the Targum as a support for the
rendering, "He crushes me for a hair." The Hebrew has, "He
crushes me with a storm" Job 9:17.

The first line of Psalm 78:54 in the Hebrew reads literally:
"And He brought them to His holy border." The NJV, however,
translates, "He brought them to His holy realm." The rendering
"realm" evidently does not rest on a variant Hebrew reading,
but on an extended meaning of the word for "border," to include not only the frontier itself, but the territory enclosed by it.
A note calls attention to the variant reading, "hill," found in
some MSS of the Septuagint and supported by the learned Jew,
Saadia Gaon, of the tenth century, who made the first important
rendering of the Bible into Arabic. "Hill" is the reading
adopted by the NEB in its translation, "He brought them to his
holy mountain."

Resources Used

In arriving at the meaning of a word or a sentence the translators made use of every resource available, Jewish and non-
Jewish, from ancient to modern times. They also availed themselves of the results of recent studies in the languages and
cultures of the Near East. In the area of linguistics (comparative
Semitics) one can see reflected in the text and notes the uses of
Akkadian (Song of Songs 3:8), Ugaritic (Job 12:19), Punic (Eccl.
12:6), Syriac (Ruth 4:7; Eccl. 6:12), Aramaic (Job 38:24; Song of
Songs 1:4; Eccl. 6:12), Arabic (Ruth 4:7; Lam. 2:20; Eccl. 12:12),
in addition to Postbiblical Hebrew (Eccl. 7:18; 12:1, 5, 10), and
Mishnaic Hebrew (Ps. 57:7; Job 24:14; Neh. 3:15).

One would naturally expect that Jewish scholars translating
for Jewish readers would pay close attention to readings in the
Aramaic Targums, and such is the case. In addition to the cita-

tion of Targumic readings in notes (see Ps. 84:12; 106:27; Eccl. 1:7) the version adopts several readings on the basis of the Targums. Note the italicized words in the following:

> The words you *inscribed* give light. (Ps. 119:130)
> Fair Babylon you *predator*. (Ps. 137:8)
> Who makes *peoples* subject to him. (Ps. 144:2)
> But if *you* will not redeem, tell me. (Ruth 4:4)
> And *glides* back to where it rises. (Eccl. 1:5)
> How the life-breath passes *into* the limbs. (Eccl. 11:5)
> *"by denying myself."* (1 Chron. 22:14)

Among the medieval Jewish scholars of the Hebrew Bible who influenced the translators the footnotes refer to the following: Saadia, a gaon (head) of a Babylonian Talmudic academy of the early tenth century and translator of the Bible into Arabic (Ps. 28:8; 30:8; 78:54; 88:16; 144:2); Ibn Janah, a grammarian and philologian of the eleventh century in Spain (Song of Songs 7:7); Rashi, best known commentator, late eleventh century (Ps. 22:17; 64:17; 139:11; 144:8; Eccl. 1:7; 7:14); Ibn Ezra, a grammarian and commentator of the twelfth century in Spain (Ps. 139:11; Song of Songs 7:6); Rashbam, a commentator of the early twelfth century (Eccl. 1:3); and Kimhi, a grammarian and commentator of the late twelfth and early thirteenth centuries in France (Ps. 7:11; 106:27; Neh. 3:15).

But in spite of the rich resources available for the study of the original Hebrew and Aramaic texts and their interpretation, together with the technical expertise of the translators in the original languages and other cognate languages, there still remain passages where the text and its meaning are unclear. The reader may be surprised to discover that the footnote, "Meaning of Hebrew obscure" or its equivalent, occurs some 190 times in the translation of The Writings. This is especially true of the poetic books. A note to Job 24:18 is particularly surprising: "From here to the end of the chapter the translation is largely conjectural." One can certainly hope that future discoveries and research will result in a clearer and more definite understanding of the meaning of obscure passages.

The translators of this version chose to word it in "modern literary English." Many examples of literary beauty could be given, but two must suffice:

Psalm 93:3–4

The ocean sounds, O Lord,
  the ocean sounds its thunder,
  the ocean sounds its pounding.
Above the thunder of the mighty waters,
  more majestic than the breakers of the sea
  is the Lord, majestic on high.

Psalm 139:9–10

If I take wing with the dawn
  to come to rest on the western horizon,
  even there Your hand will be guiding me,
  Your right hand will be holding me fast.

This translation contains many interesting and striking renderings. At the very beginning of The Writings the righteous man is described as one who shuns the course of evil, "rather, the teaching of the Lord is his delight, and he studies that teaching day and night" (Ps. 1:2). Two renderings here are worthy of comment. The first is the translation of the Hebrew word Torah as "teaching": a translation that is to be preferred to the traditional "law," which is too restrictive in meaning. Torah is a general term for divine instruction and direction, and is by no means confined to legal matters. The translation "studies" rather than the traditional "meditates" is quite striking. According to a note it is based on the literal meaning of the Hebrew verb, which means "utters," hence "recites," or "studies." According to the Talmud ('Erubin 53b-54a) students in Jewish schools were urged to study their lessons aloud as an aid to comprehension and retention. It would be interesting to know how much earlier than Talmudic times this method was practiced. It is worth noting that although the Hebrew verb here considered occurs in three other passages in the Psalms (63:7; 77:13; 143:5), this is the only place it is translated "studies," though in Psalm 143:5 it is rendered "recites."

According to this version, the eighth Psalm, which celebrates man's God-given dignity, affirms,

> You have made him master over Your handiwork,
>   laying the world at his feet. (v. 7)

What an awesome responsibility human beings have!
The NJV adds new freshness to Psalm 23:

> He makes me lie down in green pastures;
>   He leads me to waters in places of repose;
>   He renews my life;
>   He guides me in right paths
>   as befits His name.
> Though I walk through a valley of deepest darkness,
>   I fear no harm, for You are with me;
>   Your rod and Your staff—they comfort me.
> Only goodness and steadfast love shall pursue me
>   all the days of my life,
>   and I shall dwell in the house of the LORD
>   for many long years. (vv. 2–4, 6)

Although there is no change in the meaning from the traditional interpretation of Proverbs 6:6, that meaning is now expressed in language that is modern and arresting:

> Lazybones, go to the ant;
> Study its ways and learn. (cf. v. 9)

The same can be said of the translation of Proberbs 17:22:

> A joyful heart makes for good health;
> Despondency dries up the bones.

In the Book of Ruth, the story of Naomi's arrival in Bethlehem with her daughter-in-law, after a sojourn of a number of years in the land of Moab, is vividly pictured with the words: "The whole city buzzed with excitement over them" (Ruth 1:19).

The description of the horrible effects of the famine within Jerusalem while it was under siege is indeed shocking:

> Alas! Women ate their own fruit,
> Their new-born babes!

According to a note the root of the original word translated "new-born" means just that in Arabic. But even if one prefers the alternative rendering, "dandled," the shock is little less severe (Lam. 2:20).

Koheleth, who according to a note, was probably "the Assembler," either of hearers or of sayings, begins his discourse on the meaning of life with the startling conclusion, as worded in the NJV:

Ecclesiastes 1:2–3

Utter futility! . . .
Utter futility! All is futile!
What real value is there for a man
In all the gains he makes beneath the sun?

But later he admonishes:

Ecclesiastes 9:10

Whatever is in your power to do, do it with all your might.
For there is no action, no reasoning, no learning,
    no wisdom in Sheol,
    where you are going.

Life's ending is described with poetic figures:

Ecclesiastes 12:6

The jar is shattered at the spring
And the jug is smashed at the cistern.

The rendering "jug," rather than the traditional "wheel," according to a note, is derived from the use of the root in Punic.

Two renderings worthy of note occur in Esther 1. The first concerns the seven-day festival in the palace garden when royal wine flowed freely:

Esther 1:18

And the rule for the drinking was,
"No restrictions!"

The second is given in connection with Queen Vashti's refusal to display her beauty before the inebriated banqueters and the king was at a loss as to know what to do about it:

Esther 1:13

Then the king consulted the sages learned in procedure. (For it was the royal practice [to turn] to all who were versed in law and precedent).

In describing the instruments and methods of execution used, this version's rendering of the Book of Esther strikingly departs from the traditional translations. "Hanging" gives way to "impaling," and "gallows" to "stake." Hence the two would-be assassins of King Ahasuerus were "impaled on stakes," rather than "hanged on the gallows" (Esth. 2:23). Haman, at the suggestion of his wife and his friends, put up a stake "fifty cubits high," on which he intended "to ask the king to have Mordecai impaled" (Esth. 5:14). When Haman's wicked plot to destroy all the Jews in order to dispose of the hated Mordecai was exposed by Queen Esther, this version avers, "Haman cringed in terror before the king and queen" (7:5). The exposure of this horrible plot, which would have meant the execution of the queen, so angered the king that he left the banquet for a walk in the palace garden, while Haman remained behind to plead with the queen for his life. On his return the king was further infuriated by the sight of Haman lying prostrate on Esther's couch, which the king interpreted as an attempt to rape her. At this juncture a royal servant informed the king of the "stake" that Haman had put up for the execution of Mordecai. The king now impetuously ordered, as this version translates it, "Impale him on it!" (7:9) The account continues, "So they impaled Haman on the stake he had put up for Mordecai" (7:10). A similar fate also befell the sons of Haman (9:25).

The Hebrew word for "stake," or "gallows" in the older versions, simply means "wood." Although there is no note explaining the translation "stake," the word was probably chosen because the Persians normally used this method of disposing of offenders.

One difficulty in accepting this translation is the height of this instrument of execution—seventy-five feet. Just how would a man be impaled on a stake that high?

Translation of Significant Words

Several important words in the religious vocabulary of the Kethubim are given a significantly different rendering in this version from that found in the historical English Bibles. As a conspicuous example the reader will note that the traditional rendering "soul" for the Hebrew *nephesh* is comparatively rare, though it does occur (Pss. 42; 62:2, 6; 63:2). In this regard this latest portion of the Hebrew Bible is in agreement with the earliest portion, the Torah. In the Psalms particularly, *nephesh* is most often translated by a form of the personal pronoun (Pss. 3:2; 7:2, 6; 16:10; 17:13, et al.), or by "life" (Pss. 23:3; 34:23; 35:4, et al.). It may also be rendered "whole being" (Ps. 6:4) or even "body" (Ps. 44:26).

Ḥesed, usually translated "mercy" or "lovingkindness" in the traditional English versions is a very important word in the religious vocabulary of the Hebrews. The NJV, like the RSV most often translates it as "steadfast love" (note the refrain of Psalm 136, repeated twenty-six times, "His steadfast love is eternal"), for the word has in it the double significance of love and loyalty. But the word is also rendered "faithful care" (Pss. 36:8, 11; 48:10; 88:12, et al.), etc. Such renderings indicate that the God of the Hebrew Bible is more a God of love than most people have realized.

Shalom, occurring more than thirty times in The Writings and used as a modern greeting in Israel, has a far broader meaning than the traditional rendering "peace." It means more than the absence of war or strife. It has the meaning of wholeness, of total welfare. Most often in this version it is appropriately translated "well-being" (Pss. 29:11; 72:3, 7; 85:9; 119:165, et al.). But "goodwill" (Ps. 28:3), "amity" (Pss. 34:15; 35:20), "integrity" (Ps. 37:37), and, simply, "greetings" (Ezra 4:17; 5:7) are also used.

As a name for God *El Shaddai* occurs around thirty-five times in The Writings, mostly in the Book of Job. It is translated traditionally as "the Almighty" in the early chapters of Job (Job 5: 17; 6:4; 8:3, et al.), but more often is transliterated, *Shaddai*, omitting the *El* (= "God").

In comparison with the RSV the NJV is more modern, less literal, and more interpretive. The abandonment of the old second personal pronoun, *thou, thy, thee,* and the corresponding verb forms, which the RSV retains in language addressed to Deity, is one feature of the NJV's modernity. The NJV tends to change some of the metaphors into non-metaphors, probably in the interest of clarity. In Psalm 4:7, which the RSV translates literally, "lift up the light of thy countenance upon us, O Lord," the NJV has, "bestow your favor on us, O Lord." In Psalm 18:3 the literal "horn of (my) salvation" of the RSV, becomes "(my) mighty champion." The RSV gives the literal, "I am poured out like water" in Psalm 22:15, whereas the NJV has "My life ebbs away." The RSV of Psalm 78:63 reads:

> Fire devoured their young men,
> and their maidens had no marriage song.

Compare the NJV:

> Fire consumed their young men,
> and their maidens remained unwed.

The second line of Psalm 83:3 in the RSV reads, "Those who hate thee have raised their heads," while the NJV has, "Your foes assert themselves." Instead of the RSV's "and make her arms strong" (Prov. 31:17), the NJV has "and performs her tasks with vigor." The literal, "So you would endanger my head with the king" in Daniel 1:10, RSV, is rendered, "And You will put my life in jeopardy with the king" in the NJV. The words of the Chaldeans regarding Nebuchadnezzar's dream, according to the RSV, were, "And none can show it to the king except the gods, whose dwelling is not with flesh" (Dan. 2:11), but as translated in the NJV, they were: "There is not one who can tell it to the king except the gods whose abode is not among mortals." (Lit., "flesh").

Figures of speech that are not interpreted in the text of the translation are sometimes explained in footnotes (see Lam. 2:8; Eccl. 4:5). According to the RSV rendering of Ezra 5:1, Haggai and Zechariah "prophesied to the Jews who were in Judah and Jerusalem, in the name of the God of Israel who was over them." In the NJV they prophesied "inspired by the God of

Israel," an interpretation of the clause that says literally, "with the name of the God of Israel upon them" (see footnote). The RSV translates Nehemiah 9:6, in part, "Thou hast made heaven, the heaven of heavens. . . ." The NJV renders this, "You made the heavens, the highest heavens." According to the RSV rendering of 2 Chronicles 15:7 the prophet Azariah said to King Asa "and all Judah and Benjamin," "But you, take courage! Do not let your hands be weak. . . ." The NJV translates this: "As for you, be strong, do not be disheartened. . . ." A note of the last clause indicates, literally, "do not let your hands be slack."

The term "kidneys," or "reins" (KJV) was not only used literally for physical organs, but metaphorically as a center of psychic and moral life. For the metaphorical sense the NJV three times translates the word as "conscience" (Pss. 7:10; 16:7; 139:13) and "heart" three times (Ps. 26:2; Prov. 23:16; Job 19:27). In Lamentations 2:11 the liver is also used as a seat of psychic life. The sentence that the NJV translates, "My being melts away" literally says (see note), "My liver spills on the ground." The bowels are also used metaphorically to refer to strong emotions. In Song of Songs 5:4 the NJV translates "and my heart was stirred for him" (or, according to many manuscripts "within me"). Compare the KJV: "And my bowels were moved for him." Lamentations 1:20 reads, "My heart is in anguish" where the KJV has again, "My bowels are troubled" (see also Ps. 22:15).

Notes

Reference has been made frequently to the notes in the new version. They are of various kinds, including textual, translational, and explanatory. While the latter are not numerous, they are helpful. Some are brief, consisting of only a word or two, as when giving the meaning of names. Such notes help one to understand Ruth 1:20, for example: Ruth's mother-in-law said, "Do not call me Naomi [i.e., 'Pleasantness'] . . . Call me Mara [i.e., 'Bitterness'] for Shaddai [usually rendered 'the Almighty'] has made my lot very bitter." A note to Ruth 4:11 explains, "Ephrathah is another name for Bethlehem." According to the notes, "His footstool" in Lamentations 2:1 refers to the Temple, and "His booth" in verse 6, to the Tabernacle. The language of Ecclesiastes 12:2–4 is taken as symbolic of decrepitude. "The guards of the house" are the arms, "the men of valor," the legs, "the maids that grind," the teeth, "the ladies that peer through the window," the eyes, and "the door to the street," the ears.

A note to wisdom in Proverbs 1:20 explains: "In Proverbs wisdom is personified as a woman." Job 12:17 (cf. v. 19) avers: "He [God] makes counselors go about naked," "a sign of madness."

Longer explanatory notes are occasionally found in the translation of some of the books. In Ruth 2:20 Naomi explains to Ruth that Boaz "is one of our redeeming kinsmen." A note refers to Leviticus 25:25 and Deuteronomy 25:5–6 and states, "The fact that Boaz was a kinsman of Ruth's dead husband opened up the possibility of providing an heir for the latter." In Ruth 3:9 Ruth's request of Boaz, "Spread your robe over your handmaid for you are a redeeming kinsman," is explained as "a formal act of espousal" (cf. Ezek. 16:8). Boaz's exclamation to Ruth, "Your latest deed of loyalty is greater than the first, in that you have not turned to younger men, whether poor or rich," (v. 10) is interpreted to mean, "she sought out a kinsman of her dead husband. . . . Her first act of loyalty had been to return with Naomi." When another man nearer of kin to her dead husband than Boaz declined to act as the "redeeming kinsman," he gave as his reason "lest I impair my own estate" (Ruth 4:6). A note explains: "by expending capital for property which will go to the son legally regarded as Mahlen's; see Deut. 25:5–6."

A different kind of note explains that Ecclesiastes 4:9–5:8 "consists of a series of observations of which each one is introduced by some slight association with what precedes. The theme of 4:4–8 is not resumed until 5:9."

The reference to the fact that stillbirths were not accorded a burial in Ecclesiastes 6:3 is explained in a note: "Stillbirths were cast into a pit or hidden in the ground in no recognizable graves." These examples are sufficient to indicate the value of the explanatory notes. More of them could have been included. For one, the reader would appreciate a note explaining who the Persian king Ahasuerus was.

CONCLUSION

In conclusion, the publication of The Writings in 1982 marked the end of a quarter of a century of careful planning and diligent labor in the production of a new Jewish version of the Hebrew Bible in modern English. The NJV is a monument to careful scholarship, particularly in dealing with the traditional Hebrew text. Its fidelity to that text is unquestionable. Combined with it is a concern to break away from the traditional English translations and produce a version that is clothed in contemporary idiomatic English. In both of these attempts the version is successful. It ranks as one of the best translations of the Hebrew Bible available. It will not only meet the religious needs of English-speaking Jews, particularly in America, but will probably be widely read and studied by Christians as well. It seems appropriate to conclude with words printed on the jacket: "The message of the Bible is eternal. This new translation is designed to preserve that message, in all its majesty and meaning for our generation."

8

The Amplified Bible

ITS BACKGROUND AND PURPOSE

The Amplified NT was published in 1958 by the Lockman Foundation and Zondervan Publishing House. Four years earlier, in 1954, The Amplified Gospel of John had been published. The Amplified OT came out in two parts, Part Two in 1962 and Part One in 1964. In 1965 all of these parts appeared in one volume, The Amplified Bible (AB), published by Zondervan. The leading figure in the preparation of this translation was Frances E. Siewert, a research secretary, who also wrote the introductions to the earlier publications.

The desire to make the Bible understandable is admirable and translators of the Bible have used different methods to accomplish this common aim. The Amplified Bible does this by amplification. "Its purpose is to reveal, together with the single-word English equivalent to each key Hebrew and Greek word, any other clarifying shades of meaning that may be concealed by the traditional word-for-word method of translation." Its justification is that "amplification merely helps the English reader comprehend what the Hebrew and Greek listener understood as a matter of course." Whether it has succeeded will be determined after careful investigation.

The symbols used in the translation for the various types of amplification are explained at the beginning. There are four types:

Parentheses () and dashes — : signify additional phases of meaning included in the original word, phrase, or clause of the original language.

Commas are used to set off titles of Deity.

Brackets [] : contain justified clarifying words or comments not actually expressed in the immediate original text.

Italics point out certain familiar passages now recognized as not adequately supported by the original manuscripts. Also, "and," "or," and other connectives in italics indicate that the word itself is not in the original text, but it is used to connect additional English words indicated in the same original word.

The format is unfortunate. The verses are arranged as in the KJV: each verse is set off as a separate paragraph in two columns in the one-volume edition. This format militates against understanding the verses in context and leads to reading each verse as a separate, isolated oracle. It would have been better to arrange the verses in normal paragraphs, with the verse numbers less pronounced in smaller type. Also by the present arrangement poetic sections of the Bible cannot be indicated. Unfortunately, no quotation marks are used. There are no headings of any kind. Cross references, found in brackets after the verse, sometimes refer to certain parts of the verse and this method does not allow the specific indication needed. It would be much better to place these in the margin or at the bottom of the page.

Most of the notes in the NT provide the source for the translation or for the expansion. Apparently, the translators relied most heavily on Vincent, Thayer, and Cremer. Most of the notes in the OT are explanatory comments and are much longer than the NT notes. Many of the notes are apologetic in tone, showing how archaeology has "proved" the Bible, how the ark was built to prevent the animals from multiplying, how Noah had many years in which to interest travelers in securing animals for him. There are more notes in Genesis than any other book. On the one hand, one gets the feeling from reading these notes that the translators were pious, and on the other hand, one detects some insecurity on their part in not letting that Bible stand on its own feet.

The books of the Bible are listed not only in canonical but also in alphabetical order. Perhaps it is anticipated that people who are not informed readers of the Bible will turn to this translation.

ITS CHARACTERISTICS

We give a few sample passages to illustrate the kind of amplification found in this translation:

Genesis 1:1–6

1 In the beginning God (prepared, formed, fashioned,) *and* created the heavens and the earth. [Heb. 11:3.]

2 The earth was without form and an empty waste, and darkness was upon the face of the very great deep. The Spirit of God was moving, (hovering, brooding) over the face of the waters.

3 And God said, Let there be light; and there was light.

4 And God saw the light, that it was good—suitable, pleasing— *and* He approved it; and God separated the light from the darkness. [2 Cor. 4:6.]

5 And God called the light Day, and the darkness He called Night. And there was evening and there was morning, one day.

6 And God said, Let there be a firmament [the expanse of the sky] in the midst of the waters; and let it separate the waters [below] from the water [above].

Psalm 23:1–3

1 The Lord is my shepherd [to feed, guide and shield me]; I shall not lack.

2 He makes me lie down in (fresh, tender) green pastures; He leads me beside the still *and* restful waters. [Rev. 7:17.]

3 He refreshes *and* restores my life—my self; He leads me in the paths of righteousness—uprightness and right standing with Him—[not for my earning it, but] for His name's sake.

Matthew 5:16–22

16 Let your light so shine before men that they may see your moral excellence *and* your praiseworthy, noble *and* good deeds, and recognize *and* honor *and* praise *and* glorify your Father Who is in heaven.

17 Do you think that I have come to do away with *or* undo the Law and the prophets; I have come not to do away with *or* undo but to complete *and* fulfill them.

18 For truly, I tell you, until the sky and earth pass away *and* perish not one smallest letter nor one little hook [identifying certain Hebrew letters] will pass from the Law until all things [it foreshadows] have been accomplished.

19 Whoever then breaks *or* does away with *or* relaxes one of the least important of these commandments and teaches men so, shall be called least important in the kingdom of heaven; but he who practices them and teaches others to do so shall be called great in the kingdom of heaven.

20 For I tell you, unless your righteousness (your uprightness and your right standing with God) is more than that of the scribes and Pharisees, you will never enter the kingdom of heaven.

21 You have heard that it was said to the men of old, You shall not kill; and whoever kills shall be liable *so* that he cannot escape the punishment imposed by the court. [Exod. 20:13; Deut. 5:17; 16:18.]

22 But I say to you that every one who continues to be angry with his brother *or* harbors malice [enmity of heart] against him shall be liable to *and* unable to escape the punishment imposed by the court; and whoever speaks contemptuously *and* insultingly to his brother shall be liable to *and* unable to escape the punishment imposed by the Sanhedrin, and whoever says, "You cursed fool!—You empty-headed idiot!" shall be liable to *and* unable to escape the hell (Gehenna) of fire.

An analysis of the above examples indicates that some amplifications are unnecessary such as the words in brackets in Psalm 23. They have not added anything; the meaning is clear without them. Throughout the Bible there are many such examples. A few further examples from Matthew are: 1:11, removal (deportation); 1:17, Exile (deportation); 2:6, Ruler (Leader); 4:23, good news (Gospel); 7:17, healthy (sound); 7:23, openly (publicly); 10:8, freely (without pay); freely (without charge). See also Mark 1:3: "A voice of one crying in the wilderness—shouting in the desert—Prepare the way of the Lord, make His beaten-tracks straight (level and passable)!"

At times there are unjustifiable amplifications that are not derived from the Greek text, such as in Matthew 2:13: "Get up! [Tenderly] take . . . the young Child" and 7:7, "keep on knocking [reverently]." Not only are such explanations not derived from the Greek text but they are clearly unnecessary. The Greek text does not need them; neither does the English text. For another striking example of a translation that gives a meaning not found in the Greek, see Mark 8:35: "For whoever wants to save his [higher, spiritual, eternal] life, will lose [the lower, natural, temporal which is lived (only) in earth]; and whoever gives up his life [which is lived (only) on earth], for My sake and the Gospel's, will save [his higher, spiritual life in the eternal kingdom of God]."

There are also additions that are completely redundant since in those instances the one English word is sufficient, as in Matthew 6:19, "gather *and* heap up *and* store"; Matthew 10:37, "loves *and* takes more pleasure"; and Mark 2:19, "Can the wedding guests fast (abstain from food and drink) . . . ?"

When a repeated word is given the same or similar amplification, the style becomes very tedious. Such is the case in Matthew 5:3–11 with the Beatitudes. Notice the monotonous repetition: "Blessed—happy, to be envied and spiritually prosperous [that is, with life-joy and satisfaction in God's favor and salvation, regardless of their outward conditions] . . . . Blessed *and* enviably happy, [with a happiness produced by experience of God's favor and especially conditioned by the revelation of His matchless grace]. . . . Blessed—happy, blithesome, joyous, spiritually prosperous [that is, with life-joy and satisfaction in God's favor and salvation, regardless of their outward conditions]. . . . Blessed *and* fortunate *and* happy *and* spiritually prosperous [that is, in that state in which the born-again child of God enjoys His favor and salvation]. . . . Blessed—happy, to be envied, and spiritually prosperous [that is, with life-joy and satisfaction in God's favor and salvation, regardless of their outward conditions]. . . . Blessed—happy, enviably fortunate, and spiritually prosperous [that is, possessing the happiness produced by experience of God's favor and especially conditioned by the revelation of His grace, regardless of their outward conditions]. . . . Blessed—enjoying enviable happiness, spiritually prosperous [that is, with life-joy and satisfaction in God's favor and salvation, regardless of their outward conditions]. . . . Blessed *and* happy *and* enviably fortunate and spirtually prosperous [that is, in the state in which one enjoys and finds satisfaction in God's favor and salvation, regardless of his outward conditions]. . . . Blessed—happy, to be envied, and spiritually prosperous [that is, with life-joy and satisfaction in God's favor and salvation, regardless of your outward conditions]. . . . " Thus it goes unremittingly from the first "Blessed" to the last. And it may be seriously questioned whether the simple Greek word *makarios* means all this. Another similar repetition within one verse is found in Matthew 12:33: "Either make the tree sound (healthy and good), and its fruit sound (healthy and good), or make the tree rotten (diseased and bad) and its fruit rotten (diseased and bad); for the tree is known and recognized and judged by its fruit." In Genesis 1 the word "good" is amplified seven times with a combination of "suitable," "pleasing," "admirable," "fitting," or "pleasant."

On the other hand, there are some noticeable lacks in amplification. The word "daily" in Matthew 6:11 and "Cananaean" in 10:4 could have been given some explanation. This is the only translation that has "I AM" instead of "I am he" in Matthew 14:27. It has surely gone too far here. It is not suitable to the context. The "piety" of the translators is seen also in capitalization of all pronouns or nouns referring to Jesus even in those instances where such an intention is not present (see for example Matthew 12:24): "But the Pharisees hearing it said, This Man drives out demons only by *and* with the help of Beelzebub, the prince of demons." The footnote gives this explanation: "Capitalized because of what He is, the spotless Son of God, not what the speakers may have thought He was." (See John 5:11f. for another example.) This method is at best confusing.

The translation is in reality a mini-commentary. Some will laud this; others will be critical of it. A person's translation theory will determine how he will react. Inevitably, however, interpretive elements will be included in such a translation. While clarity of meaning is the goal of this type of translation, one wonders if it sacrifices too much in literary beauty and objective accuracy. In her introduction to the NT, Frances

Siewert wrote, "One does not expect literary beauty and finesse in a work which must give the plain, unchanged words of various authorities without embellishment." Perhaps this version has its place in individual study but those who do not know the original languages should check it with other translations and a good commentary. Otherwise their choice of a rendering is purely subjective.

In the NT, according to the preface, "the Greek text of Westcott and Hort was pursued with meticulous care." If "pursued" means "followed," the assertion is highly misleading, for there are numerous departures from the text of Westcott and Hort in the direction of the traditional text. These departures are printed in italics, to indicate that these words are "not adequately supported by the original manuscripts." The inclusion of such readings is no doubt due to the piety of the translators and their concern for the readers who have become accustomed to them. These include Matthew 6:13; 17:21; 18:11; 21:44; Luke 4:18, et al. Mark 16:9–20 is included as part of the regular text with no differentiation. Other endings of Mark are not indicated. A short note is found in the footnotes, stating: "Verses 9 to 20 not in the two earliest manuscripts." For a modern Bible this is hardly acceptable. At John 5:3–4 we find a strange thing. The last part of verse 3 is included in italics but verse 4 is omitted altogether, yet those two parts generally go together in the MSS. John 7:53–8:11 is found in the traditional position without any differentiation. The note does not indicate that it is found in different places in the MSS; it only indicates that it "is not found in the older manuscripts, but it sounds so like Christ that we accept it as authentic, and feel that to omit it would be most unfortunate." Even 1 John 5:7–8 is included in the text with italics. It is strange, however, to find that Revelation 22:14 has "who cleanse their garments" instead of the KJV reading "that do his commandments." For other examples of departure from the Westcott and Hort text, see Matthew 6:4, 6, 8; Acts 8:37; 9:5f.; Colossians 1:14.

The OT, according to the introduction, "is based primarily on the accepted Hebrew text." The traditional Hebrew text, however, is sometimes modified by additions and changes derived from the Septuagint and other ancient versions or the Qumran scrolls (see Gen. 4:8; 44:4; Ps. 37:23–24; Prov. 7:22; 10:10; 11:16; 18:9, 19, et al.). The most striking example in the 1962 edition is the insertion in italics of a substantial passage from the Septuagint between Job 2:9 and 10.

The AB purports to be "free from private interpretation" and "independent of denominational prejudice." But there are, nevertheless, passages that appear to reflect a theological bias. Isaiah 7:14 reads, "Therefore the Lord Himself shall give you a sign, Behold, the young woman *who* is unmarried *and* a virgin shall conceive and bear a Son, and shall call his name Immanuel—God with us." Note also 1 Peter 3:19–20: "In which He went and preached to the spirits in prison, [the souls of those] who long before in the days of Noah had been disobedient. . . . " Another example is Matthew 16:18: "And I tell you, you are Peter [Petr*os,* masculine, a large piece of rock], and on this rock [petr*a,* feminine, a huge rock like Gibraltar] I will build My church, and the gates of Hades (the power of the infernal region) shall not overpower it—or be strong to its detriment, or hold out against it." Unfortunately, in spite of brackets, parentheses, or other signs, most readers will consider that what is in the text, including the explanations or interpretations, is part of Scripture.

The Greek word *thumiaterion* in Hebrews 9:4 is wrongly translated "altar of incense," since the note seems to be referring to the golden censer when it refers to the fact that it was not permanently kept in the Holy of Holies, but taken in on the Day of Atonement.

In checking 1 Corinthians 1:1–9 closely with the Greek we find the following amplifications:

1:1 will *and* purpose
apostle (special messenger)

1:2 church (assembly)
consecrated *and* purified *and* made holy
[who are] selected *and* called
saints (God's people)
"any place" instead of "every place"
call upon *and* give honor

1:3 Grace (favor and spiritual blessing)
(heart) peace

1:4 grace (the favor and spiritual blessing)

1:5 [So]
in full power *and* readiness of speech (to speak of your faith)
complete knowledge *and* illumination (to give your full insight
into its meaning)

1:6 [our]
confirmed *and* established *and* made sure

1:7 not (consciously) falling behind *or* lacking
spiritual endowment *or* Christian grace (the reception of which
is due to the power of divine grace operating in your souls by
the Holy Spirit)
wait *and* watch (constantly living in hope)
coming . . . *and* [His] being made visible to all

1:8 establish . . . —keep you steadfast, give you strength, and
guarantee your vindication, that is, be your warrant against all
accusation or indictment—[so that you will be]

1:9 faithful—reliable, trustworthy and [therefore] ever true to His
promise, and He can be depended on; by Him you were called
into companionship *and* participation

CONCLUSION

The translation apart from the amplification has no great
merit. It is characterized by "a determined effort to keep, as far
as possible, the familiar wording of the earlier versions." The
value is supposed to reside in the amplification. However, as
we study the amplification, the great majority of the additions
do not really add much. At times, as we have seen, they constitute a private interpretation. It would be much better to take
a faithful translation such as the American Standard Version
and use a good commentary as needed. It is contended that a
particular Greek word cannot be translated by one English
word. There is no doubt that this is true at times. However, the
English words that are used to translate have overtones and if
we were to carry out this purpose consistently, we would have
to use several English words to explain and make precise the
preceding English word, *ad infinitum.* Thus, although a single

English word seldom says all that the author intended, a multiplication of words says more than he wished to convey (e.g., see 1 Cor. 10:13). The criticism directed toward Barclay's NT is more applicable here: There is all too much danger of the ordinary man assuming that the interpretations and amplifications are part of God's revelation. Scripture is quite capable of being understood, and the Holy Spirit is still present.

9

The Jerusalem Bible

ITS BACKGROUND

The Jerusalem Bible (JB) has the distinction of being the first complete Catholic Bible to be translated into English from the original languages (1966). The Confraternity OT (now part of the complete Bible in the NAB), Spencer's NT, and other portions of the Bible had already been translated from the original before this time. Since the JB was published, the NAB has also been translated completely from the original languages. Previously all Catholic Bibles were translated from the Latin Vulgate, which was a translation itself. Such an excellent version as that of Monsignor Knox was perceptibly affected by this limitation.

One needs to keep in mind the double objective of the translators of the JB. It aims to bring the Bible into contemporary language and to deepen one's understanding of it with explanatory notes. The notes are a substantial part of this translation and serve a very important function. Unfortunately, the small print will discourage a full use of them. In an earlier day, much objection would have been raised against notes being placed in the Bible because they were usually so decidedly sectarian and even inflammatory, especially in the sixteenth and seventeenth centuries. However, helpful notes that lead to a better understanding of Scripture will be welcomed. As a whole, the notes in the JB are of this sort.

The notes are a translation from the one-volume French edition of La Bible de Jerusalem, published by the scholars of the Dominican Biblical School of Jerusalem. The first edition of this came out in 1956. The biblical text, however, is based on the original, although checked closely with the French where questions of interpretation and text arose. The translators worked under the general editorship of Fr. Alexander Jones of Christ's College, Liverpool.

Because it has such a substantial amount of notes, the first edition of 1966 was a hefty one with 2,062 pages and weighing just under five pounds. An abbreviated paperback edition with abbreviated notes was published in 1971. Besides the notes for the text itself, there are introductory notes for sections of the Bible, such as the Pentateuch, and for certain individual books. At the end there are helpful supplements, including a chronological table, a genealogical table of the Hasmonean and Herodian dynasties, an explanation of the biblical calendar, a table of weights and measures, an index of biblical themes in the notes, and maps of different periods and subjects. Cross references for texts are provided in the outside margin. Headings introduce portions of Scripture. The text itself is printed in one column, with the verse numerals in the inside margins.

ITS CHARACTERISTICS

In general, the JB is considerably freer than the RSV but not as free as PHILLIPS. It has more of the Bible in poetic form than any previous Bible, especially in the Gospel of John. Personal names are in the form found in the RSV. This removes the strangeness that the Protestant reader formerly found in reading Catholic Bibles.

This is a Catholic Bible, therefore what the Catholic calls the deuterocanonical books and the Protestant the Apocrypha are included. They are not segregated but are scattered throughout —the historical, wisdom, and prophetic books in their appropriate sections. Moreover, the additions to Esther are scattered throughout the book but are distinguished from the rest of the text by being printed in italics. In Daniel Susanna is chapter 13 and Bel and the Dragon is chapter 14. These are not in italics.

The archaic forms of the second person singular are completely eliminated even in prayer. The name of God is given as *Yahweh* as in the original. The ASV had used "Jehovah" but both the RSV and the NEB went back to the KJV practice of using LORD or GOD, the former when the word *Yahweh* stood alone or with the word for God, *Elohim,* and the latter when it stood with the Hebrew word for Lord, *Adonai. Yahweh* is the correct form of the name, but Christians no doubt will have difficulty getting accustomed to saying: "Yahweh is my shepherd, I lack nothing."

To get the flavor of the JB we will compare a section from the Gospels and the Epistles from the RSV, JB, and PHILLIPS:

Matthew 6:1–4

Beware of practicing your piety before men in order to be seen by them; for then you will have no reward from your Father who is in heaven.

Thus, when you give alms, sound no trumpet before you, as the hypocrites do in the synagogues and in the streets, that they may be praised by men. Truly, I say to you, they have their reward. (RSV)

Be careful not to parade your good deeds before men to attract their notice; by doing this you will lose all reward from your Father in heaven. So when you give alms, do not have it trumpeted before you; this is what the hypocrites do in the synagogues and in the streets to win men's admiration. I tell you solemnly, they have had their reward. But when you give alms, your left hand must not know what your right is doing; your almsgiving must be secret, and your Father who sees all that is done in secret will reward you. (JB)

Beware of doing your good deeds conspicuously to catch men's eyes or you will miss the reward of your Heavenly Father.

So, when you do good to other people, don't hire a trumpeter to go in front of you—like those play actors in the synagogues and streets who make sure that men admire them. Believe me, they have had all the reward they are going to get! No, when you give to charity, don't even let your left hand know what your right hand is doing, so that your giving may be secret. Your Father who knows all secrets will reward you. (PHILLIPS, first edition)

Romans 12:1-2

I appeal to you therefore, brethren, by the mercies of God, to present your bodies as a living sacrifice, holy and acceptable to God, which is your spiritual worship. Do not be conformed to this world but be transformed by the renewal of your mind, that you may prove what is the will of God, what is good and acceptable and perfect. (RSV)

Think of God's mercy, my brothers, and worship him, I beg you, in a way that is worthy of thinking beings, by offering your living bodies as a holy sacrifice, truly pleasing to God. Do not model yourselves on the behavior of the world around you, but let your behaviour change, modelled by your new mind. This is the only way to discover the will of God and know what is good, what it is that God wants, what is the perfect thing to do. (JB)

With eyes wide open to the mercies of God, I beg you, my brothers, as an act of intelligent worship, to give him your bodies, as a living sacrifice, consecrated to him and acceptable by him. Don't let the world around you squeeze you into its own mold, but let God remold your minds from within, so that you may prove in practice that the plan of God for you is good, meets all his demands and moves toward the goal of true maturity. (PHILLIPS, first edition)

Although it is a problem to translate weight, measure, money, and time expressions into modern equivalents, it is preferable to do this so that the reader may better understand the context. It may not be important to know the amount of money involved in the parable of the talents, but it is crucial in the parable of the unmerciful servant (Matt. 18:23–35). The JB has translated or transliterated the expressions but not with their modern equivalents. Thus talents, pounds, denarius, cubit, hour, etc., are kept in the translation. To compensate for this, however, the JB makes these explanations in its notes. Hopefully, people will go to the trouble of reading them.

The translation of the NT especially seems much freer than it needs to be. Many times this freedom does not enhance the meaning of the text, but more often it leads to a slight change in the meaning. Sometimes words are omitted or added unnecessarily. The following examples will illustrate what we mean:

The JB translates 1 Corinthians 7:1–2 in this manner: "Now for the questions about which you wrote. Yes, it is a good thing for a man not to touch a woman; but since sex is always a danger, let each man have his own wife and each woman her own husband." The expression "since sex is always a danger" does not do justice to the Greek, which is best translated as by the NEB as "because there is so much immorality." The implication in the JB translation is that Paul is giving this counsel as something due to the normal dangers existing in society, whereas Paul is giving this counsel because of an extraordinary situation. Corinth was no ordinary city. Immorality was rampant and the church was being infected by its surroundings (note 1 Corinthians 5 and 6:12–20). The JB translates Matthew 6:2 in the following way: "So when you give alms, do not have it trumpeted before you." The Greek only says, "Do not sound the trumpet before you." The JB follows PHILLIPS in reading more into the text than it actually says. PHILLIPS expresses it more directly: "Don't hire a trumpeter to go in front of you." In 1 Corinthians 12:13 the words "into one body" have been inexplicably omitted. "Will" is omitted and "send greetings" is added unnecessarily in 1 Corinthians 1:1. In 1 Corinthians 1:4 "grace" has become "graces" and "of God" has been omitted after it. In the next verse "in him" has been omitted. These examples are sufficient to indicate the inaccuracy of a translation that is meant for serious study of the Word as the notes attest.

The text of the JB is interesting to study because of its tendency to include what Protestants exclude. Take, for instance, Mark 16:9–20. Modern Protestant Bibles do not include this passage in the text, or at least not in the same type as the text. The JB includes this portion with no differentiation. In the note, explanation is given for this: It is "included in the canonically accepted body of inspired scripture." The note goes on to explain that "this does not necessarily imply Marcan authorship which, indeed, is open to question." It further explains the different endings that various MSS give to Mark. Several questions come to mind regarding the principle of accepting later additions as being also canonical. When was the Scripture canonically accepted? What MS or MSS were canonically accepted? If this principle is followed, it would seem that most of the late readings would be accepted into the text and the early readings rejected. But there is no consistency in the application of the principle. Such poorly accepted readings as those found in Luke 24:6, 12, 36, 40, 51; John 1:13; 5:3–4; and Hebrews 9:11, are included. A note added to John 5:3–4 indicates that the best witnesses omit this reading. John 7:53–8:11 is not only included, it is also found at this place in the text, even though the note states that the author of this passage is not John. And, on the other hand, certain readings that one would expect to be included on the same basis are omitted, such as Matthew 6:13; 18:11; 12:47; Luke 9:56; and Acts 8:37, to name only a few. The tendency is definitely on the side of including more questionable readings than either the RSV or the NEB. In Acts the JB has selected some interesting Western readings that few other English translations have accepted. These are: "Hades" instead of "death" in 2:24; the addition of "and by no other" in 4:10; "three days afterwards" instead of "on the third day" in 10:40; "in the first psalm" instead of "in the second psalm" in 13:33; and "seek the deity" instead of "seek God" in 17:27.

Both the NEB and PHILLIPS translate Matthew 16:18, "You are Peter the rock," but the JB translates it straightforwardly, "You are Peter," although the note brings out the above interpretation. Following the NEB, the JB translates John 1:3–4: "All that came to be had life in him," connecting the last part of verse 3 with verse 4. This is allowable on the basis of the Greek text. Another ambiguous text is Romans 9:5. It can be translated as the RSV and NEB have done it, "To them . . . according to the flesh, is the Christ. God who is over all be blessed for ever." The JB has instead: "Christ who is above all, God for ever blessed!" The JB equates Christ with God, whereas the former translations make a distinction. On 1 Corinthians 7:36 the JB follows the traditional father-daughter view. First Timothy 3:2 is translated, "He must not have been married more than once."

We have already mentioned the notes in this Bible. They are a significant part of the translation. As a whole, they are judicious and helpful. The reader will gain much and will profit in his understanding of the Bible through a reading of the notes. In the past, notes in Catholic Bibles were objectionable to Protestants. No one can say that about the notes in this Bible, though some of the notes have a distinctly Catholic flavor to them. For example, the note on Matthew 1:25 states, "The text is not concerned with the period that followed and, taken by itself, does not assert Mary's perpetual virginity which, however, the gospels elsewhere suppose and which the Tradition of the Church affirms." Compare this with the note in the Douai-Rheims version: *"Till she brought forth her firstborn son.* From these words Helvidius and other heretics most impiously inferred that the blessed Virgin Mary had other children besides Christ: but St. Jerome shews, by divers examples, that this expression of the Evangelist was a manner of speaking usual among the Hebrews, to denote the word *until,* only what is done, without regard to the future." On Matthew 12:46, where Jesus' brothers are mentioned, the note reads, "Not Mary's children but near relations, cousins perhaps, which both Hebr. and Aramaic style 'brothers.'"

First Corinthians 3:14 has been used by Catholics to support the doctrine of purgatory. The note reads, "This is not a direct reference to purgatory but several Doctors of the Church have taken it as a basis for that doctrine." The RSV, NEB, and PHILLIPS all have "wife" or "Christian wife" in 1 Corinthians 9:5, but the JB translates, "Christian woman." The note on this verse says, "Lit. 'a sister, a woman (wife?).'" The question at issue here is whether the apostles were married or not. Catholics who believe in clerical celibacy naturally presuppose the apostles to have been unmarried.

The note for Genesis 3:15, after explaining the version with reference to the Messiah, reads, "The Latin version has a feminine pronoun ('she' will crush . . .) and since, in the messianic interpretation of our text, the Messiah and his mother appear together, the pronoun has been taken to refer to Mary; this application has become current in the Church." Another passage applied to Mary is Revelation 12:1. Here the note reads, "It does not seem probable that John had Mary in mind or intended any allusion to the physical birth of the Messiah in the incarnation." However, it is instructive to see that these notes are generally nondogmatic, especially when they are compared with notes in earlier Bibles.

A very explicit note is found on Matthew 16:19: "Catholic exegetes maintain that these enduring promises hold good not only for Peter himself but also for Peter's successors. This inference, not explicitly drawn in the text, is considered legitimate because Jesus plainly intends to provide for his Church's future by establishing a regime that will not collapse with Peter's death. Two other texts, Luke 22:31f. and John 21:15f., on Peter's primacy emphasise that its operation is to be in the domain of faith; they also indicate that this makes him head not only of the Church after the death of Christ but of the apostolic group then and there." Other Catholic notes are found in Matthew 5:3; 6:11; 16:18. The note appended to Matthew 19:11–12 reads, "Christ invites to perpetual continence those who would consecrate themselves entirely to the kingdom of God."

A very definite asset, at least from the Protestant reader's point of view, is that the names of biblical characters are given in the form found in Protestant Bibles, such as the RSV and NEB. However, there is one word representing Catholic terminology that a Protestant will have to translate, the word "holocaust" for "burnt offering."

CONCLUSION

The translation is not homogeneous throughout. The translation of Matthew does not seem as free as that of Mark. In fact, the translation seems to become freer as it goes along, being freest in the Epistles. The same is true in the OT. Genesis does not seem as free as Exodus. On the whole, the translation is good, though not distinctive. There are not many striking translations. There are still some awkward spots and some bad translations in what we judge to be a generally good translation.

The feature that makes this translation valuable is the copious informative and instructive notes.

10

Barclay's New Testament

BARCLAY'S METHOD OF TRANSLATION

William Barclay, long known for his popularization of scholarly research in readable prose, also produced a translation of the NT for the average reader, which was originally published in two volumes. One of the aims listed in the foreword "was to try to make the New Testament intelligible to the man who is not a technical scholar" (1, 5). The first volume, containing the Gospels and Acts, appeared in 1968. The second, including the rest of the NT, was released in 1969. Both were published by Collins. A one-volume paperback edition was published by the Westminster Press in 1980.

A short introduction precedes each book or group of books (such as 1 and 2 Thessalonians). The arrangement of the books in each section of the NT is in chronological sequence. Thus the order for the first section is Mark, Matthew, Luke, Acts, John. The first Epistle of Paul is Galatians, followed by 1 Thessalonians, etc.

There are few notes. When they do appear, they are usually textual-critical notes indicating a different reading in some MSS for the verse indicated. There are no headings or titles. There is a short foreword in both volumes, a chapter entitled "On Translating the New Testament" at the end of Volume 1, and at the end of Volume 2 two appendices. The first of these in sixty-two pages treats various NT words in alphabetical sequence. These words are taken from the KJV and are followed by the Greek original. Each is explained by the author. The second appendix, "Notes on Passages," lists those passages the translator has expanded in the text and gives an explanation of their meaning. Throughout, the pronoun "you" is used for the second person singular.

In the foreword Barclay gives as his second aim "to make a translation which did not need a commentary to explain it" (1, 5). As he admits, this is an impossibility. But in trying to do this he has at times moved away from a legitimate translation to a paraphrase or commentary. Barclay will accept this criticism, for he contends that translation is to some extent interpretation and that "the aim of the translator must be to produce a translation which can stand by itself, and which needs no commentary to make it intelligible" (1, 317). He also maintains that translation "will necessarily involve what is known as paraphrase" (1, 317). We can expect, then, a bit of freedom in this translation. How we judge it will depend on where we stand on the spectrum of translation theory.

Barclay illustrates his method by his translation of certain words. The word "adulterous" in "an evil and adulterous generation" (Matt. 16:4) was translated "apostate generation," since the meaning is not that it is a generation characterized by sexual sin but one that has fallen away from God. "Can ye be baptized with the baptism that I am baptized with?" (Mark 10:38) is modified into "Can you be submerged in the sea of troubles in which I must be submerged?" The word "cup" in "Are ye able to drink of the cup that I shall drink of . . . ?" (Matt. 20:22) is translated, "Can you pass through the bitter experience through which I must pass?"

ITS CHARACTERISTICS

Illustrations of Barclay's use of expansion are found in Matthew 9:17 and 11:7 (the italicized words indicate the expanded portions): "No more do people pour new *fermenting* wine into old wineskins *that have lost their elasticity*"; and " 'What did you

go out to the desert to see?' he said, 'Was it to see what you can
see any day there—the long grass swaying in the wind?'"

There are two expressions in the Greek that Barclay feels may
be omitted in the translation without any loss of meaning. One
of these is the word or words usually translated "lo" or "behold." The other is the phrase "it came to pass."

Barclay feels also that manners and customs have to be taken
into consideration in translation. The translation should explain
the custom or at least make clear its meaning. For example,
Barclay says that Matthew 3:12 in the KJV—"Whose fan is in his
hand, and he will thoroughly purge his floor. . . ."—is not intelligible to Westerners. The "fan" was a tool that was used to
toss the grain into the air; the chaff was blown away by the
wind and the heavy grain fell to the floor. Barclay simply translates, "He is going to winnow the chaff from the corn, and he
will clear every speck of rubbish from his threshing-floor." The
American needs to translate "corn" into "grain."

Another example of expansion to explain the local custom is
found in Matthew 10:14: "And whosoever shall not receive you,
nor hear your words, when ye depart out of that house or city,
shake off the dust of your feet," which Barclay translates, "If
anyone refuses you a welcome or a hearing, as you leave that
house or town, shake the last speck of its dust from your feet, as
if you were leaving a heathen town." According to Barclay, it
was a custom that whenever a Jew left a Gentile city, he would
shake the dust off his feet to remove the pollution of that city.
Mark 7:11 reads, "It is Corban, that is to say, a gift, by whatsoever thou mightest be profited by me." Barclay translates it
like this: "'This money that I might have contributed to your
support is Korban' (that is, a gift dedicated to the service of God
and usable for no other purpose)." The explanation is included
in the translation.

Barclay has also reshaped certain Greek sentences to put them
into idiomatic English. This includes the use of subordination
where Greek does not use it, and vice versa; changing the imperative, which is used more freely in Greek, to a form with
"must"; changing the vocatives, which are hardly ever used in
English, into another form; changing clauses that begin with

"he that," "whoever," "everyone," etc. to an infinitive clause; and the inversion of certain Greek sentences when translated into English.

The Greek text from which Barclay translates is that of the United Bible Societies (UBS). However, he has deviated from that text in some instances. In Matthew 27:16–17 the prisoner is called Jesus Barabbas, but in the UBS text "Barabbas" is enclosed in single brackets, indicating that it is of dubious textual validity. Barclay has given no indication of this but includes it as though it were part of the original text. The passage concerning the adulterous woman, John 7:53–8:11, is included at the end of the Gospel of John in the UBS text, but Barclay has placed it in the traditional position in the same size type as the rest of the text. He distinguishes it from the preceding and following texts by indentation and a note indicating that the best and most ancient MSS do not contain the story.

It is interesting to check a few ambiguous passages to see which meanings Barclay selects. In Matthew 16:18 he clearly makes Peter the rock on which the church is built, as in the NEB: "I tell you, you are Peter—the man whose name means a rock—and on this rock I will erect my Church. . . ." In Mark 15:39 the Roman centurion ("company commander" according to Barclay) confesses, "This man was indeed a son of God!" contrary to the RSV (2nd edition) and AV but in agreement with PHILLIPS and the NEB. In John 1:4 he connects part of verse 3 with verse 4 to read, "As for the whole creation, the Word was the life principle in it. . . . ," as in the NEB. In Romans 9:5 he agrees with the NEB and RSV in opposition to PHILLIPS and the KJV in not explicitly identifying Christ with God: "Theirs are the fathers, and in human descent it is from them that the Messiah comes. God who is over all be blessed for ever and ever! Amen." In 2 Timothy 3:16 he agrees with the NEB and KJV, RSV, and PHILLIPS in reading, "Every divinely inspired scripture is . . ." instead of "All Scripture is inspired of God."

Something of the freedom in Barclay's translation may be seen as it is compared carefully with the original in 1 Corinthians 1:1–10. The left column gives the original translation and the right Barclay's translation.

1:1 Paul	This is a letter from Paul
the brother	our colleague
1:2 church	congregation
sanctified in Christ Jesus	those whose union with Christ has consecrated their lives to God
called *to be* saints	those whom God has called to be his own
1:3 peace	every blessing
1:4 for the grace	I thank him for his grace
in him	through your union with him
with all speech and all knowledge	with the result that you are equipped with every kind of knowledge and with complete ability to communicate
1:6 as the testimony of Christ was confirmed among you	You are in fact the proof that what Christ promised has happened
1:7 the revelation of our Lord Jesus Christ	the time when our Lord Jesus Christ will again burst upon the stage of history
1:8 in the day of our Lord Jesus Christ	on the day when our Lord Jesus comes
blameless	no one will be able to level any charge against you
1:9 God is faithful	You can rely on God
Fellowship of his son	share the life of his Son

Some interesting translations of Barclay from Matthew follow, compared with the RSV:

Barclay	RSV
3:15	
'For the present,' Jesus answered 'let it be so, for the right thing for us to do is to do everything a good man ought to do!'	But Jesus answered him, "Let it be so now; for thus it is fitting for us to fulfil all righteousness."
3:17	
This is my Son, the Beloved and Only One.	This is my beloved Son.
4:17	
Kingdom of Heaven is almost here	kingdom of heaven is at hand

5:16

lovely things — good works

6:24

God of heaven and of the god of this world's wealth — God and mammon

6:33

Make the Kingdom of God, and life in loyalty to him, the object of all your endeavour — But seek first his kingdom and his righteousness

10:4

Simon, the Nationalist — Simon the Cananaean

12:42

there is a greater event than Solomon here — something greater than Solomon is here

16:1

some visible divine action — a sign from heaven

19:8

if it had not been that your hearts are quite impervious to the real commandment of God — for your hardness of heart

21:33

a pit in which the juice could be extracted from the grapes — a winepress

22:18

Jesus was well aware of their malicious motives. 'You are not out for information,' he said to them, 'you are out to make trouble in your two-faced maliciousness. . . .' — But Jesus, aware of their malice, said, "Why put me to the test, you hypocrites?"

26:28

This means my lifeblood, through which the new relationship between man and God is made possible — for this is my blood of the covenant

26:41-42

'Sleeplessly watch and pray, for you may well all have to face your ordeal of temptation. I know that you mean well and that you want to do the right — "Watch and pray that you may not enter into temptation; the spirit indeed is willing but the flesh is weak:". . . . "if this cannot pass unless I drink it. . . ."

thing, but human nature is
frail.' . . . 'if there is no escape
from this situation unless I go
through it to the bitter end. . . .'

28:1

Late on the Sabbath   Now after the Sabbath

The following longer passages from the Gospels and one from
the Epistles, give more of the flavor of this translation:

Matthew 23:5-15

'Their every action is designed for self-display. They wear outsize
prayer-boxes, and exaggerate the size of the tassels of their robes.
They like the top places at banquets and the front seats in the
synagogues. They like to be deferentially greeted as they move
through the market-places, and to be called Rabbi by ordinary
people. You must not let anyone call you Rabbi. There is One who is
your teacher, and you are all brothers. You must not call any man on
earth father. There is One who is your Father, and he is in heaven.
You must not let anyone call you leaders. There is One who is your
leader, I mean the Messiah. Your top-ranking man must be your
servant. If a man exalts himself, he will be humbled; and, if he
humbles himself, he will be exalted.'

'Tragic will be the fate of you experts in the Law and you Pharisees
with your façade of ostentatious piety! You shut the door of the
Kingdom of Heaven in men's faces. You will not go in yourselves,
and you will not allow those who are trying to get in to go in.

'Tragic will be the fate of you experts in the Law and you Pharisees
with your façade of ostentatious piety! You roam sea and land to
make one convert, and when he has become a convert, you make
him twice as much hell-begotten as yourselves.'

John 1:1-3

When the world began, the Word was already there. The Word was
with God, and the nature of the Word was the same as the nature of
God. The Word was there in the beginning with God. It was through
the agency of the Word that everything else came into being. Without the Word not one single thing came into being.

Romans 8:1-6

We can therefore say that there is now no condemnation for those
whose life is one with the life of Christ. For, when through union

with Christ Jesus I came under the law of the life-giving Spirit, I was emancipated from the law of death-bringing sin. For what the law was unable to do—that is to say, to effect this emancipation from sin—because human nature rendered it impotent and ineffective, God did. He did it by sending his own Son with a human nature like our sinful nature. He sent him to deal with sin, and to deal with it as a human person. He thus left sin without a case, and, because he won the victory over sin, the legitimate demand of the law is satisfied in us too, in us whose lives too are no longer directed by our lower nature, but by the Spirit. Those who have allowed their lower nature to become the rule of their lives have an attitude to life which is dominated by their lower nature; those who have taken the Spirit as the rule of their lives have an attitude to life which is dominated by the Spirit. To have a mind dominated by our lower human nature is to turn life into death; to have a mind dominated by the Spirit is to have real life and every blessing.

Notable is the fact that Barclay has set more of the NT in poetry than previous versions, especially in the Sermon on the Mount (Matt. 5–7) and in the Book of Revelation. It is also evident that he has sought to bring out the force of the Greek tenses, especially in the imperative. Thus we have the following constructions: Matthew 6:25, "Stop worrying"; Matthew 7:1, "Don't make a habit of judging others"; and Matthew 7:7, "Keep on asking."

CONCLUSION

Several criticisms have been made against this version. A. D. Harvey's observation is accurate when he says that "the total impression is a perplexing mixture of the new with the traditional, the technical with the non-technical. . . . The style, too, is a curious mixture. Sometimes it is frankly colloquial ('That's your look-out,' Matt. 27:4), sometimes strangely archaic ('When the devil had exercised his every tempting wile,' Luke 4:13; 'Share my vigil,' Matt. 26:38)" (*Theology* LXXII [1969], 368).

The most serious criticism against Barclay's translation is his interpretive comments added in the translation, which Harvey calls "this highly personal and sometimes even idiosyncratic translation" and which the editor of the *Churchman* calls "academic arrogance." Referring to the "Notes on Passages," the latter says:

> Here a number of brief passages are singled out for expansion and short comment. Dr. Barclay concedes that this strays over into interpretation, but thinks it has to be done for the non-technical reader. No doubt the intention is good, but is there not an (unintentional, of course) academic arrogance about this? Have modern scholars ceased to believe in the perspicuity of Scripture, and is twentieth-century man so devoid of spiritual perception that he must now exchange reliance on an infallible teaching church for Scripture mediated by scholars? It is our conviction that a high doctrine of Scripture must mean that translation and interpretation are to be kept rigidly separate. There is all too much danger, as Charles Cranfield has recently pointed out in our columns, of the *ordinary* man whom Dr. Barclay seeks to help assuming that Dr. Barclay's interpretations are part of God's revelation. Scripture is quite capable of speaking for itself, and the Holy Spirit has not departed. It is probably a sign of the inadequacy of so much modern systematic theology (even in Reformed Scotland) that scholars imagine ordinary readers *must* have their aids. What such a situation reveals is the inadequate doctrine of Scripture and the Spirit held by those who so imagine. (*Churchman* LXXXIII [1969], 253–54)

Interpretive translations are unavoidable to a certain extent. However, the danger of personal, subjective, and idiosyncratic translations arising in a one-man effort is much greater than it is in a group translation where one is checked by others.

11

The Good News Bible, Today's English Version

THE NEW TESTAMENT

Its Background

On 15 September 1966, the American Bible Society published a new modern speech translation of the NT with the title, Good News for Modern Man: The New Testament in Today's English Version (TEV). The TEV soon outstripped in popularity even the NT of the NEB. A second edition was published on 1 October 1967, "incorporating," the translator tells us, "many changes both in style and substance, aimed at making the translation more faithful and accurate, more natural, and easier to understand." A third edition, embodying further improvement, was published in 1971. During the first six years of its existence, some thirty-five million copies of the TEV have been sold world-wide. This phenomenal record may be due, in part, both to its reasonable price and its promotion by the American Bible Society. But it is obvious it has an inherent worth that has given it a wide appeal to English-speaking people everywhere.

The translation was prepared by Robert G. Bratcher, Research Associate of the Translations Department of the American Bible Society. He had previously produced a new translation of the Gospel of Mark, entitled "The Right Time," and was requested by the American Bible Society to translate the entire NT. The

Bible societies customarily sponsor versions in the world's major languages to meet the needs of people who have little formal education or who, regardless of education, are not familiar with the archaic language of the traditional church versions. Bratcher's basic text was submitted for suggestions and approval to translation consultants of the American Bible Society, and to the Translation Department of the British and Foreign Bible Society.

The Fourth Edition

In 1976 the fourth edition of this Good News New Testament was combined with the newly completed TEV Old Testament to form the Good News Bible (GNB).* This fourth edition of the New Testament differs considerably from the first three in wording and in its adherence to the basic Greek text: the United Bible Societies' The Greek New Testament (1st ed., 1966; 2nd ed., 1968; 3rd ed., 1975) prepared by an international committee of NT scholars. The third edition of this Greek Testament was the base from which the fourth edition of the GNB NT was made.

The third edition of the translation of the NT was without footnotes, but included an appendix of four pages of "Other Readings and Renderings," listing some of the more important variant readings in Greek manuscripts and ancient versions, as well as alternative possible translations of a number of passages. In the fourth edition this information is given in footnotes including 135 textual notes listing variants in Greek manuscripts and ancient translations. In the UBS Greek text there are numerous single words and phrases, several clauses, and longer passages consisting of a verse or more that are enclosed in single square brackets to indicate that they have "dubious textual validity." The third edition of the TEV ignored these brackets and included the enclosed readings as part of the translation without any indication of doubt regarding their

---

*A note dated 12 July 1982 from the publishers of this version, the American Bible Society, indicates that the preferred designation for it is GNB rather than TEV. In this chapter the designation TEV that was used in the 1975 edition of *So Many Versions?* is retained for the first three editions of the NT, while GNB is used for the whole Bible, the OT, and the fourth edition of the NT.

textual validity. The fourth edition, however, contains foot-notes to indicate that some manuscripts lack the bracketed material (see Matt. 12:47; 16:2b–3; Mark 10:7b; 14:68c; Luke 11:33b; John 3:31c). The bracketed phrases and clauses in a few passages of the Greek text appear to have been missed, since there are no footnotes to indicate that some manuscripts lack them (e.g., Mark 3:16, "These are the twelve he chose"; Mark 3:22, "and sisters"). Unfortunately, there is no footnote to indi-cate that in the double name "Jesus Barabbas," given to the notorious criminal chosen to be freed in place of Jesus Christ by the Jewish mob (Matt. 27:16–17), "Jesus" rests on slender sup-port and was therefore placed in single brackets by the editors of the Greek text.

In the UBS Greek text a few passages are enclosed in double square brackets to indicate that they were "regarded as later additions to the text, but . . . are of evident antiquity and im-portance" (Matt. 21:44; Luke 22:43–44; 23:34; Mark 16:9–20; John 7:53–8:11). In the first three editions of the TEV these pas-sages were enclosed in single brackets to indicate that they "are not in the oldest and best manuscripts." In the fourth edition, Matthew 21:44 is removed from the text, but given in a footnote introduced by the words: "Some manuscripts add verse 44." Luke 22:43–44 and 23:34 are retained unbracketed in the text, but a footnote informs the reader that some manuscripts lack these passages. The longer ending of Mark (Mark 16:9–20) is printed in single square brackets under the title in boldface capital letters: "AN OLD ENDING TO THE GOSPEL." An ac-companying footnote explains: "Some manuscripts and ancient translations do not have this ending to the Gospel (Verses 9–20)." After verse 20 of this ending, the shorter ending is also included in single square brackets with the heading: "ANOTHER OLD ENDING." No notice is given of the fact that one Old Latin manuscript (Codex Bobbiensis, *k*) has this end-ing only, nor is there note taken of the expanded form of the longer ending found in Codex Washingtonianus. The pericope of the adulteress (John 7:53–8:11) is also included in single brackets with a footnote explaining: "Many manuscripts and early translations do not have this passage (8.1–11); others have it after 21.24; others have it after Luke 21.38; one manuscript has it after John 7.36."

The third edition of the TEV NT included a number of passages in single brackets in the text, which "are not in the oldest and best manuscripts" but were cited as important variants in the critical apparatus of the UBS Greek text (Matt. 17:21; 18:11; 23:14; Mark 7:16; 9:44, 46; 11:26; 15:28; Luke 17:36; 23:17; John 5:3b–4; Acts 8:37; 15:34; 24:6b–8a; 28:29; Rom. 16:24). All of these were removed from the text of the fourth edition, but are cited in footnotes that begin, "Some manuscripts add. . . ." From the viewpoint of critical scholarship, the fourth edition is therefore far superior to its predecessors, and more closely follows the critical judgment of the editors of the UBS Greek text.

In a number of passages, the GNB follows different manuscript readings from those preferred by the editors of the UBS Greek text (see Mark 6:33; Luke 21:19; John 14:17; Acts 7:46; 12:25; 13:40; Rom. 8:2, 28; 1 Cor. 10:9; 13:3; 2 Cor. 8:7; 1 Thess. 2:7; 1 Peter 1:22, 3:18; 2 Peter 3:10). Three of these are worthy of note. The GNB follows those MSS that have "God" as the subject of the first clause in Romans 8:28 and translates, "We know that in all things God works for good with those who love him, those whom he has called according to his purpose." In 1 Corinthians 13:3 the GNB has reverted to the more traditional reading, "to be burned," rather than accepting the UBS reading, "that I may boast." In 2 Peter 3:10 the GNB has adopted the reading of one manuscript, "will vanish," rather than to try to translate the oldest extant, but meaningless, reading of the UBS text, "will be found."

The Concept of Translation

The TEV is based on a concept of translation known as "dynamic equivalence." Eugene Nida of the American Bible Society describes it thus: "To translate is to try to stimulate in the new reader in the new language the same reaction to the text the original author wished to stimulate in his first and immediate readers." This is, to be sure, an unattainable goal that can be only approximately achieved. But in striving toward it, the translator is less concerned with a literal word-by-word rendering and more concerned with the meaning of the original and the way that meaning can best be stated in natural English. "This means," Bratcher says, "that no attempt is made to translate a given Greek word by the same word in English, but always to use the English word or expression that most faithfully and naturally represents this meaning of the Greek word in the context in which it is used." The translator is primarily concerned with faithfulness to the message of the original. Having determined what that message is, he asks himself, "How would the author have said this if he were writing in English?" This principle has been used not only in the GNB, but also in the NEB and other recent translations.

But one of the hallmarks of the GNB is its use of common language English. By this is meant that part of the English language understood by people from all walks of life and all levels of education who read and write English. Although no arbitrary limit is set on the vocabulary, a studious effort is made to keep the language simple and direct. The Bible must be made understandable not only to Christians with little formal education, but also to non-Christians who are unfamiliar with technical religious vocabulary. Not only must the language of the elite be avoided, but also slang. Regional and provincial expressions, as well as idioms, are kept to a minimum.

To make it more intelligible to the common man, expressions are modernized wherever practicable. "Caesar" becomes "Emperor" or "Roman Emperor" (Luke 2:1; 3:1; 20:22ff.; Acts 25:8ff.; 26:32, et al.). "Centurion" is given as "army officer" (Matt. 27:54, et al.), "Roman officer" (Matt. 8:5), "captain in the Roman army" (Acts 10:1), "officer in the Roman army" (Acts 27:1), or simply "commander" (Acts 23:17, 23), or "officer" (Acts 22:25–26). "Publicans" are "tax collectors" (Matt. 5:46, et al.), not a flattering comparison for modern collectors of internal revenue. The "captain of the temple" is the "officer in charge of the temple guards" (Acts 4:1; 5:24, 26). The "Sanhedrin" is the "Council" (Matt. 26:59; John 11:47), defined in the "Word List" in the back of the NT as "the supreme religious court of the Jews," but the authority of that body went beyond religious matters, and included legislative as well as judicial powers.

The modern equivalents are given for expressions of time (Matt. 14:25; 20:3, 5, 9; 27:46; John 1:39; 4:52), distances (John 21:8; Acts 1:12; 27:28; Rev. 21:17), capacity (Matt. 13:33; Luke 16:6, 7; John 2:6; Rev. 6:6), and money. Monetary equivalents are especially difficult and often only a rough approximation is attempted as in the parable of the unforgiving servant who owed "millions of dollars" but would not be patient with a fellow who owed him "a few dollars" (Matt. 18:24, 28). In the story Jesus told Simon the Pharisee about the two debtors, the third edition of the TEV reads, "one owed five hundred dollars and the other fifty dollars" (Luke 7:41). In the fourth edition this has been changed to: "one owed him five hundred silver coins and the other fifty." Similarly, in what is usually designated the parable of the talents, one servant, according to the third edition, received "five thousand dollars, another two thousand dollars, and a third one thousand dollars (Matt. 25:15). The fourth edition, however, reads, "To one he gave five thousand silver coins, to another he gave two thousand, and to another he gave one thousand."

Wherever practicable, the GNB avoids the use of the technical religious terms of the standard versions, "Antichrist," for example, is given as the "enemy of Christ" (1 John 2:18, 22); "bishops" are "church leaders" (Phil. 1:1; 1 Tim. 3:2; Titus 1:7); "deacons" are "church helpers" (Phil. 1:1; 1 Tim. 3:8, 12); "raca" is translated as "you good-for-nothing" (Matt. 5:22) and "mammon" as "money" (Matt. 6:24). Where such modernizations did not seem feasible, the old terms are retained and briefly explained in the word list at the back of the NT.

The translator has also sought to clothe the great gospel ideas of the NT in words the common man, unused to theological language, can understand and appreciate. Thus, "repent" of the standard versions usually becomes "turn away from your sins" (e.g., Matt. 3:2; 4:17; Mark 1:15; Acts 2:38, et al.), though "repent" is retained in a number of passages (e.g., Luke 15:7, 10; Acts 3:19; Rev. 2:22, et al.). Apart from a few passages where "repentance" is rendered as "opportunity to repent" (Acts 5:31; 11:18), "turning away" (Heb. 6:1), "a change of heart" (2 Cor. 7:20), or simply "repentance" (Luke 24:47), the noun is translated by such verbs as "repent" (Matt. 3:11; Luke 5:32, et al.), "turn from" (Matt. 3:8; Acts 13:24, et al.), "turn away from" (2 Peter 3:9; Heb. 6:1), "change" (2 Cor. 7:9; Heb. 12:17), or "change your ways" (2 Cor. 7:9). To the Pharisees and Sadducees who came to be baptized, John said, "Do the things that will show that you have turned away from your sins" (Matt. 3:8). The Lord "does not want anyone to be destroyed, but wants all to turn away from their sins" (2 Peter 3:9). The great Pauline word "justify" is usually translated as "put right with God" (Rom. 2:13; 3:20, 24, 26; 5:1, 9; Gal. 2:16, et al.). The words "foreknew," "predestined," "called," "justified," and "glorified" of Romans 8:29–30 became respectively "already chosen," "set apart," "called," "put right with himself," and "shared his glory." The gospel truth contained in the words "reconcile" and "reconciliation" is beautifully expressed by the metaphor of "changing us from God's enemies into his friends" (2 Cor. 5:18–20). "We were God's enemies, but he made us his friends through the death of his Son" (Rom. 5:10f.). For "adoption" it reads "made God's children or sons" (Rom. 8:15, 23; 9:4; cf. Eph. 1:5). "It is through Christ that all of us, Jews and Gentiles, are able to come in the one Spirit into the presence of the Father" (Eph. 2:18). "Advocate" is given as someone "who pleads with the Father on our behalf" (1 John 2:1), and "propitiation" is given as "the means by which our sins are forgiven" (1 John 2:2; cf. Rom. 3:25).

Usually the noun "resurrection" is rendered "rise from death" (Matt. 22:23; Mark 12:18; Luke 14:14; 20:35) or "rise to life" (Matt. 22:30; Mark 12:23; Luke 20:33) or similar expressions, though "resurrection" is retained in John 11:25. In addition to translating "Gehenna" (Matt. 5:22, 29, 30, et al.) and "Hades" (Matt. 11:23; Luke 10:15) as "hell," and the verb using "Tartarus" as "threw them into hell" (2 Peter 2:4), the noun "destruction" is also so given in four passages. According to the GNB, Jesus declared that "the gate to hell is wide and the road that leads to it is easy, and there are many who travel it" (Matt. 7:13). Peter tells Simon Magnus, "May you and your money go to hell" (Acts 8:20). And according to Paul, those who make their bodily desires their god "are going to end up in hell"

(Phil. 3:19). And the "Wicked One" who comes at the "final Rebellion" "is destined to hell" (2 Thess. 2:3). Although the Greek noun for "destruction" and its corresponding verb may refer to total and definitive destruction (especially when contrasted with being saved), these words are not an equivalent to the present-day notions of "hell." The latter has overtones (and temperature) not implied by the Greek.

The objective of keeping the language of the TEV direct and simple has resulted in other translational procedures. Long and involved sentences are broken up into smaller units. Romans 1:1–7 is one sentence in the Greek but is translated as six sentences. The still longer Greek sentence of Ephesians 1:3–14 is broken up into fourteen English sentences. Rhetorical questions are sometimes translated as simple statements. Thus in Matthew 5:46, "Do not even the tax collectors do that?" is rendered, "Even the tax collectors do that!" Likewise in verse 47, "Do not even the pagans do that?" becomes "Even the pagans do that!" Instead of the question "Is there anything a man can give to regain his life?" is the statement "There is nothing a man can give to regain his life" (Mark 8:37).

At times metaphors are changed to similes. In Luke 11:34, instead of saying as the RSV does, "Your eye is the lamp of the body," the GNB reads, "Your eyes are like a lamp for the body." Other examples are the following: "Their words are full of deadly deceit; wicked lies roll off their tongues, and dangerous threats, like snake's poison, from their lips" (Rom. 3:13). "But thanks be to God! For in union with Christ we are always led by God as prisoners in Christ's victory procession. God uses us to make the knowledge about Christ spread everywhere like a sweet fragrance. For we are like a sweet-smelling incense offered by Christ to God . . ." (2 Cor. 2:14f.). The simile of the mother hen is used in Matthew 23:37 to express Jesus' love for the people of Jerusalem: "Jerusalem, Jerusalem! . . . How many times I wanted to put my arms around all your people, just as a hen gathers her chicks under her wings, but you would not let me!" At other times metaphors are changed into non-metaphors. "The finger of God" becomes "God's power" (Luke 11:20). "Cut to the heart" (RSV) is changed to "deeply troubled"

(Acts 2:37). "He does not bear the sword in vain" becomes "his power to punish is real" (Rom. 13:4). "Have put on Christ" is converted to "and now you are clothed, so to speak, with the life of Christ himself" (Gal. 3:27).

THE GNB OLD TESTAMENT

Translation Procedure

The work of translating the Old Testament was begun in September, 1967, and completed in 1975. The translation was done by a committee of six who were chosen for their competence as biblical scholars, their professional experience as translators in mission work abroad, and their adherence to the principles that produced the Good News New Testament. The committee consisted of Roger A. Bullard, Keith R. Crim, Herbert G. Grether, Barclay A. Newman, Heber F. Peacock, and John A. Thompson. This panel of translators was chaired by Robert G. Bratcher of the American Bible Society, the translator of the New Testament. In 1971 a British consultant Brynmor F. Price of the Translations Department of the British and Foreign Bible Society was added.

In the translation procedure, each member of the committee prepared a draft of the books assigned him together with a series of extensive notes explaining his choice of the particular textual readings, and his renderings of the text. The preliminary draft and notes of each translator were then circulated to the committee members, who in turn prepared written suggestions. These suggestions from the members were collated with the initial draft, and the results were revised in detail line by line, and verse by verse. The revised draft was then read aloud, and further revised. Copies of the resulting revision were then sent to more than two hundred consultants in various parts of the world for their criticism. A special panel of eight biblical scholars, linguists, and churchmen reviewed the suggestions sent in and further revised the translation. This, in turn, was reviewed in the light of stylistic considerations. It was then submitted to the Translations Committee of the American Bible Society for final approval.

Between 1970 and 1975 a number of portions of this translation were published as separate booklets: The Psalms for Modern Man, December, 1970; Job for Modern Man, with the sub-title Tried and True, August, 1971; Wisdom for Modern Man (Ecclesiastes and Proverbs), 1972; The Man Who Said "No"! (Jonah), 1973; Justice Now (Hosea, Amos, Micah), 1974; and Let My People Go (Exodus), 1975.

The Hebrew Text

The basic text used by the translators of the OT was the traditional Masoretic Hebrew text as printed in the third edition of Rudolf Kittel's Biblia Hebraica. Departures from this basic text are of various types that are indicated in the preface:

> In some instances the words of the printed consonantal text have been divided differently or have been read with a different set of vowels; at times a variant reading in the margin of the Hebrew text (qere) has been followed instead of the reading in the text (kethiv); and in other instances a variant reading supported by one or more Hebrew manuscripts has been adopted. Where no Hebrew source yields a satisfactory meaning in the context, the translation has either followed one or more of the ancient versions (e.g., Greek, Syriac, Latin) or has adopted a reconstructed text (technically referred to as a conjectural emendation) based on scholarly consensus; such departures from the Hebrew are indicated in footnotes.

The reader may be interested in examples of each type of these changes in the traditional text. To understand them one should keep in mind that the Hebrew alphabet consists exclusively of consonants, twenty-two in number. Hence the text in the earliest Hebrew manuscripts was written in consonants only, the vowels being supplied by the reader. The Masoretes became the custodians of the traditional Hebrew text from the sixth to the eleventh centuries A.D. About the seventh century they developed a system of vowel signs, called points (as well as accentual marks) that were inserted above, below, and sometimes within the consonantal text. Hence, it is not surprising that the consonantal text is regarded as having greater authority than the vowel system developed by the Masoretes hundreds of years later.

In dividing the consonantal text into words, the ancient scribes may have occasionally erred. The GNB along with several other recent versions, divides the consonants of Amos 6:12b differently. The Masoretic word-division would be translated, "Do men plow there [i.e., on the rock] with oxen?" A change in the word-division yields the translation, "Do men plow the sea with oxen?" In Jeremiah 23:33 the three-word Hebrew clause translated in the KJV as "What burden?" can be divided into two words, meaning, "You are the burden." This variant word-division that was adopted by the GNB translators has the support of the Greek and Latin versions. Hence the rendering, "You are a burden to the Lord." It is generally agreed that in Isaiah 2:20 the Masoretes inadvertently divided a single word into two that may mean "to a hole of rats." The GNB agrees with most English translations in taking the two as a single word meaning "to the moles." Such changes in word-division are not indicated by footnotes.

In a number of passages the GNB has read the consonantal text with a different set of vowels than those supplied by the Masoretes. By differently vocalizing the consonants of "Calneh" in Genesis 10:10, KJV, one gets the reading "all of them." Hence the rendering of the GNB, "all three of them in Babylonia." The Hebrew consonants for "sword" and "drought" are identical; the difference is in the vowels used to pronounce the letters. The GNB agrees with most English versions (even the NJV) in rendering God's threatened judgment on Israel described in Deuteronomy 28:22 as drought rather than a sword (KJV). A different vocalization in Judges 5:5 yields the translation given by the GNB, "The mountains quaked" rather than "flowed" (or "melted," KJV), and in Proverbs 22:20 "thirty sayings" in place of "excellent things." Such changes in vocalization are not indicated by footnotes.

The Masoretes were not at liberty to change the consonantal text (*kethiv*, "that which is written"), but they did frequently suggest a divergent reading in the margin (*qere*, "that which is to be read"). Occasionally the GNB follows the reading preferred by these scribes. The *qere* of Numbers 1:16 yields the meaning "chosen" which is adopted in preference to the *kethiv* "renowned." The *kethiv* of Psalm 100:3 reads "He [God] made us and not we ourselves." But the *qere* would be rendered, "He made us and we are his," or as the GNB translates the last clause, "and we belong to him." In 2 Samuel 22:51 the *kethiv* is rendered by the KJV as, "He is the tower of salvation for his king." The *qere* that the GNB follows is translated, "God gives great victories to his king." In Ezekiel 3:20 the GNB also prefers the *qere*, "righteous deeds," to the *kethiv*, "righteousness." There are no footnotes to indicate that the translators are following these divergent readings suggested by the Masoretes.

A few examples can be cited in which the GNB follows a variant from the MT supported by one or more Hebrew manuscripts. At Mount Sinai, according to the GNB translation of Exodus 19:18 "all the people trembled violently," whereas the MT reads "the whole mountain trembled violently." The GNB text is read by a few Hebrew manuscripts and the Greek version. The MT of Joshua 9:4 states that the Gideonites disguised themselves as envoys. But the GNB follows the reading of some Hebrew manuscripts along with the Latin Vulgate and the Syriac version: "They went and got some food." When Hannah took her boy Samuel to Shiloh, according to the MT of 1 Samuel 1:24, she took along three bulls to offer as a sacrifice, but the GNB follows the Dead Sea Scrolls and the Greek and Syriac versions in reading "a three-year-old bull." When David, according to 2 Samuel 18:3, proposed to accompany his loyal troops in the struggle to crush Absalom's revolt, his subjects protested. According to a couple of Hebrew manuscripts, along with some Greek and Latin manuscripts, they replied, as the GNB translates it, "but you are worth ten thousand of us." The GNB also follows the reading of the famous Isaiah Scroll from the Dead Sea cave in reading the second question of Isaiah 49:24, "Can you rescue the prisoners of a tyrant?" instead of the MT reading, "Or the captives of a just one delivered?" The GNB also follows the Isaiah Scroll, supported by the Greek and Latin versions, and the Aramaic Targum, in adding "by night" to the second clause of Isaiah 60:19, "Or the moon be your light by night." With the exception of 1 Samuel 1:24, there is no textual note to indicate that a different manuscript tradition is being followed. There is a footnote to Job 14:6 indicating that the second clause of the sentence "Look away from him and leave him alone" has the support of one Hebrew manuscript.

There are numerous passages in which, in the opinion of the GNB translators, the Hebrew textual sources failed to yield a satisfactory meaning in the context. Hence they consulted such ancient translations as the Greek, Latin, and Syriac. Many readings supported by one or more of these ancient versions were adopted. The announcement of the third plague on the land of Egypt, for example, was accompanied by the prediction that while the houses of the Egyptians would be full of flies, there would be none in Goshen where the Israelites were living. Exodus 8:23 in the GNB quotes God as saying to Pharaoh, "I will make a distinction between my people and your people." The reading "distinction," which comes from the Greek and Latin versions, suits the context better than the traditional Hebrew that reads "redemption" or "ransom." According to the MT of 1 Samuel 20:19, Jonathan instructed David to hide "by the stone Ezel." The GNB follows the Greek version in reading, "behind the pile of stones there." Similarly in Psalm 19:4 the Greek and Latin versions are the source of the GNB translation "their *voice* goes out to all the world" rather than the MT's reading, "their line."

There is evidence to indicate that scribes in copying manuscripts sometimes transposed the order of the letters in a word. This probably happened in the MT of Psalm 49:11 that reads in the KJV, "Their inward thought *(qirbam)* is that their house shall continue for ever . . . ." Instead of "their thought" the Greek and Syriac versions and the Aramaic Targum have "their grave," *(qibram* in Hebrew), which differs only in having the "r" and "b" transposed. This reading is more suitable in the context and is adopted by several recent versions, including the GNB, which translates:

> Their graves are their homes forever,
> there they stay for all time.

But the most striking divergencies from the MT consist of additions of material not found in the Hebrew text. In Genesis 4:8 the MT states that Cain spoke to his brother, Abel, but it does not report what he said. The Samaritan Pentateuch, and the Old Greek and Syriac versions supply this lack, which in the GNB is translated, "Let's go out in the fields." According to the Greek version of Genesis 44:4, 5, Joseph's servant not only asked the Hebrew patriarch "Why have you paid back evil for good?" but, "Why did you steal my master's silver cup?" (GNB), a question not found in the Hebrew. The Greek version also supplies material that seems to have dropped out of the Hebrew text of Judges 16:13–14, which the GNB includes. This version also makes additions to the MT derived from the Greek in 1 Samuel 3:15; 4:1; 9:25–26; 10:1, 21; 12:7–8; 13:15; 14:41; 2 Samuel 13:27, 34; 15:8; 17:3; 1 Kings 8:12; 2 Kings 23:16; and Psalm 145:13b. In all of these cases footnotes call the reader's attention to the textual changes.

According to the preface, when the translators, after consulting all the ancient sources, were left with passages that defied explanation, they "adopted a reconstructed text (technically referred to as a conjectural emendation) based on a scholarly consensus." Such reconstructions of the Hebrew text are footnoted with the words "Probable Text." About a third of the nearly seven hundred textual footnotes in the OT concern such departures from the Hebrew. Only a few examples can be cited here. In Psalm 29:9 in place of the Hebrew, "The Lord's voice makes the deer give birth," a reconstructed text yields the translation, "The Lord's voice shakes the oaks." Psalm 56:7 is translated, "Punish them, O God, for their evil," whereas the Hebrew has the verb "save" or "deliver," rather than "punish." In Isaiah 8:6 the Hebrew "rejoice" is emended to read "tremble." "Cruel men attack like a winter storm" is read in Isaiah 25:4 rather than "like a storm against a wall." In Proverbs 11:30 "violence" makes more sense than "a wise man" (Hebrew). No attempt was made to reconstruct the text of 1 Samuel 13:1, which has suffered irreparably in transmission. The GNB follows the Greek version in omitting the verse altogether.

Concepts of Translation

The translators of the OT followed the same two basic concepts of translation as were used in the production of the NT:

dynamic equivalence translation, and common language translation. The procedure may be reviewed by quoting the preface:

> After ascertaining as accurately as possible the meaning of the original, the translators' task was to express the meaning in a manner and form easily understood by the readers. . . . Every effort has been made to use language that is natural, clear, simple, and unambiguous. Consequently there has been no attempt to reproduce in English the parts of speech, sentence structure, word order, and grammatical devices of the original languages.

In this version, as one of the OT translators, Keith R. Crim, has put it, "Simplicity and readability were considered more important than literary quality." This suggests that in exalted, highly literary passages such as are found in the Psalms, and in the Prophets, the idea of dynamic equivalence must yield to common language translation. The language idiom used is primarily spoken rather than written, colloquial rather than literary.

In order to make the meaning of the original clear today, modern idioms are at times substituted for ancient ones. Thus whereas the Hebrew of Genesis 26:35 literally says that Esau's Hittite wives were "a bitterness of spirit" to Isaac and Rebekah, his parents, the GNB has, "They made life miserable for Isaac and Rebecca." Rebekah's later exclamation, "I am weary of my life because of the Hittite women" (Gen. 27:46) is rendered, "I am sick and tired of Esau's foreign wives." When the Israelites during their wilderness wanderings tired of manna and strongly craved meat, Moses promised, "the Lord will give you meat. You shall not eat one day . . . but a whole month, until it comes out at your nostrils and becomes loathsome to you" (Num. 11:19ff.). The idiom of the last clause is modernized by the GNB to read, "until it comes out of your ears, until you are sick of it." The Hebrew text of Hosea 4:16 compares Israel's stubbornness to that of a heifer. But the GNB changes the comparison to read: "The people are as stubborn as mules." In contrast to Solomon who chastised the Israelites with whips, his son Rehoboam threatened to chastise them with scorpions (1 Kings 12:14; 2 Chron. 10:11). The GNB translates, "He beat you with whips; I'll flog you with bullwhips" (or, "a horse-whip," British ed.). "A covenant of salt" (Num. 18:19; 2 Chron. 13:5) is in this version, "an unbreakable covenant."

The translator faces an acute problem in translating mean-ingfully material involving an ancient custom no longer fol-lowed. Anointing the body or part of the body with olive oil was a common practice in ancient times. Ordinary anointing was part of the daily toilette, but official anointing was a cere-mony that accompanied the appointment of a person for a spe-cial work or office. How then should the original words for "anoint" be translated? In the GNB "anoint" was retained for the official act, or the word "chosen" was substituted for it (Isa. 61:1; Luke 4:18). But ordinary anointing was variously trans-lated as "put on some perfume" (Ruth 3:3), "comb the hair" (2 Sam. 14:2; Dan. 10:3), or "welcome one as an honored guest" (Ps. 23:5). The second line of Ps. 92:10, "You have poured fresh oil over me," is interpreted in the GNB as "You have blessed me with happiness." "God has anointed you with the oil of glad-ness above your fellows" in Psalm 45:7 becomes "God . . . has poured out more happiness on you than on any other king."

In Bible times both men and women wore long, loose, flowing garments that were confined by a belt or girdle. In the interest of maneuverability in running or working the forepart of the garment was folded up or tucked into the girdle. These facts constitute the background of the phrase that the older English versions rendered as "girding up the loins." How can this phrase be translated in a meaningful way today? The GNB translates it as "dressed for travel" (Exod. 12:11; cf. Luke 12:35), "fastened his clothes tight around his waist" (1 Kings 18:46), "stand up" (Job 38:3; 40:7), "get ready" (2 Kings 9:1; Jer. 1:17), and "prepare for battle" (Nah. 2:1).

In the interest of clarity and ease of comprehension, figura-tive language is sometimes changed to simple statements set-ting forth the truth that the figure was intended to convey. "In the sweat of your face you shall eat bread" (Gen. 3:19) becomes "You will have to work hard and sweat to make the soil produce anything." Jacob's words to his sons, "You will bring down my gray hairs with sorrow to the grave" (Gen. 42:38), are rendered,

"I am an old man, and the sorrow you would cause me would kill me." In place of "Blessed shall be your basket and your kneading-trough" (Deut. 28:5, contrast v. 17) is the simple assertion, "The Lord will bless your grain crops and the food you prepare from them." Instead of comparing the doom that would come to Israel and Judah with the degradations caused by a moth or dry rot (Hos. 5:12), one reads the simple threat, "I will bring destruction on Israel and ruin on the people of Judah." The injunction, "You shall rise up before the hoary head, and honor the face of the old man" (Lev. 19:32), is translated, "Show respect for old people and honor them." The appropriation of land in Israel by Judean princes is described in Hosea 5:10 as a removal of property lines. The GNB translates, "I am angry because the leaders of Judah have invaded Israel and stolen land from her."

This method of handling figurative language is especially notable in poetic literature and in Proverbs. Psalm 5:9 in the ASV reads:

> For there is no faithfulness in their mouth;
>> Their inward part is very wickedness;
>>> Their throat is an open sepulchre;
>>> They flatter with their tongue.

Compare the GNB translation:

> What my enemies say can never be trusted;
>> they only want to destroy.
> Their words are flattering and smooth,
>> but full of deadly deceit.

Compare the renderings of Proverbs 12:19 in these two versions:

ASV: The lip of truth shall be established forever;
      But a lying tongue is but for a moment.

GNB: A lie has a short life,
          but truth lives on forever.

As a further illustration, note the renderings of Proverbs 25:15:

ASV: By long forbearing is a ruler persuaded,
          and a soft tongue breaketh the bone.

GNB: Patient persuasion can break down the strongest
       resistance
           and can even convince rulers.

In passages using anthropomorphic language, this method of translation is particularly noteworthy. Compare Isaiah 59:1 in the KJV and GNB:

KJV: Behold the Lord's hand is not shortened, that it cannot
       save;
           neither his ear heavy, that it cannot hear.

GNB: Don't think the Lord is too weak to save you
           or too deaf to hear your call for help.

According to the Hebrew text of Deuteronomy, it was God's hand and his outstretched arm that freed the ancient Israelites from Egyptian slavery (Deut. 4:34; 5:15; 7:19; 11:2; 26:8). The GNB translates these anthropomorphic expressions as his great power and strength. These figures of God's power and victory are similarly translated in the Psalms (see Pss. 44:3; 77:15; 89:10, 13, 21; 98:1), and sometimes in Isaiah (45:12; 59:16; 62:8; 63:5, 12). The Hebrew text of the eighth Psalm speaks of the heavenly bodies as the work of God's fingers, and the world with its plant and animal life as the product of God's hands (Ps. 8:3, 6). In the GNB these created things are simply that which God has made. In the original text the ears and eyes of God are also frequently mentioned. The promised land, Palestine, is "a land which the Lord God cares for; the eyes of the Lord your God are always upon it from the beginning of the year to the end of the year" (Deut. 11:12). The GNB reads, "The Lord your God takes care of this land and watches over it throughout the year." Hanani, the seer, according to 2 Chronicles 16:9, declared, "The eyes of the Lord run to and fro throughout the whole earth to show his might in behalf of those whose heart is blameless toward him." In the GNB this becomes, "The Lord keeps close watch over the whole world, to give strength to those whose hearts are loyal to him." Nehemiah's petition, "let thy ear be attentive and thy eye open to hear the prayer of thy servant . . ." (Neh. 1:16), becomes, "Look at me, Lord, and hear my prayer" (see also Pss. 11:4; 32:8; 33:18; 34:15; Isa. 1:15). When Sennacherib, the Assyrian monarch, demanded the surrender of Hezekiah, the Judean king prayed, "Incline thy ear, O Lord, and hear; open thy eyes, O Lord, and see; and hear the words of Sennacherib, which he has sent to mock the living God" (2 Kings 19:16; Isa. 37:17). In the GNB this reads, "Now, Lord, look at what is happening to us. Listen to all the things Sennacherib is saying to insult you, the living God." (See also Pss. 17:6; 32:8; 34:15; 45:10; 71:2; 86:1; 130:2.)

The metaphorical title for God, "Rock," is frequently used in the OT. The GNB translates this title in various ways: "my protector" (Ps. 18:2), "my refuge" (Pss. 19:14; 31:2–3; 71:3), "my defender" (Ps. 18:46), "a powerful God" (Isa. 44:8), "my secure shelter" (Ps. 71:3), "mighty defender" (Deut. 32:4), and "mighty savior" (Deut. 32:15, 18).

As in most English versions, the Tetragrammaton, the distinctive, ineffable name of God usually transliterated as YHWH, is rendered by the GNB as LORD. The combination *Adonai* (Lord) *Yahweh* is translated "Sovereign LORD," "LORD of hosts" is given as "Lord Almighty," "God Almighty" as "Almighty God," "the LORD, the God of hosts" as "the Sovereign LORD Almighty," "the Most High God" (Daniel) as the "Supreme God," and "the Ancient of Days" as "the one who had been living forever."

The Hebrew noun for "mercy" and "lovingkindness" in the KJV is most often translated, "constant love" (Deut. 7:9, 12; Pss. 25:6; 36:7; 40:10; 42:8–9, etc.), but "unchanging love" (Num. 14:19), "eternal love" (1 Chron. 16:41), "unfailing love" (Isa. 63:7), and "great love" (1 Kings 3:6) are also used. This exemplifies the great emphasis that the GNB places on the love of God in the OT—a needed corrective for those who have thought of the OT God as cruel and avenging.

In a number of OT passages, God is characterized as "a jealous God," as in the second commandment of the Decalogue (Exod. 20:5; Deut. 5:9). The assertion, "I the LORD your God am a jealous God" is translated in the GNB as "I am the LORD your God and I tolerate no rivals" (see also Exod. 34:14; Deut. 4:24; 6:15; Josh. 24:19; Neh. 1:2). Elijah's declaration, "I have been very jealous for the LORD God of hosts" (1 Kings 19:10, 14), is given as "LORD God Almighty, I have always served you—you alone." God's promise in Ezekiel 39:25, "and will be jealous for my holy name," is rendered "I will protect my holy name." "Then the LORD will be jealous for his land," becomes "Then the LORD showed concern for his land" (Joel 2:18). Through the prophet Zechariah, God declared, "I am jealous for Jerusalem and for Zion with a great jealousy" (Zech. 1:14, cf. 8:2), this is interpreted as "I have deep love and concern for Jerusalem, my holy city."

Readers of the GNB who are familiar with the traditional "biblical English" of the KJV, RV, ASV and their successors, the RSV and NASB, will be challenged by changes, particularly in terms connected with Israelite worship. A partial list will illustrate what is meant. Compare the traditional term (given first) with the counterpart used in the GNB:

> firmament/dome; (Noah's) ark/boat; ark of bulrushes/basket of reeds; rod/walking stick; sanctuary/sacred Tent; tabernacle/Tent; tabernacle of the LORD/LORD's tent; tent of meeting/Tent; of my [or, the LORD's] presence; court/enclosure; laver/bronze basin; bread of the Presence/sacred bread offered to God; My Glory/the dazzling light of my presence; ark of the covenant/Covenant Box; mercy seat/lid; cherub/winged creature; breast plate (or, -piece) of judgment/breast piece to use in determining God's will; peace offering/fellowship offering; cereal offering/grain offering; guilt (trespass) offering/repayment offering; feast of weeks/Harvest Festival; feast of tabernacles (ingathering)/ Festival of Shelters; Year of Jubilee/Year of Restoration; first fruits/first grain; congregation/ community; golden calf/gold bull.

The OT term for repentance and conversion is to turn back, or to return, to God. The GNB translation of Isaiah 55:7 forcefully expresses what this involves:

> Let the wicked leave their way of life
> and change their way of thinking.
> Let them turn to the Lord, our God;
> he is merciful and quick to forgive.

That this turning is not just a work of the human will, but requires divine aid is underscored by the prophet Ezekiel. The GNB translation of Ezekiel 36:26 is:

I will give you a new heart and a new mind.
I will take away your stubborn heart of stone
    and give you an obedient heart.

Jeremiah's appeal, "Amend your ways and your doings" (Jer. 7:3; cf. v. 5; 26:13, 35:15), is forcefully rendered as "Change the way you are living and the things you are doing." However "correct" or "rectify" would more adequately represent the Hebrew that means "make good" or "make right." In this regard "amend," though not common language English, would be a more accurate translation than "change." To walk with God means, in this version, to live in fellowship with God (Gen. 5:22, 24; 6:10).

There can be no question that the translation given by the GNB is simple, clear, and unambiguous. The OT is clear even when the Hebrew is uncertain or ambiguous. This raises the possibility that the translation may not always give the correct interpretation.

READER AIDS

Notes, Appendices, and Other Aids

In addition to its translation in common language English, the GNB provides a number of helps for the Bible reader. The translation of each book in the Bible is preceded by a succinct "Introduction," usually about a half-page in length, which sets forth the major theme or teaching of that book. Each introduction concludes with a brief "Outline of Contents" of the document with chapter and verse references for each section.

The text of each book is arranged in paragraphs, or, if poetry, in stanzas, rather than being chopped up into separate verses as in the KJV. The verse numbers, however, are given in small type at the beginning of each verse. The paragraphs are, in turn, arranged in larger sections with topical headings printed in boldface type to indicate their contents. These headings are helpful in most of the books of the Bible, but are less satisfactory in the Epistles, and at times break up a continuous argument. References to parallel passages in other parts of the Bible, where such parallels exist, are listed in parentheses below the sectional headings.

The first three editions of the GNB NT contained no footnotes or marginal references, but the fourth edition has nearly 300 notes, and the entire Good News Bible, as published in 1976, contains over 1,775. More than 40 percent of these deal with textual problems in manuscripts of the original languages and ancient versions. Others give possible alternative translations of the original text (see the notes to Exod. 3:14; Num. 11:31; Ps. 45:6, Isa. 1:18; Matt. 6:27; 18:22; Luke 2:36–37; John 4:9, as examples). A few translational notes call attention to the fact that one (or more) words in the original was not translated because its meaning is uncertain (see notes to Isa. 28:25; 34:12; Dan. 7:15; Hab. 3:1). Others advise the reader that the meaning of the original of an entire verse is not clear (see notes to 1 Sam. 13:1; 1 Chron. 3:21; Job 19:20). There are also notes explaining ancient persons, places, customs, etc. (See the notes to Exod. 28:30; Hos. 1:11; 4:14. In the NT see the notes to Acts 13:1; 1 Peter 5:13; and 2 John 1.) Footnotes to individual Psalms give the translation of the Hebrew title to the Psalm where one occurs.

Small italic letters in the text call attention to the notes. The notes for each book begin with the letter "a" and on through the alphabet. The 26 letters of the alphabet are used for notes more than 4 times (107 notes) in Genesis, and in the Psalms nearly 9 times (228 notes). Underneath these footnotes cross references by chapter and verse are given in larger type to other portions of Scripture "where identical or similar matters or ideas are dealt with." Intermingled with the text are appropriate maps for convenience of reference.

Following the translation of the books of the NT, the Good News Bible contains six appendices of helpful information. The first is a "Word List" of 163 alphabetically arranged biblical words and expressions that are explained in simple, direct English. Included are definitions of such biblical words as amen, anoint, apostle, Christ, covenant, demon, disciple, elders, fast, Hades, Lord, Messiah, Nazirite, parable, Day of Preparation, prophet, Sabbath, Scriptures, and vows. The list also contains notes on the Jewish months, pagan deities, precious and semiprecious stones, agricultural products, plants, animals, and constellations that are mentioned in the Bible. The explanations provided of OT religious observances, festivals, and priestly attire are especially helpful, as are the notes on the parties and sects of NT times.

The second consists of eighty-six NT passages that quote or paraphrase the Greek Old Testament (the Septuagint) and that differ significantly in meaning from the traditional Hebrew. Thus even the reader who does not know the original languages of the Bible is helped to "understand some otherwise puzzling differences in quotation."

The third contains a chronological chart of the events of the entire Bible in three pages. Many Bible students will not agree with the thirteenth-century B.C. date suggested for the Exodus.

The fourth consists of ten pages of maps of the Bible lands during the successive periods of sacred history. Most of these maps were printed also at various points within the sacred text. Inside the front cover there is also a two-page map of the ancient world. Inside the back cover there are maps of Jerusalem in New Testament times and Palestine in the time of Jesus.

The fifth appendix contains a subject index with nearly 350 entries covering "some of the more important subjects, persons, places, and events in the Bible." References to biblical passages are given in page numbers rather than by book, chapter, and verse.

Presentation of Poetry

A large part of the OT is arranged in poetic form, including all of the Psalms, Song of Songs, and Lamentations. In the translation of the Psalms, free verse was used and an attempt was made, as the preface to the original publication of them states, to put them "in easy-flowing rhythmical lines that can be effective in public worship as well as in private devotion." Note this sample of their work (Ps. 90:1–2):

> O Lord, you have always been our home.
>   Before you created the hills
>   or brought the world into being,
>   you were eternally God,
>   and will be God forever.

While this lacks the poetic grandeur of the rendering of these verses in the older versions, its simplicity has a beauty all its own (compare Ps. 84:1–2).

The first three verses of Psalm 1 will serve as a further illustration:

> Happy are those
> > who reject the advice of evil men,
> > who do not follow the example of sinners
> > or join those who have no use for God.
> Instead, they find joy in obeying the Law of the Lord,
> > and they study it day and night.
> They are like trees that grow beside a stream,
> > that bear fruit at the right time,
> > and whose leaves do not dry up.
> They succeed in everything they do.

In the six love poems (or, songs) that constitute the Song of Songs (or, of Solomon), each song has portions assigned to "The Man," "The Woman," and in the last three to "The Women."

With the exception of five verses, all of Joel is arranged as poetry. All of Job except the prologue (1:1–2:13) and the epilogue (42:7–17) are also printed in poetic form. Zophar is given as the speaker of chapter 24:18–25; Bildad of chapter 26:5–14; and Zophar of chapter 27:13–23. But it is uncertain whether these identifications not found in the Hebrew text are correct. All but seven of the books of the OT (Leviticus, Ruth, Chronicles, Ezra, Esther, Haggai, and Malachi) have material arranged in poetic form. Chapter 8 of Proverbs is printed as poetry. Chapters 1–7 and 9 are prose, and chapters 10–31 have the form of short prose maxims.

A number of NT passages are also arranged as poetry. Among these in the Gospels are the Beatitudes (Matt. 5:3–10), the Lord's Prayer (Matt. 6:9–13, the Magnificat (Luke 1:46–55), the Benedictus (Luke 1:67–79), and the Nunc Dimittis (Luke 2:29–32). In the Pauline Letters such passages as Philippians 2:6–11; 1 Timothy 3:16; and 2 Timothy 2:11–13 are also poetic form. A half a dozen passages in the Apocalypse are also printed as poetry (Rev. 4:11; 5:9–10, 12–13; 11:17–18; 15:3–4; 18:4–8).

In the OT italics are used for the names of ancient books cited as giving historical accounts, such as "The Book of Jashar" (Josh. 10:13), "The Book of the Lord's Battles" (Num. 21:14), "The History of the Kings of Israel" (1 Kings 14:19), "The History of the Kings of Judah" (1 Kings 14:24), etc.

In the NT italics are used for transliterations of Aramaic expressions (Mark 5:41; 15:34; 1 Cor. 16:22) and occasionally for emphasis (1 Cor. 16:21; Col. 4:18; 2 Thess. 3:17, Philem. 19). Quotation marks are freely used in both Testaments for direct address of speakers, OT passages quoted in the NT, and explanations of names (e.g., Matt. 1:23). Exclamation points are used generously.

As in the NT approximate modern equivalents are given for weights and measures. Linear measurements are given in inches (Exod. 28:16; 1 Kings 7:26), feet (Gen. 6:15; Esth. 5:14, etc.), and yards (Exod. 27:9, 12–16, 18; Ezek. 47:3–5). The only measurement for area is the acre (1 Sam. 14:14; Isa. 5:10). For dry capacity use is made of the quart (Exod. 16:36), and the bushel (1 Sam 1:24; 25:18). Liquid measures are given in pints (Lev. 14:10), quarts (Exod. 29:40), and gallons (1 Kings 7:26; Isa. 5:10). Weights are given in pounds (Ruth 2:17; 1 Sam. 17:5, 7) and tons (Esth. 3:9).

An outstanding feature, peculiar to the Good News Bible, is its more than six hundred imaginative and artistic line drawings by a Swiss-born artist living in Paris, Mlle. Annie Vallotton. These line drawings are designed to illustrate and draw the reader's attention to the biblical text. They add much to the appeal of this translation and help to make it speak to modern humankind.

BRITISH USAGE EDITION

Brynmor F. Price, as the British consultant for the OT committee of translators, had the responsibility of checking on British usage in grammar, vocabulary, and spelling in preparation for the publication of a British Usage Edition. Although differences in spelling between Britain and America do not affect the meaning, they are worthy of note. The ending of a group of words which in America is spelled -or, is spelled -our in Britain. Among those found in the GNB are: armour, behaviour, colour, favour, flavour, glamour, harbour, honour, labour, neighbour, odour, rumour, saviour, and splendour. (Compare also mouldy and smoulder.) The ending of a few other words which in America is written as -er, is spelled -re in Britain, such as centre, metre, sceptre, and theatre. Note also the British spelling of axe, briars, counsellors, conquerers, controlling, defence, draught, grey, jewelry, judgement, marvellous, offences, plough, quarelling, shrivelled, travelling, and worshipped.

The ending of the past tense of some verbs that in America is -ed is in Britain -t, such as burnt, dreamt, leapt, learnt, and spilt. In place of "around," the British generally prefer "round." Whereas Americans use the suffix -ward, the British prefer -wards, as in "afterwards," "downwards," "eastwards," "towards," "westwards," etc. The British also prefer "eldest," to "oldest."

A comparison of a number of words, phrases, and clauses found in the British edition with those in the American edition (listed first) will serve to illustrate the changes in vocabulary:

aliens/foreigners; at evening/in the evening; back and forth/to and fro; bother/annoy; Big and Little Dipper/Great and Little Bear; brag/boast; brush fire/fire among thorns; coals/embers; crazy/mad (or, daft); develop/produce; die of starvation/die by famine; dip water/scoop water; dirt/earth (or, mud); drool/dribble; drunk/drunken man; faraway/distant; fix/prepare; fix the scales/tamper with the scales; flagpole/flagstaff; from far away/from afar; from head to toe/from head to foot; garbage/refuse; garbage dump/refuse heap; garbage is dumped/refuse is thrown; gathered/assembled; got/fetched; grabbed/seized; grain/corn; heads of grain/ears of corn; his insides/his entrails; hogs/pigs; it isn't so/it isn't true; keep from/avoid; lamp/candle; laugh at/mock; mama/mummy; maybe/perhaps; mistreat/ill-treat; plant (seed)/sow; pool/pond; porch/passage; property line/boundary line; raised/reared; reach out/stretch out; rooster/cock; set the table/laid the table; sling/catapult; a trumpet blows/a trumpet sounds; smart/clever (or, sensible); sick/ill; spit/spew; stalk of grain/ear of corn; suit yourselves/please yourselves; traded/exchanged; trim (verb)/prune; trip/journey; washbowl/washbasin; woodsmen/woodmen; woodworker/woodcarver; work horse/draught horse; you smart aleck/you cheeky brat.

The British Usage Edition in general strikes an American as a bit less colloquial than its American counterpart. The British edition, it should be pointed out, also uses the metric system of weights and measures. In the parable of the unforgiving servant, it also substitutes pounds for dollars.

CONCLUSION

In conclusion, although one might wish that a word here and there, or certain verses, had been translated differently (e.g., Gen. 6:2, 4), the GNB effectively meets the objectives of the American Bible Society set for it. Most of the criticisms leveled against it do not take into consideration the principles of dynamic equivalence and common language translation that constantly guided the translators. There are both gains and losses in this kind of translation. The GNB is an honest attempt by skilled translators to clothe the message of the Bible in language that is simple, plain, and meaningful to modern people. Through it the Bible has come alive to many a person who never has read, and never would read, a version in sixteenth-century English. Anyone who reads English can comprehend this version. A sentence from the preface appropriately asserts:

The Bible is not simply great literature to be admired and revered; it is Good News for all people everywhere—a message both to be understood and to be applied in daily life.

12

The New English Bible

ITS HISTORY

In 1946, the year in which the Revised Standard Version of the NT was published in the United States, plans were laid in the British Isles for the production of the New English Bible (NEB). As the result of the initiative taken by the annual General Assembly of the Church of Scotland in approaching other churches regarding a new version, delegates from the Church of England, the Church of Scotland, and the Methodist, Baptist, and Congregational churches met in conference in October. It was decided to undertake the production of a completely new translation.

In the following year representatives of these churches were appointed to form a "Joint Committee on the New Translation of the Bible," which met in July, 1947. At its third meeting in January, 1948, the committee invited also the Presbyterian Church of England, the Society of Friends, the Churches in Wales, the Churches in Ireland, the British and Foreign Bible Societies, and the National Bible Society of Scotland to appoint representatives.

At a later time representatives of the Roman Catholic Church in England and Scotland also attended as observers.

Three panels were assigned to translate respectively the OT, the Apocrypha, and the NT. The work of each panel was submitted for scrutiny to a group of literary advisors to make recommendations regarding the English style.

The first edition of the NT was published in 1961. The complete Bible was published in March, 1970, in two editions: a Library Edition of three volumes, OT, Apocrypha, and NT (second edition); and the Standard Edition in one volume, with or without the Apocrypha. The new Bible is an "authorized" version in the sense that it was produced under the official auspices of the leading Protestant churches of the British Isles. It therefore has a status and an authority no private translation could have.

DISTINCTIVES OF THE NEB

The NEB differs from the RSV in three chief respects. In the first place, it purports to be a completely new rendering of the original Hebrew, Aramaic, and Greek, and not just a revision of the older English versions. As its name implies, the RSV is a revision of the American Standard Version, which was the American edition of a revision of the King James Version. The KJV was itself a revision of older English revisions of the work of William Tyndale, the real father of all these English Bibles. The New English Bible has abandoned the Tyndale–King James tradition, and attempted an entirely fresh translation into clear and contemporary English.

The second difference, closely related to the first, concerns the method of translation. The translators of the Tyndale tradition sought to present a literal word-for-word rendering, as far as they were able to do so consistent with English idiom. In fact, from The Geneva Bible on down to the KJV, English words that were not actually representative of corresponding words in the original but were regarded as necessary to make sense in our language were put in italics.

The method of translation used in the NEB is much freer. Instead of being a word-for-word translation, it is a "meaning-for-meaning" rendering. Professor C. H. Dodd, in his "Introduction to the New Testament," describes it thus:

> We have conceived our task to be that of understanding the original as precisely as we could (using all available aids), and then saying again in our own native idiom what we believed the author to be saying in his. . . . In doing our work, we have constantly striven to follow our instructions and render the Greek, as we understand it, into the English of the present day, that is into the natural vocabulary, constructions, and rhythms of contemporary speech. (p. vii)

The Greek Text

In the third place, the NEB NT differs from the RSV in many passages in its underlying Greek text. The Greek MSS and early versions of the NT confront the translator with a variety of readings, and he must in a given verse choose either to follow one of the standard Greek editions or assume the role of textual critic and decide on his own which reading to follow. The latter course was followed by the NEB translators. C. H. Dodd states this point as follows:

> There is not at the present time any critical text which would command the same degree of general acceptance as the Revisers' text did in its day. Nor has the time come, in the judgement of competent scholars to construct such a text, since new material constantly comes to light and the debate continues. The present translators therefore could do no other than consider variant readings on their merits, and having weighed the evidence for themselves, select for translation in each passage the reading which to the best of their judgement seemed most likely to represent what the author wrote. . . . (p. v)

On the basis of this eclectic principle, the translators reconstructed the Greek text as they went along. In the vast majority of cases they accepted readings that have been adopted by the major critical Greek texts of our time. But frequently they daringly adopted Greek readings that are supported by a very small group of MSS of the so-called Western type, of which Codex Bezae (D) and the Old Latin version are representative. Their Greek text, edited with introduction, textual notes, and appendix by R. V. G. Tasker, was published in 1964 under the title The Greek New Testament. A few important differences between it and the critical editions of Westcott-Hort, Nestle-

Aland, and the United Bible Societies, as well as the Received Text lying behind the KJV, will serve to illustrate its occasional daring acceptance of "Western" readings.

No known Greek MS omits the name "Jesus" from Matthew 1:18, but the NEB follows the Old Latin, the Old Syriac, and the Vulgate versions in leaving it out; hence the rendering, "This is the story of the birth of the Messiah." Matthew 5:11 in the NEB reads, "How blest you are, when you suffer insults and persecution and every kind of calumny for my sake." The last part of the verse in the RSV reads, "and utter all kinds of evil against you falsely on my account." In the Greek text used by the NEB the word "falsely" is omitted on the basis of D, six MSS of the Old Latin, the Old Syriac, and the Georgian versions, plus a few early Fathers. Nevertheless, the translation "calumny" implies false accusations maliciously reported. The NEB omits all of Matthew 9:34 following D, three Old Latin MSS, and the Sinaitic Syriac, on the assumption that this verse is an assimilation to Matthew 12:24. "Lebbaeus" is substituted for "Thaddaeus" in the list of the twelve apostles in Matthew 10:3 on the basis of D and a couple of Old Latin MSS.

In place of "moved with pity" in Mark 1:41, the NEB follows the reading "being angry" of D and a few Old Latin MSS, which it translates weakly as "in warm indignation." Among the variety of forms in which MSS give the charge of Jesus to the blind man healed at Bethsaida in Mark 8:26, the NEB has adopted the simple one found in no currently known Greek MS, but in one important Old Latin document: "Do not tell anyone in the village."

In Luke 5:17 the NEB substitutes "and there were come together" for "who had come," on the basis of D and one Old Latin MS. The verse is then translated as two sentences: "One day he was teaching, and Pharisees and teachers of the law were sitting around. People had come from every village of Galilee and from Judaea and Jerusalem. . . ." Instead of "Consider the lilies, how they grow; they neither toil nor spin" in Luke 12:27, the NEB with D, the Old Syriac, and two Old Latin MSS have "Think of the lilies: they neither spin nor weave."

In Acts 1:26 the reading of D and its Latin counterpart, "the twelve apostles" is read instead of "the eleven apostles." "By his holy prophets" is read in Acts 3:21, with D and a couple of Old Latin MSS, instead of "by his holy prophets from of old." In Acts 4:25 the phrase "by the Holy Spirit" is inserted, with D, before "by the mouth of," resulting in the translation "who by the Holy Spirit, through the mouth of David thy servant, didst say."

There are other interesting readings in the NEB Greek text that are not peculiarly Western. In Mark 8:38, as in its parallel of Luke 9:26a, "words" is omitted with the resulting translation, "If anyone is ashamed of me and mine [i.e., my followers] in this wicked and godless age, the Son of Man will be ashamed of him, when he comes in the glory of his Father and of the holy angels." The striking reading found in some "Caesarean" type MSS that give the name of the notorious prisoner released in place of our Lord as "Jesus Bar-Abbas" is adopted in Matthew 27:16f. In Luke 10:1, 17 the NEB has the interesting reading "seventy-two" rather than "seventy," and in this is supported by Codex Vaticanus as well as Western and other MSS. John 13:10 reads, "A man who has bathed needs no further washing." But the omission here of "needs only to wash his feet" rests on weak MS evidence.

The Hebrew Text

The textual basis for the OT of the NEB is the traditional Masoretic Hebrew (and Aramaic) text as printed in Rudolf Kittel's Biblia Hebraica (third edition). Originally this traditional text was written in consonants only, and the vowels were supplied by the reader. In later times, however, the rabbis added the vowel signs to preserve what they regarded as the true pronunciation. Through the centuries this traditional text has suffered from copyists' errors and scribal emendations and consequently does not always represent what was originally written. Where errors in the text were apparent, the translators tried to recover the original by consulting the portions extant in the Dead Sea Scrolls and, for the first five books, the Samaritan Pentateuch, which differs considerably from the Hebrew, mostly in minor and unimportant ways, but that occasionally has cogent readings. Use was also made of such ancient versions as the Septuagint, the Syriac, the Vulgate, and the Aramaic Targums in the endeavor to recover pre-Masoretic readings. In instances where such research failed to provide satisfactory solutions, the translators resorted to emendation of the text, first by substituting other vowels, and then, if they regarded it as necessary, by changing the consonants as well. Emendations in the consonantal text are designated in the footnotes as *"Prob. rdg."* (i.e., probable reading). It is to be expected that some exegetes of the Bible will regard this or that surgical operation on the sacred text as too hasty and unnecessary.

The translators have also occasionally changed the order of materials in the text. For example, in Genesis 26, verse 18 is placed between verses 15 and 16. Verses 6 and 7 of Isaiah 41 are inserted between verses 20 and 21 of Isaiah 40. In Jeremiah 12 part of verse 14 and all of verse 15 are given after verse 17. Verses 13 and 14 of Jeremiah 15 are removed from the text and put in a footnote. Amos 5:7 is transposed to follow verse 9. In several places in Joel 3:9–12 the order of the lines has been rearranged. Zechariah 2:13 is followed by chapter 4:1–3 and verses 11–13. The remaining verses (4–10) of chapter 4 are left in their normal place after chapter 3:10. In Zechariah 13, verses 7–9 are transposed to follow 11:17. A legitimate question may well be raised at this point: Is such a rearranging of the materials in harmony with modern concepts of sequential thought the proper function of translators, or should translators confine their activity to rendering the text in the order in which it has been handed down?

Another deviation from custom has been the complete omission of the superscriptions from the Psalms. These ancient editorial titles were part of the traditional text and are found in the oldest Hebrew MSS known. Their great antiquity is shown by the fact that as early as the time of the translation of the Greek OT, the significance of some of the technical musical terms was already unknown as their rendering in the LXX reveals. Many Bible students will regard the omission of these ancient titles as unfortunate. The translators of the NEB have no antipathy to headings as such, for they have inserted many of them in the text of other parts of the Bible.

The NEB, like the RSV, has returned to the practice of the KJV in normally translating the sacred, covenant name YHWH as "LORD." This sacred name, called the Tetragrammaton and occurring some 6,800 times in the OT, came to be regarded as too sacred to be pronounced. Hence, the practice arose of substituting the Hebrew word *Adonai,* meaning "Lord," for it when reading the sacred text. When the vowel signs were added to the consonantal text, the Masoretes pointed the Tetragrammaton with the vowels used to pronounce *Adonai.* The late medieval form "Jehovah" is an artificial form combining these vowels with the consonants of the Tetragrammaton. Scholars today are generally agreed that the correct form is "Yahweh." Nevertheless, the customary form "Jehovah," which had already been used four times in the KJV (Exod. 6:3; Ps. 83:18; Isa. 12:2; 26:4) was retained in the NEB in a few passages where the name is explained (Exod. 3:15; 6:3; 33:18f.; 34:5–6), with a footnote explaining its pronunciation. It is also used in such place names as Jehovah-jireh (Gen. 22:14), Jehovah-nissi (Exod. 17:15–16), Jehovah-shalom (Judg. 6:23–24), and Jehovah-shammah (Ezek. 48:35).

The NEB rendering of the first two verses of the Bible is, to say the least, debatable: "In the beginning of creation, when God made heaven and earth, the earth was without form and void, with darkness over the face of the abyss, and a mighty wind that swept over the surface of the waters." A footnote gives the traditional rendering, "In the beginning God created heaven and earth." Another footnote gives "and the spirit of God hovering," for "a mighty wind that swept." These footnotes indicate that the translators were not in complete agreement on the new renderings. The arguments pro and con for the new or the traditional translation are too technical to be dealt with here, but suffice it to say that a comparison with other modern versions and recent commentaries indicates that Bible scholars of equal repute can be cited for either interpretation.

At the conclusion of the creating activity of each day of creation week is the statement appropriately translated, "Evening came, and morning came, a second day" (v. 8), "a third day" (v. 13), "a fourth day," (v. 18), "a fifth day," (v. 23), and "a sixth day" (v. 31). "Thus the heavens and the earth were completed with all their mighty throng" (Gen. 2:1). In the following sentence the NEB follows the Samaritan Pentateuch and the LXX in reading "the sixth day," rather than the Hebrew, which has "the seventh day." "On the sixth day God completed all the work he had been doing, and on the seventh day he ceased from all his work" (Gen. 2:2). It is doubtful that this change is justifiable. The activities of the sixth day have already been described. Also, if we follow the well-known principle of textual critics that the more difficult reading is to be preferred, we would retain the Hebrew "the seventh day." God completed His work on the seventh day by inaugurating the Sabbath. This He did by desisting from His creative work and by blessing and sanctifying the seventh day.

ITS CHARACTERISTICS

For the most part, the NEB translators have done an outstanding piece of work in conveying the thought of both Testaments into modern English. They have been aware of modern trends in understanding and interpreting the text. Showing a sensitivity to the meaning of the various Greek tenses, they have tried, where practicable, to put the meaning into English. It may be helpful at this juncture to give a few samples of their translations.

Micah 6:6–8

What shall I bring when I approach the LORD?
How shall I stoop before God on high?
Am I to approach him with whole-offerings or yearling calves?
Will the LORD accept thousands of rams
or ten thousand rivers of oil?
Shall I offer my eldest son for my own wrongdoing,
my children for my own sin?

God has told you what is good;
and what is it that the LORD asks of you?
Only to act justly, to love loyalty,
to walk wisely before your God.

Luke 10:41–42

But the Lord answered, 'Martha, Martha, you are fretting and fussing about so many things; but one thing is necessary. The part that Mary has chosen is best; and it shall not be taken away from her.'

Luke 3:14

'Exact no more than the assessment.' Soldiers on service also asked him, 'And what of us?' To them he said, 'No bullying; no blackmail; make do with your pay!'

Matthew 5:3

'How blest are those who know their need of God; the kingdom of Heaven is theirs.'

Matthew 6:7–8

'In your prayers do not go babbling on like the heathen, who imagine that the more they say the more likely they are to be heard. Do not imitate them. Your Father knows what your needs are before you ask him.'

Matthew 22:15–18

Then the Pharisees went away and agreed on a plan to trap him in his own words. Some of their followers were sent to him in company with men of Herod's party. They said, 'Master, you are an honest man, we know; you teach in all honesty the way of life that God requires, truckling to no man, whoever he may be. Give us your ruling on this: are we or are we not permitted to pay taxes to the Roman Emperor?' Jesus was aware of their malicious intention and said to them, 'You hypocrites! Why are you trying to catch me out?'

2 Corinthians 2:14, 15

But thanks be to God, who continually leads us about, captives in Christ's triumphal procession, and everywhere uses us to reveal and spread abroad the fragrance of the knowledge of himself! We are indeed the incense offered by Christ to God, both for those who are on the way to salvation, and for those who are on the way to perdition.

The language of the NEB is, of course, English. But what kind of English? According to the "Introduction to the New Testament," the object of the translators was to give "a faithful rendering of the best available Greek text into the current speech of our time" (p. v). They were commissioned "to make the attempt to use consistently the idiom of contemporary English" (p. vi). Similarly, in the "Introduction to the Old Testament" (p. xviii) we are told, "They have tried to keep their language as close to current usage as possible, while avoiding words and phrases likely soon to become obsolete."

How well have the translators succeeded in carrying out these objectives? This is a difficult question to answer, since current English in the United Kingdom may differ in many respects from current speech in America. It is to be expected that the NEB will use the "Queen's English," and therefore some words and expressions used may sound unusual to American ears. The British character of the language will frequently challenge the American reader, and he may at times wonder if "current" and "contemporary" English means twentieth-century English or includes nineteenth-century English as well. At any rate, he will note a number of differences between his own language and that of the "Queen's English."

Although differences in spelling have little significance, the alert American reader will note a large number of words ending in -our instead of -or, such as armour, colour, clamour, favour, honour, labour, and neighbour. He will also note that some words that he prefers to end with -er end in -re, such as sceptre (Gen. 49:10, et al.), theatre (Acts 19:29, 31), and reconnoitre (Josh. 2:1). Some words that the American reader spells with an "s" are spelled with a "c," such as offence (2 Cor. 6:3; 11:7), defence (Acts 19:3), and pretence (Phil. 1:18). "Mouldy" (Josh. 9:5, 12) he spells without the "u." "Plough" (Deut. 22:10), "ploughing" (Luke 17:7), and "ploughman" (1 Cor. 9:10) he spells with "ow" rather than "ough." He notes both "jailer" (Acts 16:23, 27) and "gaoler" (Isa. 10:4). "Caldron" is spelled "cauldron" (Job. 41:20; 1 Sam. 2:14).

British usage is reflected also in the vocabulary. Amounts of money are sometimes given in British terms: "Are not sparrows five for twopence?" (Luke 12:6). "Presently there came a poor widow who dropped in two tiny coins, together worth a farthing" (Mark 12:42). "Are we to go and spend twenty pounds on bread to give them a meal?" (Mark 6:37). "Why this waste? The perfume might have been sold for thirty pounds and the money given to the poor" (Mark 14:5). "He met a fellow-servant who owed him a few pounds" (Matt. 18:28). Likewise some expressions of time reflect British life: "I stayed with him for a fortnight" (Gal. 1:18). "But I shall remain at Ephesus until Whitsuntide" (1 Cor. 16:8).

One of the most common differences between British and American English is in the use of the word "corn." "Corn" in Britain means grain, particularly wheat, whereas in the United States and Canada (also Australia) it refers to Indian corn or maize. The latter was, of course, unknown in the Middle East in Bible times and the NEB naturally follows the British usage, as does the KJV. Americans should think of wheat when they read, "Once about that time Jesus went through the cornfields on the Sabbath; and his disciples, feeling hungry, began to pluck some ears of corn and eat them" (Matt. 12:1). "A sower went out to sow. . . . Some seed fell on rocky ground, where it had little soil, and it sprouted quickly because it had no depth of earth; but when the sun rose the young corn was scorched, and as it had no root it withered away" (Matt. 13:4–6). "A man sowed his field with good seed; but while everyone was asleep his enemy came, sowed darnel among the wheat, and made off. When the corn sprouted and began to fill out, the darnel could be seen among it" (Matt. 13:25f.). "But Samson said, 'This time I will settle my score with the Philistines; I will do them some real harm.' So he went and caught three hundred jackals and got some torches; he tied the jackals tail to tail and fastened a torch between each pair of tails. He then set the torches alight and turned the jackals loose in the standing corn of the Philistines. He burnt up standing corn and stooks as well, vineyards and olive groves" (Judg. 15:3–5).

A number of other words appear in the NEB that are evidently in use in Britain but quite unknown to most Americans. One is "stooks," meaning "shocks," in the above Samson story. Another is the use of "weeds" for mourning garments in the expression "widow's weeds" (Gen. 38:14, 19; Isa. 47:8; Rev. 18:7). As a term for a heap of stones piled up as a memorial, the

Scottish word "cairn" occurs six times in the story of Laban and Jacob's meeting that resulted in making a covenant (Gen. 31:46ff.). "In spate," meaning "in flood," is also chiefly Scottish (Job 6:17; 40:23; cf. 11:2). One wonders if the following represents a Scotticism: "Do not be haughty, but go about with humble folk" (Rom. 12:16). The word "hind" means "female deer" (Ps. 42:1; Hab. 3:19), for which Americans use "doe."

When the translators speak of using current speech and contemporary English, one is tempted to ask, contemporary for whom? One has the feeling that at times terms are used that would be known only to the educated. And perhaps "contemporary" includes also the nineteenth century. Note the italicized words in the following quotations:

Now his sons used to *foregather* (Job 1:4)
the stronger man seizes it from the *panniers* (Job 5:5)
they reach them only to be *balked* (Job 9:21)
Of myself I *reck* nothing (Job 9:21)
not for him to *swill down* rivers of cream (Job 20:17)
I do not *descry* him (Job 23:9)
I broke the fangs of the *miscreant* (Job 29:17)
tormented by a ceaseless *ague* in his bones (Job 33:19)
and its lair in the *saltings* (Job 39:6)
Can you pull out the whale with a *gaff* (Job 41:1)
strangers will *batten* on your wealth (Prov. 5:10; cf. Rev. 17:16)
he will get nothing but blows and *contumely* (Prov. 6:33)
and give them to his *lackeys* (1 Sam. 8:14–15)
your *runnels* of water pour into the street (Prov. 5:16)
he and the king of the south will make *feints* at one another (Dan. 11:40)
does that mean that Christ is an *abettor* of sin? (Gal. 2:17)
What are they all but *ministrant* spirits? (Heb. 1:14)
Moses, then, was faithful as a *servitor* (Heb. 3:5)
to fetch cedar-wood from the Lebanon to the *roadstead* at Joppa (Ezra 3:7)
And there shall be a *causeway* there (Isa. 35:8)
Alas, alas for the great city . . . *bedizened* with gold and jewels and pearls (Rev. 18:17)
Do you bring in the lamp to put it under the *meal-tub* . . . ? (Mark 4:21)
You strain off a *midge*, yet gulp down a camel! (Matt. 23:24)

On the other hand, the English of the NEB is often brisk, tangy, and arrestingly good:

The men in charge of them took to their heels (Mark 5:14)
This touched them on the raw and they ground their teeth with fury (Acts 7:54)
So they fell foul of him (Mark 6:4)
You are the people who impress your fellow-men with your righteousness; but God sees through you (Luke 16:15)
He saw how crafty their question was, and said, 'Why are you trying to catch me out?' (Mark 12:15)
while I was with you, if I ran short, I sponged on no one (2 Cor. 11:9)
Out! Pester me no more! (Exod. 10:27)
Up with you! Be off, and leave my people, you and your Israelites (Exod. 12:31)
But if you go on fighting one another, tooth and nail, all you can expect is mutual destruction (Gal. 5:15)
the long-winded ramblings of an old man (Job 8:2)
and begins to bully the other servants (Matt. 24:49)
he began to feel the pinch (Luke 15:14)
I count it so much garbage (Phil. 3:8)

Some readers may regard some expressions as a bit too familiar for the sacred Scriptures:

Your calf-gods stink, O Samaria (Hos. 8:5)
Do you think you can hoodwink men like us? (Num. 16:14)
and answer with a bellyful of wind (Job 15:2)
This is more than we can stomach (John 6:60)
Not indulging in double talk, given neither to excessive drinking nor to money-grubbing (1 Tim. 3:8)
they got wind of it (Acts 14:6)
that I may not be left picking lice (Song of Sol. 1:7)

On the other hand, in the story of Paul the prisoner one notes the use of technical legal language:

and they laid an information against Paul before the Governor (Acts 24:1)
When the prisoner was called, Tertullus opened the case (v. 2)
and when I was in Jerusalem the chief priests and elders of the Jews laid an information against him, demanding his condemnation (Acts 25:15)

But Paul appealed to be remanded in custody, for His Imperial
Majesty's decision (v. 21)
I stand in the dock today (Acts 26:6; cf. Phil. 1:7)

Occasionally the language has a pedantic flavor:

at parricides and matricides . . . in his eternal felicity (1 Tim.
1:9–11)
inculcate abstinence from certain foods (1 Tim. 4:3)
I call him a pompous ignoramus. He is morbidly keen on mere
verbal questions and quibbles . . . all typical of men who have let
their reasoning powers become atrophied (1 Tim. 6:4)
It is an intractable evil, charged with deadly venom (James 3:9)
the smoke of her conflagration (Rev. 18:18)

In relation to the original, the English rendering is sometimes quite paraphrastic and interpretive. What is literally "to
those who have believed on his name" is given as "to those
who have yielded him their allegiance" (John 1:12). The literal
"If you abide in my word" is made to read, "If you dwell
within the revelation I have brought" (John 8:31). The literal
rendering "that the works of God might be displayed in curing
him" becomes "so that God's power might be displayed in
curing him" (John 9:3). The translation of Exodus 11:1 is certainly paraphrastic: "After that he will let you go; he will send
you packing, as a man dismisses a rejected bride." Note also
verse 7: "Not a dog's tongue shall be so much as scratched."
The insertion of the word "phylactery" into Exodus 13:16 is
unquestionably in the nature of an interpretation and most
probably is incorrect: "You shall have the record of it as a sign
upon your hand, and upon your forehead as a phylactery. . . ."
The literal phrase "by [or, in] his blood" becomes "by his
sacrificial death" (Rom. 3:25), or "by Christ's sacrificial death"
(Rom. 5:9). The Greek word rendered "propitiation" in the
KJV becomes in 1 John 2:2 and 4:10 "the remedy for the defile-
ment of our sins" and in Romans 3:25 "the means of expiating
sin."

The version is printed in an attractive form with one column
to the page. The verse numbers are given in the left-hand margin. Subject headings are given in large type. The poetic por-

tions of Scripture such as the Psalms, Proverbs, and a large part of the prophets, are printed in poetic form. Quotation marks are used throughout.

CONCLUSION

Before the complete Bible was printed, the translators took the opportunity of reviewing the renderings given in the 1961 edition of the NT, particularly in the light of criticisms that had been made. Although the basic translation remains the same, some four hundred revisions were made. This means that when the NEB NT is quoted, one should state which edition is being used. It is anticipated that the thorough revision of the entire Bible, now in process, will be completed in the mid-eighties.

By and large, the NEB gives a valid reproduction of the thought of the sacred Scriptures. The reader must bear in mind, however, that the intention of the translators was to give a thought-by-thought and not a word-by-word translation. This often results in paraphrastic and interpretative renderings. The reader who knows his Greek New Testament will also note that the application of the eclectic principle followed in dealing with MSS frequently led to the adoption of readings with very little MS support. The strongest point of the NEB is its vigorous and colorful English style, though the American reader will find it necessary to refer occasionally to his dictionary of the English language.

13

The New American Bible

ITS HISTORY AND TEXTUAL BASIS

Just as it was inevitable that the NEB should be published as the English Protestant counterpart of the American RSV, so also it was inevitable that the NAB should be published as a counterpart of the English Catholic JB. However, this NAB has been in process for over three decades, being originally known as The Confraternity Version. In fact, the NT, a revision of Rheims-Challoner based on the Latin Vulgate, was published in 1941. When in 1943 the famous encyclical on Scripture studies was issued by Pope Pius XII recommending translation from the original text, work on the OT was begun, based on the original text. By 1969 the OT was complete, including the Apocrypha. Of course, the NT had to be retranslated, this time from the Greek text. With the publication of the NAB in 1970, there exists for the first time a complete American Catholic Bible translated from the original languages. The translation team included fifty-nine Catholic and five Protestant scholars.

The OT is based on the Hebrew and Aramaic (the Masoretic text), but no critical modern translation slavishly follows the MT in every instance. In 1 Samuel the NAB has "251 notes citing the Qumran Scroll, the Septuagint, and a combination thereof, together with some indicating a conjectural change without versional or manuscript evidence. (Keith Crim, *Interpretation*, 26 [1972], 78). The NAB departs from the MT more frequently than the RSV (58 times) and the NEB (104 times).

The Greek text used in the NT is Nestle-Aland's Novum Testamentum Graece (25th ed., 1963), with some assistance from the United Bible Societies' Greek NT. Here again it has not followed this text in every instance. Unfortunate is its use of brackets to indicate what are called "doubtful readings of some merit." Such readings are found, for example, in Matthew 5:5; 17:21; 21:44; 24:36; John 5:3; Ephesians 1:1. Some readings not found in the Nestle-Aland text have been included in the translation. These include Luke 24:12; 24:40; 24:51. At the end of Mark it has followed the Nestle-Aland text by including both longer and shorter endings within the text section. There is a line, however, between these endings and no line between Mark 16:8 and the longer ending. Besides these two endings it has also included, separated by a line from the shorter ending, the ending found in the Freer Logion. According to the note at this place, the longer ending "has traditionally been accepted as an inspired part of the gospel" although "vocabulary and style argue strongly that it was written by someone other than Mark." The story of the woman taken in adultery is found in brackets at its traditional position in John even though the explanation in the footnote indicates it is out of place there. This passage is found in different places in different MSS but is missing in the best early MSS.

READER AIDS

The NAB has short introductions to the different parts of the OT—the Pentateuch, the Historical Books, the Wisdom Books, and the Prophetic Books. It also has an introduction to each book of the Bible. These are moderately liberal in tone. The text is set in two columns in very readable type. It is in paragraph form with verse numbers in very light, small type, perhaps a bit too light. The names of biblical personages and places (except for "Gethsemane") are those customarily found in Protestant Bibles. At the end of the Bible are included the "Dogmatic Constitution on Divine Revelation," a "Glossary of Biblical Theology Terms,"

"A Survey of Biblical Geography," and some maps.

The NAB has fewer footnotes than the JB that are often even less Catholic in flavor. For example, in Genesis 3:15 no mention is made of Mary. This is true also in Revelation 12:1. No mention of purgatory is made in 1 Corinthians 3:13. In Matthew 13:55 and Mark 6:3 the Greek words *adelphos* and *adelphē* are translated "brother" and "sister" respectively. No note concerning this is appended to the former passage, but in Mark 6:3 we find the following: "The question about the brothers of Jesus and his sisters (v. 3) cannot easily be decided on linguistic grounds. Greek-speaking Semites used the terms *adelphos* and *adelphē*, not only in the ordinary sense of blood brother and sister, but also for nephew, niece, half-brother, half-sister, and cousin." Then follows clearly where the writer stands: "The question of meaning here would not have arisen but for the faith of the church in Mary's perpetual virginity." It is a bit more apologetic regarding the perpetual virginity of Mary as the note on Matthew 1:25 indicates: "The evangelist emphasizes the virginity of the mother of Jesus from the moment of his conception to his birth. He does not concern himself here with the period that followed the birth of Jesus, but merely wishes to show that Joseph fully respected the legal character of the paternity imposed on him by the divine will. Moreover the New Testament makes no mention anywhere of children of Joseph and Mary."

ITS CHARACTERISTICS

The use of "thou," "thee," "thine," and related verb forms has been dropped. "You" is used for both singular and plural forms. Unlike the JB with its use of "Yahweh," the NAB has gone back to the more acceptable "LORD."

There is some rearrangement of verses in the NAB. In Jeremiah, for instance, 11:19–23 is placed between 12:6 and 12:7. More drastic is the rearrangement in Ezekiel. The order, beginning with 8:3, is 8:5–18; 9:1–11; 11:24–25; 8:1–2, 4; 10:20–22, 14–15, 9–13, 16–17, 8, 18–19; 11:22–23, 1–21. More such changes are made in Hosea. The JB also did some rearranging, especially in Hosea. Previously the translation known for this was that of Moffatt.

The translation itself is simple, clear, and straightforward and reads very smoothly. It is good American English, not as pungent and colorful as the NEB. Its translations are not striking but neither are they clumsy. They seem to be more conservative in the sense that they tend not to stray from the original. That is not to say that this is a literal translation, but it is more faithful. It does not make daring transcultural translations such as the PHILLIPS "Shake hands with everyone" for "Greet one another with a holy kiss." The following passages illustrate these characteristics:

Psalm 91:1–3

You who dwell in the shelter of the Most High,
    who abide in the shadow of the Almighty,
Say to the LORD, "My refuge and my fortress,
    my God, in whom I trust."
For he will rescue you from the snare of the fowler,
    from the destroying pestilence.

Isaiah 40:1–2

Comfort, give comfort to my people,
    says your God.
Speak tenderly to Jerusalem, and proclaim to her
    that her service is at an end,
    her guilt is expiated;
Indeed, she has received from the hand of the LORD
    double for all her sins.

Matthew 5:31–32

"It was also said, 'Whenever a man divorces his wife, he must give her a decree of divorce.' What I say to you is: everyone who divorces his wife—lewd conduct is a separate case—forces her to commit adultery. The man who marries a divorced woman likewise commits adultery."

Romans 12:1–2

And now, brothers, I beg you through the mercy of God to offer your bodies as a living sacrifice holy and acceptable to God, your spiritual worship. Do not conform yourselves to this age but be transformed by the renewal of your mind, so that you may judge what is God's will, what is good, pleasing and perfect.

Some striking translations of this version are:

In the beginning, when God created the heavens and the earth, the earth was a formless wasteland, and darkness covered the abyss, while a mighty wind swept over the waters (Gen. 1:1–2).
"Dome" for "firmament" (Gen. 1:6).
"sky" for "heaven" (Gen. 1:8).
When they heard the sound of the LORD God moving about in the garden at the breezy time of the day . . . (Gen. 3:8).
Reform your lives! The reign of God is at hand (Matt. 3:2).
When he saw that many . . . were stepping forward for this bath (Matt. 3:7).
The mouth speaks whatever fills the mind (Matt. 12:34).
You . . . leave the inside filled with loot and lust! (Matt. 23:25).
To the presiding spirit of the church in Ephesus . . . (Rev. 2:1).
He shall rule them with a rod of iron and shatter them like crockery (Rev. 2:27).

In certain ambiguous passages, interesting translations appear. Matthew 16:18 reads, "I for my part declare to you, you are 'Rock,' and on this rock I will build my church." This is not altogether surprising, since Protestant Bibles already had moved in this direction. In John 1:4 the NAB has followed the NEB in joining verse 3 and verse 4 so that it reads, "Whatever came to be in him, found life, life for the light of men." The NAB is the only translation we know that chooses to translate 1 Corinthians 7:21 in the following way: "Even supposing you could go free, you would be better off making the most of your slavery." It has chosen to keep the word "virgin" in 1 Corinthians 7:36, but the word obviously means "betrothed" as in the RSV instead of "daughter" as in the KJV. Unlike the ambiguous form of the translation of 1 Corinthians 9:5 in the JB "to take a Christian woman round with us," with the note "Lit. 'a sister, a woman (wife?).' To look after the apostle's needs," the NAB translates it more unambiguously than even Protestant translations: "Do we not have the right to marry a believing woman like the rest of the apostles and the brothers of the Lord and Cephas?" Catholic translators have sought to avoid admitting that the apostles were married because of their teaching on celibacy. First Timothy 3:2, as expected, has the phrase "married only once."

"Little while" is included in Hebrews 2:7: "You made him for a little while lower than the angels," thus clearly indicating that this passage from Psalms is understood messianically by the writer. The translators chose not to identify Christ with God in their rendering of Romans 9:5, since they isolated the benediction from what precedes. Thus it reads, "Blessed forever be God who is over all! Amen."

THE NAB AND THE JB

In a comparison of the NAB with the JB, note the differences:

NAB	JB
Ps. 23:1–3	
The LORD is my shepherd; I shall not want.	Yahweh is my shepherd, I lack nothing.
In verdant pastures he gives me repose;	In meadows of green grass he lets me lie.
Beside restful waters he leads me; he refreshes my soul.	To the waters of repose he leads me; there he revives my soul
He guides me in right paths for his name's sake.	He guides me by paths of virtue for the sake of his name.
Rom. 7:7–8	
What follows from what I have said? That the law is the same as sin? Certainly not! Yet it was only through the law that I came to know sin. I should never have known what evil desire was unless the law had said, "You shall not covet." Sin seized that opportunity; it used the commandment to rouse in me every kind of evil desire. Without law sin is dead. . . .	Does it follow that the Law itself is sin? Of course not. What I mean is that I should not have known what sin was except for the Law. I should not for instance have known what it means to covet if the Law had not said *You shall not covet.* But it was this commandment that sin took advantage of to produce all kinds of covetousness in me, for when there is no Law, sin is dead.
Matt. 6:1–2	
Be on guard against performing religious acts for the people to see. Otherwise expect no recompense for your heavenly Father.	Be careful not to parade your good deeds before men to attract their notice; by doing this you will lose all reward from your Father in

When you give alms, for example, do not blow a horn before you in synagogues and streets like hypocrites looking for applause. You can be sure of this much, they are already repaid.

heaven. So when you give alms, do not have it trumpeted before you; this is what the hypocrites do in the synagogues and in the streets to win men's admiration. I tell you solemnly, they have had their reward.

One immediate observation we make is the overall brevity and the directness of the American translation. In the first passage the JB favors the prepositional phrase, whereas the NAB prefers the shorter adjectival modifier. In the second passage the directness of the NAB shows through. It is not only shorter, it has a sentence in the positive form that the JB has in the negative. In the last passage, the American version is plain and straightforward, whereas the British version is more colorful and spicy. These are typical differences between the two translations.

A close check of the translation of 1 Corinthians 1:1–10 with the Greek indicates that it is a faithful translation. Where it is not following the Greek literally, usually the translation is derivable from the context or makes explicit that which is implicit in the original; for example, the addition of "send greetings" and "you" in verse 2, the omission of "of God" after "favor" in verse 4 and "concerning you" after "informed" in verse 11.

CONSISTENCY OF TRANSLATION

Besides some of the observations we have made above concerning the text and footnotes, the translators have been criticized for a lack of consistency and for not having an adequate plan for the work as a whole.

Regarding the question of consistency, Bruce Metzger (*Princeton Seminary Bulletin,* 64 [1971], 92) mentions the translation of the word *makarios* (blessed) and the word *basileia* (kingdom). It is not necessary or even desirable that a certain Greek or Hebrew word be always translated by the same English word. Words do change meanings as they are used in different texts. However, certain technical words or words used in the same contexts should not be translated with different

English words. In the Beatitudes in Matthew 5 and Luke 6, *makarios* is translated "blest," but in the seven times it is found in Revelation it is translated "happy." Other translations of this word are "go well with" (Luke 12:37–38), "fortunate" (Luke 12:43), "pleased" (Luke 14:14). This last verse is followed by the translation of the same word with "happy" in the next verse (Luke 14:15). In the OT the Hebrew word for "blessed" is translated "happy" in most cases, but "blessed" is found in Ecclesiastes 10:17, Isaiah 30:18, and Daniel 12:12.

The same inconsistency is found in the translation of the Greek word for "kingdom." Matthew 3:2 reads, "Reform your lives! The reign of God is at hand," but Matthew 4:17 reads, "Reform your lives! The kingdom of heaven is at hand." Again Matthew 4:23 refers to the proclamation of "the good news of the kingdom," while Matthew 9:35 refers to the proclamation of "the good news of God's reign." In Matthew 13 it is "the reign of God" that is always likened to something, except in verse 45 where it is "the kingdom of heaven." Not only is the word *basileia* translated in two different ways, but "God" is substituted for "heaven" in an arbitrary manner. The translation "reign" is not a good one in Matthew 26:29: "I tell you, I will not drink this fruit of the vine from now until the day when I drink it new with you in my Father's reign." Other words used to translate *basileia* are "kingship," "dominion," and "nation." For "burnt offering" NAB has used the unfortunate translation "holocaust," which today signifies something quite different from the sacrifice of burnt offering. Only in Mark 12:33 is the word translated "burnt offering."

The translation of the word *dikaiosune*, usually translated "righteousness," has always been a problem for translators. The cognate Greek verb appears to be translated "to justify," but the noun is translated in various ways, depending on the context. In Matthew 3:15 it is translated "God's demands," but in the rest of Matthew as "holiness." "All that is right" and "uprightness" are some other translations. In Romans, however, it seems to be consistently translated "justice." This does not seem to be the best translation in certain cases such as Romans 4:5, 6, "But when a man does nothing, yet believes in him who justifies the sinful, his faith is credited as justice. Thus David congratulates the man to whom God credits justice without requiring deeds"; Romans 4:9, "For we say that Abraham's faith was 'credited as justice'"; and Romans 6:13, "Rather, offer yourselves to God as men who have come back from the dead to life, and your bodies to God as weapons for justice." This is also true in Romans 5:17 and 6:16.

Another point Dr. Metzger makes is the reference to pronouncements of Councils in the footnotes. He refers to John 3:5; 20:22–23; 20:28; James 5:15. Of most interest to readers will be that found in connection with John 21:15ff., where this annotation is found: "The First Vatican Council cited this verse in defining that the risen Jesus gave Peter the jurisdiction of supreme shepherd and ruler over the whole flock."

Keith Crim's criticism (*Interpretation*, 26 [1972], 77), it seems, is well founded. It would be interesting to note the changes that will be made when the entire work is reviewed for revision. He writes:

> The beginning of the work is usually dated to the issuance of the Encyclical *Divino afflante Spiritu* in 1943, so that the project was spread over almost three decades. Those years have seen so many changes in the life of the church, so much advance in biblical studies, so great an increase in our knowledge of linguistics and translation procedures that a total reworking would have been required to make the earlier books consistent with those translated later. Some books were revised or even retranslated, but this only increases the feeling that there was no adequate plan for the work as a whole.

Nevertheless, this translation is a remarkable achievement. As we have mentioned before, this is the first complete American Catholic Bible translated from the original languages.

14

The New American Standard Bible

ITS PURPOSE

The Lockman Foundation is a nonprofit Christian corporation formed in 1942 in La Habra, California, to promote Christian Education, Christian Evangelism, and above all, Bible translation in several languages. In English it has produced two noteworthy translations: The Amplified New Testament and the New American Standard Bible.

The publication of the latter began with the Gospel of John in 1960, followed by the four Gospels in 1962, the NT in 1963, and the entire Bible in 1971. The "Preface to the New American Standard Bible A.D. 1963" briefly sets forth the principles and objectives on which the revision was made. It begins, "The producers of this translation were imbued with the conviction that interest in the American Standard Version should be renewed and increased." Certainly the ASV was a monument to the best British and American scholarship and biblical learning of the latter half of the nineteenth century. The Lockman Foundation was disturbingly aware that this "monumental product of applied scholarship, assiduous labor and thorough procedure . . . was fast disappearing from the scene." The recognized value of that version, it was felt, "deserves and demands perpetuation. . . . Recognizing a responsibility to posterity, the Lockman Foundation felt an urgency to rescue this noble achievement from an inevitable demise, to preserve it, as a heritage for coming generations, and to do so in such a form as the demands of passing time dictate."

To achieve this objective the revision must be put "in clear and contemporary language." The twofold purpose of the editorial board was "to adhere to the original languages of the Holy Scriptures as closely as possible and at the same time to obtain a fluent and readable style according to current English usage." Accordingly, a group of sixteen men worked on each Testament. The goal of using contemporary English in the revision often required a departure from the word-for-word literalness of the ASV, one of its chief faults.

THE NEW TESTAMENT

With regard to the NT, which was published first, we are told that "consideration was given to the latest available manuscripts with a view to determining the best Greek text." In most instances the twenty-third edition of the Nestle Greek NT was followed. Thus, the underlying Greek text differs in a number of passages from that on which the ASV was based. Furthermore, in Matthew the doxology of the Lord's Prayer (6:13) and two whole verses (18:11; 23:14) are printed in brackets, though they are found only in the footnotes of both the ASV and the Nestle Greek text. Contrary to Nestle, but like the ASV, Luke 24:12 is printed in the text, but also in brackets. The NASB also follows the ASV, contrary to Nestle, in printing the long ending of Mark in the text (16:9–20) in brackets, as well as the shorter ending in italics with the title "Addition." It also has in brackets the story of the woman discovered in the act of adultery (John 7:53–8:11). John 1:18 follows Nestle in reading "the only begotten God" rather than "the only begotten Son" as in the ASV. For other differences from the text of the ASV, see Mark 1:29; 2:4, 16; 6:14; 7:4, 24; 12:33; Luke 9:2, 59; 10:42; 24:36, 40, 51; John 8:16; 10:18; 13:32; 15:8; et al.

Arrangement of Text

Several features of the general format of the version are worthy of note. For one thing, there is only one column of text on

223

each page. Unfortunately, however, it does not follow the ASV in arranging the text in sense paragraphs. Rather, each verse, like the KJV, is printed as a separate unit. Such an arrangement tends to blind the reader to the connection of verses with one another, and gives the false impression that each verse is a unit by itself. It is true that paragraphs are designated by boldface numbers, but some readers may tend to overlook them.

Translation of Greek Verbs

Except in language addressed to Deity, the use of "thou," "thee," and "thy" has been replaced by "you" and "your." To avoid ambiguity, this pronoun in the 1963 edition of the NT was designated "you^s" or "you^{pl}" when it could not be determined from the context whether a singular or plural was meant. Thus, the 1963 edition of the NT of Matthew 5:21f. reads: "You^{pl} have heard that the ancients were told, 'You^s shall not commit murder;' . . . but I say to you^{pl} . . . If therefore you^s are presenting your offering . . ." and so on through the chapter. This distinction is sometimes important for a correct exegesis (e.g., the plural in 1 Cor. 3:16), but the practice was evidently found to be too clumsy to be retained when the whole Bible was published in 1971. Personal pronouns referring to God the Father, Jesus Christ, and the Holy Spirit begin with a capital letter. This is true when they refer to Jesus Christ, irrespective of the speaker's attitude toward our Lord (e.g., the mob, Matt. 26:68; 27:22; Herod, Matt. 2:8; the high priest, Matt. 26:63; Pilate, Matt. 27:11–14, et al.).

The translators of the NASB NT gave careful attention to the rendering of Greek tenses. Often in the Greek text of the Gospels the present tense is used to describe a past event with the vividness of a present happening. There are 151 uses of this "historical present" in the Gospel of Mark alone. The usage of the present is translated by an English past tense marked with an asterisk.

In translating the Greek past tenses, the NASB translators sought to distinguish between the undefined action of the aorist and the continuous action of the imperfect. As in other translations, the aorist tense was translated by the English past, or, in some instances, by the perfect, or even by the past perfect. At times, when the aorist emphasizes the entrance into an act or state (ingressive aorist), they tried to reproduce this idea in English; e.g., "He became afraid" (Matt. 14:30), "they all got drowsy" (Matt. 25:5), "they became silent" (Luke 20:26), "for this brother of yours was dead and has begun to live" (Luke 15:32) (compare these passages in the RSV).

The imperfect tense is used to indicate continuous action in past time. It is often rendered in the NASB by the English past progressive (or past continuous); e.g., "he was doing." However, the repeated use of the past progressive results in a very stilted and unidiomatic English style. No English writer today would say: "And He was teaching them many things in parables, and was saying to them in His teaching, 'Listen *to this!*'" (Mark 4:2–3); "And with many such parables He was speaking the word to them as they were able to hear it; and He was not speaking to them without parables; but He was explaining everything privately to His own disciples" (Mark 4:33–34); ". . . and many of the Corinthians when they heard were believing and being baptized" (Acts 18:8).

The translators did much better with the customary imperfect: "All who were owners of lands or houses would sell them and bring the proceeds of the sales, and lay them at the apostles' feet; and they would be distributed to each, as any had need" (Acts 4:34–35). "And a certain man who had been lame from his mother's womb, . . . whom they used to set down every day at the gate of the temple . . ." (Acts 3:2; see also Mark 15:6; Luke 2:41; 21:37).

But apparently the prevailing use of the imperfect in the NT in the minds of the translators was the inceptive that signifies the beginning of an action. Usually they translated this as, e.g., "*began* to do." "Began" is italicized, according to the preface, to distinguish it from the Greek verb meaning "begin." Inadvertently, however, "began" is not in italics in Matthew 16:7; Mark 1:31; and Luke 12:17. Matthew 15:36 is translated, "He broke *them* [the seven loaves] and started [no italics] giving *them* to the disciples." But in Luke 7:5, "Now Jesus *started* on His way with them," "started" is italicized. The number of imperfects interpreted as having an inceptive meaning is far greater than most grammarians could accept. A quick check indicates that there are some 170 in the Gospels and Acts, with about 100 in Luke-Acts.

Several imperfects are translated in a tendential (or conative) sense; e.g., "and they tried to give Him wine" (Mark 15:23), "John tried to prevent Him" (Matt. 3:14), "they were going to call him Zacharias" (Luke 1:59; see also Mark 9:38; Luke 9:49; Acts 7:26; 18:4; 25:11). But in such cases, "tried" and "were going" are not in italics.

The future perfects in Matthew 16:19; 18:18 are rendered, "Whatever you shall bind on earth shall have been bound in heaven, and whatever you shall loose on earth shall have been loosed in heaven." Similarly the perfects in John 20:23 are translated, "If you forgive the sins of any, *their sins* have been forgiven them [marginal note: "I.e., have previously been forgiven"]; if you retain the *sins* of any, they have been retained."

In their treatment of questions, the translators have tried to reproduce the nuances of the Greek. Questions introduced by the Greek particle *ou (ouk, ouchi)* expect an affirmative answer and are generally so worded (see Matt. 7:22; 13:27, 55; Luke 12:6; 17:17; Acts 13:10; Rom. 2:26; 1 Cor. 9:1; 14:23; for exceptions, see Mark 14:60; Acts 21:38). Questions introduced by the particle *mē (mēti)* expect a negative answer. These are translated by a double clause—one a negative statement, the other a question: "Grapes are not gathered from thornbushes, nor figs from thistles, are they?" (Matt. 7:16); "You do not want to go away also, do you?" (John 6:67); "When the Christ shall come, He will not perform more signs than those which this man has, will He?" (John 7:31; see also Matt. 16:25; John 7:47, 51; 21:5; Rom. 11:1; 1 Cor. 6:3; 12:28–30, et al.).

THE OLD TESTAMENT

For the OT, which was published in 1971 after about ten years of labor, the revisers used as their basic text the latest edition of Kittel's Biblia Hebraica. In general, they stuck closely to this Hebrew text, though occasionally correcting it by the use of

Hebrew MSS and ancient versions. In Judges 16:13–14, for example, to the words "'If you weave the seven locks of my hair with the web'" they added in square brackets these words from the Greek: "'and fasten it with a pin, then I shall become weak and be like any other man.' So while he slept Delilah took the seven locks of his hair and wove them into the web."

The OT book in which the most changes in the traditional Hebrew text were made is Isaiah, where some thirty changes occur. Like the RSV, for example, the NASB has "you" in 1:29 rather than "they." It also agrees with the RSV in reading, "deep as Sheol or high as heaven," rather than the traditional "either in the depth or in the height above" (ASV) in 7:11. In 14:4 the "golden city" (ASV) becomes "the fury" (by changing *madhebah* to *marhebah*). In several instances, the readings of the copy of Isaiah in the Dead Sea Scrolls were followed (e.g., 37:20, 27; 56:5, 10). In 49:17 the translators followed the ancient versions and the Dead Sea Scrolls in reading, "Your builders hurry" rather than, "Your sons hurry."

A major departure of the NASB from the ASV is in abandoning the use of "Jehovah" to designate the personal covenant God, the God of revelation. It is now known that "Jehovah" is an incorrect transliteration of the Tetragrammaton YHWH. Like the RSV, the NASB has gone back to the ancient practice of translating it as LORD or sometimes as GOD (see the marginal notes on Exod. 3:14; 6:3). Such place-names as "Jehovah-jireh" (Gen. 22:14), "Jehovah-nissi" (Exod. 17:15), and "Jehovah-shalom" (Judg. 6:24) in the ASV are translated respectively, "The LORD Will Provide," "The LORD is My Banner," and "The LORD is Peace" (see marginal notes for each).

The Semitic idiom translated in the ASV "and it came to pass" has been retained in the NASB, but slightly modernized as "and it came about" or "and it happened." The RSV committee, on the other hand, regarded this Hebrew idiom as "meaningless" in English, and "in the interest of simplicity and directness," left it untranslated.

The NASB has followed the ASV in transliterating the Hebrew word for the place of the dead as "Sheol." The corresponding term in the NT, "Hades," is likewise transliterated.

227

"Gehenna," however, is translated as "hell" (Matt. 5:22, 29–30; 10:28, et al.) or "the eternal fire" (Matt. 18:9).

READER AIDS

The NASB has retained the practice, begun in the Geneva Bible and continued through the KJV and ASV, of printing in italics words for which there are no exact equivalents in the original but that have been added to make the translation conform to English idiom. Neither the KJV nor the ASV were successful in achieving complete accuracy or consistency in this use of italics, nor has the NASB achieved this well-nigh impossible goal. For example, when there is an ellipsis of the Greek word for "day," should it be italicized in English? In Matthew 28:1 and John 20:1, 19, the NASB reads "the first *day* of the week"; but in Mark 16:2, 9; Acts 20:7; and 1 Corinthians 16:2, "the first day of the week." In Luke 13:31 it has "the third *day*"; but in Acts 27:19, "the third day"; while in Hebrews 4:4, "the seventh *day*." Day is italicized in the expression "the next *day*" in Luke 13:33, but it is not in a number of similar constructions in Acts (20:15; 21:1, 8, 18; 23:32; 25:17; 27:3, 18–19). There is an ellipsis of the word for "water" in both Matthew 10:42 and James 3:11. The former is given as "a cup of cold water" and the latter as "both fresh and bitter *water*." The verb "to be" is often not expressed in the original. In a translation should it, therefore, be in italics? In Galatians 1:5 we have "to whom *be* the glory," but 1 Corinthians 15:57 et al., "thanks be to God." The Greek of John 5:12 has simply "take up and walk." By italicizing *your* in the rendering, "Take up *your* pallet, and walk," the NASB gives the impression that "pallet" is in the original but *your* is not, whereas both are lacking.

A prominent feature of the NASB is its marginalia and cross references placed in a column more than an inch wide on the outer edge of each page. Superscript numbers in the text refer to the marginalia, which are arranged by verses. Several kinds of marginal notes are included. Some are textual, i.e., they call attention to readings in MSS that vary from the text followed in the translation (e.g., Matt. 6:13; 19:9; Mark 1:1, 29; 9:44, 46; Luke 22:19; 24:36). Such textual notes are less numerous than in the ASV. Translational notes are far more frequent, particularly those that give the literal meaning of the original language when a freer rendering was preferred (see Matt. 7:28; 9:15; 18:6; Luke 19:22, et al.). Other translational notes suggest an alternative rendering for a word or phrase (Matt. 5:45; Luke 7:25; Rom. 4:1; 1 Cor. 2:13; 2 Tim. 3:16; Rev. 22:1, et al.). There are also explanatory notes on the meaning of geographical and personal names (Gen. 4:24; 12:9; 14:18–20; 16:14; 17:1, 5; 24:10; 25:26; 28:19; 29:32, 34–35; 30:8, 11, 13, 18; 31:47, 49; 32:2, 28; Exod. 2:10, et al.).

Notes are included explaining the value of such coins as the talent (Matt. 18:24), denarius (Matt. 18:28; 20:9; Luke 10:35; John 6:7; 12:5; Rev. 6:6), drachma (Luke 15:8), didrachma (Matt. 17:24), stater (Matt. 17:27), mina (Luke 19:13), assarion (Matt. 10:29; Luke 12:6), and lepton (Luke 12:59). Others define measures and weights, as cubit (Gen. 6:15), log (Lev. 14:10), span (Isa. 40:12), bath (Isa. 5:10), ephah and hin (Lev. 19:36), homer (Num. 11:32), and kab (2 Kings 6:25). Still others explain such obscure terms as raca (Matt. 5:22), Mammon (Matt. 6:24; Luke 16:9, 11, 13), magi (Matt. 2:1), tax-gatherers (Matt. 5:46; 9:10; Luke 19:2), and Twin Brothers (Acts 28:11). A note to Titus 1:12 suggests the author of the quotation "Cretans are always liars, evil beasts, lazy gluttons." The paranomasia of Jeremiah 1:11–12, between the "almond tree" (*shaked*) and "watching" (*shoked*) is also explained. A note defines the sinners of Luke 15:1 as "irreligious or non-practicing Jews," and "the Fast" of Acts 27:9 as "the Day of Atonement in October."

Finally, there are interpretive notes such as the explanation of "hate" in Luke 14:26 as meaning "by comparison with his love" for Christ, and "through the Spirit" in Acts 21:4 as signifying "because of impressions made by the Spirit." The "signs" Jesus did are explained in John's Gospel as *"attesting miracles, i.e.,* one which points to the supernatural power of God in redeeming grace"* (John 2:11). In the ASV all marginalia are given as footnotes on each page.

Small superscript letters in the text refer to the cross references, also arranged by verses. A sample check here and there indicates these have been taken over from the ASV. Some are printed in italics to indicate they are parallel passages. These carefully selected cross references are of great value to the serious Bible student. The wide column containing them, along with the marginal notes, make the page less attractive to the general reader.

CONCLUSION

In conclusion, one may say that the NASB represents a conservative and literal approach to the translation of the Scriptures. In the OT, the traditional Hebrew text is only occasionally modified by readings from Hebrew MSS and ancient versions. In the NT, while the twenty-third edition of the Nestle Greek NT forms the basic text, that text has been considerably modified in the direction of the "Received Text" of which the KJV is a translation. A number of verses resting on doubtful MS authority have been reintroduced into the text from the margin. There is a hesitancy to follow a modern critical Greek text. But the version does represent an honest attempt to be faithful to the Hebrew text and to the Greek readings adopted. It seeks to give an accurate literal rendering of the Hebrew and Greek. Unfortunately, however, it has failed to reach its stated goal of putting the Scriptures in "a fluent and readable style according to current English usage." Its stilted and nonidiomatic English will never give it a wide popular appeal. It does, however, have great value as a study Bible, and this is perhaps its significant place as a translation.

15

The Living Bible

ITS HISTORY

For a number of years the need for putting the thoughts of the Bible writers into modern understandable English had been growing on the mind of a Wheaton, Illinois, businessman, Kenneth Nathaniel Taylor. He first became acutely aware of the need for a modern speech Bible when he was a speaker for Inter-Varsity on various college campuses in the United States and Canada. Later in his own growing family he noted the puzzled expressions on the faces of his children, now ten in number, as he read to them from the classic KJV. When he questioned them regarding their understanding of what he had read, he found they had failed to get the message. So he began to explain the passages in simple, everyday English they could understand. Thus, each day he gained experience in rewording the Bible in a simple, conversational style.

This led to his first systematic attempt, in 1956, to produce a written paraphrase of a book of Scripture. Riding a commuter train each day from his home in Wheaton to his work in Chicago, where he was the director of the Moody Literature Mission of the Moody Press, he conceived the idea of using commuter time, which most people wasted, in the production of a new modern speech rendering of the Scriptures. He began with the Book of

Romans, using as his basis the extremely literal ASV.

Taylor has his roots in conservative evangelical Christianity. He received his Bachelor of Arts degree from Wheaton College in 1938, studied at Dallas Theological Seminary from 1940 to 1943, and received the Master of Theology degree from Northern Baptist Theological Seminary in 1944. He was with the Moody Literature Mission of the Moody Press from 1947 to 1962. Then he decided to form his own publishing company to promote the paraphrases he was producing. He called his new firm Tyndale House after William Tyndale, the father of the English Bible.

Taylor gives this adequate definition of what he understands by paraphrasing the Scriptures: "To paraphrase is to say something in different words than the author used. It is a restatement of an author's thoughts, using different words than he did." His diligence in carrying on this task is shown by the publication of portions of his paraphrase in the years that followed his first efforts in 1956. In 1962 he published a rendering of the NT letters with the title, Living Letters. This was followed by Living Prophecies in 1965, Living Gospels in 1966, and the Living New Testament in 1967. It is obvious that he hoped to make the Bible a living book with a vibrant message for today's world. In 1967 he also put out Living Psalms, followed by Living Lessons of Life and Love in 1968, Living Books of Moses in 1969, and Living History of Israel in 1970. The complete Living Bible (LB) came from the press in 1971.

Because of its readability, this new rendering into modern idiomatic English has been well received and widely acclaimed. Its circulation has been enhanced by the Billy Graham Evangelistic Association, which has publicized it on television and has given away hundreds of thousands of copies. Taylor has succeeded in making the Bible come alive for vast numbers of people, particularly for the young. In 1965 Wheaton College conferred on him the honorary degree of Doctor of Literature.

ITS TEXTUAL BASIS

According to the preface of the Living New Testament, the basic text for this new rendering was the ASV of 1901. The Greek text used for the NT of the ASV, as for its 1881 English counterpart, was a marked improvement over the Received Text used as a basis for the KJV. Even so, in the light of MS discoveries and textual studies since 1881, it is clear that further improvements in the Greek text are needed. It is therefore disappointing to note that the LB does not even fully accept the critical text used for the ASV. A few of the passages in the NT that are of doubtful authenticity and were therefore removed from the ASV text and placed in footnotes are restored to the text by the LB (see Matt. 17:21; 18:11; Mark 15:28; John 5:3b–5; Acts 8:37; 24:6b–8a; Rom. 16:24). In most of these cases the LB has a footnote calling the reader's attention to the fact that many ancient MSS omit the passage. It is difficult to understand why Taylor restored John 5:3b–4; however, he did place it in parentheses.

In the OT there is also at least one departure from the basic text. In Genesis 4:8 the LB reads, "One day Cain suggested to his brother, 'Let's go out into the fields.'" The ASV has simply, "And Cain told Abel his brother." The Hebrew does not contain the words "Let us go into the fields," but they are found in the Samaritan Pentateuch, the LXX, and the Syriac versions. The LB, however, has no footnote revealing this fact.

ITS CHARACTERISTICS

For the most part, the LB is a simplified, easy-to-follow rendering in effective and idiomatic, present-day English. Colossians 1:16–17 will serve as an example: "Christ himself is the Creator who made everything in heaven and earth, the things we can see and the things we can't; the spirit world with its kings and kingdoms, its rulers and authorities; all were made by Christ for his own use and glory. He was before all else began and it is his power that holds everything together."

Added Details

At times the text is greatly expanded by imaginative details for which there is no warrant in the original. A clear example is in Amos 1:1–2. Here the ASV gives a literal word-for-word translation of the Hebrew. It gives the title as "The words of

Amos who was among the herdsmen of Tekoa. . . ." In the LB this becomes two full sentences: "Amos was a herdsman living in the village of Tekoa. All day long he sat on the hillsides watching the sheep, keeping them from straying." The ASV continues, ". . . which he saw concerning Israel." In the LB this becomes: "One day in a vision, God told him some of the things that were going to happen to his nation, Israel. . . . This is his report of what he saw and heard."

Literary Shortcomings

On the other hand, the paraphrase at times does less than justice to what the original says. Psalm 19:7–9, which extols the wonders of God's law in a beautifully structured piece of literary art, will serve as an example. The original has six different names for the written revelation and ascribes six different characteristics and functions to it. In the LB the literary beauty of the poem has given way to simple assertions: "God's laws are perfect. They protect us, make us wise, and give us joy and light. God's laws are pure, eternal, just."

One of the literary masterpieces of the OT is Isaiah 40. On the whole, the thought of the chapter is quite adequately represented in the LB. But after the appeal in verse 26, "Look up into the heavens! Who created all these stars?" an analogy completely untrue to the original is given: "As a shepherd leads his sheep, calling each by its pet name, and counts them to see that none are lost or strayed, so God does with stars and planets!" A footnote to the word "shepherd" says, "Implied," but there is nothing in the Hebrew implying this figure of speech. Rather, the actual analogy is far more majestic, designed to display, as the prophet declares, the greatness of God's might and the force of His power. Unfortunately, this intent of the verse is completely missing in the LB. The analogy is not that of a shepherd, but of a great general reviewing his army, for that is what the word "host" used in the ASV means. God as the Lord of hosts leads forth the stars as a general summons his forces. He is a supreme general who knows by name every star in infinite space, and not one in that vast multitude fails to respond to its master.

Interpretations

Taylor cannot be faulted for his simple, direct rewording of the ASV into everyday English. But when he assumes the role of a commentator, and freely interprets or reinterprets a passage, his fidelity to the original is often subject to question. Above everything else, a translation must be faithful to the text of the original. It should be seriously questioned whether a translator has the right to read his own interpretation into the text. Was the forbidden tree in the Garden of Eden, for example, a "Tree of Conscience"?

Taylor interprets "the sons of God" in Genesis 6 as "evil beings from the spirit world." He holds that they were God's "created, supernatural beings, but no longer godly in character" (footnote), who fell in love with women on earth, "the daughters of men." Hence he translates:

> Now a population explosion took place upon the earth. It was at this time that beings from the spirit world looked upon the beautiful earth women and took any they desired to be their wives. . . . In those days, and even afterwards, when the evil beings from the spirit world were sexually involved with human women, their children became giants, of whom so many legends are told (Gen. 6:1–2, 4).

He does, however, admit in the footnote: "Some commentators believe that the expression 'sons of God' refers to the 'godly line' of Seth, and 'daughters of men' to the men of the line of Cain."

Christians of various persuasions have long debated the correct translation of the Hebrew word *'almah* in Isaiah 7:14. Taylor translates, "A child shall be born to a virgin." But then in a footnote he writes:

> The controversial Hebrew word used here sometimes means "virgin" and sometimes "young woman." Its immediate use here refers to Isaiah's young wife and her new-born son (Isa. 8:1–4). This, of course, was not a virgin birth. God's sign was that before this child was old enough to talk (verse 4) the two invading kings would be destroyed. However, the Gospel of Matthew (1:23) tells us that there was a further fulfillment of this prophecy, in that a virgin (Mary)

conceived and bore a son, Immanuel, the Christ. We have therefore properly used this higher meaning, "virgin," in verse 14, as otherwise the Matthew account loses its significance.

The interpretation given of the opening words of the last book of the Bible is questionable: "This book unveils some of the future activities soon to occur in the life of Jesus Christ" (Rev. 1:1). From the viewpoint of grammar, it is true that the title as given in the ASV, "The Revelation of Jesus Christ," could theoretically mean either "a revelation given by Jesus Christ" or "a revelation about Jesus Christ." But the rest of the verse makes it obvious that the first of these is intended, not the second. And even if we were to take the second interpretation, it would still be far from referring to "some of the future activities soon to occur in the life of Jesus Christ." The last clause of verse 1 also is not true to the original: ". . . and then an angel was sent from heaven to explain the vision's meaning."

Verse 10 in the ASV begins, "I was in the Spirit on the Lord's day." In the LB this becomes, "It was the Lord's Day and I was worshiping." Certainly this is an unusual interpretation of being "in the Spirit." It occurs again in 4:2; 17:3; and 21:10 and means the Spirit took control of him, i.e., he was given a vision.

The LB rendering of the first beatitude does less than justice to Jesus' words: "'Humble men are very fortunate!' he told them, 'for the Kingdom of Heaven is given to them'" (Matt. 5:3). While humility is a Christian virtue, there is something deeper implied here. The "poor in spirit" are those who have a deep sense of spiritual poverty (see Isa. 66:2). They are not only humble but have a feeling of spiritual destitution, and recognize their need of God, in contrast to those who feel rich in spiritual achievement and religious understanding.

The careful student of the Gospels also feels compelled to protest the distorted picture of Jesus' messianic claims as set forth in the LB. It is a well-known fact that Jesus was very reticent about referring to himself as the Messiah. When others designated him as such, he did not refuse to accept it, but he evidently preferred not to be thus addressed. There can be little doubt that this was because of the political overtones associated with the word "Messiah." That term did not give the people an adequate picture of his mission. Hence, Jesus preferred to be known as the "son of man" (see Mark 9:29–31; Matt. 26:63–64, ASV). This was his own characteristic self-designation, used more than eighty times in the Gospels. Since the title never appears on the lips of Jesus' followers, its usage must go back to Jesus himself. In all probability it stems from the designation of the heavenly figure in Daniel 7:13. Unfortunately, in the LB this characteristic self-designation has disappeared from the text of the Gospels. In its place one finds "the Messiah" (Mark 9:13; Luke 21:27; 24:6), "I, the Messiah" (Matt. 8:20; 9:5; 11:19; 12:8, et al.), or simply "I" (Matt. 10:23; 13:42; 16:13, et al.). Thus, according to this paraphrase, our Lord freely and repeatedly claimed to be the Messiah.

Theological Bias

In his preface, Taylor frankly admits there are dangers in paraphrases:

> For whenever the author's exact words are not translated from the original languages, there is a possibility that the translator, however honest, may be giving the English reader something that the original writer did not mean to say. This is because a paraphrase is guided not only by the translator's skill in simplifying but also by the clarity of his understanding of what the author meant and by his theology. For when the Greek or Hebrew is not clear, then the theology of the translator is his guide along with his sense of logic. . . . The theological lodestar in this book has been a rigid evangelical position.

It may be seriously questioned whether a translator should be guided by his theology in translating the Word of God. Should he not rather submit his theology to the Word? The function of a translator is to determine as accurately as possible what the original writer said, and then to state this as precisely as possible in effective English. Taylor, however, did not work directly from the original Hebrew, Aramaic, and Greek documents, but from a standard English translation of the late nineteenth and early twentieth centuries. The LB, therefore, suffers from the limitation of being a secondary translation, i.e., it is a translation of a translation. It is further limited by the fact that the translator frankly states he was guided by his theology. It would no doubt be helpful for the reader to know what Taylor means by "a rigid evangelical position." But this is not spelled out.

One can, perhaps, guess at some aspects of it by noting certain renderings in the LB along with footnotes that are given. The ASV gives a literal translation of Psalm 115:17, "The dead praise not Jehovah, neither any that go down into silence." But in the LB this becomes, "The dead cannot sing praises to Jehovah here on earth." The ASV rendering of Psalm 6:5 reads, "For in death there is no remembrance of thee: In Sheol who shall give thee thanks?" The LB translates, "For if I die I cannot give you glory by praising you before my friends," apparently implying that he could praise God in heaven. In the LB, Ecclesiastes 9:5 is "For the living at least know that they will die! But the dead know nothing; they don't even have their memories." But a footnote declares, "These statements are Solomon's discouraged opinion, and do not reflect a knowledge of God's truth on these points!" Psalm 73:24 in the ASV reads, "Thou wilt guide me with thy counsel, and afterward receive me to glory" (possibly meaning "honor"). The last clause in the LB is "and afterwards receive me into the glories of heaven."

In the NT Paul's famous saying, "For I am already being offered, and the time of my departure has come" (2 Tim. 4:6, ASV) is translated, "My time has almost run out. Very soon now I will be on my way to heaven." First Thessalonians 4:14 in the LB reads, "For since we believe that Jesus died and then came back to life again, we can also believe that when Jesus returns, God will bring with him all the Christians who have died." The ambiguous wording of this paraphrase makes it doubtful as to what Taylor had in mind. In the light of other passages, such as those quoted above, this translation is probably intended to convey the idea that God will bring these departed ones back from heaven with Jesus when he returns. While some commentators follow this interpretation, a more probable one is that God will bring back to life those Christians who have died. Faith in the resurrection of Christ thus calls for faith also in the resurrection of those who have fallen asleep in death as Christians.

The Hebrew word for the place of the dead, *Sheol,* is consistently transliterated in the ASV. The LB, however, frequently translates it as "hell," as though it were a place of punishment —contrary to Hebrew thought. "The wicked shall be sent away to hell" (Ps. 9:17). "Hell is licking its chops in anticipation of this delicious morsel, Jerusalem" (Isa. 5:14). "But they don't realize that her former guests are now citizens of hell" (Prov. 9:18). "The denizens of hell crowd to meet you as you enter their domain" (Isa. 14:9).

In other places *Sheol* is translated "grave." Psalm 16:10 is adequately rendered, "For you will not leave me among the dead; you will not allow your beloved one to rot in the grave." However, when this passage is quoted in Acts 2:27, the meaning is distorted by inserting the word "body" in contrast to "soul": "You will not leave my soul in hell or let the body of your Holy Son decay." Thus a false dichotomy, foreign to OT thinking, is introduced into the quotation. This is made abundantly clear in verse 31 where the word "soul" is inserted and "flesh" is rendered "body": "The Messiah's soul would not be left in hell and his body would not decay."

In arguing for the resurrection, Jesus asked the Sadducees, "Have you not read in the book of Moses . . . how God spake unto him saying, I am the God of Abraham, and the God of Isaac, and the God of Jacob?" (Mark 12:26, ASV, quoting Exod. 3:6). Then he added, "He is not the God of the dead, but of the living" (v. 27). This comment of Jesus is given in the LB as follows: "God was telling Moses that these men, though dead for hundreds of years, were still very much alive; for he would not have said, 'I *am* the God' of those who don't exist! You have made a serious error." In the parallel in Luke 20:38 the LB has, "To say that the Lord *is* some person's God means that person is *alive*, not dead! So from God's point of view, all men are living." In Matthew 22:32, the other Gospel parallel, the LB reads, "So God is not the God of the dead, but of the living." But a footnote explains: 'I.e., if Abraham, Isaac, and Jacob, long dead, were not alive in the presence of God, then God would have said, 'I *was* the God of Abraham, etc.'" Thus in all three passages Taylor interprets Jesus' comment as meaning that Abraham, Isaac, and Jacob are alive in the presence of God.

While this interpretation is given by several commentaries, it cannot be the correct one, and it points out the danger in a translator's trying to interpret Scripture for the reader rather than letting the Word speak for itself. Clearly in this context the subject under discussion is the resurrection of the dead, which the Sadducees denied (Matt. 22:23, 31; Mark 12:18, 26; Luke 20:27, 37). Jesus is quoting from Exodus 3:6, not to argue for the immortality of the soul, but to show that the Sadducees were wrong in denying a resurrection. And we may well ask, How would the continuous existence of the ancient patriarchs prove the resurrection? A note in the Oxford Annotated Bible (p. 1201) gives a better explanation: "The idea here is that men who are related to God in faith have life even though physically dead. Resurrection is the divine act by which men will achieve the fulness of life intended in creation and lost through sin and death."

In Luke 20:34ff. Jesus sets forth the common NT theme of two antithetical ages: the present age and the age to come. In the present age there is marriage, the production of children, and ultimately death. "But those who are accounted worthy to attain to that age and to the resurrection from the dead neither marry nor are given in marriage, for they cannot die any more, because they are equal to angels, and are sons of God, being sons of the resurrection" (Luke 20:35–36, RSV). By the fact of "physical birth men are a part of this age, which continues until the parousia of Christ" (Matt. 24:3; 13:49f.). They become a part of the age to come by the resurrection, and it is "those who are accounted worthy" who attain to that age. It was in anticipation of this resurrection that Jesus could speak of the God of the partriarchs as the God of the living. He beheld the results of his redemptive work as though it were already existing.

In view of a coming resurrection—in view of the certainty of the fact that there is to be one—they all live unto God. The argument is similar to Paul's explanation that God had made Abraham the father of many nations (Rom. 4:17), the latter part of which the LB appropriately translates, "And this promise is from God himself, who makes the dead live again and speaks of future events with as much certainty as though they were already past."

There are numerous other readings whose fidelity to the original is questionable. "For Moses gave us only the Law with its rigid demands and merciless justice, while Jesus Christ brought us loving forgiveness as well" is the translation given of John 1:17. But this not only reads a great deal into the passage that is not there, but it also gives a distorted view of the Pentateuch. Salvation means more than bringing people to heaven (Rom. 1:16–17), and the righteousness of God is more than a "way to heaven" (Rom. 3:21–22). Taylor admits that his translation of Matthew 13:52, "Those experts in Jewish law who are now my disciples have double treasures—from the Old Testament as well as from the New," is "highly anachronistic" (footnote). But if it is anachronistic, what defense is there for using it to translate Jesus' words? The rendering of 1 Corinthians 16:2 is also anachronistic: "On every Lord's Day each of you should put aside something from what you have earned during the week. . . ." The Greek has simply "on the first day of the week," and there is no evidence that it was called "the Lord's Day" in the first century. The translation of Acts 20:7 is also questionable: "On Sunday, we gathered for a communion service." Again, the Greek has, "On the first day of the week. . . ." The meeting referred to was obviously a night farewell service. It is not entirely clear whether the days are reckoned on the Jewish basis from sundown to sundown, or on the Roman basis from midnight to midnight. But the former seems most likely, in which case the meeting was held on Saturday night (see NEB, TEV). Moreover, it is not clear that this was a communion service. The original has "to break bread." This expression can mean either an ordinary meal (Acts 2:42, 46) or the Lord's Supper. In any case, it was not called a "communion service" in NT times. Other questionable interpretations are given in Hebrews 5:7; 13:10; 2 Corinthians 7:14; 1 Peter 3:18f.; 5:1; 2 Timothy 2:8; 3:16, et al.

CONCLUSION

Taylor is to be congratulated for producing an appealing and readable paraphrase that may well arouse a new interest in the Bible. Although his vernacular at times borders on vulgarity (e.g., 1 Sam. 20:3, the first edition), the language is, in the main, highly readable and effective. For an accurate rendering of the teaching of the sacred Word, however, it often comes far short. It is a secondary version inasmuch as it is a translation of a translation. Furthermore, although the Greek text on which the NT of the ASV is based was a marked improvement on the Received Text of the KJV, there are better Greek texts available. Taylor could therefore have produced a more accurate translation had he chosen a modern critical edition of the Greek text and faithfully followed it. Furthermore, in his paraphrasing Taylor takes many liberties in leaving out or adding materials, and it is, therefore, unsafe to build one's concept of biblical truth on so free a version. He himself suggests, "For study purposes, a paraphrase should be checked against a rigid translation." By a "rigid translation" he perhaps means some literal version like the ASV. Certainly it is unsafe to follow the LB without first checking it against a more faithful translation, or, better yet, against a good critical text of the original Hebrew, Aramaic, and Greek.

16

The New International Version

The most recent of the major modern-speech Bibles is The New International Version (NIV), the NT of which was published in September 1973. It is a completely new translation made directly from the original languages of the Bible. The decision to produce it was formalized by a group of biblical scholars meeting in Chicago in 1965. This was the culmination of several years of exploratory study by Evangelicals from a number of different churches beginning in the 1950s, before the flood of modern translations began. This study was initiated when interested groups from the Christian Reformed Church and the Commission on Education of the National Association of Evangelicals found each other. The project launched in Chicago in 1965 received a new impetus in 1967 when the New York International Bible Society agreed to sponsor it financially.

Though a number of modern-speech versions have appeared since the project was first conceived, there is still a distinctive place for a new translation suitable for private reading as well as public worship. Some of the modern versions have language that is too informal, regional, or colloquial to be suitable for liturgical or church use. In others, the English is not idiomatic, but artificial and wooden. Some are excessively free or paraphrastic and lack fidelity to the sacred original text. Some are one-man productions, which have not been subjected to the checks and balances of a large committee and therefore contain idiosyncrasies.

The NIV is called an "International" version because, in the first place, the committee producing it consisted of distinguished Bible scholars from such English-speaking countries as Canada, England, Australia, and New Zealand, as well as the United States. In the second place, English is today an international language, and the translators have sought to use vocabulary common to the major English-speaking nations of the world. They have sought to avoid the use of Americanisms on the one hand and Anglicisms on the other. Their success in avoiding the former is evident from the fact that, though a British edition was published in 1974, few changes in vocabulary were felt necessary, though British spelling was adopted. The version is also transdenominational in character. The translators came from many denominations, including Baptist, Brethren, Church of Christ, Episcopalian, Lutheran, Mennonite, Methodist, Nazarene, Presbyterian, Christian Reformed, and others. An interchange among such a wide variety of religious persuasions was an effective safeguard against sectarianism.

The governing body of the project consists of fifteen members, most of whom are well-known biblical specialists in the U.S.A. The Executive Secretary of this committee until his untimely death in 1980 was Dr. Edwin H. Palmer. His successor is Dr. Kenneth Barker who is also the secretary of the Committee for Bible Translation of the New York International Bible Society. Among the one hundred translators whose services have been enlisted are a number of world-renowned scholars, including Gleason Archer, Roland K. Harrison, William Hendriksen, E. M. Blaiklock, Elmer B. Smick, William Lane, Leon Morris, Ralph Earle, Donald J. Wiseman, to name but a few.

The initial translation of each book was the work of a small team of scholars. After they had done their best with the text, their work was submitted for restudy and revision, with constant reference to the original, by an Intermediate Editorial Committee. It then went to the General Editorial Committee for further review and thorough revision. Inasmuch as a sensitive feeling for English style does not always go with scholarship in biblical languages, the work was next submitted to literary consultants and tested for clarity and idiom. The suggestions made were kept in mind by the governing body as the translation was reviewed and further revised. Before being issued in final form, it was again read by literary consultants.

Few translations since the KJV of 1611 have been as carefully done as this one. At each stage of the process there has been a wrestling of various minds with the sacred text and an honest attempt to say in simple, clear English what the Bible writers express in the originals. It is difficult to conceive a plan that could have better checks and balances than the one used. Along with this, attention has been given to the literary quality of the English and an attempt has been made to achieve a version worthy of memorization.

In reading this translation, one will find very few awkward constructions. The translation as a whole is straightforward, clear, and reliable. It is generally written in a dignified manner; only rarely does one find something he might judge to be too colloquial. Before examining the translation more closely, let us examine the Greek text used for this translation.

THE NEW TESTAMENT

The Greek Text Used

According to the preface, the Greek text is "an eclectic one" based on "accepted principles of New Testament textual criticism" in consultation with "the best current printed texts of the Greek New Testament" (p. ix). A careful examination of the NIV New Testament shows that in general its text follows modern critical Greek texts such as Nestle-Aland and the United Bible Society text but not always. Exactly what is meant by the designation "eclectic" is difficult to say. Most of the harmonizing passages that were added in Matthew and found in the KJV have been omitted (such as those found in Matt. 5:44; 17:21; 18:11; 23:14; Mark 9:44; 11:26; Luke 9:54–56; 23:17). Obviously late readings (found in the KJV) have also been omitted, such as the second half of Matthew 6:13, "For thine is the kingdom and the power and the glory forever. Amen"; John 5:3–4; Acts 8:37; and 1 John 5:7–8. Unfortunately, however, Matthew 21:44; Luke 24:6a, 12, are included in the text. The longer passages, Mark 16:9–20 and John 7:53–8:11, are also still placed in the text, according to their verse numeration, in the same print. Lines are drawn before and after the passages and notes indicate that early MSS omit these passages. In the case of the passage in Mark, none of the other endings are given either in the same print or in the footnotes. In regard to the passage in John, no explanation is given as to the fact that when it is included it is sometimes found at the end of the Gospel of John or after Luke 21:38. In Romans 8:28 the NIV has "in all things God works for the good of those who love him." There are some passages that are disputed by scholars. In regard to these, the NIV has included Matthew 16:2–3; Luke 22:19b, 20; 22:44; parts of 24:36, 40, 51. It has "Gerasenes" in Luke 8:26, "seventy-two" in Luke 10:17, "Bethesda" instead of Bethzatha" in John 5:2, included "in Ephesus" in Ephesians 1:1, omitted "Jesus" before "Barabbas" in Matthew 27:16; has "filled with compassion" instead of NEB's "in warm indignation," in Mark 1:41.

Characteristics of Translation

Certain passages are ambiguous in the Greek text and thus have been translated differently by different versions. The NIV translation is given first, followed by the alternative translation or translations:

Mark 15:39

Surely this man was the Son of God!
Truly this man was a son of God. (NEB, RSV, first edition)

John 1:3–4

. . . without him nothing was made that has been made. In him was life, and that life was the light of men.
No single thing was created without him. All that came to be was alive with his life, and that life was the light of men. (NEB)

John 1:9

The true light that gives light to every man was coming into the world.

That was the true Light, which lighteth every man that cometh into the world. (KJV)

Romans 9:5

Theirs are the patriarchs, and from them is traced the human ancestry of Christ, who is God over all, forever praised! Amen.
. . . to them belong the patriarchs, and of their race, according to the flesh, is the Christ. God who is over all be blessed for ever. Amen.
(RSV, NEB)

1 Corinthians 7:36

If anyone thinks he is acting improperly toward the virgin he is engaged to, and if she is getting along in years and he feels he ought to marry, he should do as he wants. He is not sinning. They should get married.
In the KJV, it is implied that the "virgin" is the father's daughter. In the RSV, the "virgin" is the man's betrothed and in the NEB she is a man's "partner in celibacy."

1 Thessalonians 4:4

. . . that each of you should learn to control his own body in a way that is holy and honorable.
That each one of you know how to take a wife for himself in holiness and honor. (RSV)

1 Timothy 3:2

. . . the husband of but one wife . . .
. . . married only once . . . (RSV); . . . faithful to his one wife . . . (NEB)

A very interesting passage in recent translations has been Matthew 16:18. The NIV has "And I tell you that you are Peter, and on this rock. . . ." However, the note reads *"Peter* means *rock."* It is not as explicit as the NEB's "You are Peter, the Rock," but is not far from it. This is rather surprising for a conservative version. The traditional conservative position is that "Peter" means a rolling stone.

Reading this version in isolation, one discovers few expressions that are unusual, because of archaic, awkward, or too-colloquial language. In the Gospel of Matthew, the following were noted: In 1:18 "to be with child" does not seem modern enough, though most of the modern versions still use that phrase. PHILLIPS has "to be pregnant," which seems more appropriate for a modern translation. In 1:25 "he had no union with her" is not the idiom of today. It is better than "knew her not" of the RSV, but PHILLIPS, NEB, and JB read, ". . . had no intercourse with her," which is a much better reading. Putting a lamp "under a bowl" (5:14) sounded a bit strange. There are differences here in the translations, to be sure, such as "meal-tub" (NEB), "bushel" (RSV), "tub" (JB), and "bucket" (PHILLIPS), but somehow "bowl" does not seem to be right. Without a qualifying adjective, it implies something too small. "Do not murder" (v. 21), found earlier in the NEB, is the modern way of expressing "Thou shalt not kill," but somehow it does not seem to be strong enough. The JB has "You must not kill." "Put up with you" in 17:17 and "he grabbed him" in 18:28 seem a bit colloquial to us, although other earlier versions have used these expressions. "Capstone" in 21:42 is not the same as "corner-stone." "Spices" in 23:23 is an unnecessary addition. "Yes, it is you" in 26:25 seems a bit too direct for what is intended and fails to capture the Oriental manner of expressing statements in an indirect way. "Gave up his spirit" in 27:50 is not modern idiom.

The above is not a long list, indicating that the version generally reads well. It has very few awkward expressions, but on the other hand not many striking ones either.

Some interesting NIV translations are "the darkness has not understood it" (John 1:5), "lived for a while among us" (John 1:14), "one and only Son" (John 3:16, 18), "verdict" (John 3:19), "how dare you lecture us" (John 9:34), "this is getting us nowhere" (John 12:19), "Counselor" (John 14:16), "the one doomed to destruction" (John 17:12), "sacrifice of atonement" (Rom. 3:25), "evil is right there with me" (Rom. 7:21), "the Lord will carry out his sentence on earth with speed and finality" (Rom. 9:28), "who are coming to nothing" (1 Cor. 2:6). "who will expose the motives of men's hearts" (1 Cor. 4:5), "we are in rags" (1 Cor. 4:10), "we have become the scum of the earth" (1 Cor. 4:13), "got up to indulge in pagan revelry" (1 Cor. 10:7), "it keeps no record of wrongs" (1 Cor. 13:5), "their extreme poverty welled up in generosity" (2 Cor. 8:2), "eternally condemned" (Gal 1:8, 9), "the whole world is a prisoner of sin"

(Gal. 3:22), "who cut in on you" (Gal. 5:7), "being in the very nature of God" (Phil. 2:6), "basic principles of this world" (Col. 2:8, 20), "The Lord's message rang out from you" (1 Thess. 1:8), "nor did we put on a mask to cover up greed" (1 Thess. 2:5), "the kind who worm their way into homes" (1 Tim. 3:6), "not malicious talkers" (1 Tim. 3:11), "The Son is the radiance of God's glory" (Heb. 1:1), "fix your thoughts on Jesus" (Heb. 3:1), "hurled their insults at him" (1 Peter 2:23), "be clear minded and self-controlled" (1 Peter 4:7), "love each other deeply" (1 Peter 4:8), "they are experts in greed" (2 Peter 2:14), "they mouth empty, boastful words" (2 Peter 2:18), "to stimulate you to wholesome thinking" (2 Peter 3:1), "without the slightest qualm" (Jude 12), "take to heart what is written in it" (Rev. 1:3), "the maddening wine of her adulteries" (Rev. 14:8).

In any translation there will be differences of opinion regarding the validity or appropriateness of certain translations. Bruce has questioned the translation of John 1:5 and 14 (*Christianity Today*, 28 September 1973, pp. 25–26). Questionable also is the translation of "verdict" in John 3:19. What follows it does not read like a verdict. The JB's "on these grounds sentence is pronounced" is an excellent translation of this. Bruce also noted that the same Greek word translated "righteousness" in Romans 3:21–22 is translated "justice" in 3:26. The same type of thing has happened in Matthew 16:25–26 where the NIV has translated the same Greek word as "life" in verse 25 but "soul" in verse 26. In Acts 1:10–11 the same Greek word is translated "sky" in verse 10 but "heaven" in verse 11. The interpretive translation, "But woman will be kept safe through childbirth" in 1 Timothy 2:15, instead of the more usual, "Yet woman will be saved through bearing children" (RSV), is quaint.

To see exactly what differences or similarities it had with several different types of translations, a careful comparison was made between selected passages in this translation and those of the RSV and NEB. The first passage compared was Matthew 5:3–10. Here NIV deviated from the RSV only slightly. "Shall" of the RSV was changed to "will." In 5:6 the RSV had "satisfied"; the NIV, "filled." In 5:7 the RSV had "shall obtain mercy"; the NIV "will be shown mercy." In 5:10 the RSV had "for righteousness' sake"; the NIV, "because of righteousness." The NEB differs so much that it is not possible to make this type of comparison. This indicates the conservative nature of the NIV.

The second passage analyzed was Luke 15:11–32. Here there are many more differences from the RSV than in the previous passage. The NIV has moved away from the literalism of the RSV, especially in regard to the translation of the conjunction "and." Sometimes it has a different conjunction; sometimes it simply drops it. "And he said" of the RSV in 15:11 has been changed radically to "Jesus continued." The NIV has taken liberties here by adding "Jesus," which is not in the Greek and altered "said" to "continued." While some of the changes are not improvements, it is surprising, when one makes a close comparison, to note how the NIV modernizes more than the RSV. These include the NIV's "my share of the estate" for "the share of the property that falls to me," "property" for "living," "set off for a distant country" for "took his journey into a far country," "wild living" for "loose living," "there was a severe famine" for "a great famine arose," "food to spare" for "bread enough and to spare," "here I am starving to death" for "I perish here with hunger," "set out" for "arise," "against you" for "before you," "finger" for "hand," "let's have a feast and celebrate" for "let us eat and make merry," "what was going on" for "what this meant," "fattened" for "fatted," "pleaded with" for "entreated," "so I could celebrate" for "that I may make merry," "squandered" for "devoured," "everything I have" for "all that is mine," "we had to celebrate" for "it was fitting to make merry."

It is interesting to compare the above NIV changes with the NEB readings. For those changes noted above the NEB reads, "my share of the property," "the whole of his share," "left home for a distant country," "reckless living," "a severe famine fell," "more food than they can eat," "here am I, starving to death," "set off," "against you," "finger," "let us have a feast to celebrate the day," "what it meant," "fatted," "pleaded with," "for a feast," "running through your money," "everything I have," and "how could we help celebrating." There are a good number of similarities between the NIV and NEB.

Besides those above, we note the following (the first reading is that of the NEB): "younger" — "younger one," "flung his arms around him" — "threw his arms around him," "Quick! fetch a robe, my best one" — "Quick! Bring the best robe," and "I have slaved for you" — "I've been slaving for you." The reading of "pigs," "he came to his senses," "still a long way off," and "sandals," is identical in both.

Some NEB influence seems apparent from the above examination. What is worthy of note also is the extremely conservative nature of the RSV translation. In spite of all the criticism leveled at it when it was first published, looking back from our vantage point today, it seems to be a very conservative translation. It is obvious from our examination that it failed to modernize the language adequately. The NIV has done this, but the NEB had already done so some time before.

The final passage we examine is Romans 7:4–12. The NIV improves on the RSV in 7:4 with "So, my brothers" for "Likewise, brethren," and "sinful nature" for "flesh" in 7:5. However, although there are considerable changes, no significant improvements were observed. Again the NEB is much freer than the NIV.

The NIV preface mentions that "brackets are occasionally used to indicate words or phrases supplied for clarification." These brackets are in reality the lower half of square brackets printed in inconspicuous type. Their use is very rare in the NT and appears to be confined to a few passages in Paul's letters. The brackets are not intended to take the place of italics as used in the KJV. Nevertheless, the same type of inconsistency arises with the use of brackets and one wonders why brackets were felt to be necessary in the places where they are added and not necessary at other places. For example, Galatians 2:4 reads, " This matter arose because some false brothers had infiltrated our ranks." In Galatians 4:17 we have "What they want is to alienate you ⌊from us⌋." However, Romans 11:11 reads, "Did they stumble so as to fall beyond recovery?" "Beyond recovery" is implied but is not in the Greek text; yet it is not bracketed. It is unfortunate that this policy was followed, because it is difficult to know exactly what should be bracketed and what should not. But if brackets are to be used it would be especially appropriate to enclose the very questionable explanatory addition "of their prayer shawls" with them in Matthew 23:5. In the same Gospel one might also suggest bracketing: "whose mother had been . . . wife" (1:16), "it be so" (3:15), "than others" (5:47), and "the door" in 7:7, to mention only a few.

The NIV has also been inconsistent in translating expressions of time, money, measure, and distance. In Matthew 18:24 the servant owed the king "ten thousand talents," explained in a note as "several million dollars," and his fellow-servant owed him "a hundred denarii," explained as "a few dollars." The laborers received "a denarius for the day" (Matt. 20:2), and the "denarius" is the sample for tribute money (Mark 12:15). "Talents" and "minas" are also used in Matthew 25:14–30 and Luke 19:11–27 respectively. But in John 12:5 the perfume was worth "a year's wages" (300 denarii), and in John 6:7 "eight months' wages" (200 denarii) "would not buy enough bread for each one to have a bite!" In John 1:39 "tenth hour" is used and "seventh hour" in John 4:52. Luke 24:13; John 6:19; and 11:18 translate "stadia" into "miles," but this is not done in Revelation 14:20 (1,600 stadia) and 21:16 (12,000 stadia), although in each case the note indicates the approximate number of miles. In John 21:8 "cubits" is translated into "yards" but in Revelation 21:17 "144 cubits" is used. These are used instead of modern equivalents.

The NIV has followed the current practice of replacing the obsolete "thou," "thee," "thy," and "thine" with the forms of "you" even when Jesus or the Father is addressed. By this many problems are avoided where one has to decide whether Jesus is being addressed as merely a man or as a divine person. Also quotation marks are used for direct address. While this is a good practice, it leads inevitably to differences in a few places. Especially is this true in John 3 in Jesus' conversation with Nicodemus. Following the NEB, JB, NAB, and PHILLIPS, the NIV has ended the quotation of Jesus after verse 21. The RSV ended the quotation after verse 15.

PUBLICATION OF THE WHOLE BIBLE

In 1978; five years after the publication of the NT, the entire NIV came from the press. Preliminary editions of portions of the

OT had been previously published, including Isaiah in 1975, Daniel in 1976, and Proverbs and Ecclesiastes in 1977. The entire OT was completed in 1978 and was published together with a fresh revision of the NT in October of that year.

Revisions of the New Testament

A collation of the revision with the original printing of 1973 indicates that nearly three hundred changes in the text of the NT have been made. The reasons for these changes are known only to the committee, but one can hazard some suggestions. A number were evidently made to insure that the translation more precisely represents the Greek text. By comparing the October, 1978, printing of Matthew 3:16, 19:11; Mark 1:10; 5:42; 6:17; Luke 12:3; 18:12 with the original printing of 1973, the reader can observe this type of change. Any changes that make a translation more accurate are welcome. In a number of other revisions one can detect a trend toward a more literal rendering. Note the following changes: "heart" for "mind" in Luke 2:5, Mark 6:52; "under heaven" for "in the world" in Acts 2:5, "see decay" for "undergo decay" in Acts 2:27; 13:35, 37, "O house of Israel" for "O Israel" in Acts 7:42, "stiff-necked people" for "stubborn people" in Acts 7:51, "full of the Holy Spirit" for "filled with the Spirit" in Acts 7:55, and "whose I am" for "to whom I belong" in Acts 27:23. Whether one regards such literalness as an improvement or not depends on the theory of translation one holds. In 1 Corinthians 9:26, the reading of the revision "I do not fight like a man beating the air" is not as striking as that of the 1973 printing, "I do not fight like a man shadow boxing."

The revision also appears to be more in the direction of the traditional wording of the older standard English Bibles, such as the KJV. "Imposter" is changed to "deceiver" (Matt. 27:13), "put out" becomes "quenched" (Mark 9:48), "grinding of teeth" gives way to the familiar "gnashing of teeth" (Matt. 8:12; 13:42, etc.), "prove the world wrong about" gives way to "convict the world of" (John 16:8), "pioneer" is changed to "author" (Heb. 2:10; 12:2), "just like Melchizedek" becomes "in the order of Melchizedek" (Heb. 5:6, 10; 6:20; 7:17), "the chest of the covenant" is again "the ark of the covenant" (Heb. 9:4–5; Rev. 11:19), "many sins" are once more "a multitude of sins" (James 5:20), and "on the cross" in 1 Peter 2:24 is again "on the tree." A few changes appear to reflect a desire to get away from colloquial language: "Never, Lord!" rather than "Perish the thought, Lord!" (Matt. 16:22), "a great deal of money" rather than "a lot of money" (Acts 16:16), and "strike" rather than "hit" (John 8:23).

When OT passages are quoted the tendency seems to be to make the wording in the NT quotation conform to the wording of the OT as far as the Greek text will allow. The reader can see this by comparing the printings of Matthew 8:17 with Isaiah 33:4; Matthew 12:20 with Isaiah 43:3; Romans 4:7–8 with Psalm 32:1–2; and Romans 9:7 with Genesis 21:12.

"The one doomed to destruction" is a marked improvement over "the child of hell" in John 17:12. "Child of hell" was an unfortunate translation, which failed to take account of the Hebrew idiom reflected in the Greek phrase, as well as mistranslating the Greek word for "destruction" as "hell." Both errors have now been corrected. In three passages in the Book of Revelation (2:26; 12:5; 19:15) the 1973 printing followed the standard English versions in rendering literally the symbol of power over the nation as "a rod of iron." In the 1978 printing this was changed to "a scepter of iron," in harmony with its translation of Psalm 2:9. Whether or not this is the correct rendering is debatable. In John 19:30 the change from "gave up his life" to "gave up his spirit" (cf. Matt. 27:50) is not an improvement. The new printing consistently substitutes the modern "grumble" for "murmur."

THE OLD TESTAMENT

The Text

Although an eclectic Greek text formed the basis of the NT of the NIV, the OT translators based their work on the standard Masoretic Hebrew and Aramaic text "as published in the latest editions of Biblia Hebraica" (preface, p. viii). Occasionally a variant reading in the margin suggested by the Masoretes was adopted in place of a word or words in the text itself. Since these variants, like the text itself, belong to the Masoretic tradition, it was not deemed necessary to indicate such changes in footnotes. The first line of 2 Samuel 22:51 in the Hebrew, for example, reads, "He is a tower of deliverances for his king," The NIV, following the marginal reading of the Masoretes, which is in agreement with the deuterograph in Psalm 18:50, translates, "He gives his king great victories." The marginal reading of Numbers 1:16, to cite another example, yields the NIV rendering, "These were the men appointed from the community," rather than the reading translated by the KJV as "These were the renowned of the congregation." The NIV agrees with most recent versions in giving the second line of Psalm 100:3 as "It is he who made us, and we are his" rather than reading the last clause as "and not we ourselves." Ancient scribal traditions regarding textual variants are sometimes cited in footnotes whether followed in the text (as in Job 7:20), or not (see Gen. 18:22; 1 Sam. 3:13; Job 32:3; Hos. 4:7).

In a very few passages the consonants of the Hebrew text were divided differently than in the Masoretic tradition. A division of one word into two in Psalm 73:4 yields the translation, "They have no struggles;/their bodies are healthy and strong," rather than, "There are no struggles in their death;/their bodies are healthy" (see the footnote). Although there is no footnote to indicate it, the rendering "the great king" in Hosea 5:13; 10:6 is also based on a change in word division. Footnotes mention a few other possible renderings based on differences in dividing the consonants which were not adopted in the text (see the notes to Num. 24:23; Prov. 30:1; Amos 4:3).

The Dead Sea Scrolls which represent an earlier stage of the Hebrew text than that of the Masoretic period were also consulted, and a few readings found in them were adopted in the text. In Isaiah 33:8, for example, the reading "witnesses" (*'edîm*) suits the sense better than "cities" (*'arîm*). The differences between the consonants of the two is a "d" rather than an "r," two letters often confused because of their similarity in the square Hebrew characters. Hence the NIV renders the second half of the verse: "The treaty is broken,/its witnesses are despised,/no one is respected." The MT of Isaiah 53:11 has no direct object for the verb "he shall see." The two Isaiah scrolls from Qumran have the word "light" as the object, as does the old Greek version. The NIV accepts this reading and adds the interpretive phrase, "of life" in its rendering: "After the suffering of his soul,/he will see the light of life and be satisfied." In Isaiah 21:8 the great Isaiah Scroll, from cave 1, supported by the Syriac, is the source of the rendering, "and the lookout shouted," rather than, "and he cried as a lion" as the MT reads. Similarly, that scroll, supported by the Greek and Syriac versions, is the source of the reading, "How his fury has ended!" in Isaiah 14:4, whereas the KJV reads "the golden city ceased!" In Isaiah 49:24 the NIV also follows the great Dead Sea Scroll of Isaiah along with three ancient versions in reading. "Can plunder be taken from warriors,/or captives rescued from the fierce?" in place of the reading of the MT in the final clause, "or the captives of a just one be delivered?" Several recent versions, including the NIV, have added two lines to Psalm 145:13 that had apparently dropped out of most of the Hebrew manuscripts:

> The Lord is faithful to all his promises
> and loving toward all he has made.

A footnote gives the information that these two lines are found in one Hebrew MS, the Dead Sea Scrolls, and the old Greek and Syriac versions. Some other passages affected by the wording of the Dead Sea Scrolls include: 1 Samuel 1:24; 2 Samuel 22:33; Psalms 119:37; 144:2; 145:5; Isaiah 37:20, 25, 27; 45:2; 51:19.

Readings in the Samaritan Pentateuch, particularly when supported by one or more of the ancient versions, were also occasionally followed. In Genesis 4:8 the NIV includes the words of Cain to Abel, "Let's go out to the field," which the MT lacks, but that are found in the Samaritan Pentateuch as well as the Septuagint, Vulgate, and Syriac versions. The reading of the Samaritan Pentateuch, a number of Hebrew manuscripts, the Septuagint and Syriac versions, "he saw a ram caught by its horns" in Genesis 22:14 is preferred to the reading of most Hebrew manuscripts, "he saw a ram behind him." The NIV also follows the Samaritan text and the Greek version of Genesis 47:21 in reading, "and Joseph reduced the people to servitude," in preference to the Hebrew, "and he moved the people into the cities." A number of other readings adopted from the Samaritan with other sources concern the spelling of names that have historical importance, but have little bearing on the essential message of the Bible (see Gen. 10:4; 36:39; 37:36; 46:13, 16; Num. 2:14; 26:39–40; 33:8). Some other readings of the Samaritan Pentateuch are cited in footnotes but not adopted in the text (see Gen. 36:16; Exod. 12:40; 14:25; Num. 3:9). The Samaritan readings that are peculiarly sectarian in nature, however, are not cited.

According to the preface, readings from such important early versions as the Septuagint, Syriac, and Vulgate, as well as the Aramaic Targums, were also "occasionally followed where the Masoretic Text seems doubtful and where accepted principles of textual criticism showed that one or more of these textual witnesses appeared to provide the correct reading" (p. ix). The Septuagint is the most important of these. Passages have already been cited in which this version supports the Dead Sea Scrolls, a few Hebrew manuscripts, or the Samaritan Pentateuch in readings that have been accepted. In addition there are a few readings that have been adopted that are found in the Greek version alone. The most noteworthy example is the long addition to the MT in Judges 16:13–14, which completes Samson's explanation of how he might be tied up, and begins the account of how Delilah carried out his suggestion. This part of the story may have accidently been dropped from the Hebrew text. Several other additions to the MT from the Greek have been accepted by recent versions such as those to Gen. 44:4; 1 Sam. 3:15; 4:1; 10:1; 12:8; and 14:41, but were not adopted by the NIV. In this regard, as in the matter of translation it is a conservative version, revealing extreme care and caution in modifying the traditional text. It does, however, follow a number of Septuagint readings as in Exodus 8:23; Joshua 18:18; 1 Samuel 13:1; 1 Chronicles 16:15; Job 28:11; Psalms 35:16; 44:4; 49:11; Ezekiel 40:6, 14, 37, 44, 48–49, et al.

In Hosea 4:7 the NIV follows the Syriac in reading "they exchanged their glory for something disgraceful," in place of the Masoretic Text's, "I will exchange. . . ." "And their backs were wrenched" in Ezekiel 29:7 is based on the Syriac rather than the

MT that has "and you caused their backs to stand." (See also Ezek. 23:21.)

In Ezekiel 43:3 the NIV follows the Vulgate along with some manuscripts in reading, "when he came to destroy the city," whereas the MT has "when I came to destroy the city." The reading of Ezekiel 19:7, "He broke down their strongholds" follows the Aramaic Targum; the traditional Hebrew would yield, "He knew their strongholds." "Of cypress wood" in Ezekiel 27:6 is also based on the Targum. A note states, "the Masoretic Text has a different division of the consonants."

In general the translators tried to avoid conjectural emendations. Nevertheless some changes were almost unavoidable. In 2 Kings 10:25 the final clause reads, "and then they entered the inner shrine of the temple of Baal." The Hebrew text, however, does not read "inner shrine" but "city" which does not seem to make sense in the context. Hence the translators apparently substituted *debîr* "innermost room" for *'îr* "city." The Hebrew of Psalm 40:2 reads "He lifted me up from the pit of roaring," whereas the NIV translates, "He lifted me out of the slimy pit." The Hebrew for, "They are full of superstitions from the East," in Isaiah 2:6, lacks the word for "superstitions," but the context calls for some sort of pagan practice or practices. Versions vary on the term to be supplied among which are: "diviners" (RSV), "influences" (NASB), "traders" (NEB), "soothsayers" (JB), "customs" (AB), and "practices" (NJV). The last clause in the prayer of repentance Hosea suggests for Israel reads, "that we may offer the fruit of our lips" (Hos. 14:2). But instead of "fruit" the Hebrew text has "bulls," which can be emended to "fruit" by leaving off a single letter.

The translators of the NIV treated the Hebrew text with great respect, and kept all changes to a minimum. It is evident, however, that the original text has suffered in the process of transmission, and some emendations can hardly be avoided if the translator is to make sense of every passage.

Translation Goals, Principles, and Methods

The translators of the NIV, according to the preface, sought to produce a version that would be characterized by accuracy, clarity, and literary quality. Accuracy means that the version must faithfully communicate in English the thought that the original writers put in Hebrew, Aramaic, and Greek. A faithful communication of the thought of the originals is the goal of all translators, but there are differing views regarding the method by which it is to be achieved. There are two components of language that Beekman and Callow (*Translating the Word of God*, Grand Rapids: Zondervan, 1974, pp. 19f.) have emphasized: form and meaning. "Form" refers to the message these linguistic elements are designed to communicate. All translators of the Bible seek to communicate the meaning of the originals. But must the translator preserve the form of the original to convey the meaning? Those who answer this question in the affirmative produce what is known as a "formal" translation. On the contrary, those who maintain that what a translator should do is to grasp the meaning of the original and express that meaning in the natural form of the receptor language produce what is known as a dynamic translation. Hence translations may be divided into those that are formal and those that are dynamic. The NIV is a middle-of-the-road version in which a high degree of "formal correspondence" is combined with renderings that are "dynamically equivalent." The preface informs us that the translators

> have weighed the significance of the lexical and grammatical details of the Hebrew, Aramaic and Greek texts. At the same time, they have striven for more than a word-for-word translation. Because thought patterns and syntax differ from language to language, faithful communication of the meaning of the Bible demands frequent modifications in sentence structure and constant regard for the contextual meanings of words (p. viii).

Though modifications in the linguistic elements of the originals were made, it is evident that the translation is not completely divorced from the form of the originals. In fact, fidelity to the original was regarded by the translators as including a reflection of the various styles of the Bible writers. Their goal in this regard is plainly stated: "When the original is beautiful, its beauty must shine through the translation; when it is stylistically ordinary this must be apparent" (*The Story of the New International Version*, New York International Bible Society, p. 13).

Clarity means that the translation should be put in "clear and natural English." It "should be idiomatic but not idiosyncratic, contemporary but not dated" (preface, p. viii). The use of the traditional pronouns "thou," "thee," "thy," and "thine," together with the corresponding archaic verb forms, in language addressed to the Deity was abandoned, because it would not be contemporary. Furthermore, their use would not be accurate since "Neither Hebrew, Aramaic, or Greek uses special pronouns for the persons of the Godhead" (preface, p. viii).

The literary quality desired was one that would make the version "suitable for public and private reading, teaching, preaching, memorizing and liturgical use" (preface, p. viii). A version designed for use in public worship calls for language that is dignified and elegant, yet direct and simple. Not all the English of the NIV has this literary quality. The recorded conversations between human beings are, as a matter of fact, usually rendered in a colloquial style with frequent use of such contractions as can't, didn't, don't, hasn't, haven't, he's, I'll, I'm, isn't, she's, won't, and you've. But in the translation of the poetic portions of the OT, such as the Psalms, Job, and large portions of the prophets, special attention was given to the literary quality. Here especially the version is well-suited for public reading in worship services. In Samuel and Kings it is just as well that the uncouth way in which the male members of the households of Nabal, Jeroboam, Baasha, and Ahab are contemptuously described is not translated literally, as in the King James Version (1 Sam. 25:22, 34; 1 Kings 14:10; 16:11; 21:21; 2 Kings 9:8). The version also agrees with other recent translations in abandoning the use of the names of such internal organs as the bowels, the reins, and the liver as metaphors for the center of strong emotions. In the KJV "bowels" was used not only in a literal sense for the intestines (2 Chron. 2:15; Acts 1:18), but for the internal organs of reproduction, both male and female (Gen. 15:4; 25:23; 2 Sam. 16:11; Ps. 71:6) and metaphorically as the center of the emotions (Isa. 63:15; Jer. 4:19; 31:20; Lam. 1:20, etc). In place of "bowels" to designate the internal genitals, the NIV uses "body" (Gen. 15:4; 2 Sam. 7:12), "flesh" or even "own offspring." In the metaphorical sense as the center of emotions it uses "heart" (Jer. 31:20; Lam. 1:20). For "reins," an old word meaning "kidneys," when used metaphorically the version also has "heart" (Ps. 26:2; Jer. 12:2). Lamentations 2:11 in the KJV reads, "My liver is poured upon the earth for the destruction of my people." The NIV shows a marked improvement in its rendering: "My heart is poured out on the ground/because my people are destroyed."

Throughout the NIV the traditional and the modern are intermingled. Modern features include the complete abandonment of some Hebrew idioms or their translation into an appropriate English equivalent. As an example of the former is the complete omission of the common idiom translated "and it came to pass" from both Testaments (e.g., Gen. 6:4; Luke 2:1). An example of the latter is the translation of the idiom "to lift up the eyes" with "to look up" (Gen. 13:10; 18:2; 22:4). Similarly, "to lift up the voice and weep" is usually rendered, "to weep audibly," or "to raise the voice" (Gen. 27:38; 29:11; Judg. 2:4; 21:2). "To obey God's voice" is usually rendered "to obey God" (Gen. 22:18; 26:5), while "to hearken to his voice" becomes "to listen to what he says" (Exod. 23:21–22). "To call his/her name" so-and-so becomes "To name him/her" (Gen. 3:20; 4:25; 5:3, et al.). "To gird up the loins" becomes "to tuck the cloak in one's belt" (Exod. 12:11; 1 Kings 18:46). When the adjective "uncircumcised" is used in a metaphorical sense it is frequently interpreted. "I am of uncircumcised lips" is rendered "I speak with faltering lips" (Exod. 6:12, 30). "Their ears are uncircumcised," as in the RSV, becomes, "Their ears are closed/so they cannot hear" (Jer. 6:10). The fruit of newly planted trees was to be considered "uncircumcised" for three years, which is interpreted to mean "forbidden," as in the RSV (Lev. 19:23). The passages that deal with a spiritual "heart circumcision," however, are translated quite literally (Deut. 10:16; 30:6; Jer. 4:4; 9:26; Rom. 2:29; Col. 2:11).

Some idioms in the traditional biblical English are likewise modernized. "To hold one's peace" is rendered "to be silent" or "to keep quiet" (Gen. 24:21; 34:5; Lev. 10:3; Neh. 8:11). "To breathe one's last" is certainly an improvement over the KJV, "to give up," or "to yield up the ghost," since "ghost" today hardly suggests the seventeenth-century meaning, "breath" (Gen. 25:8, 17; Job 14:10; Acts 5:5, 10). "Begat" in the genealogies is usually translated "was the father of" (Gen. 4:18; 10:8, 13, 15). "Behold" in the Aramaic portions of Daniel is rendered "and there before me/you" (Dan. 2:31; 4:10, 13; 7:2, 5–8, 13).

The NIV is a new translation made directly from the originals, and in no sense is a revision of any of the historic English versions. Nevertheless the translators "sought to preserve some measure of continuity with the long tradition of translating the Scriptures into English" (preface, p. viii). As the result it is not a completely different Bible that sounds strange to the reader familiar with the KJV or RSV. Its religious vocabulary is for the most part already familiar to the church-goer. More modern religious terms are introduced only when the traditional ones are regarded as inadequate.

Much of the traditional terminology connected with the Israelite people, their center of worship, religious festivals, and sacrificial system has been retained. But some changes are worthy of note. Since the meaning of "peculiar" has drastically changed, Israel is spoken of as God's "treasured possession" (Exod. 19:5; Deut. 14:2), rather than God's "peculiar people." Instead of the "congregation" of Israel, the version uses the word "community." The "court" of the ancient tabernacle is designated "courtyard" (Exod. 27:9ff.; 38:9), the "laver" where the priests washed is called a "basin" (Exod. 30:18, 28). The "ark of the Testimony" is introduced as a "chest" (Exod. 25:10), though the term "ark" is usually retained (Exod. 25:16, et al.). The cover of the ark, which the traditional versions followed Tyndale in calling the "mercy seat" (after Luther's *Gnadenstuhl*), is usually designated "the atonement cover" (Exod. 25:17; 26:34, et al.), but is also called "the place of atonement" (1 Chron. 28:11; Heb. 9:5), or simply, "the cover" (Exod. 25:18ff.; 37:8). The "shewbread" (KJV), as in the RSV, is called "the bread of the presence" (Exod. 25:30). The "breastplate of judgment" worn by the high priest is a "breastpiece for making decisions" (Exod. 28:15). The "meat" (KJV), or "cereal" (RSV), offering is called a "grain offering" (Lev. 2:1), the traditional "peace offering" is designated a "fellowship offering" (Lev. 3:1), while the "trespass offering" (RSV) is named a "guilt offering" (Lev. 5:15; 6:6). While the designation "Feast of Unleavened Bread" is retained, the term "yeast" is used in the observance instruction, "For seven days you are to eat bread made without yeast. On the first day remove the yeast from your houses, for whoever eats anything with yeast in it from the first day to the seventh must be cut off from Israel" (Exod. 12:15; cf. 23:15). "Scapegoat" is retained with the explanatory note, "That is, goat of removal" (Lev. 16:8, 10, 26). The traditional injunction for the people's observance of the Day of Atonement, "afflict your souls" is rendered "deny yourselves" (Lev. 16:29, 31; 23:27, 32). Moses' rod used in delivering Israel was a "staff" (Exod. 4, et al.). The "signs" he showed to convince Pharaoh of his mission are called "miraculous signs" (Exod. 4:8; 7:3), a term also used in the NT for Jesus' miracles (John 2:11; 4:48).

Unlike the GNB; the NIV retains the anthropomorphic language of the Hebrew Bible. It speaks of the arm, the hands, the fingers, the feet, the eyes, and ears of God. It was "by the word of the LORD" and the "breath of his mouth" that the heavens with their hosts of stars were brought into existence (Ps. 33:6). The heavens are also the work of God's fingers and the things on the earth were made by his hands (Ps. 8:3, 6). Heaven is God's throne, while the earth is his "footstool" (Isa. 66:1). God brought Israel out of Egypt "with a mighty hand and an outstretched arm" (Deut. 5:15). He will yet "lay bare his holy arm in the sight of all nations" (Isa. 52:10). To show God's special care for the land of Palestine, Deuteronomy 11:12 asserts, "the eyes of the LORD your God are continually on it from the beginning of the year to its end." God's arm is not "too short to save, nor his ear too dull to hear" (Isa. 59:1). Moses, Aaron, Nadab, Abihu, and seventy elders of Israel on Mount Sinai "saw the God of Israel" under whose feet was something resembling "a pavement made of sapphire, clear as the sky itself" (Exod. 24:10). Hanani the seer affirmed: "The eyes of the Lord range throughout the earth, to strengthen those whose hearts are fully committed to him" (2 Chron. 16:9). The NIV also retains the metaphor of God's "wing" as a place of refuge and protection (Ruth 2:12; Pss. 36:7; 57:1; 61:4; 63:7; 91:4).

The translation follows the KJV and most recent English versions in rendering YHWH, the sacred Tetragrammaton, the covenant name of God, as "LORD," spelled with capital letters, to distinguish it from the translation of *adonai*, "Lord," spelled with lower-case letters. YHWH is rendered "LORD" even in such place names as "The LORD will provide" (Gen. 22:14). "The LORD is my Banner" (Exod. 17:15), "The LORD is Peace" (Judg. 6:24), and "The LORD is there" (Ezek. 48:35). Wherever the compound name *Adonai YHWH* occurs (e.g., nearly 225 times in Ezekiel), it is translated as "Sovereign LORD." As an equivalent for the appellatives, "the LORD of hosts" and "God of hosts," which affirms God's universal sovereignty over the powers of earth and heaven, the version uses, "The LORD Almighty" and "God Almighty." *El Shaddai* is also translated "God Almighty," but is everywhere footnoted (see Gen. 17:1; Exod. 6:3, et al.). Other divine appellations, such as, "God Most High" (Gen. 14:19–20, 22), "the Most High" (Deut. 32:8; Ps. 107:11, et al.), and "the Ancient of Days" (Dan. 7:9, 13) are given the traditional renderings.

The NIV has, of course, discarded the obsolete and antiquated words found in the KJV. But, in addition, the careful reader will observe a number of other changes in the vocabulary, among which only a few conspicuous examples can be given. The "firmament" of the creation story (Gen. 1:6, 7, 14–17, 20) is called an "expanse." "Adam named his wife Eve, because she would *become* the mother of all the living" (Gen. 3:20). "The windows of heaven" in the account of the flood are called "the floodgates of the heavens" (Gen. 7:11; 8:2), "The LORD rained down burning sulfur on Sodom and Gomorrah," not "brimstone and fire" (Gen. 19:24). Joseph's "coat of many colours" (Gen. 37:3, 32) is called a "richly ornamented robe." Moses as a baby was placed in "a papyrus basket," "coated with tar and pitch," rather than "an ark of bulrushes" "daubed with slime and with pitch." It was placed "among the reeds along the bank of the Nile," not among "the flags by the river's brink" (Exod.

2:3). The plague of lice in Egypt was a plague of gnats as in the RSV (Exod. 8:16ff.). The "tables" of stone on which God wrote the Ten Commandments were "tablets of stone" (Exod. 24:12; 32:16). The commandment forbidding the taking of God's name "in vain" is translated "You shall not misuse the name of the LORD your God" (Exod. 20:7; Deut. 5:11). Baalam's "ass," and all other "asses" in the Bible, are "donkeys" (Num. 22:21–33). The "swine" of the KJV are all "pigs" (Isa. 65:4; 66:17, et al.). "Strong drink" is most often "beer" (Prov. 20:1; 31:4, 6; Isa. 28:7), but also "other fermented drink" (Lev. 10:9; Judg. 13:4, 7, 14). A "scribe" in the OT is a "secretary," (2 Kings 19:2), while in the NT he is a "teacher of the law." The "abomination of desolation" is "the abomination that causes desolation" (Matt. 24:15; cf. Dan. 11:31; 12:11). Pagan places of worship are still called "high places," but the "groves" (KJV) are "Asherah poles," and "images" (as a translation of *maṣṣebōth*) are "pillars" (Deut. 12:13). "To make one's son or daughter pass through the fire" is now clearly rendered "to sacrifice his son or daughter in the fire" (Deut. 18:10; 2 Kings 17:17).

The significance of the ancient city gate together with the open area near it as a community center for legal business, social and cultural activities must be kept in mind to appreciate the NIV translation of words rendered "gate" in the KJV. The traditional translation is naturally most often used. But "gateway" also occurs, as in the story of Lot who was sitting in the "gateway" of Sodom when he saw the two angels enter (Gen. 19:1ff.). In several passages "gate" is regarded as a figure *(synecdoche)* standing for the whole city (see Deut. 28:52, 55, 57). Hence, the promise to Abraham "thy seed shall possess the gate of his enemies" (Gen. 22:17, KJV) is translated, "Your descendants will take possession of the *cities* of your enemies." But a similar promise in the blessing given Rebekah is rendered, "may your offspring possess/the *gates* of their enemies" (Gen. 24:60). In Jeremiah 14:2, "gates" is again rendered cities, "Judah mourns,/her cities languish." The phrase "within your gates," so common in Deuteronomy, is usually translated "in your towns" (Deut. 12:12ff.; 14:21, 27–29, et al.). Finally, since legal transactions and court procedures were carried on at the city gate, the NIV sometimes translates "gate(s)" as "court(s)" (Isa. 29:21; Amos 5:10, 12, 15).

The similes and metaphors of the Hebrew Bible are usually retained. This is particularly true of the highly literary passages in the Psalms and the Prophets (e.g., Ps. 91:1, 3; Isa. 40:12). The version translates God's assertion as given in Psalm 60:8 quite literally: "Moab is my washbasin/upon Edom I toss my sandal." Hosea compares Israel's evanescent love to the morning mist (Hos. 6:4). "Walking" as a metaphor for living is usually retained. Moses, according to the Book of Deuteronomy (8:6; 10:12; 11:22), appealed to the Israelites to walk in the ways of God. "To walk humbly with your God," is one of the basics of religion, according to Micah (Mic. 6:8). Enoch and Noah were men who "walked with God" (Gen. 5:22, 24; 6:9). The term "horn" is also retained as a symbol of "strength" (1 Sam. 2:1; 2 Sam. 22:3), a strong one (Pss. 89:27; 132:17), power (Ps. 75:10), and dignity (Ps. 112:9), according to the notes.

Sometimes a figure is modified, such as, "I gave you empty stomachs" rather than "I gave you cleanness of teeth" (Amos 4:6), or the figure is made more specific as, "They consult a wooden idol," in place of "inquire of a thing of wood" (Hos. 4:12). "Ships of Tarshish" is sometimes rendered "trading ships" (1 Kings 10:22; 22:48; Isa. 2:16), and sometimes retained (Ps. 48:7; Isa. 23:1, 14). Rarely is figurative language rendered literally. One example is Joseph's words to his brothers (Gen. 45:12) where in place of the literal rendering, "and now your eyes see, and the eyes of my brother Benjamin see, that it is my mouth that speaks to you," the NIV gives, "You can see for yourselves, and so can my brother Benjamin, that it is really I who am speaking to you." Another example is Leviticus 19:32, "Rise in the presence of the aged" rather than "You shall rise up before the hoary head."

In instances where a person or place has two or more different names, the policy of the translators is in general to use the more familiar one (preface, p. x). For this reason, the Hebrew for "Chaldeans" is usually rendered "Babylonians," with the footnote reading, "Or, Chaldeans" (2 Kings 25:4, 13, 25–26; Isa.

13:19; Jer. 33:5). The ancient city of Ur, however, is still called "Ur of the Chaldeans" (Gen. 11:28, 31; 15:7; Neh. 9:7). In Daniel the Aramaic for "Chaldeans" is translated, "astrologers" several times (Dan. 2:4–5, 10; 3:8; 4:7; 5:7, 11). "Nebuchadrezzar" in Jeremiah and Ezekiel is given the more familiar spelling "Nebuchadnezzar" (e.g., Jer. 21:2; Ezek. 26:7). The Persian ruler, "Ahasuerus" is given the more familiar name "Xerxes" (Ezra 4:6; Esth. 1:1; Dan. 9:1). The city of "Noph" in Egypt becomes "Memphis" (Isa. 19:13; Ezek. 30:13), and "No" is rendered "Thebes." "Syria," "Syrian" and "Syrians," however, are given as "Aram," "Aramean," and "Arameans," respectively—a literal rendering of the Hebrew (2 Sam. 8:6; 1 Kings 20, et al.). The version follows the Hebrew in giving both "Azariah" (2 Kings 14:21; 15:1, 6–8) and "Uzziah" (2 Kings 15:13, 30, 32, 34, and the Prophets) as the name of the tenth king of Judah. Unfortunately, only 2 Kings 14:21 has a note to "Azariah" identifying him as identical with "Uzziah." In none of the passages having "Uzziah" is there a note to identify him with "Azariah."

In the NT it is impossible to follow the logic behind the treatment of Simon Peter's Aramaic name. In 1 Corinthians 15:5 and Galatians 1:18; 2:9, 11, 14, Cephas is rendered "Peter," with the note, "Greek *Cephas.*" But in 1 Corinthians 1:12; 3:22; and 9:5, "Cephas" is retained with the note, "That is, Peter." One wonders why the latter was not done consistently. "Prisca" in Paul's letters is rendered "Priscilla" (1 Cor. 16:9; 2 Tim. 4:19) with the note, "Greek *Prisca,* a variant of *Priscilla.*" "Silvanus" is given as "Silas" with the note, "Greek *Silvanus,* a variant of *Silas*" (2 Cor. 1:19; 1 Thess. 1:1; 2 Thess. 1:1; 1 Peter 5:12). A number of other proper names are similarly treated. The traditional "Beelzebub" is retained in the New Testament even though it is not found in any Greek manuscripts, which read "Beelzeboul" or "Beezeboul." "Beelzebub," "lord of the fly," occurs in 2 Kings 1:2, 6, but it is doubtful that the New Testament references to "Beelzeboul" refer to the same deity. "Beelzebub" in the English New Testament apparently was taken from the Latin Vulgate of Matthew 10:25; 12:24, 27, and parallels in other synoptics.

READER AIDS

The mechanical features of the version are a model of the printer's craft. The type is clear and easy to read. The text is arranged in paragraphs, but the traditional verse numbers are retained in inconspicuous type. Poetic passages are printed in poetic form.

The preface of a little over four pages contains valuable information regarding the goals, methods, and principles that guided the translators of the version. Every user of the NIV would do well to read this informative introductory statement.

Sectional Headings

As a help to the reader, the version provides sectional headings which are printed in italics. The preface cautions: "They are not to be regarded as part of the NIV text, are not for oral reading, and are not intended to indicate the interpretation of the sections they head" (p. x). They do, however, indicate the subject matter with which the sections deal. In the Book of Habakkuk, for instance, they provide a brief outline of the contents of the book. In the Epistles of the NT they are less helpful. In the Book of Job, the speaker of each dialogue is identified by the printing of his name in italics in the margin. In the Song of Songs, the male and female speakers are also indicated as "Lover," and "Beloved." This identification was based primarily "on the basis of the gender of the Hebrew pronouns used." "The words of others are marked *Friends*." This adds interest as well as clarity to these dramatic poems.

Brackets

The practice of occasionally using half-brackets to enclose "words or phrases supplied for clarification" in the New Testament, as noted above, is also followed in the Old Testament (see examples in Gen. 24:33; Exod. 4:2; Lev. 11:26; 1 Sam. 13:1; 2 Kings 6:33; Job 26:7; Ps. 57:2; Isa. 53:11; Amos 1:3). But again the question arises as to the reason for bracketing some supplied words and phrases, while leaving others equally supplied unbracketed. The version, for example, quotes Eve at the birth of Cain as exclaiming, "With the help of the LORD I have brought forth a man" (Gen. 4:1). "With the help of" has been supplied since the Hebrew literally reads, "I have acquired a man, the LORD," which some Christians interpret as an indication that Eve expected her first-born son to be the Messiah. Whether or not this interpretation is correct, the supplied phrase could well have been bracketed. Note also a few of the unbracketed additions in the Book of Job: "who is but" and "who is only" (25:6), "nuggets of" (28:6), "use was" (30:3) and "through" (30:14). In Nahum 1:8–14 the prophetic message is like a pendulum swinging back and forth between Nineveh and Judah. The translators have inserted "Nineveh" in verses 8 and 11, and "O Nineveh" in verse 14 in lower half-brackets to indicate that the words of doom are addressed to the Assyrian capital. Similarly, "O Judah" is inserted in verse 12 to indicate that the message of relief from oppression is addressed to her. Verse 15 is also addressed to Judah, but in this verse "O Judah" is a part of the Hebrew text. One cannot but respect the conscientious scruples of the translators in using the half-brackets to mark these insertions. But since only a selected number of such additions are bracketed, perhaps a better way of informing the reader of these justifiable insertions would be by the use of footnotes.

Footnotes

The text of the NIV is supplemented with nearly 3,350 footnotes, more than 2,500 in the Old Testament and over 800 in the New Testament. These brief notes are of various kinds. Approximately 350 in the Old Testament are textual, indicating variant readings in Hebrew manuscripts, the Masoretic tradition, and ancient versions. In addition to notes citing variant readings which were adopted by translators, a large number of notes cite other variants which were not adopted. A note to Genesis 11:12–13, for example, indicates that the Septuagint adds the name "Cainan" to the genealogical list (cf. Luke 3:35–36). A note to Exodus 12:40 indicates that according to the Samaritan Pentateuch and the Septuagint the 430 years cover the period that the Israelites lived in Egypt "and Canaan." A note to Exodus 14:25 cites the reading of the Samaritan Pentateuch, Septuagint, and Syriac, "He jammed the wheels of their chariots," rather than "He made the wheels of their chariots swerve," as the MT reads.

There are about 130 textual notes in the New Testament. The text of Matthew 5:22 contains what is evidently the original form of Jesus' saying: "anyone who is angry with his brother will be subject to judgment." But some manuscripts have a softened form of the saying by the addition of "without cause" after "brother," as the note indicates. The NIV of Romans 8:28 reads: "And we know that in all things God works for the good of those who love him." A note reads: "Some manuscripts read *And we know that all things work together for good to those who love God.*" The word "some" here is an understatement, for most manuscripts do not have "God."

More than a third of the notes in the New Testament are simply references to Old Testament passages quoted, or paraphrased by the NT writer. Unfortunately, none of the synoptic Gospels has references to parallel material in the others. Nor does Ephesians have references to parallel passages in Colossians. In the Old Testament cross references are comparatively rare (see 2 Kings 9:26, 36; 14:6; 15:12; 17:12; 23:27; 25:3; Zeph. 1:9).

Many notes in both Testaments provide alternative translations to that given in the text. To illustrate, the affirmation in the *Shema* of Deuteronomy 6:4, "The LORD our God, the LORD is one," could, according to the note, be rendered, "The LORD our God is one LORD; or The LORD is our God, the LORD is one; or The LORD is our God, the LORD alone." A note suggests that Rahab, the harlot, may possibly have been an innkeeper (Josh. 2:1; 6:17). A note to Psalm 56:8 suggests that the second line, "list my tears on your scroll" could also be rendered, "put my tears in your wineskin" (cf. KJV).

In the New Testament, the NIV joins most recent versions in rendering Jesus' saying about anxiety (Matt. 6:27; Luke 12:25): "Who of you by worrying can add a single hour to his life?", rather than the alternative given in the footnote, ". . . a single cubit to his height." A note to John 1:4 gives as an alternative to "the darkness has not understood it," ". . . has not overcome it." Matthew 19:12b is translated, "others have renounced marriage because of the kingdom of God." The traditional rendering "have made themselves eunuchs" is given in a note. In the puzzling passage about marriage in 1 Corinthians 7:36–38, the NIV opts for the interpretation that Paul is talking about an engaged couple. The view that the apostle's instruction concerns whether or not a father should seek a marriage for his daughter is set forth in the alternative translation in a note. Paul's exhortation about sexual morality in 1 Thessalonians 4:4f. is another passage about which translators differ: ". . . to know how to possess [or, acquire] his own vessel in sanctification and honor." Does the Greek word for "vessel" here mean one's own body (cf. 2 Cor. 4:7), or a "wife" (cf. 1 Peter 3:7)? The NIV opts for the former: "each of you should learn to control his own body," but provides the alternative in a note: "learn to live with his own wife" or "learn to acquire a wife."

A large number of notes are explanatory in nature. A note to Genesis 2:7, for example, explains, "The Hebrew for *man* (adam) sounds like and may be derived from the Hebrew for *ground (Adamah);* it is also the name *Adam* (see Gen. 2:20)." A note to Genesis 2:23, "she shall be called woman," says, "The Hebrew word for *woman* sounds like the Hebrew word for *man*" [not *Adam*, but *'ish*]. Genesis 3:20 reads, "Adam [Note: Or *The man*] named his wife Eve [Note: *Eve* means living], because she would become the mother of all the living." A note to Matthew 23:5 explains, "phylacteries," "That is, boxes containing Scripture verses, which were worn on the forehead and arms." Other explanatory notes give the meaning of names of places and persons, the approximate modern equivalents of weights and measures, and of money.

The notes are of great value to the reader and in some cases could have been expanded. This version translates Isaiah 7:14: "Therefore the LORD himself will give you a sign: The virgin will be with child and will give birth to a son, and will call him Immanuel." There are notes to indicate that the "you" is plural in the original, and that "Immanuel" means "God with us." But, unfortunately, there is no note to indicate that the Hebrew word for "virgin," *almah,* means a young woman of marriageable age, not necessarily a virgin.

Back Matter

At the back, following the translation of the Book of Revelation, there is a useful "Table of Weights and Measures." It includes "Weights," "Length," "Dry Measure and Liquid Measure." In each section, the biblical unit together with its equivalent in other biblical terms is given together with the American and metric equivalents.

The NIV is now available in a wide variety of styles, many of which include other reader aids. A series of fourteen maps is included in many editions. While these maps are accurate and useful, the colors give them a gaudy appearance. A sixteen page section of new maps is being prepared that should soon be available. Other aids in various NIV editions include a mini-concordance, Bible reading plans, a harmony of Jesus' life in the gospel accounts, and listings of favorite Scripture passages.

CONCLUSION

In conclusion, one must say that the NIV translation is, on the whole, accurate and clear. It is a monument of Christian scholarship at its best. It does not have the color or striking characteristics of PHILLIPS or the NEB, but it is dependable and straightforward. It is more modern than the RSV, less free than the NEB, and more literary than the GNB. Its adoption for reading in public worship by the Christian Reformed Church, and its wide use by Assembly of God and Nazarene congregations, as well as its adoption as the base for some Christian education materials, are indications that it will have wide usage, particularly by conservative Christians.

17

The New King James Version

ITS HISTORY

Although several of the recent modern speech versions have been favorably received, the King James Version continues to be preferred by more than a third of America's readers of the English Bible. At the same time there is a growing awareness of the modern reader's difficulties in understanding its sixteenth-century English that, to a great extent, goes back to William Tyndale and Miles Coverdale. A new major attempt to update the language, while at the same time preserving its basic literary structure, has therefore been made. The result is The Holy Bible, New King James Version, which professes to be not a new translation but a new and improved edition of the old.

This is, of course, not the first time that the King James Version has been revised. From the very first this version was not static or fixed. Hence the KJV in use today differs markedly from the one originally printed in 1611. It differs in content, size, typography, spelling, punctuation, and to some extent in vocabulary. In addition to the sixty-six books that all Christians accept as inspired and authoritative, the first edition contained the Old Testament Apocrypha. Like its predecessor, the Bishop's Bible of which it was a revision, the first edition was printed in a large folio size using a block letter type, except for the comparatively few words printed in roman type to indicate that they had no exact equivalents in the original, but were added to make the translation conform to English idiom. In 1612, in imitation of the Geneva Bible, the whole version was printed in quarto size with roman type, and the "supplied" words in italics.

A revision containing more than three hundred differences from the 1611 edition was published in 1613. Sharp criticisms of the version by such men as Hugh Broughton forced the Cambridge University Press to publish a further revision in 1629. In 1638 an attempt was made to produce an "authentique corrected Bible" by a small committee that included two of the original translators. Fifteen years later (1653) the Long Parliament called for another revision because of errors in printing, translation, and language. But when Cromwell, the "Lord Protector," dissolved Parliament and took over the government, nothing came of the proposal. A revision in the spelling was made in 1675 by John Fell, Dean of Christ Church, Oxford.

More extensive revisions were made in the eighteenth century. In 1762 Dr. Thomas Paris of Trinity College, Cambridge, published his newly corrected edition. This was followed by the publication of the results of nearly four years of intensive work by Dr. Benjamin Blayney of Oxford in 1769. J. Isaacs gives a summary of the changes Blayney made:

> The marginal references were checked and verified, over 30,000 new marginal references were added, the chapter summaries and running headnotes were thoroughly revised, the punctuation was altered and made uniform in accordance with modern practice, textual errors were removed, the use of capitals was considerably modified and reduced, and a thorough revision was made in the form of certain kinds of words: "fetched" was substituted for "fet," "burned" for "burnt," "lifted" for "lift," "since" for "sith," in 35 instances "more" was written for "moe," and in 364 "ye" for "you." Dr. Paris had already altered "neesed" to "sneezed," "cruddled" to "curdled," and "glistering" to "glittering."[1]

This edition, which Goodspeed estimated to differ from that of 1611 in at least 75,000 details, has become the standard form of the KJV in use today.

[1]J. Isaacs, "The Authorized Version and After," *Ancient and English Versions,* H. Wheeler Robinson, ed., p. 225.

In the late nineteenth century the English RV was published, and in 1901 the ASV, both of which are described in chapter 2. The main emphasis in these revisions was on accuracy and consistency in rendering. Because of their rigid literalness they lacked the literary charm of the KJV; hence, they never achieved an acceptance by the English-speaking populace as a replacement for the KJV. Moreover they did not abandon many of the archaic features of the language of the classic version.

In 1975 an international group of some 130 scholars, editors, and religious leaders began a new revision of what is now called The Holy Bible, New King James Version. The project was initiated and sponsored by Thomas Nelson, Inc., under the leadership of its president, Mr. Sam Moore.

After a set of guidelines for the revisers was drawn up, the various books of the Bible were assigned to competent scholars who independently drew up proposed changes based on a study of the KJV as compared with the documents in the original languages. These recommended changes were then submitted to the editors who correlated and unified them. The results were submitted to the Overview Committee of clerical and lay advisors. At the same time, the Scholar Committee reviewed for accuracy the work of the editors. All changes were finally approved by an Executive Review Committee consisting of leading Christian scholars.

Dr. Arthur L. Farstad of Dallas Theological Seminary gave up his academic appointment to become the New Testament editor. Dr. James Price of Temple Baptist Theological Seminary, Chattanooga, Tennessee, served as the Old Testament editor. A Canadian professor of Florida Southern College in Orlando, William McDowell, became the English editor, whose primary concern was grammatical accuracy, punctuation, and style. The New Testament was published in 1979, and the Old Testament was published in the summer of 1982.

CHANGES FROM THE KING JAMES VERSION

The task of updating the English involved various kinds of changes—word order, grammar, vocabulary, spelling, etc. The changes in word order cannot be dealt with in detail here, but the reader can derive some idea of the extent of the changes by comparing the new version with the old in Matthew 3:8–9; 4:5; 9:14; 13:30; 18:15; Luke 19:15; Acts 3:22; 5:13; 7:7, 29, 30, 37; 9:31; 10:42; 12:5; 19:12; 20:29; 21:10; 22:29; 25:26.

Pronouns

Grammatically, one of the conspicuous features of the KJV that the new version abandoned is the use of the second personal pronouns *thou* (and its correlative forms for the other cases) and *ye*. In Old English *thou* (nominative), *thee* (dative and accusative), *thy* and *thine* (genitive) were the standard pronouns for the second person singular. The corresponding plurals were *ye, you, your,* and *yours*. In late Middle English these plurals began to supplant the singular forms, probably because of the influence of French, in which the plural was the polite form for addressing a single person. The older singular forms, however, continued to be used in familiar address among family members and friends, and in the liturgy of the church. Apart from their persistence in some dialects, these older forms eventually came to be used almost exclusively in poetry, church liturgy, and by such religious groups as the Friends (Quakers).

Originally the plural *ye* was used for the nominative and *you* for the dative and accusative. This usage, derived from earlier English versions, was preserved in the KJV (see John 14:1–3; Acts 14:15–16). In the secular English of Shakespeare's time the case distinction between *ye* and *you* was no longer consistently maintained. The confusion between the two is reflected in Shakespeare's lines:

"Stand, sir, and throw us that you have about ye."
(The Two Gentlemen of Verona, 4. 1.3)

"A southwest wind blow on ye and blister you all o'er."
(The Tempest, 1.2)

Eventually *you* became the regular form for both the nominative and objective cases, and *ye* survived only in poetry. At the same time the old singular forms *thou, thee, thy,* and *thine* continued to be used in language addressed to Deity. Even the Revised Standard Version retained them in prayers, and the

British counterpart, the New English Bible, followed the same practice. But today the trend is away from their use even in prayer, as the flood of recent modern speech versions indicates. This trend now reflected in the NKJV is defended, "these pronouns are no longer part of our language" (introduction, p. iv).

Verbal Endings

Along with these antiquated pronouns, the corresponding verbal endings *-est (-st, -t)* of the second person singular in the present and preterite tenses have also been abandoned. Likewise the inflection *-eth (-th)* for the third person singular, characteristic of several English dialects until about the sixteenth century, and found in the KJV, has given way to the originally northern inflection *-es, -s* in modern English, and hence also in the new revision.

Verb Forms

Similarly antiquated preterite forms of verbs have been modernized. Many of the strong verbs, for example, have a preterite using an *a* where now one uses an *o*. The following are examples of modernization in tense forms (in some instances substituting a different word):

KJV	NKJV	Reference
And they *awake* him	and they *awoke* him	Mark 4:38
made a great supper and *bade* many	gave a great supper and *invited* many	Luke 14:16
Which *bare* twelve manner of fruits	Which *bore* twelve fruits	Rev. 22:2
Abraham *begat* Isaac	Abraham *begot* Isaac	Acts 7:8
blessed and *brake* the loaves	blessed and *broke* the loaves	Mark 6:41
certain men *clave* unto him (past tense of cleave)	some men *joined* him	Acts 17:34
he *drave* them from the judgment seat	he *drove* them from the judgment seat	Acts 18:16
he *spake* unto them of John the Baptist	he *spoke* to them of John the Baptist	Matt. 17:13

they . . . *strake* sail	they *struck* sail	Acts 27:17
cut down branches . . . and *strawed* them	cut down branches . . . and *spread* them	Matt. 21:8
he *sware* unto her	he also *swore* to her	Mark 6:23
threw him down and *tare* him (past tense of tear)	threw him down and *convulsed* him	Luke 9:42
and *ware* no clothes	and he *wore* no clothes	Luke 8:27

Other preterite forms in the KJV are also now antiquated and the NKJV has substituted current equivalents for them, as the following illustrate:

KJV	NKJV	Reference
thus it *behoved* Christ to suffer	thus it was *necessary* for the Christ to suffer	Luke 24:46
and *digged* a winepress in it	*dug* a winepress in it	Matt. 21:33
Moses trembled and *durst* not behold	Moses trembled and *dared* not look	Acts 7:32
and *kneeled* down and prayed	He *knelt* down and prayed	Luke 22:41
they *laded* us with such things	they *provided* such things as were necessary	Acts 28:10
a light *shined* in the prison	a light *shone* in the prison	Acts 12:7
the thorns *sprung* up	the thorns *sprang* up	Matt. 13:7
they *sung* as it were a new song	they *sang* as it were a new song	Rev. 14:3
he *sunk* down with sleep	who was *sinking* into a deep sleep	Acts 20:9
they *trode* upon one another	they *trampled* one another	Luke 12:1

A few past participles also needed to be brought up-to-date, such as:

KJV	NKJV	Reference
that he should be *holden* of it	that he should be *held* by it	Acts 2:24
He had *holpen*	He was *helped*	Luke 1:54
where thou has not *strawed*	where you have not *scattered* seed	Matt. 25:24

they both were now *well stricken* in years	they were both *well-advanced* in years	Luke 1:7
I have *strived* to preach the gospel	I have *made it my aim* to preach the gospel	Rom. 15:20

Similarly, note the antiquated future passive:

KJV	NKJV	Reference
and shall be . . . *spitted* on	and will be . . . *spit upon*	Luke 18:32

As was customary in sixteenth-century English, the KJV uses the verb *be* as an auxiliary for the formation of the perfect tense of a number of intransitive verbs. Current English uses the verb *have* as an auxiliary to form the perfect tense of both transitive and intransitive verbs. The NKJV has changed the old version to correspond with this more recent practice (see Matt. 2:2, 13; 8:16, 29, 33; 9:28, 31; 11:20; 14:23, 34; 21:42; 26:20, 50, 55; Luke 13:25; John 10:10; Acts 1:6; 8:16; 12:18; 17:6; Heb. 12:2, et al.).

Relative Pronouns and the Indefinite Article

Noteworthy also is the substitution of *who* (and its correlatives) for *which* and *that* as relative pronouns when reference is made to a person. As in current usage, the NKJV also has the indefinite article *a* before words beginning with a consonant, but *an* before words beginning with a vowel. In the KJV *an* was also used before an aspirated *h* (Matt. 5:14; 8:30; 10:12; 13:8; 17:27; 26:30; Luke 1:69; 2:36; 6:48–49; 8:32; 21:18; John 10:12; 1 Cor. 6:15–16; Eph. 2:22; 1 Thess. 5:8; Heb. 4:15; 2 Peter 2:14; Rev. 11:9).

Vocabulary

Obsolete words. For the understanding of the message of the Bible the meaning of words is of far greater importance than the inflectional forms employed. Much of the vocabulary of the KJV is quite foreign to the average person today. The revisers of the NKJV have therefore endeavored to substitute modern equivalents for the obsolete or antiquated vocabulary of the older version. Some specific examples will indicate their success in achieving this objective. In the following examples the reading of the KJV is given first, followed by that of the NKJV:

Mark 1:30

and *anon* they tell him of her
and they told Him about her *at once*

Acts 9:26

he *assayed* to join himself to the disciples
he *tried* to join the disciples

Matthew 26:73

thy speech *bewrayeth* thee
your speech *betrays* you

Acts 21:15

And after those days *we took up our carriages*
And after those days *we packed*

Mark 6:25

I *will* that thou give me *by and by* in a *charger* the head of John the
    Baptist
"I *want* you to give me *at once* the head of John the Baptist on a
    platter."

Acts 28:13

And from thence *we fetched a compass,* and came to Rhegium
From there we *circled round* and reached Rhegium

Heb. 10:29

and hath *done despite* unto the Spirit of grace
and *insulted* the Spirit of grace

1 Peter 3:11

Let him *eschew* evil . . . ; let him seek peace, and *ensue* it
Let him *turn away* from evil . . . ' let him seek peace and *pursue* it

1 Peter 2:18

not only to the good and gentle, but also to the *froward*
not only to the good and gentle, but also to the *harsh*

Titus 1:9

by sound doctrine both to exhort and to convince the *gainsayers*
by sound doctrine, both to exhort and to convict those *who*
    contradict

Acts 8:3

and *haling* men and women committed them to prison
and *dragging* off men and women, committing them to prison

Matthew 18:8

it is better for thee to enter into life *halt* or maimed
it is better for you to enter into life *lame* or maimed

Acts 19:38

Let them *implead* one another
Let them *bring charges against* one another

1 Timothy 1:6

have turned aside unto vain *jangling*
have turned aside to idle *talk*

Matthew 17:12

but have done unto him whatsoever they *listed*
but did to him whatever they *wished*

Romans 16:2

she hath been a *succourer* of many
indeed she has been a *helper* of many

Matthew 7:13

Enter ye in at the *strait* gate
Enter by the *narrow* gate

Luke 17:9

I *trow* not
I *think* not

Acts 2:40

Save yourselves from this *untoward* generation
Be saved from this *perverse* generation

2 Corinthians 8:1

we *do you to wit* of the grace of God
we *make known to you* the grace of God

Acts 7:40

we *wot not* what is become of him
we *do not know* what has become of him

Words with new meanings. Even more confusing to the average person than the obsolete or antiquated vocabulary of the KJV are the numerous familiar words that have a different meaning in the older version than they have in common parlance today. Many words have either changed in meaning or have discarded some meanings they had some four hundred years ago. The following are examples of the substitution of other words in the new revision for those whose meanings are now different:

Revelation 17:6

and when I saw her I wondered with great *admiration*
And when I saw her, I marveled with great *amazement*

Luke 11:48

Truly ye bear witness that ye *allow* the deeds of your fathers
In fact, you bear witness that you approve the deeds of your fathers

Philippians 4:6

Be *careful* for nothing
Be *anxious* for nothing

Galatians 1:11

I *certify* you, brethren, that the gospel . . . is not after man
I *make known* to you, brethren, that the gospel . . . is not according
    to man

Matthew 19:1

and came into the *coasts* of Judea beyond Jordan
and came to the *region* of Judea beyond the Jordan

Romans 1:28

to do those things which are not *convenient*
to do those things which are not *fitting*

2 Peter 2:7

vexed with the filthy *conversation* of the wicked
who was *oppressed* with the filthy *conduct* of the wicked

Acts 19:19

Many of them also which used *curious arts* brought their books
Also, many of those who had *practiced magic* brought their books

Acts 17:23

as I passed by and beheld *your devotions*
as I was passing through and considering the *objects of your worship*

1 Peter 2:4

a living stone, *disallowed* indeed of men
a living stone, *rejected* indeed by men

Mark 8:3

for *divers* of them came from far
for *some* of them have come from afar

1 Thessalonians 5:14

comfort the *feebleminded*
comfort the *fainthearted*

Luke 7:42

he *frankly* forgave them both
he *freely* forgave them both

James 2:3

and ye have respect to him that weareth the *gay clothing*
and you pay attention to the one wearing the *fine clothes*

1 Peter 2:12

Having your *conversation honest* among the Gentiles
having your *conduct honorable* among the Gentiles

1 Thessalonians 4:12

That ye may walk *honestly* toward them that are without
that you may walk *properly* toward those who are outside

Luke 23:23

they were *instant* with loud voices
But they were *insistent*, demanding with loud voices

2 Thessalonians 2:7

only he who now *letteth* will *let* until he be taken out of the way
only He who now *restrains* will do so until He is taken out of the way

2 Corinthians 11:14

and no *marvel*
and no *wonder!*

1 Timothy 5:4

But if any widow have children or *nephews*
But if any widow has children or *grandchildren*

Acts 25:9

But Festus, *willing* to do the Jews a *pleasure*
But Festus, *wanting* to do the Jews a *favor*

Mark 2:4

they could not come nigh unto him for the *press*
they could not come near Him because of the *crowd*

Matthew 17:25

and when he was come into the house, Jesus *prevented* him, saying
and when he had come into the house, Jesus *anticipated* him, saying

1 Timothy 2:9

adorn themselves in modest apparel, with *shamefacedness* and
    sobriety
adorn themselves in modest apparel, with *propriety* and moderation

Matthew 3:15

Suffer it to be so now. . . . Then he *suffered* him
Permit it to be so now. . . . Then he *allowed* Him

Acts 17:22

I perceive that in all things ye are too *superstitious*
I perceive that in all things you are very *religious*

Philippians 3:21

who shall change our *vile* body
who will transform our *lowly* body

Matthew 10:19

take no thought how or what ye shall speak
do not worry about how or what you should speak

Luke 13:19

it grew, and *waxed* a great tree
it grew and *became* a large tree

Words that are modernized. To further illustrate the modernization in vocabulary, compare the NKJV rendering with that of the KJV in the following list. The rendering of a particular word may not always be consistent, but usually is throughout the New Testament.

KJV	NKJV
abide	stay
any man	anyone
barbarian	native
befall	happen
beseech	beg
bewail	weep
bottles	wineskins
brethren	brothers
candle	lamp
candlestick	lampstand
cast	throw
certain (pro.)	some
chamber	room
charity	love
cock	rooster
conceits	opinion
corn	grain
damnation	condemnation
damsel	girl
declare	explain
demand	ask
devil	demon
dumb person	mute
ears of corn	heads of grain
earthy	of dust
espouse	betroth

So Many Versions?

KJV	NKJV
evidently	clearly
forth	out
fowls	birds
give place	make room
glistering	glistening
God forbid	certainly not
good man	master
haply	perhaps
heady	headstrong
hell (grave)	hades
high minded	haughty
hire	wages
Holy Ghost	Holy Spirit
in no wise	by no means
interpret	translate
lucre	monetary gain
manner	kind
meat	food
motions	passions
napkin	handkerchief
naught	nothing
nigh	near
on this wise	in this way
particularly	in detail
passion	suffering
privily	secretly
quicken	give life
raiment	clothing
rend	tear
salute	greet
savour (vb)	be mindful
sepulchre	tomb
shamefacedness	propriety
ship	boat
shoe	sandal
smite	strike
straightly	sternly
straightway	immediately
tarry	stay
unto	to

KJV	NKJV
verily	assuredly
victuals	food
winked at	overlooked
whole	well
wrought	worked

The following is a list of sixty words, primarily conjunctions and adverbs, from the vocabulary of the KJV New Testament that have been discarded by the revisers. Many of these words are known to today's reader, but they do give an antique flavor to the KJV.

afore	howbeit	uttermost
aforehand	insomuch	whence
aforetime	notwithstanding	whensoever
albeit	peradventure	whereat
as concerning	thence	whereby
as pertaining	thenceforth	wherefore
as touching	thereabout	wherein
contrariwise	thereat	whereinsoever
forasmuch	therein	whereof
forsomuch	thereinto	wheresoever
forthwith	thereof	whereto
hence	thereon	whereunto
henceforth	thereout	whereupon
henceforward	thereto	wherewith
herein	thereunto	wherewithal
hereof	thereupon	whither
heretofore	therewith	whithersoever
hereunto	thither	withal
hither	thitherward	whosesoever
hitherto	unto	yonder

Correction of Prepositions. The NKJV is to be credited with correcting a number of misleading uses of prepositions in the KJV. The familiar "strain at a gnat" (Matt. 23:24), is generally regarded as simply a misprint for "strain out a gnat," as the revision gives it. "Make to yourselves friends *of* the mammon of unrighteousness" (Luke 16:9) is more accurately rendered:

"make friends for yourselves *by* unrighteous mammon."
"Nothing worthy of death is done *unto* him" (Luke 23:15) is
correctly given as "nothing worthy of death has been done *by*
Him." "*Against* the day of my burying hath she kept this" (John
12:7) becomes, "she has kept this *for* the day of My burial."
Paul's "I know nothing *by* myself" is better rendered, "I know
nothing *against* myself" (1 Cor. 4:4). "Without" in 2 Corinthians 10:13 has the archaic meaning of "beyond," and the
italicized "our" should be left out. Hence the rendering "We,
however, will not boast *beyond* measure" (so also in v. 15). The
preposition "of" formerly had several meanings not now current, among which is "by," as the new revision puts it (Luke
9:7–8, 22; 14:8).

Correction of translation. In the first printing of the revision, the
misleading translation of the verdict of the Sanhedrin with
reference to Jesus, "He is guilty of death" (Matt. 26:66) was
unfortunately retained. This has since been corrected to "He is
deserving of death," in agreement with the translation of the
same sentence in Mark 14:64.

Translation of idioms. It is also of interest to note how some of the
idioms in the kjv have been modernized in the new revision.
Note the following examples:

KJV	NKJV	Reference
cast the same in his teeth	reviled Him with the same thing	Matt 27:44
gave up the ghost	breathed his last	Acts 5:5
they held their peace	they kept silent	Luke 14:4
made their minds evil affected against	poisoned their minds against	Acts 14:2
had kept his bed	had been bedridden	Acts 9:33
would have set them at one again	tried to reconcile them	Acts 7:26
set at naught	rejected	Acts 4:11
many taken with palsies	many who were paralyzed	Acts 8:7
taken with diverse diseases and torments	afflicted with various diseases and torments	Matt. 4:24

to use them despitefully and to stone them	to abuse and stone them	Acts 14:5
spitefully entreated	insulted	Luke 18:32
cast a trench	build an embankment	Luke 19:43
thrust him from them	rejected	Acts 7:39

Changes in spelling. Changes in spelling include the American spelling of such words in the KJV as "armour" (Eph. 6:11, 13), "clamour" (Eph. 4:31), "favour" (Luke 2:52), "Saviour" (Luke 2:11), "sceptre" (Heb. 1:8), "theatre" (Acts 19:29, 31), "offence" (2 Cor. 6:3), "defence" (Acts 19:33), "pretence" (Phil. 1:18), "plough" (Luke 9:62), et al. Another departure from the KJV is in the capitalization of pronouns referring to Deity. The new edition has also brought consistency in the spelling of names, particularly between the Old Testament and the New: the Old Testament spelling has been adopted in the New Testament. Compare the following proper names in the NKJV with the KJV given in parentheses: Ahaz (Achaz), Balak (Balac), Elijah (Elias), Gomorrah (Gomorrha), Haran (Charron), Hezekiah (Ezekias), Hosea (Osee), Immanuel (Emmanuel), Isaiah (Esaias), Jehoshaphat (Josaphat), Jephtha (Jephthae), Jeremiah (Jeremias, Jeremy), Jonah (Jonas), Josiah (Josias), Judah (Judas), Manasseh (Manasses), Melchizedek (Melchisedic), Messiah (Messias), Noah (Noe), Phares (Perez), Rahab (Rachab), Ramah (Rama), Rehoboam (Roboam), Shechem (Sychem), Sinai (Sina), Uriah (Urias).

Vocabulary difficulties that remain. While in general the revisers of the NKJV have done well in modernizing the English of the KJV, occasionally words were retained that do not convey the sense of the original to modern readers. According to a brochure advertising the revision, "No word has been changed unless that change genuinely improves the understanding of God's Word for our time." This conservative attitude, commendable as it may be, has at times resulted in the retention of words which, though in use today, have a different connotation than they had in the sixteenth and early seventeenth centuries.

A few examples will illustrate this tendency. "Possess" once had the meaning of obtain or come into possession of. Hence to

So Many Versions?

retain the translation, "I give tithes of all that I possess" (Luke
18:12), does not give the correct meaning. Tithe was not paid on
what one owned, but on what one acquired or gained. Similarly, "possess" in 1 Thessalonians 4:4 should most likely be
translated "procure." The crucial problem in understanding the
verse is the meaning of "his own vessel." Translators continue
to divide themselves into those who understand the phrase to
refer to one's own body, on the one hand, or to "his own wife"
on the other. The primary meaning of the Greek verb, acquire,
obtain, suggests the second option. "Possess" would suggest
the former. In Matthew 6:30 (and Luke 12:28) "thrown into the
oven," would be better translated as "thrown into the furnace."
"Prevail," used in the first printing of the new revision in the
clause "when Pilate saw that he could not prevail at all" (Matt.
27:24) has the antiquated meaning of "avail." Fortunately, the
translation now reads "was accomplishing nothing." "Admired" in 2 Thessalonians 1:10, has also now more accurately
been rendered as "marveled at." "Sulphur" is more understandable today than "brimstone," formerly a common vernacular term (Luke 17:29; Rev. 9:17–18; 14:10; 20:10; 21:8, et
al.). In Matt. 3:12 (and Luke 3:17), "fork" or "shovel" would be
more meaningful today than "fan," and "clean out" would be
better than "purge." In 1 Timothy 1:12, a better rendering of
"who has enabled me" would be "who has strengthened me."
"Innocent" would be preferable to "simple" in Romans 16:19.
The best Greek lexicons indicate that the Greek adverb for "dis-
orderly" in 2 Thessalonians 3:6–7, 11 really means "in idle-
ness." Rather than "did I do it lightly?" in 2 Corinthians 1:17,
Paul means "was I vacillating?" or, "was I fickle?" In Titus 3:8,
the thought of "I want you to affirm constantly" would be better
expressed by "I want you to insist on." In 1 Timothy 4:15, the
new revision correctly substituted "your progress" for "thy
profiting." It should also have substituted "practice" for
"meditate upon." A better rendering than "wholesome" in
1 Timothy 6:3 would be "sound" as in 1 Timothy 1:3. "Deserving of death" in Luke 23:15 would be better than "worthy of
death" since "worthy" implies worth or merit. In Matthew 22:6,
"disgracefully" would be preferable to "spitefully." In spite of

the sacred associations connoted by "Calvary" (Luke 23:33), it is not a geographical name in the vicinity of Jerusalem, but an anglicized form of the Latin translation of the Greek word for "skull" that, in turn, is a translation of the Aramaic "Golgotha." These examples show the difficulty the revisers had in trying to preserve as much of the old as possible while at the same time making it meaningful today. Further improvements will no doubt be made in the wording as time goes on.

THE TEXTUAL QUESTION

The New Testament of the NKJV, like its classic predecessor, is based on the Greek text known as the Textus Receptus (TR). That this text is a crucial matter with the revisers is indicated by the "Introduction" to the new revision that clearly states:

> Of greater importance than the beauty of language in the King James Version is the textual base from which the work was translated. The New Testament of the New King James Bible is a useful and accurate revision, based on the traditional Greek text underlying the 1611 edition of the English Bible. (p. v)

This does not mean that the revisers of the New Testament are necessarily convinced that the TR is the best Greek text available. It was done, it appears, to placate those who hold that the KJV is *the* Bible, and hence the Greek text on which it is based must of necessity be the correct text.

Dr. Alfred Martin formerly of the Moody Bible Institute, a member of the New Testament Executive Review Committee of the revision, has said:

> Those of us who hold to the Traditional or Majority Text prefer the King James Version because of the textual base from which it is translated. It follows the *Textus Receptus* (Received Text), a term used to describe a consensus of several of the earliest printed editions of the New Testament, which have been based on manuscripts of the majority text. (Alfred Martin, *The New King James Bible New Testament: Monograph 2* [Nashville: Thomas Nelson, 1979])

This statement must not be understood as implying that the "Traditional or Majority Text" and the Textus Receptus are identical. Although these two texts have much in common the TR is a late and somewhat corrupt form of the "Traditional Text" or "Majority Text." The TR and Majority Text, however, differ markedly from the critical text, as we will see later.

The Textus Receptus and the New King James Version

The printed editions used by the famous forty-seven scholars who produced the KJV were, according to the best evidence available, Theodore de Beza's fourth edition of 1598, and Robert Stephanus's fourth edition of 1551. Both of these were revisions of the editions of Desiderius Erasmus of Rotterdam who edited the first Greek text to be published in Basel by Johannes Froben in 1516. In editing his New Testament, Erasmus, of course, could only use the manuscripts that were available to him. He used less than half a dozen, and these were from the late Middle Ages. Unfortunately, the later editors who had access to many more manuscripts retained many of Erasmus's errors.

Dr. Martin concedes: "We admit that the Textus Receptus is a somewhat corrupt form of the traditional type of text." But if such corruptions exist and can be identified, one would expect that in the interest of sacred truth they would be removed from the Greek text before it is translated into English! Some of the corruptions in the TR are not difficult to discover. The warning not to subtract anything from the last book of the New Testament ends with the threat according to the NKJV:

Revelation 22:19

God will take away his part from the book of life, from the holy city, and from the things which are written in this book.

A footnote in the latest printing calls attention to the reading "tree of life" rather than "book of life." This variant reading is supported not only by the majority of Greek manuscripts, but, so far as is known, by all the Greek manuscripts. From what source, then, did the reading "from the book of life" come? It is a well-known fact that when Erasmus edited his Greek NT he had access to only one manuscript (1_r) for the Book of Revelation. Unfortunately, the last page of that manuscript, containing the last six verses, was missing. In order to supply this missing part he retranslated these six verses from the Latin Vulgate into Greek. Evidently his Latin manuscript, or manuscripts, read *libro* ("book") rather than *ligno* ("tree").

Similarly, in Revelation 15:3 the TR follows a reading that has practically no support in Greek manuscripts for the title "King of saints!" The Greek manuscripts are about equally divided between the readings *nations* or *ages*. Though two Greek manuscripts (296, 2049) read "saints" they were not available in the sixteenth or seventeenth centuries when the TR was published. The reading of the TR, therefore, according to Dr. Metzger, "appears to have arisen from confusion of the Latin compendia for *sanctorum (sctorum)* and *saeculum (sclorum),* 'i.e., ages'" (Bruce M. Metzger, A Textual Commentary on the Greek New Testament, [New York: United Bible Society, 1971] pp. 755f.).

But examples can be given where more than a word is involved. The TR text of Acts 9:5–6 contains two entire sentences not found in Greek manuscripts. The NKJV renders them:

> "*It is* hard for you to kick against the goads."
> So he, trembling and astonished said,
> "Lord, what do you want me to do?"

These two sentences evidently came from the Latin Vulgate. Most textual scholars regard them as an insertion in Acts 9 from the accounts in chapters 22 and 26 (see 22:10; 26:14). In any case, their presence in Acts 9 is due to their translation into Greek by Erasmus and their insertion by him into his first edition of the Greek New Testament.

In the original printing of the NKJV, the famous Trinitarian passage in 1 John 5:7–8a had the only textual footnote—one that advised the reader that these words "are from the Latin Bible, although three Greek mss. from the fifteenth century and later also contain them" (the note has since been revised to read "four or five very late Greek manuscripts. . . ."). It is well known that the first and second editions of Erasmus's Greek New Testament lacked this passage because he did not find it in any Greek manuscripts available to him. He was so certain that it was a recent addition to the text that when he was criticized for not including it he promised to insert it in his next edition if anyone could produce a single manuscript that contained it. Such a manuscript (Codex Montfortianus, #61 of the sixteenth century) was finally shown him in England, and he kept his promise in his third edition of 1522. But this passage clearly had no place in the autograph of John's first epistle. The above are examples of corruption that have crept into the TR Greek text.

The brochure advertising this revision gives as the purpose of the project "to preserve and improve the purity of the King James Version." To improve the purity would surely include the removal from the text of any scribal additions that were not a part of the autographs. No devout reader of the Bible wants any portion of the sacred text as penned by the original authors removed. But neither should he want later additions, which in some passages have crept into the text, published as part of the Word of God.

The Critical Text Notes of the NKJV

One redeeming feature has been added since the original printing of the NKJV New Testament in 1979: the addition of more than 880 textual notes. For the most part, these textual notes call attention to variant readings adopted by a current critical text, and/or variants supported by the majority of Greek manuscripts. The critical text chosen is designated "NU-Text," the "N" standing for the twenty-sixth edition of the Nestle-Aland, *Novum Testamentum Graece* published in 1979, and the "U" referring to the third edition of *The Greek New Testament* published by the United Bible Societies in 1975. These two are cited together since their Greek text is now practically identical. For the readings of the majority of the Greek manuscripts, designated "M-Text," use was made of the product of many years of work on Greek manuscripts by Dr. Zane Hodges, assisted by Dr. Arthur Farstad et al. This majority text was published in 1982 by Thomas Nelson Publishers.

A few passages in the "NU-Text" are enclosed in double, square brackets to indicate that they "are regarded as later additions to the text, but that are of evident antiquity and importance" (*The Greek New Testament*, "Introduction," p. xlvii).

One of the two longest of the double-bracketed passages is the so called longer ending of Mark, Mark 16:9–20. The textual note regarding the ending in the NKJV does not mention the "NU-Text" but affirms: "Verses 9–20 are bracketed in most critical texts. They are lacking in *Codex Sinaiticus* and *Codex Vaticanus*, although nearly all other manuscripts of Mark contain them." No mention is made of the fact that many of the manuscripts that include the passage contain scribal notes stating that older Greek copies lack it, or of others that mark it with asterisks or obeli expressing doubts about its genuineness as part of Mark. Nor is there any indication that in manuscripts of several ancient versions the passage is missing, and that Eusebius and Jerome witness that it was lacking in most of the Greek copies of Mark known to them. The NU-Text, in addition to having the longer ending of Mark in double brackets, also contains the shorter ending, also in double brackets.

The other major passage double-bracketed in the NU-Text is the pericope of the adulteress, John 7:53–8:11. A note in the NKJV asserts that the words of this passage "are lacking in some ancient manuscripts. They are present in over nine hundred." There is no indication given that the passage is found in varying places in various manuscripts: after John 7:36; after 7:44; after 21:25; or even after Luke 21:38, or that in many manuscripts where it is found it is marked with asterisks or obeli to indicate the doubt scribes had regarding its status. Nor is the evidence from early versions included. While this story, as Metzger states, "has all the earmarks of veracity" this does not necessarily mean that it belongs to John after 7:52. And while it may be found in "over nine hundred manuscripts" the number is not significant to those who hold to the principle set forth by J. J. Wettstein, in the middle of the eighteenth century, that manuscripts should be weighed rather than counted; in other words, quality of manuscript is more important than quantity.

Two briefer passages in Luke are also double-bracketed in the NU-Text: Luke 22:43–44 and 23:34a. Notes in the NKJV simply state: "NU brackets. . . ."

No system has been devised in the NKJV to indicate in English those words in the NU-Text that are placed in single square brackets because their "presence of position in the text is regarded as disputed" (*The Greek New Testament*, "Introduction," p. xlvii). For example, a note to Matthew 27:16 states that the name of the famous criminal Pilate presented to the people, according to the NU-Text, was *Jesus Barabbas*. There is no way for the ordinary reader to know that *Jesus* is printed in single double brackets to indicate that the presence of this name in the text is debatable. The same is true of verse 17 where the NU-Text reads, "Whom do you want me to release to you? Jesus Barabbas or Jesus who is called Christ?" The NU-Text includes Matthew 12:47 in single square brackets. The same is true of Matthew 16:2b–3. In Mark 3:14 the NU-Text, after "Then He appointed twelve," adds, with many Greek manuscripts, "whom He also named apostles," but because of the possibility that the clause could be an interpolation from Luke 3:14 it is enclosed in single brackets. In the NU-Text, Mark 3:16 begins with the words enclosed in single brackets, "and he appointed the twelve," which are not noted in the NKJV. "In Ephesus" in the NU-Text is likewise single bracketed in Ephesians 1:1. Other words in single brackets in the NU-Text include "the Son of God" (Mark 1:1), "and a rooster crowed" (Mark 14:68), and "who had spent all her livelihood on physicians" (Luke 8:43).

It is too much to expect that the NKJV would have notes to all the passages where the NU-Text differs from the TR. Most of the significant variants are noted. The fact that there is no note to Luke 17:36, which the NU-Text omits, is no doubt an oversight. The NU-Text omits the phrase "and was carried up into heaven" in Luke 24:51. In John 16:16 this text also omits the clause "because I go to the Father." Neither of these is noted. There are many other interesting variants not adopted by the NU-Text, some of which are found in manuscripts of the "Western" tradition, but most of which cannot seriously claim to be the reading of the original. There are sufficient notes to open the eyes of the careful reader to some of the defects of the TR, particularly when it departs from the "M-Text," and this is a gain.

Evaluating the Greek Text of the NKJV

A study of the NU-Text makes it clear that the Greek text behind the NKJV differs from that found in the majority of the manuscripts some 315 times. This means that although the Received Text has a closer affinity with the majority text than with one of the other two or three text types represented by the Greek manuscripts, it is not identical with it.

The NKJV is the only recent translation of prominence that is based on the Received Text rather than on one form or another of a modern critical text. A critical text is a reconstruction by textual scholars applying critical principles and methods, gradually developed during the past century and a half, to the sources: the Greek manuscripts, the early versions, and the quotations of the NT in early Christian writers. The present-day proponents of the "majority text" theory deny the validity of these methods, and advocate that the true method to determine the original text is by following the reading of the majority of the Greek manuscripts. Since the Western church followed the Latin Vulgate from the time of Jerome (c. A.D. 340–420) it is not surprising that the majority of Greek manuscripts should be found in the Greek-speaking Eastern church, where the Bible they were using would be repeatedly copied over the course of centuries. But the majority of the Greek manuscripts were produced in the Eastern church between the tenth and fifteenth centuries, and so the majority text results in a text of the late Middle Ages—the working Bible of the Eastern church, not the text of the early church.

In order to understand and appreciate the problem of determining the exact wording of the New Testament a few well-known facts must be reviewed. The first is that the autographs of all the books of the New Testament have disappeared. The term "autograph" is used to designate the original manuscripts produced by the authors of the various documents. All of these have perished, probably by being handled and read until they fell to pieces. The second fact to remember is that before the invention of printing, around 1455, every copy of every book had to be laboriously produced separately by hand. That is why these copies are called "manuscripts," meaning "written by hand." Fortunately, before the autographs of the New Testament disappeared they were copied, and these copies in turn became exemplars or models for other copies, and so on. This process of copying and recopying was constantly repeated until the printing press supplanted the scribe. It is well to recognize also that it is practically impossible for any scribe to copy perfectly a handwritten document. This is especially true when the copying is done by an untrained scribe, as most probably happened in the earliest days of the Christian church. The textual student who examines the manuscripts will never find one free from errors, no matter how carefully it was written. Also, no two manuscripts are ever exactly alike. Errors once made were reproduced as fresh copies of the faulty manuscripts were written, and new errors were added by the copyist. Hence the more copyings that intervene between a given manuscript and the autographs the more errors it will have. For this reason the majority of textual scholars hold that the earliest manuscripts are apt to have far less errors than those copies in the late Middle Ages. But it must be understood that the important point is not the time of the writing of the manuscripts, but the age of the text it contains, which is determined by the exemplar copied; or to put it another way, the less copying that intervenes between it and the autograph the better the copy.[2]

In addition to the accidental and unintentional changes in wording of various kinds that crept into the text, well-intentioned scribes also made deliberate changes by attempting to correct supposed errors made by previous scribes. These changes consisted in grammatical and stylistic improvements, the clearing up of historical difficulties and the removal of obscurities. They also tended to harmonize the wording of parallel passages to make them agree, particularly in the Gospels and between biblical quotations in the NT and the OT text. Some scribes also changed the text to agree with the church

---

[2]For detailed information on the whole subject of the transmission of the New Testament and its modern reconstruction, consult Bruce M. Metzger, *The Text of the New Testament*, 2nd ed. (New York and Oxford, 1968), and his *A Textual Commentary on the Greek New Testament* (London and New York: United Bible Societies, 1971).

liturgy, even occasionally inserting simple explanatory glosses or writing notes in the margin that a later scribe sometimes copied into the text.

The various copies of the NT, each one with its own peculiar variants, were carried to various lands and cities. Some of the major cities of the Mediterranean world where the church had gained a strong Christian community became centers from which missionaries with the New Testament in their hands went forth to spread the faith in the surrounding areas. This would be true of such cities as Alexandria, Antioch, Constantinople, Carthage, and Rome. The copy of copies of the New Testament in such centers became the exemplars from which other copies were made for the surrounding territory. There thus developed various families of manuscripts, often called "local" texts, each of which was characterized by a common group of variants. In some of these centers, most probably, efforts were made to standardize the text. Hence there developed four major types of text, generally designated as: the Alexandrian in Egypt; the Western in Italy, Gaul, and North Africa (especially Carthage); the Caesarean in Egypt, Caesarea, Jerusalem, and Georgia; and the Byzantine in Antioch and Constantinople and the Byzantine Empire. Some scholars doubt that the Caesarean group of MSS are sufficiently homogeneous to be recognized as a text type.

The Byzantine text type is mentioned last because it is the latest of the four to be developed. In other words, the characteristic readings of this type are not found in the earliest Greek manuscripts, the earliest versions, or in the quotations made by the earliest Christian writers. By contrast, the Alexandrian type can be traced back to the second century. Among the Bodmer Papyri was a codex (P[75]), dated near the end of the second century or a bit later, that contains much of the Gospels of Luke and John in a form of text essentially the same as the parchment Codex Vaticanus (B), which has been the main witness to the Alexandrian text type. Another papyrus codex from the same collection (P[66]) of about the same date as P[75] or a trifle later also contains an Alexandrian text. The Western text can also be traced back to the second century, for it was used by Marcion (d.c. 160), Tatian (c. 160), Irenaeus (140–210), Tertullian (c. 150–248), and Cyprian (d. 258). The Old Latin versions from about the last quarter of the second century also bear witness to it, as do the Old Syriac Gospels from about the end of the second century or later. The Caesarean text seems to have originated in Egypt since the Chester Beatty Papyrus P[45] from the early third century reflects it. It was perhaps brought to Caesarea by Origen (c. 185–254). But the Byzantine type of text seems to have originated in Antioch and from there was taken to Constantinople from where it was dispersed throughout the Byzantine Empire. The Freer Codex (W) of the Gospels of the fourth and fifth century has this type of text in Matthew and Luke. It is also represented by Codex Alexandrinus (A) of the fifth century in the Gospels. Westcott and Hort called this type of text *Syrian;* von Soden used the designation *Koine;* Lake, the *Ecclesiastical* Text; and Ropes, the *Antiochian.* The Textus Receptus, or Received Text, is a late form of it.

In Western Europe the church increasingly used the Latin Bible, the old form of which dates back to c. 200. About 382 Pope Damasus requested Jerome to revise it. The result was the Latin Vulgate that served Western Christianity until the sixteenth century and still has an official status in Roman Catholicism. Knowledge of the Greek New Testament and of the Greek classics almost completely died out in the West, hence from the seventh century on the Greek New Testament was transmitted only in the Greek church. Thus while the Eastern church had as its Bible the Byzantine text, the West had a Bible based on the Western text. Far more copies, approximately eight thousand, are extant of the Vulgate than the Bible of the Eastern church—a fact ignored by the advocates of the majority text.

Recent proponents of the traditional text hold the theory that where variations occur the true reading is to be obtained by consulting the majority of the manuscripts. These two viewpoints amount to the same thing and reflect the views vigorously advocated in the nineteenth century by John W. Burgon, Dean of Chichester in England and his "literary executor," Edward Miller. Burgon's argument was based on the theological premise he had earlier set forth from the pulpit of the Oxford University Church that not only every book, chapter, and verse of the Bible "is the direct utterance of the Most High" but even every word, syllable, and letter. From this presupposition he was led to the conclusion that God would not allow his word to become corrupted down through the centuries. He must therefore have guided the church in the selection of the proper text, and also in the elimination from it of any errors which had crept in from earlier times. Hence, since the church had used the traditional form of the text from the fourth to nineteenth centuries, that text must be substantially correct.

But such a conclusion would require us to interpret "the church" as meaning the Eastern Orthodox Church, which has no more claim to this status than the church in the West. Furthermore, there is no evidence that the Eastern church ever made a conscious choice of the Byzantine type of text or even gave consideration to the matter of what text to use at all. Whatever choice was made was informal, gradual, and by default because of the absence of other types of Greek manuscripts.

To have validity, this theory would also require that the text of the majority be transmitted in absolute purity from its origin. But this is not the case. While the general characteristics of the Byzantine text were faithfully transmitted through the centuries from the fourth century on, a great deal of variation and development has taken place. We may well cling to the belief that God had guided in the transmission of the New Testament to the extent that the gospel of salvation through Jesus Christ has been faithfully preserved. But this is true of all the manuscripts no matter what their text type may be. Although there are variants in them that have a bearing on Christian belief, no doctrine of the Christian faith hinges on a disputed reading. We can be thankful that this is so.

Finally, with regard to the vast majority of the actual words in the New Testament there is no question. The debate concerns a relatively small portion of the total text of the New Testament.[3]

---

[3]For both sides of the recent debate on the Critical Greek Text versus the Majority Text consult works listed in the Bibliography.

THE FORMAT OF THE NKJV

Page Style

Unfortunately, the NKJV has followed the KJV in printing the numbered verses as separate units, rather than arranging the text in paragraphs. There are sectional headings that break up the text into larger units designated "Paragraph headings" in the "Introduction." Perhaps a more satisfactory designation would be "Pericope headings," for many of these sections are very long as paragraphs. Several contain twenty verses or more, and one consists of thirty-six verses (Matt. 23:1–36). "The Genealogy of Jesus Christ," consisting of Matthew 1:1–17, naturally divides itself into three paragraphs: (1) Abraham to David, verses 1–6; (2) David to the Captivity, verses 7–11; and (3) the Captivity to Christ, verses 12–17. Many other sections could appropriately be subdivided into paragraphs.

The text is arranged in two columns per page. A clear, easy-to-read typeface is used. For ease in identification, quotations from the Old Testament are printed in an oblique typeface. In the 1979 printing of the New Testament, no use was made of italics to indicate words for which there were no exact equivalents in the original but that have been added to make the translation conform to English idiom. But the translators and editors have since yielded to popular pressure by going back to the system of printing such words in italics. This system seems to rest on the false assumption that for every word in the original there is an equivalent in English, and that the ideal translation is a literal word-for-word rendering.

Use of Italics

Interpretive words that have been added to the translation need to be indicated in some way. But the use of italics for this purpose can be very confusing since this kind of type is often used to call special attention to something the author wishes to emphasize. Some of the interpretive words in the KJV have been dropped or modified in the NKJV because of a different understanding of the meaning of the Greek. Instead of rendering Hebrews 2:16, "For verily he took not *on him the nature* of angels; but he took on him the seed of Abraham," the NKJV has "For indeed he does not give aid to angels, but He gives aid to the seed of Abraham." In 1 Peter 5:3, the KJV has, "Neither as being lords over *God's* heritage . . . ," whereas the new revision reads, "Nor as being lords over those entrusted to you." The KJV rendering of 1 Peter 5:13, "The *church that* is at Babylon . . . saluteth you," has been revised to read, "She who is in Babylon . . . greets you." In 1 John 3:16a the KJV has, "Hereby perceive we the love *of God,* because he laid down his life for us." The NKJV omits the supplied words, "of God," because they are not necessary. The meaning is rather, "By this we know love," in the absolute sense, "because He laid down his life for us." There is no need to add *"God"* as the object in Acts 7:59 for Stephen is addressing Jesus Christ, not God the Father. A more probable translation of Colossians 1:19 would be, "all the fulness (of deity) was pleased to dwell in Him," making unnecessary the insertion of *"the Father"* as subject.

In a few passages, the missing concluding clause of a conditional sentence (the apodosis) is supplied in italics. An example is the insertion of *"well"* as the implied conclusion to the conditional clause, "If it bears fruit," in Luke 13:9. In Matthew 15:6, *"is released* from honoring . . ."* is a free rendering of the Greek (cf. Mark 7:11). The insertion of "that day will not come" in 2 Thessalonians 2:3 goes back to the Geneva Bible as compared to Tyndale's, "for the Lord commeth not."

Luke 1:64 illustrates the insertion of an italicized word to clear up a special type of ellipsis known as zeugma, in which one verb is used with two subjects (or objects) but is suitable only for one. The verb "opened" suites "mouth" but not "tongue," hence the verb "loosed" is supplied with the resulting translation, "Immediately his mouth was opened and his tongue loosed. . . ." In 1 Corinthians 3:2, a similar difficulty is solved by translating the verb, properly meaning "I gave to drink," as "I fed." The zeugma of 1 Timothy 4:3 is solved by the insertion of a second participle, "and commanding," with the resulting, "forbidding to marry, *and commanding* to abstain from foods which God created to be received . . ." (see also Acts 14:22 and 1 Cor. 14:34).

But the majority of the italicized words in both the KJV and the NKJV are trivial in nature, and in a large percentage of the cases there is room for a difference of opinion as to whether they are actually added words, or whether they are really inherent in the original. In both Hebrew and Greek, there is very frequently an ellipsis of the copulative verb "to be." When this verb is inserted in the English translation, should it be italicized as though the translator had added it? Or, should it be regarded as implicit in the original?

In the Greek New Testament, one of the ways of expressing the idea of possession is by the dative case with the verb "to be." This idiom is preserved in the familiar English translation of Luke 2:7, "because there was no room for them in the inn," meaning, "they had no place in the inn." This idiom is very common in giving the name of a person or a place. According to Mark 5:9, NKJV, Jesus asked a demon, "What is your name?", literally, "what name to you?" The reply was, "My name *is* Legion," literally "Name to me Legion." In both cases, as is usually the case, the copula is understood but not expressed. English idiom requires the use of the copula. Should it then be italicized as though the translator had added it? None of the versions that follow the practice of using italics for supplied words is entirely consistent. The NKJV usually italicizes the copula, as in the examples above, and others (see Luke 1:5, 27b; John 1:6; Acts 13:6; Rev. 9:11). But in a number of passages the copula is not italicized (Mark 14:32; Luke 1:27a; 2:25; 24:18; Rev. 6:8; 8:11). Which is really correct?

In John 14:10 the Greek lacks the copula in the clause, "that I am in the Father," but the NKJV does not italicize the "am." However, in the identical clause in verse 11 "am" is in italics. The copula is lacking in the Greek of both occurrences of the clause, "I am the Alpha and the Omega" (Rev. 21:6; 22:13) but in neither case is it italicized in the NKJV. This is also true of "are" in Philippians 3:15, and "is" in Romans 1:15. In ascriptions of praise to God, the supplied copula is usually italicized (1 Cor. 15:57; 2 Cor. 8:16; 9:15; Gal. 1:15; Eph. 3:20–21; 1 Tim. 1:17; 1 Peter 5:10–11; Jude 24–25; Rev. 1:5–6; 5:13b; 7:12). But the last part of 1 Peter 4:11 is an exception, "that in all things

God may be glorified through Jesus Christ, to whom belong the glory and the dominion forever and ever. Amen" (no italics). "Therefore it was necessary," in Hebrews 9:23, has "it was" in italics, but in a similar expression in 9:16, "there must also of necessity be" no word is italicized. In Romans 3:1, "What advantage has the Jew, or what *is* the profit of the circumcision?", "has" is just as truly added as is *"is,"* yet the latter alone is italicized. Similarly, in 2 Corinthians 6:14 one would expect "has" to be italicized in both clauses: "For what fellowship has righteousness with lawlessness and what communion has light with darkness?"

The Greek article is often sufficient to indicate the idea of possession. When, in such cases, the article is translated as a possessive pronoun should the pronoun be italicized? Like the KJV the new revision often does (see Matt. 4:20; 8:3; 27:24; Mark 10:16; Luke 13:13; 18:13; John 11:41; Acts 16:33; 21:24; 2 Cor. 10:10), but quite often it is not italicized (see Mark 5:23; 6:5 [1979 ed.]; 7:32; 8;23; 14:47; Acts 21:40 [1979 ed.]; 1 Cor. 12:18; Col. 3:19). Which is correct?

Greek is a highly inflected language in which the article with an adjective modifying some well-known noun may stand alone with an ellipsis of the noun itself, particularly when the context makes it evident what noun is understood. In such cases when the translator supplies the missing word is he really adding something to the text, and should that word therefore be italicized? A common word such as "day" is often understood but is normally italicized in the NKJV and in the old (see Matt. 28:1; Mark 16:2, 9; Luke 13:32–33; 24:1; John 20:1, 19; Acts 20:7; 27:19; 1 Cor. 16:2). In such titles of Jesus as "the Holy and Just One," "One" is not italicized (Mark 1:24; Acts 3:14; 7:52; 22:14). Nor is "man" italicized in such expressions as "a righteous man" (Rom. 5:7; 1 Tim. 1:9; James 5:16; 2 Peter 2:8), but in the plural one finds "Righteous *men*" in Matthew 13:17. No italics are used for "the young women" in Titus 2:4, "the poor man" in James 2:6, or for "your left hand" or "your right hand" in Matthew 6:3. But in Luke 17:34, 36 and Matthew 24:40–41, one finds "two *men*" and "two *women*." In some passages it is not certain whether the adjective "evil" is masculine or neuter. In

Matthew 5:37 the NKJV has opted for the masculine, "For what-ever is more than these is from the evil one," with no italics. Verse 39 is correctly rendered, "But I tell you not to resist an evil person," with no italics. The last petition in "the Lord's Prayer" also opts for the masculine, "But deliver us from the evil one" (no italics) (Matt. 6:13; Luke 11:4). The masculine is also chosen in John 17:15, but "one" is in italics, "that you should keep them from the evil *one*." (cf. 1 John 5:19). For some strange rea-son the NKJV follows the KJV in italicizing "man" in Luke 10:30 even though the Greek has the equivalent noun (cf. Luke 15:30). "Things" in 1 Corinthians 9:22 is not italicized as "men" is, though both are supplied. "Man," "men," and "women" are all supplied in 1 Timothy 5:1-2, but are not italicized. A very striking inconsistency in italicizing words is in Luke 17. Verse 27 reads "and destroyed them all." In verse 29 the very same words are rendered "and destroyed *them* all."

There are problems also in the translation of tenses. Grammarians recognize that the present tense may be used for an action attempted, but not actually completed. An example is found in Galatians 5:4, which the NKJV translated, "You who *attempt* to be justified by law." In such a conative or tendential use of the tense should "attempt" be italicized as though the translator were adding it? This lack of fulfillment should also have been recognized in John 10:32; Acts 26:28; Romans 2:4; and Galatians 6:12. The imperfect tense is similarly used of the past, as in Luke 1:69, "they would have called him" (with no italics); Matthew 3:14, "and John *tried* to prevent him" (note italics, and compare Acts 7:26). This tense usage should have been recognized in Mark 9:28; 15:23; Acts 18:4; and 26:11. The aorist tense of Revelation 2:8 is correctly interpreted as an in-gressive, hence the translation "who was dead, and came to life" (no italics). The durative force of the present tense is brought out in 1 John 3:9, "he cannot continue sinning" (no italics). The perfect tense can well mean *"standing* open" as in Revelation 4:1, but why the italics? And why is *"were"* italicized in Revelation 7:5–8?

Sufficient illustrations have been given to show that it is very difficult to carry out the ideal of italicizing "supplied" words accurately and consistently. None of the English versions have been able to achieve this desirable goal. For this reason and others, most recent English versions have abandoned the attempt, laudable as the system may be.

CONCLUSION

In conclusion to this long chapter, let it be said that the NKJV is a diligent attempt by a large group of committed and competent biblical scholars to produce an English Bible that retains as much of the classic KJV as possible, while at the same time bringing its English up-to-date. This is a difficult objective to achieve. It may well meet the religious needs of those Christians who sincerely believe that the KJV is *the* English Bible, but at the same time find its antiquated vocabulary and grammatical structure a handicap to understanding the message the Bible carries. Time alone can tell how well the new version will be used and accepted. It may be that many people who are familiar with the KJV, and have read it during their religious lives and are familiar with its classic English, will feel that the "old wine" is better. Those who hold to the majority text will need to accommodate themselves to the many instances in which the NKJV follows the TR instead of the majority text. Defenders of the KJV will be pleased to have a clearer rendering of the TR, but may be unhappy to find notes referring to critical texts included in the Bible. On the other hand, there may be others who will feel that modernizing the KJV has not gone far enough. It seems evident that those who are seeking a completely modern version will not choose the NKJV, particularly those who are convinced that a version is no better than the original text on which it is based and a modern critical Greek New Testament based on the ancient manuscripts is to be preferred to the Textus Receptus. In any case, one can join with the publishers in the wish that God may use this version "for the blessing of many, as He has been pleased to use the beloved 1611 King James Version across the span of the centuries."

18

The Reader's Digest Bible

ITS BACKGROUND

In September 1982 The Reader's Digest Association published its 767-page condensation of the RSV of the Holy Bible, which is known as The Reader's Digest Bible (RDB). After several years of planning and experimentation, the formidable task of condensing the whole Bible was undertaken by a team of seven editors who were highly skilled in the techniques of condensation. In addition to their experience in condensing various kinds of literature, these editors were given special training in the application of Digest techniques to the sacred Scriptures. They were required to follow closely a fifty-page guide analyzing, describing, and giving examples of each facet of the techniques involved. The carrying out of this assignment required three years of diligent labor with meticulous attention to every word of the text. The work was supervised by Bruce M. Metzger, Professor of New Testament Language and Literature at Princeton Theological Seminary, one of America's best-known Bible scholars and the current chairman of the RSV committee, who was chosen as the General Editor of the Reader's Digest project. At the very outset it was decided that some well-known passages such as the Ten Commandments, the Twenty-third Psalm, the Lord's Prayer, and other familiar passages would remain untouched. The rest of the biblical text was significantly shortened by the use of methods and skills developed over more than half a century by Reader's Digest editors.

The Revised Standard Version was chosen as the basic text because of its wide usage, impeccable scholarship, established familiarity, and direct linkage with the King James Version, "a relationship that gives it a strong echo of the elevated and dignified tone cherished by so many generations" (preface, p. xi). The reader should be aware that for the New Testament, use was made of the Second Edition of 1971, which differs in some passages from earlier printings (see Matthew 12:1; 15:29; 17:20; Mark 3:21; 5:42; Luke 11:17; 22:29; 23:42; John 10:33; 16:8–11; 1 Corinthians 4:6; 7:26; 15:19; 16:12; 2 Corinthians 3:5, 6; 5:19). In the last three chapters of Luke some six verses given in footnotes of the RSV (2nd ed.) because their authenticity is debatable are incorporated in the text of the RDB (see Luke 22:43–44; 23:17; 24:5, 12, 36).

HISTORY OF SHORTENED BIBLES

A number of abridgments of the English Bible have been produced in the twentieth century. As early as 1909 J. M. Dent and Sons in London published The Shorter Bible, an abridgment and editing of the KJV, "designed for use in schools and home reading." The same title was given to another abbreviation of the Bible published in 1921 by Charles Scribner's Sons. It was translated and arranged by Charles Foster Kent "with the collaboration of Charles Cutler Torrey, Henry A. Sherman, Frederick Harris, and Ethel Cutler. In 1928 The Living Bible was published in New York by Alfred Knopf. Edgar Johnson Goodspeed made an abridgment of the Bible, An American Translation, which was published in 1933 by the University of Chicago Press as The Short Bible. In 1936 Simon and Schuster in New York published an arrangement and editing of the KJV (except for Proverbs, Job, Ecclesiastes, and Song of Songs, which were based on the ERV), known as The Bible Designed to be Read as Living Literature. Among its deletions were the whole of Chronicles, the "Minor Epistles," genealogies, repetitions, and passages regarded as "unimportant." The Dartmouth Bible was edited by Roy B. Chamberlain and Herman Feldman and published in 1950 by Houghton Mifflin Company of Boston. The length of the biblical text was cut approximately in half by the omission of "repetitions" and "material of interest only to technical students." A Shortened Version of the Modern Readers Bible, edited by Robert A. Ballou, was published as The Living Bible in 1952 by the Viking Press, New York. Also in 1952 the Olive Pell Bible, an abridgment of the KJV, was published by the Exposition Press in New York. In 1955 another abridged edition known as the Compact Bible was published by Hawthorne Books, Inc., of New York.

The RDB differs from these earlier abridgments. The goal of the Digest editors was to produce "a text significantly shortened and clarified, yet which retains all sixty-six books, carefully preserves every incident, personality and teaching of substance; and keeps, as well, the true essence and flavor of the language" (preface, p. ix). The Digest has drawn a basic distinction between abridgment and condensation. Abridgment reduces the length of the text by eliminating sizeable sections of books. "Condensation concerns itself with every individual word of the text, every phrase, sentence, paragraph, and chapter, as well as the larger portions or blocks of text, in relation both to the immediate context and to the whole" (preface, p. ix).

CATEGORIES OF DELETIONS

The extent that nonessential words are pruned from the text varies from book to book, and the amount of condensation of each book was determined by the character of the book itself. The final result is that the OT was cut by about fifty percent, and the NT by about twenty-five percent. With the exception of the brief epistles of Philemon, 2 John, 3 John, and Jude, every book of the Bible was condensed to a greater or lesser degree.

This shortening process was never haphazard, but followed definite, predetermined guidelines. Deletions, whether long or short, belong to three well-defined categories, though it may be difficult for one not trained in Digest techniques to identify with certainty the category to which a deletion in a given passage belongs. As a matter of fact, in a single passage one or more deletions may belong to one category, and another to a different one. But whatever the category, the reader should know that extreme care was taken to preserve the basic teaching of the passage, as well as its essential literary character.

Repetition

The first of the three categories of deletion is repetition, whether it be of the same words or phrases, or of the same idea stated in different words. "The device of repetition—in word, thought and incident," the preface points out, was a practice "favored in ancient times." Today, however, it tends "to confuse and exhaust the reader's attention." Hence, repetitions are often deleted. Under repetitions are included tautology, the unnecessary repetition of a word, a statement, or an idea.

A good example of condensation where the category of repetition accounts for most of the deletions can be seen by comparing the RDB condensation with the full text of the RSV in Daniel 5:2–3 (RDB 470). The setting is a huge banquet given by King Belshazzar in the midst of which he

RSV	RDB
. . . commanded that the vessels of gold and of silver which Nebuchadnezzar his father had taken out of the temple in Jerusalem be brought, that the king and his lords, his wives, and his concubines might drink from them. Then they brought in the golden and silver vessels which had been taken out of the temple, the house of God in Jerusalem; and the king and his lords, his wives, and his concubines drank from them. . . .	. . . commanded that the vessels of gold and of silver which had been taken out of the temple in Jerusalem be brought. Then the king and his lords, his wives, and his concubines drank from them . . .

The seventy-five word account as found in the RSV has been condensed by more than half to thirty-five words. In addition to deletions due to repetition, the omission of the historical reference to Nebuchadnezzar's seizure of the gold and silver vessels is probably due to its lessened immediate relevancy.

The deletion of some thirty words from the RSV text of Matthew 15:29–31 is also mainly due to repetition:

RSV	RDB
And Jesus went on from there and passed along the Sea of Galilee. And he went up on the mountain, and sat down there. And great crowds came to him, bringing with them the lame, the maimed, the blind, the dumb, and many others, and they put them at his feet, and he healed them, so that the throng wondered, when they saw the dumb speaking, the maimed whole, the lame walking, and the blind seeing; and they glorified the God of Israel.	Passing along the Sea of Galille, Jesus went up on the mountain, and great crowds came to him bringing the sick, and he healed them. And the throng wondered, when they saw the dumb speaking, the maimed whole, the lame walking, and the blind seeing; and they glorified the God of Israel.

In the story of Peter's arrival in Cornelius's home in Caesarea, the apostle asked why he had been summoned there (Acts 10:23–29 [RDB 643]). Cornelius's reply (verses 30–33) was a repetition of the details of Peter's divinely given vision, already recorded (verses 3–9), and the RDB condensation deletes this eighty-five word repetition, but summarizes the experience in six words: "Then Cornelius told Peter his vision," the word "vision" being taken from verse 3.

Dispensable Rhetoric

The second category of deletions concerns the practice in ancient times of "the multiplying of words for rhetorical effect" (preface). This would include redundancy or the use of more words than necessary to convey the idea. It also includes embroidery, that is the use of extra words to emphasize the point made, or the inclusion of picturesque details to enhance it.

Apparently dispensable rhetoric accounts for the deletions in Genesis 2:1–3, the account of the institution of the Sabbath. The RSV in this passage contains sixty-six words, but this number is reduced to thirty-seven in the condensation.

RSV	RDB
Thus the heavens and the earth were finished, and all the host of them. And on the seventh day God finished his work which he had done, and he rested on the seventh day from all his work which he had done. So God blessed the seventh day and hallowed it, because on it God rested from all his work which he had done in creation.	Thus the heavens and the earth were finished, and on the seventh day God rested from all his work. God blessed and hallowed the seventh day because on it he rested from all his work of creation.

The deletions from the RSV of Mark 4:1–3 are also to be regarded as due to dispensable rhetoric. By eliminating them the passage is shortened from sixty-four words to thirty-four:

RSV	RDB
Again he began to teach beside the sea. And a very large crowd gathered about him, so that he got into a boat and sat in it on the sea; and the whole crowd was beside the sea on the land. And he taught them many things in parables, and in his teaching he said to them: "Listen! A sower went out to sow."	Again he taught beside the sea, and a large crowd gathered, so that he got into a boat, and the crowd was on the land. "Listen!" he said. "A sower went out to sow."

Reduced Relevancy

The third category concerns material judged to have reduced relevance for today's reader. Material that is regarded as lacking in immediate importance for the modern reader is deleted. As an example compare the condensation of Genesis 40:1–3 with the full text in the RSV:

RSV (fifty-eight words)	RDB (twenty-five words)
Some time after this, the butler of the king of Egypt and his baker offended their lord the king of	Some time after this, Pharaoh was angry with his chief butler and chief baker, and put them in the

Egypt. And Pharaoh was angry with his two officers, the chief butler and the chief baker, and put them in custody in the house of the captain of the guard, in the prison where Joseph was confined.

prison where Joseph was confined.

In Acts 2:5–13 the listing of the various countries from which the Jews at Pentecost came does not seem to have immediate relevance to the average reader today. This list was reduced to "every nation under heaven," and this change, combined with deleted dispensable rhetoric, reduced this passage from one hundred forty-one words to fifty-seven in the RDB.

METHODS OF SHORTENING AND CLARIFICATION
Poetry

About forty percent of the OT is written in poetry. And there are also poetic passages in the NT, including many of the sayings of Jesus. In the RSV these poetic sections of the Bible are set in poetic form. How does the RDB condensation handle them? Only the Psalms, the Songs of Solomon, the Song of Moses and Miriam in Exodus 15, and the Song of Deborah and Barak in Judges 15 are run as poetry. The other poetic passages are printed as prose. Hebrew poetry differs markedly from Western poetry and its characteristics are generally beyond the knowledge of the average person for whom the RDB is intended.

The most prominent characteristic of biblical poetry is what is known as parallelism of members. The basic unit is the line which is followed by a second line (or even two lines) in one way or another parallel with the first. Several kinds of parallelism have been identified, the most common being synonymous, antithetic, and synthetic. In the process of condensation synonymous parallelism is the most difficult to handle. In it the second line, using different words, repeats the thought of the first. When this kind of parallelism occurs in any of the eighty Psalms that the RDB retains, all of which are set in poetic form, both lines are preserved. The classic example of synonymous parallelism is Psalm 24 (RDB 279), which begins:

The earth is the LORD's and the fullness thereof, the world and those who dwell therein; for he had founded it upon the seas, and established it upon the rivers.

But when synonymous parallelism is run as prose, its character is decidedly changed. One of the lines becomes tautological and may therefore be deleted. Frequently the second line is cut out as in the following examples:

Jeremiah 4:24

RSV: I looked on the mountains, and lo, they were quaking, and all the hills moved to and fro.

RDB: I looked on the mountains, and they were quaking (p. 403).

Jeremiah 15:21

RSV: I will deliver you out of the hand of the wicked, and redeem you from the grasp of the ruthless.

RDB: I will deliver you out of the hand of the wicked (p. 408).

(For other examples see Genesis 49:1–2 [RDB 28]; Isaiah 40:12, 17 [RDB 384]; 43:2 [RDB 386]; 51:12 [RDB 390]; 59:1–2 [RDB 394].)

Rarely is the first line of the parallelism deleted as in the introduction to the "song" attributed to Moses in Deuteronomy 32:2:

RSV: May my teaching drop as the rain, my speech distil as the dew, as the gentle rain upon the tender grass, and as the showers upon the herb.

The editors of the RDB evidently regarded some of this language as rhetorical embroidery, and deleted most of line one and all of line four. The words "teaching" and "drop" were transferred from the first line to the third. The result is a beautiful poetic prose sentence.

RDB: May my speech distil as the dew, and my teaching drop as gentle rain upon the tender grass (p. 103).

(Compare also the second half of Jeremiah 9:2 [RDB 404].)

Frequently in running synonymous parallelism as prose, words and phrases of both lines are combined into a single statement. To illustrate: Shortly before his death the patriarch Jacob summoned his sons for a final blessing, given in poetic

315

form. The poem begins with symonymous parallelism (Genesis 49:2):

> RSV: Assemble and hear, O sons of Jacob, and hearken to Israel your father.

When this line is set as prose, both the repetition and tautology are pruned. The result is the simple prose sentence:

> RDB: Assemble and hearken to Israel your father (p. 28).

Another example is Jeremiah 4:31 that, put into prose, would be characterized by both tautology and embroidery, both of which are pruned in the condensation:

> RSV: For I have heard a cry as of a woman in travail, anguish as of one bringing forth her first child.
> RDB: I heard a cry as of one bringing forth her first child (p. 403).

Worthy of note is the choice of "bringing forth her first child" in preference to "as of a woman in travail." (See also Exodus 15:2 [RDB 40]; Isaiah 40:10 [RDB 384]; and Isaiah 42:7 [RDB 385].)

Block Cuts

In addition to the line by line pruning of words, phrases, and clauses, the Digest editors cut out verses and much larger blocks of text such as whole chapters and large sections of chapters, particularly from the OT. To illustrate: Five full chapters and all but two verses of another chapter were cut out of Genesis. Some ten chapters were deleted from the Book of Leviticus. At least eleven full chapters and major portions of others were eliminated from 1 Chronicles. Seventy of the Psalms are completely absent, but an attempt was made to have all the various types of Psalms represented. Thirteen chapters were deleted from Isaiah, and the last five chapters of Daniel were cut out.

Some of these deletions come under the category of repetitions. There are a number of duplications in the Bible, not only of incidents but also of wording, in several books. It is obvious that one of these accounts could easily be cut without serious loss. Psalm 14 of Book I of the Psalter is closely paralleled by Psalm 53 in Book II, and hence only one of these, namely Psalm

14, is retained. Second Samuel 22 is a duplicate of Psalm 18 and is deleted, while Psalm 18 is retained. Second Kings 18:13–20:19 is largely duplicated in Isaiah 36–39, but in this case both books retain a condensation of all three incidents: Sennacherib's invasion of Judah, the miraculous deliverance, and Hezekiah's illness and recovery. In both books, however, the account of Hezekiah's illness and recovery precedes the other two, an arrangement that is probably chronologically correct. The account of Zedekiah's reign and the fall and destruction of Jerusalem is found in Jeremiah 52, as well as in 2 Kings 18:13–25:21 and 25:27–30. The RDB deletes it from the Book of Jeremiah.

A conspicuous example of blocks of material that have been deleted because of reduced relevancy for our time are the genealogical lists, not only in the OT but also in Matthew 1:1–14 and Luke 3:23–38. Genealogies were extremely important in the Israelite society, which was based on a tribal system. One's personal identity, his membership and status in the community, and his legal right to an inheritance were all tied in with his ability to show his family and tribal ancestry. This was especially true of the priests, who could serve only if their descent from the family of Aaron could be demonstrated, and the royal descendants of David, from among whom a messianic ruler was expected. But for the average reader of today the genealogical lists in the Bible are simply names, some of which he has trouble in pronouncing. This explains the absence, for example, of Genesis 10; 25:12–18; 36; and 1 Chronicles 3–9.

"Also, of course," says the preface, "a certain percentage of the Old Testament text, particularly details concerning the ritual and history presented in some of the earlier books, holds a less immediate relevance for Christian belief and practice" (p. x). As a specific example, Leviticus 13, dealing with various forms of skin eruptions that were to be examined by the priests who served as the health officers of ancient times, has a more remote relevance today than it had in those days. The same can be said of the regulations dealing with bodily discharges in Leviticus 15, the regulations regarding the slaughter of animals in chapter 17, the rules governing the life and conduct of the priests in chapter 21, and details of the construction of the tabernacle, its

317

coverings, and furniture. Hence, much of this material is considerably pruned, as we shall see.

Transposition of Material

In Exodus 25–30 there is not only a substantial shortening but also a rearranging of the order of the directions for the construction of the tabernacle, its furniture, and the courtyard surrounding it. Following the instruction regarding the free will offering to be taken for this religious center (Exodus 25:1–9), the directions for the construction begins with the ark of the covenant (verses 10–22 [RDB 47]). It is noteworthy that the RDB, for the benefit of the average reader, gives the dimensions of the ark in inches. In the interest of clarity it also has, "and in the ark you shall put the *tables of the law* that I shall give you," whereas the RSV has "the testimony" (verse 16). The substitution of "tables of the law" for "tables of the testimony" is also made in Exodus 31:18 and 32:15. Following the directions regarding the making of the ark the RDB, instead of continuing with the two remaining sections of Exodus 25 that give directions for the making of the table for the bread of the Presence (verses 23–30) and the lampstand (verses 31–40), inserts abbreviated directions for the construction of the tabernacle itself derived from Exodus 26:1, 7, 14, 31–33. The account begins, "Make the tabernacle (the tent of meeting to enclose the ark) with ten curtains. . . ." The inserted explanation in parentheses suggests that the Digest editors take Exodus 26 as providing directions for the construction of the Most Holy Place of the Tabernacle. If this is the intent of the insertion, it is in error. The "tent of meeting" consisted of two apartments separated by a veil, and verses 31–35 clearly show that the chapter is intended to include both. Just why the order of the materials was transposed is not clear. Such transposition is very rare in the RDB.

Following this instruction from Exodus 26, the RDB (p. 48) returns to chapter 25 to give directions concerning the table (verses 23–30) and lampstand (verses 31–40). Because of the reduced relevance of this material it is greatly condensed. The eight verses dealing with the table are summarized by a single sentence with words derived from verses 23–24, and 30: "Make a table of acacia wood (verse 23), and overlay it with gold (verse 24); and you shall set the bread of the Presence on the table before me always (verse 30)." For the same reason the number of verses dealing with the lampstand is reduced from ten to a single sentence: "Make a lampstand of pure gold (verse 21), with six branches, three on each side (verse 32), and make seven lamps for it (verse 37)." The RDB continues with a summary sentence of Exodus 27:1–8 regarding the altar of burnt-offering: "Make an altar of acacia wood for burnt offerings and overlay it with bronze." This is followed by a single sentence reduction of Exodus 30:1–10 regarding the altar of incense: "Make an altar to burn incense upon of acacia wood overlaid with pure gold (verse 1, 3)." The laver (Exodus 30:17–21) is also given a single sentence: "And you shall also make a laver of bronze with its base of pure bronze, for washing hands and feet" (cf. verses 17, 19). The condensation then returns to Exodus 27:9–18 to deal with the court in two sentences: "Make the court of the tabernacle, enclosed with hangings of fine twined linen. The length of the court shall be a hundred and fifty feet, the breadth seventy-five, and the height of the hangings seven and a half feet" (cf. verses 9, 18). Note the measurements that the RSV gives in cubits are given in feet, which are more meaningful to the average reader.

Synoptic Gospels

In the NT there is a large body of material common to all three synoptic Gospels—Matthew, Mark, and Luke. It consists of the same stories told in much the same order and using a large percentage of the same words. The Introduction to the New Testament in the RDB informs the reader that "in the present version some of this repetition from Gospel to Gospel has been eliminated" (p. 518). From this body of common material twelve pericopes consisting of about eighty verses were deleted from Matthew but preserved in Mark. Six of these pericopes, and five others, consisting of a total of eighty-five verses were also deleted from Luke. Again, all of these were perserved in Mark and a few of them in Matthew as well. Some material that is found in two of the Synoptics was also deleted from one of them. About half of Luke's Gospel and about twenty-eight percent of Matthew consists of material found only in these Gospels. With some minor exceptions these materials were all preserved.

Clarification of the Text

According to the preface the editors not only shortened the text but clarified it. One can detect several ways in which this was done. Perhaps the most common method is the frequent substitution of its antecedent for a pronoun to avoid ambiguity. The RSV had already done this a number of times and carefully noted each occurrence in a footnote (see Mark 1:44–45; 5:9, 17; 6:14; 9:21; Luke 22:8; John 11:17), but it is far more frequent in the RDB. In each of the examples below the pronoun read by the RSV is shown in parentheses following its antecedent (read by the RDB):

RDB 388 (Isa. 45:13)	I have aroused Cyrus [him] in righteousness
RDB 522 (Matt. 2:22)	but when Joseph [he] heard that Archelaus reigned over Judea
RDB 533 (Matt. 14:12)	Then John's [his] disciples took the body and buried it
RDB 549 (Matt. 26:74)	Then Peter [he] invoked a curse
RDB 576 (Luke 1:56)	And Mary remained with Elizabeth [her]
RDB 576 (Luke 1:64)	Immediately Zechariah's [his] tongue was loosed
RDB 577 (Luke 2:33)	The child's [his] father and mother marveled
RDB 577 (Luke 2:39)	And when Joseph and Mary [they] had performed everything
RDB 643 (Acts 10:23)	Peter [he] called them in to be his guests
RDB 644 (Acts 10:42)	And Jesus [he] commanded us to preach

At times words derived from the context or made evident by it are added for clarity. In Matthew 8:18, for example, "he gave orders to go over to the other side," the RDB (528) adds "of the Sea of Galilee." In Matthew 11:2 the RDB (530) reads, "when John *the Baptist* heard in prison about the deeds of Christ. . . ." The title, "the Baptist," is added evidently to make clear which John is being talked about. In John 1:19 (RDB 607) it is not merely the Jews who sent the delegation of priests and Levites to interview John the Baptist, it was the *"Pharisees in Jerusalem"* and the place where they interviewed the Baptizer was *"Bethany beyond the Jordan"* (cf. vv. 24, 28). When Jesus set out for the centurion's home in Capernaum (Luke 7:6) to heal that Roman officer's slave, according to the RDB he was "followed by a great crowd" (p. 582). This information comes from verse 9. The RDB (583) of Luke 7:36 has "One of the Pharisees, *named Simon,* asked Jesus to eat with him." The italic words are supplied from the context (vv. 40, 43–44). Luke 10 opens with the instructions given the seventy missionaries sent out by Jesus. Near the close of his instructions, he pronounced a woe upon the cities of Chorazin, Bethsaida, and Capernaum (vv. 13–14). In verse 16 he makes a further statement to the seventy. The RDB (586) begins with the added words, "To the seventy he said. . . ." "At Mount Olivet" is added to Acts 1:6: "When the disciples had come together at Mount Olivet . . ." (RDB 635). The place is derived from verse 12. In the RDB Acts 2:4 reads: "All were filled with the Holy Spirit, *and they left the house* and began to speak in other tongues. . . ," an inference drawn from the context.

In a few places modern equivalents are given for expressions of time. In John 4:6 "about noon" is substituted for "about the sixth hour" (RDB 610). In Acts 2:15 in place of "it is only the third hour of the day" the condensation has "it is still early morning."

In a few passages the translation has been altered in the interest of clarity. Some of the rendering may be regarded as definite improvements.

Genesis 12:3

By you all the families of the earth shall be blessed. [The marginal reading of the RSV, which has in the text,] shall bless themselves.

Exodus 32:25

Moses saw that the people were out of control (for Aaron had let them get out of control to their shame). [RSV had] broken loose . . . let them break loose.

Matthew 1:21

You shall call him Jesus. [RSV gives the literal rendering of this idiom] You shall call his name Jesus [cf. Luke 1:13, 31].

Mark 1:21

From that moment his fame began spreading. [RSV] And at once his fame spread everywhere.

2 Corinthians 2:3

I might not suffer pain. [RSV] I might not be pained.

Also in the interest of clarity the RDB has inserted a few explanatory additions. As examples, note:

Exodus 21:12

Whoever strikes a man willfully so that he dies. [RSV] Whoever strikes a man, ["willfully" is transposed from v. 14].

Jeremiah 11:18

The Lord made known to me the evil deeds of my neighbors. [RSV] The Lord made known to me and I knew it; then thou didst show me their evil deeds. ["Neighbors" is transposed from Jer. 12:14].

Mark 5:12

and the demons begged Jesus, "Send us to the swine." [RSV] And they begged him. . . .

1 Corinthians 6:12

"All things are lawful for me," you say. [RSV] All things are lawful for me, ["You say" is a slogan of the liberals, not Paul's verdict].

Some stylistic improvements have also been made over the RSV. One of the characteristics of Hebrew syntax is a succession of coordinate clauses tied together by the conjunction usually translated "and." The RSV had already made a beginning in substituting for "and" other words such as "when," "then," "so," and "for" in harmony with the context. In the NT this Hebrew syntax is to some extent imitated in the Greek gospels (see "and" in Luke 1:6, 16, 18, 20, 21, 22, 23, 24, 28, 30, 34, 35, 36, 41, 50, 59, 63, 65, 67, et al.). The RDB normally omits the "and" or substitutes another word for it.

Another stylistic change is the subordination of one clause to another as justified by the context. Compare the RSV and RDB in the following examples:

Genesis 19:1

RSV: The two angels came to Sodom in the evening; Lot was sitting in the gate of Sodom.

RDB: When the two angels came to Sodom in the evening, Lot was sitting in the city gate.

Genesis 37:25

RSV: Then they sat down to eat; and looking up they saw a caravan of Ishmaelites coming from Gilead. . . .

RDB: As the brothers sat down to eat, they saw a caravan of Ishmaelites coming. . . .

Mark 3:3

RSV: And they watched to see whether he would heal him on the sabbath day, so that they might accuse him. And he said to the man who had the withered hand, "Come here."

RDB: While the Pharisees watched to see whether he would heal on the sabbath, so that they might accuse him, Jesus said to the man, "Come here."

In the interest of style the word order of the RSV is also occasionally altered (see Luke 3:7, 23; 4:1). The record of conversations in Scripture are made more interesting by modernizing their arrangement. Compare the RSV of John 1:19–23 with the same conversation as given on page 607 of the RDB:

This is the testimony of John, when the Pharisees in Jerusalem sent priests and Levites to Bethany beyond the Jordan, where John was baptizing, to ask him, "Who are you?"

"I am not the Christ," he confessed.

"What then?" they asked. "Are you Elijah or the prophet?"

"I am not," he answered.

"Then who are you?" they said. "Let us have an answer for those who sent us. What do you say about yourself?"

"I am the voice," he said, "of one crying in the wilderness, 'Make straight the way of the Lord,' as the prophet Isaiah said."

"Then why are you baptizing," they asked, "if you are neither the Christ, nor Elijah, nor the prophet?"

"I baptize with water," John answered, "but among you stands one whom you do not know, even he who comes after me, the thong of whose sandal I am not worthy to untie."

SUMMARY

Among the numerous modern versions, what place does the RDB have? A proper evaluation can be made only on the basis of the purpose for which it was produced. That purpose is clearly stated in the preface:

> Not in any way intended to replace the full Biblical text, which will always be available, *The Reader's Digest Bible* offers the general reader a more direct means of becoming acquainted with the *whole* body of the Scriptures. It can be read more rapidly and with swifter comprehension, for instruction, even for pure, heart-lifting enjoyment—the Bible is, after all, an unsurpassed collection of marvelous and stirring events linked to the divine will and purpose, compelling tales of men and women caught up in a courageous effort to live good and godly lives (p. xi).

That the RDB is not intended as a substitute for the complete and uncondensed Bible such as the RSV is worthy of emphasis. It is rather designed to be a shortened, simplified, and easy-to-read summary of the contents of the entire biblical text. To the average person who approaches the Bible for the first time the reading of the complete text in one of the historic versions appears as a formidable task. It might prove alarming were we to learn how few of those who attend church regularly make use of the complete Bible as a guide for living.

Even the form in which the historic English versions are printed, with two columns to the page and the text chopped up into individual verse units, is a deterrent to continuous reading. The layout and printing of the RDB, however, with its page-wide lines and its text separated into paragraphs makes it far more attractive to read, for it appears like a modern novel.

Furthermore, each book of the Bible is preceded by an introduction approximately a half page in length. The sacred text of the volume is followed by a thirty-one page index of persons, places, events, and teachings. The references in the index are to page numbers.

Although the text is significantly shortened, the preface maintains that not only all sixty-six books are retained, but also "every incident, personality and teaching of substance" is carefully preserved. But no matter how carefully the process of shortening is done, there will be those who are familiar with the complete Bible who will decry the absence of a favorite Psalm or a favorite verse. But fortunately, major doctrines of the Christian faith do not hinge on a single verse of Scripture, but rather on the teaching of the Bible as a whole. Nor was this condensation designed for people who are familiar with the complete Bible and have favorite chapters and verses. These students of Scripture should continue to read and study the complete Bible.

This condensation was designed for the vast number who do not read the Bible at all, or who do so sporadically, and may have become discouraged by genealogical lists and other material that seem not to have relevance for them. The RDB was designed as a popular Bible for ordinary people, young and old. Professor Metzger suggests that it should also appeal "to the college student specializing in English and European literature which abounds in Biblical references and to the Sunday School youngster who needs a simple introduction to the complexities of life in Bible times."

We therefore join the editors "in the confident hope that readers young and old will find in its quickened pace, its sharper focus, its smoothly flowing narratives an irresistible invitation to draw closer to the spiritual heart of the greatest book mankind possesses" (preface, p. xi).

19

Some Colorful Versions

No one controls the production of Bible translations. One does not need any special qualifications to put forth a translation. A knowledge of Hebrew and Greek and the intricacies of textual criticism are not prerequisites to translation. Anyone who has a special burden for a kind of translation that has not yet been done or for the improvement of a translation of a type that is already in existence can enter the field of Bible translation. As a result of this there have been some queer and interesting translations that tend to neglect accuracy in order to obtain what they may feel is relevant or what they feel is a special need, idiosyncratic as it may appear to others. In some cases the translators are well equipped in the knowledge of biblical languages and textual criticism but more often they are not. Some of the Bibles discussed in our book can come under this classification. This phenomenon however is not of recent vintage. In 1768 Edward Harwood, a Presbyterian minister, translated the New Testament into a very stilted style popular in the eighteenth century in England. Notice these portions from Luke 15 and John 3:16:

> A Gentleman of a splendid family and opulent fortune had two sons. One day the younger approached his father, and begged him in the most importunate and soothing terms to make a partition of his effects betwixt himself and his elder brother—The indulgent father,

overcome by his blandishments, immediately divided all his fortunes betwixt them, etc. (Luke 15:11ff.)

For the supreme God was affected with such immense compassion and love for the human race, that he deputed his son from heaven to instruct them—in order that everyone who embraces and obeys his religion might not finally perish, but secure everlasting happiness.

Rodolphus Dickinson published a similar type of translation at Boston in 1833 called A New and Corrected Version of the New Testament. These are his translations of some passages:

And it happened, that when Elizabeth heard the salutation of Mary, the embryo was joyfully agitated (Luke 1:41).

His master said to him, Well-done, good and provident servant! you was faithful in a limited sphere, I will give you a more extensive superintendence; participate in the happiness of your master (Matthew 25:21).

Festus declared with a loud voice, Paul, you are insane! Multiplied research drives you to distraction (Acts 26:24).[1]

EXPANDED TRANSLATION OF THE GREEK NEW TESTAMENT

In more recent years however, we have had several very interesting translations. The first of these is Wuest's Expanded Translation of the Greek New Testament published in 1956–1959. The translator intends to bring out the nuances of the Greek for the English reader. Those who know Greek will feel that he overtranslates. Kenneth S. Wuest was a teacher of New Testament Greek at the Moody Bible Institute. We give now a few examples of his translation:

Moreover, also your hairs, the ones on your head, all of them, have been counted and the result tabulated (Matt. 10:30).

Everyone therefore who is of such a character that he will confess me before men in the realization of and in testimony to his oneness with me, I also will confess him before my Father who is in heaven in the realization of and testimony to my oneness with him (Matt. 10:32).

---

[1]The selections from these two Bibles are taken from Bruce M. Metzger, "The Revised Standard Version," *Duke Divinity Review* 44 (1979): 71–72.

And behold, a leper having come, fell upon his knees and touched the ground with his forehead in an expression of profound reverence before Him, saying, Master, in the event that you may be having a heartfelt desire, you are able to cleanse me (Matt. 8:2).

Moreover, as for myself, I also am saying to you, You are Rock (*petros*, masculine in gender, a detached but large fragment of rock), and upon this massive rock (*petra*, feminine in gender, feminine demonstrative pronoun cannot go back to masculine *petros*; *petra*, a rocky peak, a massive rock) I will build my Church (Matt. 16:18).

And, having turned around, He (with His back turned to Peter and Satan) said to Peter, Be gone under my authority, and keep on going, behind me, out of my sight, Satan (Matt. 16:23).

Then Jesus said to His disciples, If anyone is desiring to come after me, let him forget self and lose sight of his own interests, and let him pick up his cross and carry it, and let him be taking the same road with me that I travel, for whoever is desiring to save his soul-life shall ruin it, but whoever will pass a sentence of death upon his soul-life for my sake, shall find it (Matt. 16:24–25).

And he went into all the country around the Jordan making a public proclamation with such formality, gravity, and authority as must be listened to and obeyed, announcing a baptism that had to do with repentance, this baptism, a testimony because of the putting away of sins, as it stands written in the book of the words of Isaiah the prophet. A voice of one shouting in the uninhabited region, Make ready the Lord's road (Luke 3:3–4).

Offspring of vipers, who gave you a private, confidential hint that you should flee from the divine and righteous wrath against sin and sinners which is about to break at any moment? (Luke 3:7).

Then when they had breakfasted, Jesus says to Simon Peter, Simon, son of Jonas, do you have a love for me called out of your heart by my preciousness to you, a devotional love that impels you to sacrifice yourself for me? Do you consider me more precious and thus love me more than these (fish)? He says to Him, Yes, Lord, as for you, you know positively that I have an emotional fondness for you. He says to him, Be feeding my little lambs. He says to him again a second time, Simon, son of Jonas, do you have a devotional love for me called out of your heart by my preciousness to you, a love that impels you to sacrifice yourself for me? He says to Him, Yes, Lord. As for you, you know positively that I have a friendly feeling for you. He says to him, Be shepherding my sheep. He says to him the third time, Simon, son of Jonas, do you have a friendly feeling and affection for me? Peter was grieved that He said to him the third time, Do you have a friendly feeling and affection for me? And he said to Him, Lord, as for you, all things you know positively. You know from experience that I have a friendly feeling and affection for you. Jesus says to him, Be feeding my sheep (John 21:15–17).

THE COTTON PATCH VERSION

Another very interesting modern version is a translation by Clarence Jordan, The Cotton Patch Version, 1968–1973. This is a local dialect version for the South especially the area around Atlanta. Local place names are substituted for biblical ones and modern day equivalents of ideas, names, and classes of people as well are used. The following passages illustrate these points:

After they had checked out, the Lord's messenger made connection with Joseph in a dream and said, "Get moving, and take your wife and baby and highball it to Mexico" (Matt. 2:13).

This guy John was dressed in blue jeans and a leather jacket, and he was living on corn bread and collard greens. Folks were coming to him from Atlanta and all over north Georgia and the backwater of the Chattahoochee. And as they owned up to their crooked ways, he dipped them in the Chattahoochee (Matt. 3:4–6).

When John noticed a lot of Protestants and Catholics showing up for his dipping . . . (Matt. 3:7).

They said, "Where did that guy get all his learning and big-league stuff? Ain't this the carpenter's boy? Ain't his mama named Mary and his brothers Jim and Joe and Simon and Jody? . . ." (Matt. 13:54–55).

Obviously a translation of this sort has the advantage of making it very personal and pertinent to the people who live in this particular area, especially those in Georgia. Jesus is born in Gainesville, Georgia, grows up in Valdosta, is baptized in the Chattahoochee, and walks beside Lake Lanier. Everything comes close to home in this way. Analogous modern ideas make the Bible come alive, such as this translation of Matthew 9:17:

Nor do people put new tubes in old, bald tires. If they do the tires will blow out, and the tubes will be ruined and the tires will be torn up. But they put new tubes in new tires and both give good mileage.

Another good example of equivalency is found in Matthew 19:24:

> I say it again, a pig can go through a knothole easier than a rich man can get in the God Movement.

As Jordan says in his preface, this approach helps "the modern reader have the same sense of participation . . . which the early Christians must have had," and "by stripping away the fancy language, the artificial piety, and the barriers of time and distance this version puts Jesus and his people in the midst of our modern world, living where we live, talking as we talk, working, hurting, praying, bleeding, dying, conquering, along side of the rest of us. It seeks to restore the original feeling and excitement of the fast breaking *news*—good news—rather than musty history" (pp. 9–10). However, such a translation because it speaks so directly to one group will have limited appeal elsewhere. The Southern dialect comes through especially well in the conversational sections but in the narrative inconsistency appears. At times the style seems apt and suitable and at other times discordant in its staidness.

GOD IS FOR REAL, MAN

In 1966 Carl F. Burke published *God Is for Real, Man: Interpretations of Bible Passages and Stories as Told by Some of God's Bad Tempered Angels with Busted Haloes to Carl F. Burke.* This is not really a translation but a free retelling of portions of the Bible by the children of the inner city. Burke is chaplain of Erie County Jail, Buffalo, New York. In some cases he retells these stories as he heard them expressed. Psalm 23 begins: "The Lord is like my Probation Officer, He will help me, He tries to help me make it every day"; and Psalm 46: "God is a good hideout, He is stronger than the weight lifter at the Y." The story of Jesus' temptation in Matthew 4 reads thus: "Jesus went out by the docks and the man (the devil) tried to con him. He didn't eat for forty days—and was starved. After that the man came and said, 'O if you are the Son of God, let's see you make these red bricks turn into bread.' But he didn't do it. He just said, 'Cool it, man, you got to have more than bread if you want to live big.' Then the man took him to the steeple of St Joe's. The man says, 'Long way down, huh? Lots of cars too! Let's see ya jump. Don't be chicken. There's some cats with wings to catch you.' But Jesus didn't do it. He just said, 'Don't try to con God, man, cause you can't do it.'"

A similar translation was published in *Religious Education* (November-December 1969, pp. 468–70). This was translated by Charles Flagg, Willie Carmon, and Bonnie Mills of New Haven, Connecticut. Revelation 1 reads thus: "Dig this! The revealing of Jesus Christ!: God gave Christ the power to get his boys hip to what's happening. Then he rapped to an angel so that she could get the message across to his main man John, who clued everyone in on the truth of God, on what happened in Jesus Christ, and on everything he saw. Understand me, holy is the dude who reads outloud the words of cool John and holy are the cats that dig it, and abide by it; 'cause we ain't got much time." In this translation names of places are also changed, for example, the Isle of Patmos becomes Alcatraz and the seven churches become Harlem, Chicago, New Haven, Hartford, L.A., Philly, and Detroit. Freedom from sins in Revelation 1:5 becomes being saved from racism and muggings and drug addiction and scandal. The loud voice like a trumpet of 1:10 becomes "a loud voice like the Great Satchmo gettin' down on his horn."

THE WORD MADE FRESH

Another very interesting, almost hilarious, paraphrase is the three-volume work by Andrew Edington called The Word Made Fresh published in 1975. The translator is a layman, not a professionally trained biblical scholar, and this is a rather free translation. It is also an abbreviated version and often condensed. The language is quite colloquial and pungent. Accuracy is not its virtue, but it is interesting reading and down to earth. We list and illustrate some of the features in this paraphrase.

1. *Colloquialisms.* "When Noah learned of this, he chewed out his younger son" (Gen. 9:24–26); "Lot bucked at this injunction" (Gen. 19:19); "when he was too stoned to know what was happening" (Gen. 19:32); "Esau came in famished and pooped out" (Gen. 25:39).

2. *Modernization of names of people and places.* Scarlotti for Kirjathsepher, Raquel for Achsah, Sheriff of Cade County for Othniel, Rotarians for Jebusites (Judg. 1); evil king of New Orleans for Eglon, Mac the Knife for Ehud (Judg. 3); Jesse James for Sisera, Carrie for Deborah, General Maybe for Barak, Mae East for Jael (Judg. 4).

3. *Anachronisms.* "Esau had married two Hippie girls" (Gen. 26); "and he concealed it carefully by sticking it to his thigh with scotch tape" (Judg. 3); "took a huge hammer and a railroad spike and nailed Jesse's head to the ground" (Judg. 4); the angels reply to Gideon is "Bring an uncooked TV dinner and place it on the rock before me," and after this was done, fire came out and "cooked the TV dinner as if by laser beam" (Judg. 6); Gideon's attack is called planning "the first Halloween" (Judg. 7). The food given to Daniel and his companions is described as "caviar and cherry jubilee" and the person in charge is called "the Dean of Student Life" (Dan. 1). The king rewards Daniel with "a new Master-charge card" (Dan. 2). "Then Slick, the high priest, started shredding Kleenex" (Matt. 26).

4. *Remarks in footnotes.* His comments on the passage where the soldiers spit on Jesus is "If I had been God, this is about where I'd knocked some heads flying" (Matt. 26). After Judas returns to the elders and priests, confessing his wrong in betraying Jesus, they answer, "Tough stuff, man, but you can't unscramble these eggs." His comment is, "It can't even be done today. There is no un-mix master" (Matt. 27). After Philip goes to Atlanta (Samaria), men are healed and there is great rejoicing; his comment is, "Better even than the Falcons winning" (Acts 8). Commenting on the baptism of the Ethiopian eunuch (J. Con), he says, "Sounds like immersion, Presbyterians. Sorry about that" (Acts 9). Where the "order of Levi" is mentioned, he comments, "Nothing to do with pants" (Heb. 7). Regarding the observance of the three Hebrews not bowing down, he comments, "I have always been puzzled by the ability of people with their heads bowed to see those that aren't" (Dan. 3). Regarding Nebuchadnezzar's becoming insane and eating grass, he comments, "A bad situation in an election year" (Dan. 4). To give you a flavor of this translation we quote a few passages:

The next day as the terrified gangsters fled helter-skelter, the self-deferred draftees began to come out of the neighboring villages and they joined in the chase and in the slaughter. The Dalton boys themselves, the two leaders, had their heads removed and brought to Gideon's trophy room (Judg. 7).

At each crossing place, the representatives of Big Jake would say to every man that came to cross, "What number follows thirteen?"

Those who said "fourteen" were allowed to cross but those who said "foteen" were killed, for their accent betrayed their home county (Judg. 12).

"What do you do wrong? I'm glad you asked! For one thing, you bring gifts to the church, leftovers to the family night supper, and stale bread for the communion table. How does that grab you?

"What's more, you pay your church pledge with blind animals, or sick doves, and you claim more deductions than you give. You wouldn't try to cheat the IRS, would you? Why then do you try to cheat God?" (Mal. 1).

It would be better to be one legged than always kicking old ladies in the shins (Matt. 18).

THE GOSPELS IN SCOUSE

The Gospels in Scouse is a vernacular version from the Liverpool area translated by Dick Williams and Frank Shaw in 1967 and revised in 1977. Frank Shaw is a Catholic Irish customs officer and Dick Williams is a Protestant minister, both from Liverpool. There is a glossary at the end of the book. The translation follows J. M. Thompson's edition of the synoptic Gospels. We present a few selections from this gospel:

Before God did owt else e ad summat ter say. It wus is last werd. Ony it come first. An it summed up is ole attitude to everythink.

Now dis werd wus wid God. Fact it was part'n parcil uv im. So at start uv evrythink an a long time fore man was akshully made, God's werd to men wus ready an waitin.

Evrythink there is wus made by this werd. E wus God's one and ony contractor for de ole Universe job. Nowt at all as ever got made sept through this d'partm'nt uv God . . . wot we call is "werd".

Now just becus dis werd is part uv God isself, all God's life is in im. An dis life is de light what shines on evrybody. Dis is de light wot evrybody needs (John 1:1–4).

So wot I've bin sayin, like, is this. God's ole attitude to the werld became flesh. All wot God's got ter say about man became a man—Real Man. An,de Real Man lived among us. We could see just exackly wot e was like.An e wus terrific! E wus jus filled from top to bottom wid goodness and love an onesty. An you could see e wusn't juss on'y the thruth about man. E wus also the truth about God. You could. Honest (John 1:14).

Dis feller's name wus John.

E diden ave no cherch nor nowt like dat. E just wore a camel ur baydin cozzie an a purra desert wellies an wus in an out uv de River Jordan like a frogman. Sometimes e preached on de banks, an sometimes e preached in de water. An wen people were sorry fer wot day'd don wrong e'd give em a dowsin in de water to wash em clean.

E ad de gift of de gab all right. Day came from all over ter listen to im, all sorts uv people, great crowds uv dem—all along de river till youse cud walk on dare eads.

Lots of em decided to mend dare ways an get baptised. An on a busy day John would be up and down like a fiddler's elbow (Mark 1).

But wen day chucked de nets over de side Peter laughed on de other side uv is gob. De nets shot down as if day'd caught a whale or summat. Before e cud scratch is ead dare wus so many fish in de net day cudden pull it back by demselves.

"Ey, youse lot," yelled Peter to is mates in t'other boat. "C'mere!" An wen day came day filled both boats so full day nearly sank wid de weight.

You'd uv thought Peter'd uv bin as pleased as punch. But not im. E fell flat on is face in frunt uv Jesus an sed: "Don't pal up wid me, Boss, I'm jest not good enough for you" (Mark 1:16ff.).

Everybody knows the saying, "An eye for an eye and a tooth for a tooth." But get dis: you mussen ave it in fer them that's got it in fer yew! If a feller wants yer mack, give im yer jacket too. If a feller says, "Do me a favour," do im two favours. And don hang onto yer belongins wen people ask fer elp.

An oo asn't erd people say, "Love yer mates and ate yer enemies!"? But I'm telling you to love the lads oo ate yer guts, an pray fer every nasty birra werk oo does yer down. That's ow to be thrue to wot yew really are—God's own lads.

Cos if yew only love them that love yew, yewz still in the jungle wid the monkeys.

And day just won't wash with me la! You're not on. Avter be as fit for reel life as God is, and don kid yerselfs otherwise (Matt. 5).

CONCLUSION

Translations of this type will continue. While they may not serve the general public, they may serve in a more pertinent way the smaller audience for which they were written. Therefore, though they may not be needed and therefore prove useful for many, they will be useful and even necessary for some almost on a par with a foreign translation.

Some may feel that some of these translations are sacrilegious but for others brought up without a biblical background, perhaps without much education, immersed thoroughly in secular thinking, these versions may serve to bring understanding in a way that the traditional English versions could not.

These translations not only have filled a specific need but have also added color to a sometimes somber history of Bible translations.

20

Guidelines for Selecting
a Version

The Bible has been translated more often and into more languages than any other book in the world. It speaks today in over 1,200 languages. More than that, it speaks with multiple voices in many of the world's leading languages. This is especially true in English. No period of history has had such a profusion of English Bibles as the present century, and particularly the last thirty years. It may be seriously questioned whether the present generation has need of additional new English versions. However, no version of the Bible can ever be considered final. Translations must keep pace with the results of scholarly research, particularly as ambiguities and obscurities in the sacred text are removed. There is also the possibility, if not probability, that new discoveries of ancient MSS will yet be made that will throw light on the original wording. Translations must also keep abreast of the slow, subtle changes constantly taking place in the English language to make sure the Scriptures communicate to modern man.

There has never been an age when Bibles were so readily available as today. They can be bought in paperback, cloth, or leather. The great quantity and variety of versions have bewildered many a would-be reader of the sacred pages. The question is frequently asked, "What is the best version?" There is no simple answer to this question, but there are guidelines that may prove helpful.

To the younger generation it is quite clear that the KJV, for all its literary beauty, is hopelessly out of date. It may still speak to the Bible lover of the older generation who has become familiar with its sixteenth-century English, but for the majority of English-speaking people its language has become almost a foreign tongue. There is grave danger that the continued use of this version may give modern man the impression that the Bible belongs to another age, and that it is irrelevant to the twentieth century.

But if the KJV is abandoned, what version is to take its place? Perhaps no one version will be sufficient for today. This may well be an age when multiple versions are needed. If one asks, "Which version is best?" we need to add the questions, "Best for whom?" and "Best for what?" A version suitable for a child just learning to read may not appeal to a college youth. Adults accustomed to church language may not care for a version in which the familiar terms of biblical English are discarded. A version found helpful in private reading at home may not be suitable for pulpit use in public worship. A Bible suited for committed Christians may not speak with the same force to non-Christians.

THE PURPOSES OF THE VERSIONS

There are various purposes that different versions are designed to serve. It would be unfair to judge every version on the same basis. Almost every version contains an introduction that, among other things, states the objectives the translator or translators had in mind in producing the work. What are some of the purposes the new versions are designed to serve?

A number of versions are designed for private reading at home. The popular version of J. B. Phillips began as an attempt to make Paul's letters communicate to modern youth, such as those in London. The unanticipated use of this version as an authoritative text for Bible study groups so alarmed the translator that he felt compelled to produce a second edition, published in 1972. He had used a rather poor Greek text as the basis of the first edition. For the second edition he substituted the United Bible Societies' Greek Testament. Furthermore, his high regard for the truth of the sacred Scriptures frightened him when he realized the extent of the freedom he had used in his first edition. He writes, "This passion of mine for communication . . . has led me sometimes into paraphrase and sometimes to interpolate clarifying remarks which are certainly not in the Greek." Hence, in the second edition he seeks to be more loyal to the Greek text.

The Living Bible, as the author of this very free paraphrase, Kenneth N. Taylor, asserts, has value for "rapid reading" and for acquiring a "sweeping movement" of the story of redemption. But for careful study it is too free in adding, leaving out, and even changing materials to be trusted. Taylor himself has admitted, "For study purposes a paraphrase should be checked against a rigid translation."

There are recent versions particularly suitable for careful study. One of these is the New American Standard Bible, which represents a very conservative and literal approach to the text. It reveals an honest attempt to reproduce accurately the nuances of the original languages and has taken over the valuable cross references of the ASV. However, though it has great value as a study Bible, its stilted and nonidiomatic English makes it unsuitable for pulpit use.

The Amplified Bible with its multiple renderings is also not suitable for public reading, but is at times suggestive and stimulating in private study. It is in the nature of a miniature commentary. The introduction to it plainly states, "It is not a substitute for other translations. It is intended to supplement them, authentically, concisely, and in a convenient form."

For use in public worship the RSV is the best successor to the KJV. It seeks to combine the values of the historic Protestant versions with modern vocabulary and the latest in biblical scholarship. The NEB is also designed for pulpit use but is much freer and at times too colloquial. The NIV has the dignity and beauty of language that make it suitable for use in public worship, and will no doubt be widely adopted for this purpose.

Some translations are designed to serve the needs of readers with a limited English background. The Bible in Basic English, for example, has a limited vocabulary of 850–1000 words, with an additional 50 special "Bible" words. Charles Kingsley Williams in his translation, The New Testament In Plain English, uses a vocabulary of about 1,650 words, 160–170 of which are explained in the glossary. Such translations sacrifice literary beauty for simplicity and ease of understanding. No rigid limit was set for the vocabulary of the Good News Bible. Nevertheless, it uses "words and forms accepted as standard by people everywhere who use English as a means of communication."

Some translations indicate special care in bringing out the force of the Greek verbs as well as other elements of the original. Charles B. Williams's The New Testament in the Language of the People concentrates primarily on the translation of the Greek verbs, while Kenneth S. Wuest's Expanded Translation of the New Testament extends to other elements of the language as well. The latter especially has been criticized for overtranslation of the Greek. Such translations again sacrifice beauty of style to achieve their goal. This is true also of the NASB.

Inasmuch as different versions serve different purposes, it would not be fair to evaluate them all by the same standards, as we have said. These varying objectives also suggest the desirability of having more than one version available. These versions should not be chosen solely on the basis of personal appeal. It is not safe merely to say, "I like the way this version renders this verse." Obviously, it does not necessarily follow that the rendering is correct. Nevertheless, the element of personal appeal, subjective as it is, is not wholly out of place when used in connection with more basic guidelines. If a version is to be read, it must have appeal; it must speak. But there are more basic criteria. What are they?

CRITERIA FOR CHOOSING A VERSION
The Textual Basis

The first criterion concerns the underlying text from which the translation is made. The Wycliffe Bible, which was the first complete English Bible, was a translation of the Latin Vulgate. The Vulgate has been the standard Bible of Roman Catholicism for hundreds of years. The Rheims-Douai and the recent Ronald Knox versions are translations of it. This means they are translations of a translation. The NAB, however, is an excellent Catholic translation based on the originals. The Living Bible is not directly based on the originals but is a paraphrase of a translation, the ASV. The NT of all the standard Protestant Bibles from Tyndale through the KJV were based on an inferior Greek text, known as the Received Text or the TR (Textus Receptus). This text goes back to the work of Erasmus, who first published the Greek NT in 1516. His text was made from a handful of Greek MSS dating from the Middle Ages. Between them and the autographs were many copyings, with consequent errors creeping in. Many of these inaccuracies, as Sir Frederic Kenyon said, "now can be corrected with absolute certainty from the vastly wider information which is at our disposal today."

This is not to say that the TR is a bad text or that it is a heretical text. It contains the gospel of Jesus Christ. But some parts of it are not in the form which the original writers wrote. With regard to the great bulk of the words in the NT there is no dispute. Nevertheless, some important passages are affected. Some of the major differences between the TR and a modern critical text are found in the following areas: (1) the omission or inclusion of substantial passages: Matthew 16:2b–3; Mark 16:9–20; Luke 22:19b–20, 43–44; John 7:53–8:11; 1 John 5:7–8; (2) the omission or inclusion of shorter passages, such as Matthew 6:13; 17:21; 18:11; 21:44; Mark 9:44, 46; Luke 9:56; Acts 8:37; Romans 16:24; (3) the substitution of an important word or set of words for another, e.g., Acts 20:28; 1 Timothy 3:16; Revelation 22:14; and (4) the omission or inclusion of a significant word or small group of words, e.g., Matthew 6:4, 6; 1 Corinthians 6:20; 11:24; 1 John 3:1.

Most twentieth-century translations of the NT are based on one or another of the following critical Greek texts: Westcott-Hort, Nestle-Aland, and that of the United Bible Societies. The translators of the NEB, however, constructed their own Greek text from the MSS as they went along and often in the Gospels they daringly followed "Western" readings. In some modern versions there is also an occasional use of "conjectural emendations" where it was felt the true original text was not preserved in the MSS. It is in this way that the name "Enoch" came into the text of 1 Peter 3:19 in Moffatt, Goodspeed, and Schonfield's NTs. Several modern versions in John 19:29 conjecturally substitute "spear," "pike," or "javelin" (Gr. *hyssōpōi* for "hyssop." Though one MSS actually reads that way, it must be considered a conjecture (see Moffatt, Goodspeed, Authentic, Rieu, NEB, et al.). Likewise in Philemon 8, a number of recent versions substitute "ambassador" or "envoy" for "old man" or "aged" (see AMPLIFIED, NEB, Chas. B. Williams, Twentieth Century NT, Goodspeed). Others bracket 1 Timothy 5:23 or place it in a footnote, as though it were not a part of the text. But there is no MS support for this. These examples are sufficient to illustrate the fact that one needs to use a strikingly new element in a passage of a new version with caution.

The OT of most recent versions is based on the traditional Masoretic text. Translations may differ as to the extent of the use of the ancient versions—particularly the Greek, Syriac, Latin, and Targums—to correct the Hebrew where it appears to be defective. Some also make use of the newly available materials from the Qumran caves. They also differ in the frequency with which they resort to conjectural readings where the Hebrew text does not seem to make sense.

A good translation today should be based on the best Hebrew, Aramaic, and Greek texts available. This means it should be based on the earliest and best MSS that have thus far been found. In the NT there is little need for conjectural changes. Even in the OT the tendency to emend should be curbed unless it is obvious that the text is faulty.

Accuracy of Translation

The second criterion for evaluating a version is its accuracy in translation. It is not enough for a version to be based on the best available Greek and Hebrew MSS; one must further ask, "How carefully and accurately have the original texts been translated?" This is, in reality, the most essential test of a satisfactory version. A translator is under a solemn and sacred obligation to reproduce as closely as possible the thoughts, ideas, and sentiments of the original writers, not his own convictions, beliefs, or feelings.

But how is such fidelity to be measured? By what standards is accuracy in translation to be judged? There is no simple answer to this question. There are varying standards of accuracy and differing philosophies of translation. On the one extreme are those who hold that faithfulness demands a literal word-by-word translation that retains, as far as possible, the original grammatical units. Words not actually in the original, but needed to complete the sentence in English, should be indicated by italics or other literary devices. On the other extreme are those who hold that the translator is not concerned with words so much as thoughts and ideas. He should strive for the principle of equivalent effect. The translation should have the same effect on those who read it as the original produced, or produces, on its readers. The translator should seek to grasp the message of the original and then attempt to put it into whatever English he feels will express it most accurately and satisfactorily.

These differing concepts of translation have had a long history. In the fifteenth century there were two different versions that circulated under the name of John Wycliffe. The first was an extremely literal translation of the Vulgate, closely following the Latin constructions and Latin word order. The second was a freer, more natural translation made after Wycliffe's death, probably by his secretary, John Purvey. In the prologue to the second version the philosophy of translation employed is explained as follows: "First, it is to knowe, that the best translating is out of Latyn, into English, to translate after the sentence, and not oneli after the wordes, so that the sentence be as opin, either openere in English as in Latyn." By "sentence" is meant "sense," "substance," "general significance." The general significance of the English translation must be as plain as that which is translated. This means it must be idiomatic.

Eugene Nida has given this helpful definition of translation: "Translating consists in producing in the receptor language the closest natural equivalent to the message of the source language, first in meaning and secondly in style. An extremely literal translation is not necessarily the most faithful, for it may actually distort the meaning or even convey no meaning at all. Everyone who has studied languages knows there is often no exact equivalent in a given language for words in another language. Therefore an exact, meaningful word-by-word translation from one language into another is frequently impossible. On the other hand, there must be limits to the freedom the translator exercises. He should use "the closest natural equivalent." We believe that he should stick as closely as he naturally can to the letter of the original, while making sure that he sets forth its spirit. This is the happy median of a good version.

Paul Cauer has succinctly stated what we believe to be the ideal: "So frei wie nötig, so treu wie möglich!" This means that a version should be "as free as necessary, as faithful as possible." Paraphrases are particularly liable to substitute the modern writer's own opinions for the actual teaching of the sacred Scriptures. The paraphraser may feel free to add not only words, but phrases, and even whole sentences to Holy Writ. There is real danger of distortion in such a procedure.

For a translator to be accurate in rendering a passage today means also that he must avail himself of the latest information available regarding the vocabulary and sentence structure of the biblical languages. Significant discoveries in archaeology and linguistics have resulted in meaningful advances in the recovery of the languages and cultures of the Middle East. All of this new information must be brought to bear upon the meaning of a word or a passage of the Bible.

As an added safeguard to accuracy it is helpful to have a committee go over the work of a translator. The checks and balances that are thus brought in serve to smooth out one man's idiosyncracies and result in greater reliability.

Quality of English

The third basic criterion for a satisfactory version concerns the quality of its English. For one thing, it is essential that a good version have clarity of expression. It is possible for a translator to have accurately determined the sense of the original without stating it clearly in English. Accuracy and clarity are related but they are not identical. Clarity has to do with the relationship of the translation to the reader. An ideal version presents the message of the original in language that is clear as crystal.

Among other things, this means that it must use words that are understandable to the reader. The level of understanding of readers, of course, varies with their cultural and educational backgrounds. But if the version uses simple, direct, and common English, it will be understandable to both the learned and those with limited education. For American readers an ideal version should not use words and expressions that have meaning in England or Scotland but are foreign to America.

Although it is desirable that a version have a simple, direct form of English, the language must be dignified and reverent. Slang, colloquialisms, and momentarily popular expressions should be avoided. It should be a worthy vehicle for the expression of the profound truths of the Word of God.

At the same time, the version must have literary appeal. It must be readable, euphonious, and interesting. It must be clothed in language that will grip the heart. Only then can it speak with full force the words of truth the world needs to hear.

Appendix

An Annotated List of Twentieth-century English Translations

The translations are arranged under the date the entire Bible was published. Earlier parts of the translation are listed under this date. If only the NT has been translated, it is, of course, listed under its date. If no complete NT or OT exists, then the date of the first portion is used. The compilers are aware that there may be other translations not listed, especially those of individual books, particularly the Psalms. Annotations are included for those that the compilers were able to examine. Reference is made to the appropriate chapter when that translation has been treated in the book. Reprints of pre–twentieth-century Bibles are not included in the list.

The compilers were especially indebted to the following two works in putting together this bibliography: Margaret T. Hills, ed., *The English Bible in America: A Bibliography of Editions of the Bible and the New Testament Published in America, 1777–1957*. New York: The American Bible Society and the New York Public Library, 1961. A. S. Herbert, *Historical Catalogue of Printed Editions of the English Bible, 1525–1961*. London: The British and Foreign Bible Society; New York: The American Bible Society, 1968.

1900 Hayman's Epistles
      The Epistles of the New Testament. An attempt to present them in current and popular idiom by Henry Hayman. London: A. and C. Black.

1901 The American Standard Version
The Holy Bible containing the Old and New Testaments translated out of the Original Languages. The Version set forth A.D. 1677, compared with the most ancient authorities and revised A.D. 1881–1885. Newly edited by the American Revision Committee.

A.D. 1901 Standard Edition, New York: Thomas Nelson and Sons.

See Chapter 2.

1901 Modern American Bible
The New Testament. The Modern American Bible. . . . The Books of the Bible in Modern American Form and Phrase with Notes and Introduction. By Frank Schell Ballantine. . . . New York: Thomas Whittaker, 1899–1901.

Part I: S. Mark (1899?). Part II: S. Matthew, S. Peter, S. Jude, and S. James (1899?). Part III: S. Luke (Gospel-Acts) (1899?). Part IV: S. Paul (including Hebrews) (1901?). Part V: S. John (Gospel, Letters, Revelation) (1901?). Based on Textus Receptus and later Greek texts. Preceded this by translation of the Four Gospels (Good News—The Four Gospels in a Modern American Dress, 1897). Revised 1909.

1901 Moffatt's Historical New Testament
The Historical New Testament. . . . A New Translation . . . by James Moffatt. Edinburgh: T. & T. Clark.

The books are chronologically arranged. A different translation from Moffatt's later translation.

1901 Way's Epistles
The Letters of St. Paul to Seven Churches and Three Friends. Translated by Arthur S. Way. London: The Macmillan Co.

Arthur S. Way, a classical scholar, translated the Letters of St. Paul, the first edition of which appeared in 1901, and a second thoroughly revised edition, which included Hebrews, was published in 1906 and reprinted in 1951.

1901 Young People's Bible
The Young People's Bible; or, the Scriptures Corrected, Explained, and Simplified, by Harriet Newell Jones . . . with Introduction by Rev. Malcolm MacGregor. . . . Philadelphia: American Book and Bible House.

1902   Emphasized Bible (Rotherham)
The Emphasized Bible (complete), a new translation designed to set forth the exact meaning, the proper terminology, and the graphic style of the sacred originals; arranged to show at a glance narrative, speech, parallelism, and logical analysis, also to enable the student readily to distinguish the several divine names; and emphasized throughout after the idioms of the Hebrew and Greek tongues. . . . By Joseph Bryant Rotherham.

Old Testament (1902), New York, Chicago, Toronto: Fleming H. Revell Co., 3 vols. Vol I: Genesis-Ruth. Vol. II: 1 Samuel-Psalms. Vol. III: Proverbs-Malachi.

New Testament (1897), is a rewritten edition of the version first printed in 1872 and reissued in a revised form in 1878. Gospel according to Matthew (1868). Greek text of Tregelles. In 1916, published four volumes in one.

1902? Godbey's New Testament
Translation of the New Testament from the original Greek. By Rev. W. B. Godbey. Cincinnati: M. W. Knapp, Office of God's Revivalist.

Based on Tischendorf's edition of the Codex Sinaiticus. Dedicated to "The Holiness People of all lands."

1902   Twentieth Century New Testament
The Twentieth Century New Testament. A translation into Modern English. Made from the original Greek. New York: Fleming H. Revell Co.

Part I: The Five Historical Books (undated, 1898?). Part II: Paul's Letters to the Churches (1900). Part III: The Pastoral, Personal and General Letters, and the Revelation (1901). Based on Westcott and Hort's Greek text.

One-volume edition (revised) in 1904. Reprinted frequently. See chapter 1.

1903   Fenton's Bible
The Holy Bible in Modern English, containing the complete sacred Scriptures of the Old and New Testaments, translated into English direct from the original Hebrew, Chaldee, and Greek, by Ferrar Fenton.

1882, Romans; 1884, Epistles; 1895, New Testament; 1903, whole Bible. New Testament and four parts of Old Testament.

First ed. of New Testament in Modern English 1895, revised 1900. Vol. I: Pentateuch, 1901? Vol. II: Joshua-

II Kings, 1902? Vol. III: Isaiah, Jeremiah, Ezekiel, Minor Prophets, Prophets, 1902?

Ferrar Fenton was a London businessman who devoted some twenty years of his life to fulfill a pledge of making the Scriptures intelligible "through the use of modern English." This work by an amateur was popular for a time, but "its erroneous and inaccurate renderings have rather damaged its earlier favor" (Price).

1903 Weymouth's New Testament
The New Testament in Modern Speech. An Idiomatic Translation into Every Day English from the text of The Resultant Greek Testament by Richard Francis Weymouth.

The text was revised in the 1924 edition by the Rev. S. W. Green, the Rev. Prof. A. J. D. Farrer, and the Rev. Prof. H. T. Andrews, and again in 1929 by the Rev. Prof. James Alexander Robertson.

See chapter 1.

1904 Worrell's New Testament
The New Testament Revised and Translated by A. S. Worrell, with Notes and Instructions designed to aid the earnest Reader in obtaining a clear Understanding of the Doctrines, Ordinances, and primitive Assemblies as revealed in these Scriptures. . . . Louisville, Ky.: A. S. Worrell.

Based on the Greek text underlying the ERV and on Westcott and Hort as modified by Scrivener and others. "Baptize" is translated "immerse"; "church" is "assembly" or "congregation." Claims great fidelity to the Greek. "To handle the tenses carelessly," writes the translator, "is to trifle with the word of God. . . . It is the business of the translator to translate with scrupulous exactness." Contains some textual variants, alternate renderings, and explanatory notes.

1905 Lloyd's New Testament
The Corrected English New Testament. A Revision of the "Authorized" Version (By Nestle's Resultant Text). Prepared with the Assistance of Eminent Scholars and Issued by Samuel Lloyd, a Life Governor of the British and Foreign Bible Society as His Memorial of the Society's Centenary, 1904. London: Samuel Bagster & Sons, Ltd.

The corrections are of two kinds: (1) the removal of textual defects in the underlying Greek and (2) a modernization of the English. Because of the large extent to which the AV had failed, Lloyd proposed that the Bible Society produce a new revision as a memorial to its centenary. When this was not accepted, he, with the cooperation of a number of biblical scholars, independently produced this version of the NT as an illustration of the kind of revision needed. He attempted "to show the possibility of popularizing without demeaning the Sacred Scriptures and of correcting without defacing the Version so worthily beloved."

1906 Forster
St. John's Gospel, Epistles, and Revelation, translated by Henry Langstaff Forster. Adelaide: Hunkin, Ellis and King.

The Revelation (1903). Tasmania: Henry Langstaff Forster.

1907 Bourne's Gospels
The Fourfold Portrait of the Heavenly King . . . translated by "Interpreter" i.e., A. E. Bourne. London: E. Stock.

A new translation of the Gospels.

1907 Moulton's Modern Reader's Bible
The Modern Reader's Bible; the Books of the Bible with Three Books of the Apocrypha presented in Modern Literary Form; edited with Introductions and Notes, by Richard G. Moulton. New York: The Macmillan Co.

1908 Rutherford's Epistles
Paul's Epistles to the Thessalonians and to the Corinthians. A New Translation by W. G. Rutherford, London.

1909 The Bible in Modern English
The Bible in Modern English. A Rendering from the Originals by an American, making use of the best scholarship and the latest research at home and abroad. Perkiomen, Pa.

1909 Weaver New Testament
New Testament in Modern Historical and Literary Form for the church, the school, and the home, embracing the life of Jesus Christ in the words of Matthew, Mark, Luke, and John, and the Church of the Apostles according to

the Acts, the Epistles and Revelation, historically harmonized. Translated by S. Townsend Weaver. Philadelphia: University Literature Extension.

1910 Cunard's
The first Judgment of the Christians by the Spirit, Alpha and Omega. An Authorized Revision of St. Matthew, and the History of this Planet, from the First Strata to the End. Written for the Spirit at Command by F. W. Cunard. Liverpool: Cunard & Sons.

1912 Improved Bible Union Version
The Holy Bible containing the Old and New Testaments. An Improved Edition (Based in Part on the Bible Union Version). Philadelphia: American Baptist Publication Society.

The Bible Union Version was an "immersion" version begun in the middle of the nineteenth century, but of which the OT was never fully completed. The NT of that version used "immersion" for "baptism." The Improved Version has "baptism (immersion)," "baptize (immerse)," and "baptized (immersed)." The poetic portions of the OT, including those of the prophets, are printed in poetic form.

1914 Numeric New Testament
The New Testament from the Greek text as established by Bible Numerics. Edited by Ivan Panin. New Haven: Bible Numerics Co.

Based on the number value of the Greek and Hebrew letters. Awkward in many places.

Second edition, 1935, and reprinted several times.

1914 Cunnington's New Testament
The New Covenant, commonly called the New Testament of our Lord and Saviour Jesus Christ. A revision of the version of A.D. 1611 by E. E. Cunnington. London: G. Routledge & Sons.

Other editions appeared, e.g., in 1919 by T. Foster Unwin, London, under the title The Adelphi New Testament; and in 1926 with the title The Western New Testament.

1916 McFadyen
The Psalms in Modern Speech and Rhythmical Form by John Edgar McFadyen. London: James Clarke & Co.

The Wisdom Books, also Lamentations and the Song of

Songs, in Modern Speech and Rhythmical form by John Edgar McFadyen, 1917. Isaiah in Modern Speech, 1918. Jeremiah in Modern Speech, 1919.

1917 Jewish Publication Society Bible
The Holy Scriptures According to the Masoretic Text. A New Translation with the Aid of Previous Versions and with Constant Consultation of Jewish Authorities. Philadelphia: The Jewish Publication Society.

Jewish Publication Society Version. Psalms, 1903.
See chapter 7.

1918 Anderson New Testament
The New Testament. Translated from the Sinaitic Manuscript Discovered by Constantine Tischendorf at Mount Sinai, by H. T. Anderson. Cincinnati: The Standard Publishing Company.

1919 The Messages of the Bible
The Messages of the Bible, edited by Frank K. Sanders and Charles F. Kent. 12 vols. New York: Charles Scribner's Sons, 1898–1919.

Brief introductions of each book and free rendering in paraphrase.

1921 Pym
Mark's Account of Jesus. Cambridge: W. Heffer and Sons. "Common Speech" by T. W. Pym.

1921 Shorter Bible
The Shorter Bible, translated and arranged by Charles Foster Kent . . . with the Collaboration of Charles Cutler Torrey . . . Henry A. Sherman . . . Frederick Harris . . . Ethel Cutler. . . . New York: Charles Scribner's Sons.

New Testament, 1918. Old Testament, 1921. About two-thirds of the OT and one-third of the NT are omitted.

1922 Plainer Bible
A Plainer Bible for Plain People in Plain America . . . (New Testament) from the original Greek by Chaplain [Frank Schell] Ballentine. . . . Jersey City, N.J.: Plainer Bible Press.

See 1901, Modern American Bible.

1923 Riverside New Testament
The Riverside New Testament; a translation from the original Greek into the English of today, by William G. Ballantine. Boston: Houghton, Mifflin.

An eclectic rendering of Nestle's Greek text by William G. Ballantine, a former President of Oberlin College, who confesses his indebtedness to other versions, such as Weymouth's, Moffatt's, and The Twentieth Century New Testament. Produced in a very readable form with an index, this version was first published in 1923, and revised in 1934.

1923 Robertson

A Translation of Luke's Gospel with Grammatical Notes by A. T. Robertson. New York: George H. Doran Co.

1924 Labor Determinative Version

The New Covenant: a Mutual Arrangement or Testament for a true civilization founded upon brotherly labor, following the Greek title which is usually rendered the New Testament, translated out of the Greek as a Labor Determinative Version, and diligently compared with former translations herein revised for the recovery of Biblical labor standards. Jackson, Mich.: Home of the American Labor Determinative Revision Committee.

1924 Montgomery's Centenary Translation

Centenary Translation of the New Testament in Modern English. Translated by Helen Barrett Montgomery. Philadelphia: Judson Press. 2 vols.

In commemoration of the centenary of the American Baptist Publication Society, Mrs. Helen Barrett Montgomery of Rochester, N. Y., and a graduate of Wellesley College, published this translation. Many of her colloquial paragraph and chapter headings are striking, such as "Play the Game," "A 'Close-up' of Sin," "Paul's Swan Song," and "Orchestrate Your Virtues."

1925 Askwith's Psalms

The Psalms Books IV and V. Rendered into English in Rhythm Consonant with that of the Original Hebrew by E. H. Askwith. London: M. Hopkinson and Co.

1925 People's New Covenant

The People's New Covenant . . . Translated from the Metaphysical Standpoint by Arthur E. Overbury. Monrovia, Calif.: Arther E. Overbury.

This version is based on the premise of Scientific Statement of Being, as given in *Science and Health* by Mary Baker Eddy.

1925 Children's Bible
The Children's Bible. Selections from the Old and New Testaments. Translated and arranged by Henry A. Gherman and Charles Foster Kent. New York: Charles Scribner's Sons.

A translation in readable, simple English of selections from the OT and NT. Includes not only narratives, but poetic and didactic selections.

1926 Moffatt
A New Translation of The Bible, Containing the Old and New Testaments, by James Moffatt. New York and London: Harper and Brothers.

New Testament, 1913. New edition, revised, 1917. Old Testament, 1924–25, in 2 vols. Vol I: Genesis-Esther (1924). Vol. II: Job-Malachi (1925). Revision of complete Bible in 1935. See chapter 1.

1927 Kent's Student's Old Testament
The Student's Old Testament Logically and Chronologically Arranged and Translated by Charles Foster Kent. New York: Charles Scribner's Sons, 1904–27.

Six vols. I: Narratives of the Beginnings of Hebrew History from the Creation to the Establishment of the Hebrew Kingdom, 1904. II: Israel's Historical and Biographical Narratives from the Establishment of the Hebrew Kingdom to the End of the Maccabean Struggle, 1905. III: The Sermons, Epistles, and Apocalypses of Israel's Prophets from the Beginning of the Assyrian Period to the End of the Maccabean Struggle, 1910. IV: Israel's Laws and Legal Precedents from the Days of Moses to the Closing of the Legal Canon, 1907. V: The Songs, Hymns, and Prayers of the Old Testament, 1914. VI: Proverbs and Didactic Poems, 1927.

1927 Smith-Goodspeed
The Bible. An American Translation. The Old Testament Translated by J. M. Powis Smith and a Group of Scholars. The New Testament Translated by Edgar J. Goodspeed. Chicago: The University of Chicago Press.

Revised, 1935. The New Testament, An American Translation, 1923. The Old Testament, An American Translation, 1927. The Apocrypha, An American Translation, 1938. Reprinted, with Apocrypha included, 1939. See chapter 1.

1927   Christian's Bible
The Christian's Bible—New Testament. Strasburg, Pa.:
George N. Le Fevre.
    A translation from the Greek, chiefly from B and
Aleph. Not simply a translation of the Words, but under
the guidance of the Holy Ghost, His thoughts as recorded. . . . George Le Fevre is considered the translator
as well as publisher.

1928   Czarnomska Version
The Authentic Literature of Israel freed from the
Disarrangements, Expansions, and Comments of Early
Native Editors, edited with an introduction by Eliza-
beth Czarnomska. New York: The Macmillan Co., 1924–
28.

1928   Spiritualist's Matthew
The Good Message according to Matthew. For the use of
Christian Spiritualists . . . an entirely new and accurate
translation edited by J. W. Potter. London: Society of
Communion.

1929   Gowen's Psalms
The Psalms; or, the Book of Praises. A New Transcription
and Translation arranged Strophically and Metrically
from a critically constructed text, with introduction, textual notes, and glossary by Herbert H. Gowen. London:
Mowbray.

1930   Loux's Mark
Mark: To Every Man His Work, His Pay, His Rest.
Translated by DuBois H. Loux. Jackson, Mich.: Privately
printed.

1931   Wales's Psalms
The Psalms. A Revised Translation, by Frank H. Wales.
London: Oxford University Press.

1932   Chaplain Ballentine
Our God and Godhealth, our Healer. Godhealth's Messenger and Godhealth's Message of Life and Light and
Love and Law, the wisest wisdom of the wise of all ages:
translated from the original Greek, reinterpreted in the
thought-forms, language, and idioms of America today,
and arranged for reading with sustained interest from
beginning to end as a modern novel, by Chaplain [Frank
Schell] Ballentine. . . . Collegeville, Pa.: The Craigie
Publishing Co.

1932 Kleist's Memoirs of St. Peter
The Memoirs of St. Peter, or the Gospel according to St. Mark, translated into English sense-lines. By James A. Kleist, S.J. Milwaukee: Bruce Publishing Co.

Translated into sense-lines, which it is maintained is the form that resembles the original itself.

1933 Torrey's Four Gospels
The Four Gospels, a New Translation by Charles Cutler Torrey. New York and London: Harper and Brothers.

Its purpose is to show that the Gospels of Matthew, Mark, and John were composed in Aramaic.

1934 Royds' Epistles and Gospels
The Epistles and Gospels for the Sundays & chief holy days of the Christian year. A new translation by Thomas Fletcher Royds. Oxford: Basil Blackwell.

New Testament into modern English: "such English as intelligent village schoolchildren can understand without much explaining of long words." Nestle Greek text. Not continuous text. Good straightforward translation.

1934 Old Testament in Colloquial English
The Books of the Old Testament in Colloquial English, 1920–34.

Listed in E. H. Robertson's *The New Translations of the Bible*.

1934 Wade
The Documents of the New Testament. Translated and Historically Arranged with Critical Introduction by G. W. Wade. London: Thomas Murby & Co. Copies of Mark, Luke, and John issued separately in 1936.

Claims to be "an accurate, yet not literal" translation. Avoids ambiguity by presenting what the translator judges to be the most probable meaning. Literary relationships are indicated in the Synoptics, Acts, and 2 Peter-Jude. Westcott and Hort text.

1935 Westminster Version
The Westminster Version of the Sacred Scriptures, general editor, Cuthbert Lattey. Introductions and commentaries with translation.

New Testament, 1935. Smaller edition in 1948, translations with brief introductions by Father Lattey.

New Testament in parts from 1913–35, edited by Cuthbert Lattey and J. Keating.

Malachi, 1934-Lattey. Ruth, 1935-Lattey. Nahum and Habakkuk, 1937-Bevenot. Jonah, 1938-T. E. Bird. Psalms 1–41, 1939-Lattey. Psalms, 1944-Lattey. Daniel, 1948-Lattey. Obadiah, Micah, Zephaniah, Haggai, Zechariah, 1953-Sebastian Bullough.

An excellent translation by English Roman Catholic scholars under the editorship of Cuthbert Lattey, S.J., based on the original texts in both Testaments. An independent venture; not an "official" translation.

1937　Cornish's St. Paul from the Trenches
St. Paul from the Trenches, translated by Gerald Warre Cornish. Two epistles of Corinthians, part of Ephesians.

For the story behind this expanded version see F. F. Bruce, *The English Bible*, New and Revised Edition, p. 22 (New York: Oxford Press).

1937　Greber's New Testament
The New Testament. A New Translation and Explanation Based on The Oldest Manuscripts, by Johannes Greber. New York: John Felsberg, Inc. The English translation was made by a professional translator and corrected by a committee of American clergymen. A somewhat eccentric translation. It is based mainly on Codex Bezae, but at times the translator has given a version with no MS authority. Originally published in German but subsequently translated into English. Translator is a former Roman Catholic priest who came to believe in communication with the world of divine spirits.

1937　Martin's New Testament
The New Testament critically reconstructed and retranslated, by William Wallace Martin. Nashville, Tenn.: Parthenon Press.

Epistles in 2 vols. Part I: Press of Marshall and Bruce Co., Nashville, 1929. Part II: Press of the Methodist Episcopal Church, Nashville, 1930.

The twenty-one canonical Epistles have been reconstructed into thirty-six, including as authors Apollos, Barnabas, and John, son of Zebedee (as the writer of the Epistle of James).

The Psalms Complete: Their Prayers, their Collects, their Praises, in three Books. Separated, arranged, and translated by William Wallace Martin. Nashville, Tenn.: Marshall & Bruce Co.

The Book of Job in Two Versions: A Judean Version, an Ephramaean Version; and The Book of Ecclesiastes. Nashville, Tenn.: Methodist Publishing House.

Isaian Prophecies. Nashville, Tenn.: Parthenon Press.

Jeremiah-Ezekiel Prophecies. Nashville, Tenn.: Parthenon Press.

The Book of Genesis Complete. The Ephramaean Version . . . The Judean Version. Nashville, Tenn.: Parthenon Press.

Twelve Minor Prophets. Nashville, Tenn.: Parthenon Press.

1937   Spencer's New Testament

The New Testament of Our Lord and Saviour Jesus Christ; translated into English from the original Greek by the Very Rev. Francis Aloysius Spencer, O.P.; edited by Charles J. Callan, O.P. and John A. McHugh, O.P. New York: The Macmillan Co.

After publishing a new translation of the Gospels from the Latin in 1898, Father Francis Aloysius Spencer was moved to attempt a new translation from the Greek. The four Gospels were published in 1901 and the rest of the NT finished with notes shortly before Spencer's death in 1913. The whole NT, however, was not published until 1937, under the editorship of Charles J. Callan and John A. McHugh, and has been reprinted several times since. The words of Christ are printed in italics, quotations from the OT are put in small capitals, and Vulgate readings that differ from the Greek are given in brackets or footnotes.

1937   Williams's New Testament

The New Testament; a translation in the language of the people, by Charles B. Williams. Boston: Bruce Humphries. Slightly revised edition, Chicago: Moody Press, 1950. Verse numbers inserted in the text. Westcott and Hort Greek text.

A Greek professor from Union University (Jackson, Tenn.), Charles B. Williams's aim was to reproduce as far as possible the exact shades of meaning in the Greek tenses. To do this requires the use of auxiliaries and the like in English and can result in overtranslation and in the use of language that is hardly the "language of the people."

1938　Book of Books
The Book of Books. A Translation of the New Testament
Complete and Unabridged. London: R.T.S. The Lutter-
worth Press, The United Society for Christian Literature.
R. Mercer Wilson, General Secretary, The United Society
for Christian Literature translated this NT to celebrate
the centenary of the *Annotated Paragraph Bible,* which he
follows in the arrangement of his text, and the fourth
centenary of the setting up of the English Bible in the
churches. Rather straightforward simple translation.

1938　Buttenweiser's Psalms
The Psalms. Chronologically Treated with a New Translation by Moses Buttenweiser, Prof. Emeritus of Biblical
Exegesis, Hebrew Union College. Chicago: The University of Chicago Press.

1938　Clementson's New Testament
The New Testament. A Translation by Edgar Lewis
Clementson. Pittsburgh: The Evangelization Society of
the Pittsburgh Bible Institute.

1939　Oesterley Psalms
The Psalms. Translated with Text-Critical and Exegetical
Notes by W. O. E. Oesterley. London: S.P.C.K.; New
York: The Macmillan Co. 2 vols.

1940　Dakes's Gospels
Christ Jesus: The Authentic Story of the Founder of
Christianity as told by Matthew, Mark, Luke and John in
the Four Gospels. Translated from the original Greek by
John A. Dakes. Chicago: Avalon Publishing Co.
　　Dakes was a Greek businessman who felt "that a
translation made by a Greek who had learned the original language of the Gospels in the schools of Greece
might prove helpful." Certain Greek words are transliterated, such as *petros* and *petra* in Matthew 16:18,
ecclesia, aeonian, and *Logos.* A glossary appears at the
back of the book.

1940　St. Mark in Current English
St. Mark in Current English. By Mary L. Matheson. Mel-
bourne: National Council of Religious Education of
Australia.

1944　Callan's Psalms
The Psalms. Translated from the Latin Psalter, in the
Light of the Hebrew, of the Septuagint and Peshitta Ver-

sions, and of the Psalterium Juxta Hebraeos of St. Jerome. With Introductions, Critical Notes, and Spiritual Reflections by Charles J. Callan. New York: Joseph F. Wagner.

1944 Wand's New Testament Letters
The New Testament Letters, prefaced and paraphrased by J. W. C. Wand. Brisbane, Australia. Revised edition published in England, 1946.

Romans-Jude. According to the Introduction, the work "may be called either a free translation or a close paraphrase." "I have tried," says Bishop Wand, "to put the Epistles into the kind of language a Bishop might use in writing a monthly letter for his diocesan magazine."

1945 Stringfellow's New Testament
New Testament. A Translation, Harmony and Annotations by Erwin Edward Stringfellow. . . . Planographed by John S. Swift Co., Inc.

Vol. I: The Gospels (1943). Vol. II: Acts-Revelation (1945). Dubuque, Iowa: Wm. C. Brown Co.

Westcott and Hort text.

1946 Lenski
The Interpretation of the [New Testament] . . . R. C. H. Lenski. Columbus, Ohio: Lutheran Book Concern, 1931–46.

Twelve vols. Commentary with independent translation by a noted Lutheran scholar.

1947 Eerdmans's Psalms
The Hebrew Books of Psalms by B. D. Eerdmans. Oudtestamentliche Studien, IV. Leiden: E. J. Brill.

1947 Swann's New Testament
The New Testament . . . Translated from the Greek text of Westcott and Hort. By Rev. George Swann. . . . Louisville, Ky.: Pentecostal Publishing Company. Second ed., 1949.

Third ed.

1948 Letchworth New Testament
The New Testament . . . Letchworth Version in Modern English, by T. F. Ford and R. E. Ford. Letchworth, Herts: Letchworth Printer, Ltd.

A translation of the TR Greek text into current English, mainly using words of Anglo-Saxon origin, and free from colloquialisms and slang expressions. Seeks to maintain in modern dress the simple, dignified style of writing associated with the classical English versions.

1949 Basic Bible

The Basic Bible, containing the Old and New Testaments in Basic English. Cambridge: The University Press and Evans Bros. New York: Dutton.

The New Testament in Basic English, 1940. Whole Bible, 1949. Selections, 1933; Micah and Habakkuk, 1934; Mark, 1945; John, 1938.

Basic English is a system of simplified English with a primary vocabulary of 850 words devised by C. K. Ogden as an international auxiliary language and as an aid in learning English. In 1940 a committee under the direction of S. H. Hooke of the University of London produced an independent translation of the New Testament, using the 850 words in the primary vocabulary of Basic English to which 50 special Bible words and 100 others were added.

1949 Leslie's Psalms

The Psalms. Translated and Interpreted in the Light of Hebrew Life and Worship by Elmer A. Leslie. New York and Nashville: Abingdon-Cokesbury Press.

1951 Authentic Version

The New Testament . . . The Authentic Version. Plattsburg, Mo.: Brotherhood Authentic Bible Society.

Anonymous translator: "Believing that I have been given divine authority through the Holy Spirit to bring the true translation of the original Greek text, and that which has been given me through the inspiration of the Holy Spirit, I have diligently and carefully compared with the original Greek text by the use of the best Greek dictionaries and former translations, some out of the Greek and some Latin: and find that what the Spirit has given me is according to the Original Greek." Modern speech version.

1951 Vernon's Mark

The Gospel of St. Mark: A New Translation in Simple English, translated by Edward Vernon.

For the average intelligent child of twelve years old and upwards.

1952 New Testament in Plain English

The New Testament; a new translation in plain English

by Charles Kingsley Williams. London: S.P.C.K., Longmans, Green and Co.

The Life of Our Lord Jesus Christ according to St. Luke, together with some passages from the other Gospels, newly done into very simple English from the Greek of The Revised Version, 1933. Matthew, 1934.

"Plain English" is a simplified form of the English language based on a list of 1,500 "fundamental and common words that make up ordinary English speech," plus some 160 or 170 others that are explained in a glossary at the end of the volume. The translation is based on Souter's Greek Text (Oxford Press, 1910).

1952 Penguin Bible (Rieu)
The Four Gospels, a New Translation from the Greek by E. V. Rieu. London and Melbourne: Penguin Books.

Acts of the Apostles by Saint Luke, by C. H. Rieu, son of E. V. Rieu.

E. V. Rieu justifies his translation on the basis that it is from the literary standpoint more in harmony with the Greek Gospels than the KJV, whose translators "mistook fidelity to the idiom of the Greek for fidelity to its meaning" and "felt the sanctity and importance of the original so keenly that the use of normal language would have seemed a kind of sacrilege." Accurate and readable.

1952 Revised Standard Version
The Holy Bible . . . Revised Standard Version . . . being the Version Set Forth A.D. 1611. Revised 1881 and 1901 . . . and Revised 1952. New York, Toronto, Edinburgh: Thomas Nelson and Sons.

New Testament, 1946. Old Testament with Complete Bible, 1952. Apocrypha, 1957.

See chapter 2.

1954 Kissane's Psalms
The Books of Psalms. Translated from a Critically Revised Hebrew Text with a Commentary by Monsignor Edward J. Kissane. Dublin: Brown and Nolan, Ltd. Vol. I, 1953; Vol. II, 1954.

1954 Kleist and Lilly's New Testament
The New Testament rendered from the original Greek with Explanatory Notes. Milwaukee: Bruce Publishing Co.

The Four Gospels translated by James A. Kleist, S.J.,

and the Acts to Revelation by Joseph L. Lilly, C.M. Made from 1943 Bover Greek Text into modern popular English. An independent modern American translation.

1954   Kleist and Lynam's Psalms
The Psalms in Rhythmic Prose. By James A. Kleist, S.J. and Thomas James Lynam, S.J. Milwaukee: Bruce Publishing Co.

Based on Latin text of the Pontifical Biblical Institute, Rome.

1954   Moore's New Testament
The New Testament. A New, Independent, Individual Translation from the Greek, by George Albert Moore, Colonel, U.S.A. Chevy Chase, Md.: The Country Dollar Press.

Based on Souter's 1950 Greek text. Gospels issued separately in 1953.

1955   Fides Translation (Psalms)
The Psalms. Fides Translation. Introduction and Notes by Mary Perkins Ryan. Chicago: Fides Publishers Association.

Made in accordance with the new Roman Psalter.

1955   Knox
The Holy Bible; a translation from the Latin Vulgate in the light of the Hebrew and Greek originals. Authorized by the hierarchy of England and Wales and the hierarchy of Scotland. Translated by Monsignor Knox. London: Burns and Oates.

Old Testament. New York: Sheed and Ward, 1948–50, 2 vols. Vol. I: Genesis-Esther. Vol. II: Job-Maccabees.

New Testament . . . Newly Translated from the Vulgate Latin at the Request of Their Lordships, the Archbishops of England and Wales. New York: Sheed & Ward, British Trial Edition, 1944.

See chapter 3.

1955   Schonfield's Authentic New Testament
The Authentic New Testament, edited and translated from the Greek for the general reader by Hugh J. Schonfield. London: D. Dobson.

This is a work of high quality by the distinguished Jewish Scholar, Dr. Hugh J. Schonfield, who approaches these documents "as if they had recently been recovered from a cave in Palestine or beneath the sands of Egypt,

and had never previously been given to the public."
Much helpful information on the Jewish references in the
New Testament is given in the Notes and Introduction.

1956   Laubach's Inspired Letters
The Inspired Letters in Clearest English. Prepared by
Frank C. Laubach. New York: Thomas Nelson and Sons.

Romans-Jude. Written in short, clear sentences with a
limited vocabulary of about two thousand words, this
translation is intended as a preparation for the reading of
the RSV for beginning students of English. The Gospels
and Acts, the translator feels, are simple enough in the
RSV. By the world's leader in the fight against illiteracy.

1957   Concordant Version
Concordant Version. International Edition. The Sacred
Scriptures. An Idiomatic, Consistent, Emphasized Ver-
sion. . . . Los Angeles: Concordant Publishing Concern.

Old Testament—Half title: Concordant Version of the
Hebrew Scriptures. In a Beginning, commonly called
"Genesis."

[The New Testament] Concordant Version, 1919–26.
One-volume reprint, 1931.

This version is based on the belief that "every word in
the original should have its own English equivalent." It
is said to aim "at truth and accuracy rather than literary
elegance." It shows the eccentricities "of a self-taught
and opinionated 'one man' translator who has certain
peculiar views to proclaim yet is 'reverent, careful, and
thorough.'"

1957   Lamsa's
The Holy Bible from ancient Eastern manuscripts. Containing the Old and New Testaments, translated from the
Peshitta, the authorized Bible of the church of the East,
by George M. Lamsa. Philadelphia: A. J. Holman Co.

The Four Gospels according to the Eastern Version,
1933.

The Book of Psalms according to the Eastern Version,
1939.

The New Testament, 1940.

George M. Lamsa's translation purports to be produced
"from original Aramaic sources." Lamsa's original claims
for his work are generally questioned. The Peshitta is not
to be identified with the "original Aramaic." Lamsa also

adapted some questionable renderings such as "rope" for "camel" in Matthew 19:24, et al.

1958 Hudson

The Pauline Epistles: Their Meanings and Message. Introduction, Translation, Marginal Analysis, and Paraphrase by James T. Hudson. London: James Clarke & Co., Ltd.

"New translation with the missing steps in Paul's thought supplied in brackets." Omits Hebrews.

1958 Meissner's Gospels

New Testament Gospels, a Modern Translation by Lawrence Meissner. Portland, Oreg.

All the verses, 40 percent fewer words.

1958 Phillips's New Testament

New Testament in Modern English. New York: The Macmillan Co. Letters to Young Churches; a translation of the New Testament Epistles, by J. B. Phillips; with an introduction by C. S. Lewis, 1951. A corrected edition, 1957. First published in England, 1947. The Gospels, translated into modern English by J. B. Phillips, c. 1951. First published in 1952. The Young Church in Action; a Translation of the Acts of the Apostles by J. B. Phillips, 1955. Book of Revelation, 1957. Gospels, a corrected edition, 1958. Four Prophets: Amos, Hosea, First Isaiah, Micah; a modern translation from the Hebrew, by J. B. Phillips, 1963. Second revised edition of the New Testament, 1973.

See chapter 4.

1958 Tomanek's New Testament

The New Testament of Our Lord and Savior Jesus Anointed, by James L. Tomanek. Pocatello, Ida.: Arrowhead Press.

1959 Cressman

St. Mark. Toronto: Full Gospel Publishing House.

Mark, 2nd ed., 1960. John, American Bible Society, 1962.

Simplified English for Liberians by Annie Cressman of the Assemblies of God Mission.

1959 Modern Language Bible (Berkeley)

The Holy Bible, the Berkeley Version in Modern English, containing the Old and New Testaments. Translated afresh from the original languages and diligently compared with previous translations, with numerous helpful nondoctrinal notes to aid the understanding of the reader. Gerrit Verkuyl, editor-in-chief and translator of the New Testament section. Grand Rapids: Zondervan Publishing House.

Berkeley Version of the New Testament, 1945. Berkeley, Calif.: James J. Gillick & Co. Grand Rapids: Zondervan Publishing House, 1950, 1953.

See chapter 5.

1960 The Children's "King James"

The Children's "King James" Bible: New Testament. Jay Green is responsible for the wording; "Peter" Palmer for the stories. Evansville, Ind.: Modern Bible Translations.

Not KJV of 1611, but a modern version using the same text the KJ translation used. .

1961 New World Translation—Jehovah's Witnesses

New World Translation of the Holy Scriptures, rendered from the original languages by the New World Bible Translation Committee. Revised. Brooklyn: Watchtower Bible and Tract Society of New York.

The New World Translation of the Christian Greek Scriptures, 1950.

Based on Westcott and Hort, supplemented by Nestle, Bover, Merk.

New World Translation of the Hebrew Scriptures, 1953–60. Issued in five vols. Genesis-Ruth, 1953; 1 Samuel-Esther, 1955; Job-Song of Solomon, 1957; Isaiah-Lamentations, 1958; Ezekiel-Malachi, 1960. Based on 3rd ed. Kittel, 1951.

See chapter 6.

1961 Noli's Greek Orthodox New Testament

The New Testament of Our Lord and Savior Jesus Christ. Translated into English from the approved Greek text of the Church of Constantinople and the Church of Greece, by Fan S. Noli. Boston: Albanian Orthodox Church in America.

1961 One Way

One Way: The Jesus People New Testament. A Translation in Modern English. Pasadena, Calif.: Compass Press.

This is the same as Norlie's The New Testament in Modern English, 1951.

1961 Simplified New Testament (Norlie)
Simplified New Testament in Plain English for Today's
Reader. A New Translation from the Greek by Olaf M.
Norlie. With the Psalms for Today, a new translation in
current English by R. K. Harrison. Grand Rapids: Zon-
dervan Publishing House.

Dr. Olaf M. Norlie of St. Olaf College designed this
translation particularly for teenagers. It is rendered in
plain, lucid, and straightforward English.

An earlier translation of Norlie was published by the
author in 1951 in Northfield, Minn., with the title: The
New Testament . . . in Modern English translated from
the original Greek and supplied with an outline by Olaf
Morgan Norlie. Still earlier, in 1943, a translation of the
Gospel of John was published in mimeographed form in
San Antonio, Tex., by the Life Builders Press.

1961 Wuest's Expanded New Testament
Expanded Translation of the Greek New Testament by
Kenneth S. Wuest. Grand Rapids: Wm. B. Eerdmans
Publishing Co.

Vol. 1: Gospels (1956). Vol. 2: Acts through Ephesians
(1958). Vol. 3: Philippians through Revelation (1959).

Kenneth S. Wuest endeavors to reproduce for the English readers the nuances of the Greek text, both
philologically and theologically. Bible scholars may feel
that he at times overtranslates and finds shades of
meaning not actually in the Greek text. He does for all
parts of speech what Williams does for verbs.

1962 Children's Version
The Children's Version of the Holy Bible. New York:
McGraw Hill.

Printed in large, Caledonia type for easy reading. The
text is arranged in paragraphs, though the verse numbers
are retained in small type interspersed through the text.
Difficult words, names, and places are diacritically
marked and some are phonetically pronounced. The text
is a simplification and modernization of the KJV. The
preface is by Jay P. Green.

1963 Gelineau's Psalms
The Psalms: A New Translation. Translated from the He-
brew and arranged for Singing to the Psalmody of Joseph
Gelineau. Philadelphia: The Westminster Press.

1963   The Holy Name Bible
The Holy Name Bible containing the Holy Name Version of the Old and New Testaments. Revised by A. B. Traina. Irvington, N.J.: The Scripture Research Association, Inc.

The New Testament of our Messiah and Saviour Yahshua. Sacred Name Version, 1950.

This translation is understood to have been made by A. B. Traina and reprinted at his expense. The version attempts to restore Semitic proper names to their Aramaic or Hebrew form and to clear up difficulties in the text in the light of possible Semitic background.

1964   Anchor Bible
Anchor Bible, edited by William F. Albright and David N. Freedman. Individual translators for books. Garden City, N.J.: Doubleday & Co.

1964   Hadas's Psalms
The Book of Psalms for the Modern Reader: A New Translation by Gershon Hadas. New York: Jonathan David.

1965   Amplified Bible
The Amplified Bible, containing the Amplified Old Testament and the Amplified New Testament. Grand Rapids: Zondervan Publishing House.

The Amplified New Testament. Zondervan Publishing House, 1958–65. Old Testament: Part I (1964), Genesis-Esther; Part II (1962), Job-Malachi. Zondervan Publishing House. Translation by Frances E. Siwert.

See chapter 8.

1965   Bruce's Expanded Paraphrase
An Expanded Paraphrase of the Epistles of Paul. Printed in parallel with the Revised Version, with fuller references by Drs. Scrivener, Moulton & Greenup, by F. F. Bruce. Exeter: Paternoster Press.

American edition has title: The Letters of Paul: Expanded Paraphrase.

This paraphrase is designed, as Bruce states, "to make the course of Paul's argument as clear as possible." The "expanded paraphrase" is printed alongside the Revised Version of 1881, "for the convenience and interest of readers who may care to compare and contrast two renderings produced on directly opposite principles."

1966   The Bible in Simplified English
Listen . . . The Lord is Speaking: The Bible in Simplified English. Collegeville, Minn.: The Liturgical Press.

The authorized English edition of the Katholische Schulbibel, which is an abridged selection of biblical passages rearranged to provide a chronological history of the biblical period. The poetic books, duplicated historical material, and Epistles are not included. Written in simple English, this is intended for beginners in the study of the Bible.

1966   Burke
God Is For Real, Man: Interpretations of Bible Passages and Stories as Told by Some of God's Bad-tempered Angels with Busted Haloes to Carl F. Burke. New York: Association Press.

1969 edition entitled God Is Beautiful, Man.

Free treatment of selected Bible passages in American downtown slang by young people of the inner city.

See chapter 19.

1966   Jerusalem Bible
Jerusalem Bible. General editor, Alexander Jones. Garden City, New York, and London: Doubleday and Darton, Longman and Todd. See chapter 9.

1966   Living Scriptures
The Living Scriptures, a New Translation in the King James Tradition. Edited by Jay P. Green. Marshatton, Del.: National Foundation for Christian American Bible Society. New York: The Macmillan Co.

1967   Dale's New World
New World: The Heart of the New Testament in Plain English, by Alan T. Dale. London: Oxford University Press, c.1967, 1968.

1967   Liverpool Vernacular Gospels
The Gospels in Scouse, translated by Dick Williams and Frank Shaw. Revised edition, London: White Lion Publishers, 1977.

"A rollicking, carefree interpretation of some Gospel passages in the Liverpool vernacular."

See chapter 19.

1968   Cotton Patch Version
The Cotton Patch Version of Paul's Epistles, by Clarence Jordan. New York: Association Press.

The Cotton Patch Version of Luke and Acts, 1969. The Cotton Patch Version of Matthew and John, 1970. First eight chapters of John only. The Cotton Patch Version of Hebrews and the General Epistles, 1973.

A local dialect version rather than merely an English version. Intended for the South, especially the area around Atlanta. This version goes to the limit of the spectrum in translating ideas and substitutes local place names for biblical ones. Based on Nestle-Aland, 23rd ed., 1957. By the founder of an interracial farming community in Americus, Georgia, with a Ph.D. in Greek from Southern Baptist Theological Seminary.

See chapter 19.

1968 Hanson's Psalms in Modern Speech

The Psalms in Modern Speech for Public and Private Use, by Richard S. Hanson. Philadelphia: Fortress Press.

3 vols. Vol. 1: Psalms 1–41. Vol. 2: Psalms 42–89. Vol. 3: Psalms 90–150.

A fresh poetic rendering of "the Hymnbook of Ancient Israel," with special attention to its liturgical usage. Contains an informative "Introduction," introductory notes to many of the Psalms, and footnotes explaining deviations from previous translations.

1968 Restoration of Original Name New Testament

The New Testament of Our Master and Saviour Yahvah-shua the Messiah (commonly called Jesus Christ): Restoration of Original Name New Testament. Junction City, Oreg.: Missionary Dispensary Bible Research.

Rotherham's version but with changes made principally by returning to the Hebrew form of God's name and by replacing Lord and God in the New Testament by YAHVAH or, for the latter, Elohim when it is used with God.

1969 Barclay's New Testament

The New Testament: a new translation by William Barclay. London, Cleveland: Collins.

Gospels and Acts, 1968. Letters and The Revelation, 1969.

See chapter 10.

1969 Children's New Testament

The Children's New Testament. Translated by Gleason H. Ledyard. Waco, Tex.: Word Books.

1970　King James II New Testament
King James II New Testament translated by Jay P. Green. Byron Center, Mich.: Associated Publishers.

1970　The Mercier New Testament
The Mercier New Testament: A Version of the New Testament in Modern English. Part I: Matthew, Mark, Luke, John. Prepared by Kevin Condon. Cork: Mercier Press. (Identical with The Alba House New Testament.)

A fresh Catholic translation from the Greek in plain, simple, modern English. Patterned after the German Das Neue Testament für Menschen unserer Zeit (1964). Not meant to compete with the standard English versions, but to lead to a greater appreciation and use of them. Illustrated by a hundred carefully selected photographs.

1970　New American Bible
The New American Bible. Translated from the original languages, with the critical use of all the ancient sources, by members of the Catholic Biblical Association of America. New York: P. J. Kenedy.

The New Testament of Our Lord and Savior Jesus Christ translated from the Latin Vulgate. A revision of the Challoner-Rheims Version edited by Catholic Scholars under the patronage of the episcopal committee of the Confraternity of Christian Doctrine. Paterson, N.J.: St. Anthony Guild Press, 1941. (The NT in the NAB is a new translation from the Greek text.)

Genesis, 1948; Vol. I (Genesis-Ruth), 1952; Vol. III (Sapiential or Wisdom Books), 1955; Vol. IV (Prophetic Books), 1961; Vol. II (Samuel-Maccabees), 1969.

See chapter 13.

1970　New English Bible
The New English Bible with the Apocrypha. Oxford University Press and Cambridge University Press.

New Testament, 1961; 2nd ed., 1970. The Old Testament and Apocrypha, 1970.

See chapter 12.

1971　Blackwelder's Exegetical Translation
Letters from Paul. An Exegetical Translation by Boyce W. Blackwelder. Anderson, Ind.: Warner Press.

Based on Nestle's 4th ed., 1904. At times reads more like a condensed commentary than a translation. Sacrifices literary quality for exegetical values. Uses brackets in place of italics to indicate words or expressions that are added to complete the meaning of the Greek. Does not include Hebrews. By the chairman of the Department of NT at Anderson College, Anderson, Ind.

1971   Living Bible
The Living Bible, Paraphrased. Wheaton, Ill.: Tyndale House.

Living History of Israel, a paraphrase of Joshua, Judges. 1 and 2 Samuel, 1 and 2 Kings, 1 and 2 Chronicles, Ezra, and Nehemiah, 1970. Living Prophecies: the Minor Prophets paraphrased with Daniel and the Revelation, 1965, 1967. Living New Testament Paraphrased, 1967. Living Letters: the Paraphrased Epistles, c. 1962, 1967.

See chapter 15.

1971   New American Standard Bible
New American Standard Bible. Carol Stream, Ill.: Creation House.

New American Standard Bible. New Testament Pilot ed., La Habra, Calif. Produced and published by The Lockman Foundation, 1963.

See chapter 14.

1972   The Bible in Living English
The Bible in Living English. Translated by Stephen T. Byington. Brooklyn, NY: Watchtower Bible and Tract Society of New York, Inc.

See chapter 6.

1973   A Child's Bible
A Child's Bible in Colour: The Old Testament, rewritten for children by Anne Edwards. The New Testament, rewritten for children by Shirley Steen. London and New York: Pan Books and Paulist Press.

1973   Common Bible
Common Bible: The Holy Bible; Revised Standard Version, containing the Old and New Testament with Apocrypha/Deuterocanonical Books. New York: William Collins Sons.

See chapter 2.

1973   New International Version
The Holy Bible, New International Version: The New Testament. Grand Rapids: Zondervan Bible Publishers.

See chapter 16.

1973 The Psalms
The Psalms: An Exploratory Translation by Mother Maus [Lydia Gysi].
New Pagnell, Bucks.: Greek Orthodox Monastery of the Assumption.

1973 The Translator's New Testament
The Translator's New Testament. London: The British and Foreign Bible Society.
Under the direction of W. D. McHardy a team of thirty-five Bible scholars and eighteen missionary linguists prepared this translation in order "to make available, to those translators of the New Testament into their own mother tongue who depend on English for access to the sources of biblical scholarship, such help as is necessary for the making of effective translations in the languages of today." Includes Notes and a Glossary. Based on the United Bible Societies' Greek Text, 1966.

1973 The Better Version of the New Testament
The Better Version of the New Testament based on the Greek text according to eminent scholars and according to certain fundamental principles and rules of biblical interpretation, by Chester Estes. Muscle Shoals, Ala.

1974 Klingensmith New Testament
The New Testament in Everyday English, by Don J. Klingensmith, Fargo, N. Dak.: Kayes Inc.
A translation of the "simple Greek" into the simple words of everyday English. Leaves out chapter and verse divisions. In the Gospels the Pharisees are the Orthodox, the Sadducees are Liberals, scribes are scholars, disciples are students, hypocrites are stage players, Gehenna is a junk yard, and repentance is a change of thinking.

1975 The Word Made Fresh
The Word Made Fresh, a paraphrase of selected portions of the Bible by Andrew Edington. 3 vols. Atlanta: John Knox.

1976 Train Up a Child
Train Up a Child. Pt 1, Genesis, paraphrased for children by Ben Nutt. Chicago: Adams Press.

1976 Concise Jewish Bible
The Concise Jewish Bible. Edited and translated by Philip Birnbaum. New York: Sanhedrin Press.

1976 Beck's: An American Translation
The Holy Bible in the Language of Today, An American Translation by William F. Beck. Stylistic alterations and other changes dictated by the latest MS evidence made by Elmer B. Smick and Erich H. Kiehl. Nashville: Holman Bible Publishers.

The New Testament in the Language of Today, St. Louis: Concordia Publishing House, 1963.

A refreshing translation by a Lutheran scholar in simple, precise English. It is printed in readable type with orderly paragraphing and lively headings. OT quotations are printed in italics. Makes an attempt to date the events of the NT. In John 8:57 it follows P[75] and a few other MSS in its translation "and Abraham has seen you?" "Grace'" (*charis*) is usually translated as love, and "justify" as make righteous. Contains approximately twenty-five textual notes in the NT. A numbered list of OT references is given at the close of each book.

1976 Good News Bible
The Bible in Today's English Version, New York: The American Bible Society, 1976

Good News for Modern Man. The New Testament in Today's English Version. New York: American Bible Society, 1966, 1971, 1976.

Psalms for Modern Man, 1970. Job for Modern Man, 1971. Wisdom for Modern Man (Proverbs & Ecclesiastes), 1972. See chapter 11.

1976 Renaissance New Testament
The Renaissance New Testament, by Randolph O. Yeager. Bowling Green, Ky.: Renaissance Press.

Contents, v. 1. Matthew I-VIII.

1976 New Life Testament
The New Life Testament. Translated by Gleason H. Ledyard. Canby, Oreg.: Christian Literature International.

1976 The Gospel Jesus
The Gospel Jesus: The Story in Modern English by Ronald Cox. Nole Plaza, Ind.: Our Sunday Visitor.

1977 The Song of Songs
The Song of Songs: Love Poems from the Bible, translated from the original Hebrew by Marcia Falk. 1st ed. New York: Harcourt Brace Jovanovich.

1977 The Psalms
The Psalms translated [from the Hebrew] by Peter Levi, with an introduction by Nicholas de Lange. Harmondsworth: Penguin.

1977 The Gospels in Scouse
The Gospels in Scouse by Dick Williams and Frank Shaw, illustrated by Derek Alden, introduction by David Sheppard. Rev. ed. London: White Lion Publishers.

1977 Marrow Gospels
The Four Gospels; newly translated from the Greek. Luton, England: White Crescent Press.
    For the most part uses the Greek text of The British and Foreign Bible Society.

1977 The Psalms
The Psalms, a New Translation for Worship prepared by David L. Frost and a panel of Hebrew and Biblical Scholars. London: Collins Liturgical.

1977 Christian Counselor's New Testament
The Christian Counselor's New Testament; a new translation in everyday English with notations . . . by Jay E. Adams. Grand Rapids: Baker Book House, 1977. NT in Everyday English, 1979.

1977 The Holy Bible for Children
The Holy Bible for Children: A Simplified Version of the Old and New Testaments edited by Allan Hart Johsmann. Illustrations and maps by Don Kueker. St. Louis: Concordia.
    A simplified retelling . . . of selected portions of the books of the Bible.

1978 The Holy Name Bible
The Holy Name Bible, containing the Holy Name Version of the Old and New Testaments. Brandywine, Md.

1978 The New International Version
The Holy Bible, New International Version, Grand Rapids: Zondervan Bible Publishers.
    The Holy Bible, New International Version: The New Testament, Grand Rapids: Zondervan Bible Publishers.
    See chapter 16.

1978 New Testament for the Deaf
The New Testament: English Version for the Deaf, translated from the Greek Text. Grand Rapids: Baker Book House.

1979 The Psalms
The Psalms: A New Translation by Bonaventure Zerr. New York: Paulist Press.

1979 Ephesians
Ephesians by R. Paul Caudill. Nashville: Broadman Press.

1979 Lattimore's Gospels and Revelation
The Four Gospels and the Revelation. Newly translated from the Greek by Richmond Lattimore. New York: Farrar, Straus and Giroux.

1979 Sasson's Ruth
Ruth: A New Translation with a Philological Commentary and a Formalist Folklorist Interpretation by Jack M. Sasson. Johns Hopkins University Near Eastern Studies. Baltimore: Johns Hopkins University Press.

1979 Mitchell's Job
Into the Whirlwind: A Translation of the Book of Job, by Stephen Mitchell. Garden City, N.J.: Doubleday.

1982 New Jewish Version
The Writings, Kethubim: The third section of A New Translation of the Holy Scriptures according to the Masoretic Text. Philadelphia: The Jewish Publication Society of America.

The Torah: The Five Books of Moses, the first section, 1962. 2nd rev. ed., 1973. The Five Megilloth and Jonah; a new translation. Introductions by H. L. Ginsberg, with drawings by Ismar David, 1969. Psalms 1972, Isaiah 1973, Jeremiah 1974.

The Prophets, Nevi'im. Second section of a new translation, 1978.

See chapter 7.

1982 The New King James
Holy Bible. The New Kings James Version, Nashville, Camden, New York: Thomas Nelson Publishers, 1979.

The New King James Bible New Testament, Nashville, Camden, New York: Thomas Nelson Publishers.

See chapter 17.

1982 The Reader's Digest Bible
The Reader's Digest Bible condensed from the Revised Standard Version, Old and New Testament, Pleasantville, NY: The Reader's Digest Association.

See chapter 18.

Glossary

Alexandrian Text. A type of text of the Greek NT current in Egypt as early as the second century. The primary witnesses to it are Codex Vaticanus (B), Codex Sinaiticus (X), and the two Bodmer Papyri, P^{75} and P^{66}. Wescott and Hort drew a distinction between the "Neutral" and Alexandrian text types, but more recent scholars do not see sufficient differentiation between the two to justify making them separate categories.

Apocrypha. Properly a Greek neuter plural adjective meaning "hidden" with the noun "biblia," books or scrolls, understood, hence "hidden books." The term has had a varying usage such as a designation for books of esoteric wisdom that were hidden from the general reading public, or as a disparaging term for "false," "spurious," "heretical," or "extra-canonical" books. The term is used in this book in the Protestant sense to designate a group of some fifteen ancient documents not found in the Hebrew Bible, but included in some MSS of the Septuagint, and the Old Latin Version of the OT. Roman Catholics accept twelve of these as an inspired portion of the OT and call them "deuterocanonical," and use the term "apocrypha" for other extra-canonical literature such as those Protestants call "Pseudepigrapha."

Aramaic. A Northwest Semitic language closely related to Hebrew. It became a *lingua franca*, and portions of Daniel (2:4b to 7:28), Ezra (4:8 to 6:18; 7:12–26) and one verse in Jeremiah (10:11) are written in it. It became the vernacular language of the Jews in NT times, and evidently was Jesus' mother-tongue. Four Aramaic expressions from his lips are preserved even in our English versions of Mark (4:36; 5:41; 7:34; 15:34). Aramaic was also the language of the Targums.

Caesarean Text. A text-type of Greek MSS of the NT identified in the present century of which the chief representatives include Family 1, a group of related MSS of the twelfth to fourteenth centuries; Family 13, a group of about a dozen related medieval MSS; Codex Koridethi (Θ), an uncial MS of the Gospels from the ninth century; the Chester Beatty Biblical Papyrus 45 in Mark, of the third century; the Armenian and Georgian versions; and the writings of Origen, Cyril of Jerusalem, and Eusebius. This text-type lies between the Alexandrian and Western, since it has affinities with both. While it may be closer to the Western it lacks the long additions and paraphrases of that type, as well as the long additions of the TR. Streeter called it Caesarean because he noted that Origen used this text-type in Caesarea.

Codex (Pl. codices). A manuscript in the form of a leaf book, rather than a scroll, with the separate leaves fastened together on one side. The model for this type of book was evidently the multileaved Greek and Roman tablets made of thin boards fastened together by a thong hinge. The boards were slightly hollowed out to make room for black wax on which writing was done with a stylus. Before the middle of the first century B.C. the Romans took a further step by substituting sheets of parchment for the wooden leaves, and the writing was then done with a pen and washable carbon ink. These parchment notebooks were called *membranae,* a term Paul uses in 2 Timothy 4:13, in urging Timothy to come and bring his books and, as the NEB translates it, "above all my notebooks." It took some time before the next step was taken: that of using this form for literary works. But it did come and all extant MSS of the NT appear to be in the form of codices. (See *The Cambridge History of the Bible,* 2, pp. 65ff.)

Codex Bobiensis (k). A fragmentary Old Latin Codex, consisting of ninety-six surviving pages of Matthew and Mark, dated c. 400. The name is derived from the Northern Italian city of Babbio where it was preserved before it was taken to Turin, where it is today. It is regarded as the most important

representative of the African form of the Old Latin. Manuscripts of the Old Latin are designated by small letters of the
Latin alphabet, hence the "k."

Codex Washingtonianus (W). A late fourth- or early-fifth century
uncial of the Four Gospels in the so-called Western order
(Matt. John, Luke, Mark). The codex is also known as the
Freer Gospels because it was acquired by Charles L. Freer of
Detroit and is now in the Freer Gallery of Art in Washington,
D.C., hence "Washingtonianus." Its type of text varies from
Byzantine in Matthew and Luke 8:13 to 24:53, Western in
Mark 1:1 to 5:30, Caesarean in Mark 5:31 to 16:20, Alexan-
drian in Luke 1:1 to 8:12, and John 5:12 to 21:25, to a mixture
of Alexandrian and Western readings in John 1:1 to 21:12. It
is of special interest because of its expanded long ending to
Mark. After Mark 16:14 it has a long expansion, often called
the Freer Logion.

Coptic Versions. Coptic was the language of the native popula-
tion of Egypt in NT times. The language was reduced to
alphabetic writing using the Greek alphabet supplemented
by seven characters from the Demotic. Although five versions of the NT in the dialects of Coptic are known, the two
chief ones are: (1) The Sahidic of upper, i.e., Southern,
Egypt, for which sufficient fragments are known to reconstruct the major part of the NT. (2) The Bohairic, which was
current in Lower, i.e., Northern, Egypt. The entire NT has
been preserved in this dialect, which has become the Coptic
of today. Both versions of the NT are witnesses to an
Alexandrian type of text.

Deuterocanonical. "Belonging to a second canon," is a term
used by Roman Catholics to refer to those books or parts of
books that they accept as part of the OT Scriptures, but
which Protestants designate as apocryphal. The term was
introduced by Sixtus of Sienna in 1566 to distinguish these
books from the "protocanonical," i.e., those that were received by the entire church from the earliest times.

Majority Text. That form of the wording of the NT found in the
majority of the more than 5000 Greek MSS. Modern proponents of the theory of a majority text advocate that whenever
the Greek MSS differ in wording, the true text is to be determined by following the wording of the majority of these
MSS, without considering their age or textual quality. A
Greek New Testament based on this textual theory has been

constructed by Zane Hodges, assisted by Arthur Farstad.
Most Greek Testaments are built on the concept of following
the oldest and best manuscripts, which are in the minority.
"It is the quality of a New Testament that counts," wrote
Colwell, "not the quantity of its adherents. Witnesses should
be weighed, not counted." (1B, Vol. 1, p. 79).

Masoretic Text. The name of the traditional Hebrew text of OT
that is preserved in the oldest Hebrew MSS known before the
discovery of the Dead Sea Scrolls. The Hebrew text appears
to have been standardized in the first century A.D. Between
the seventh and tenth centuries A.D., this text was provided
with vowel signs, accents, and punctuation marks as well as
divided into sections. The Jewish scholars who did this work
were called Masoretes. The important Hebrew MSS from the
ninth to the eleventh century were produced by them. Hence
the traditional Hebrew text with its vocalization is known as
the Masoretic text or MT.

Minuscules. Latin—minusculus, "rather small." A term used
for manuscripts written in a script of smaller letters than the
uncials in a running hand, dating from about the ninth century on. This reformed handwriting had several advantages
over the uncials. The letters were smaller and more compact,
hence were more economical since they required less parchment. The resulting work was consequently also less bulky
and easier to handle. Also a scribe could write minuscule
letters more rapidly, and hence produce a document more
quickly.

Nestle-Aland. A critical-eclectic Greek text of the NT originally
published in 1898 by Eberhard Nestle and based on a majority of agreement between Tischendorf, Westcott and Hort, and
Weymouth (first two editions; from the 3rd on, B. Weiss),
with a small critical apparatus. Both the text and the apparatus are continually revised under the editorship in turn
of Eberhard Nestle, his son Erwin, and now Kurt Aland. The
26th edition contains a completely new form of the text and
apparatus. In wording it is identical with the 3rd edition of
the United Bible Societies text but differs in paragraphing,
orthography, and punctuation. The 23rd edition was the
basic text used by the New American Standard Bible, and the
25th edition was used for the New American Bible.

Neutral Text. A designation used by Westcott and Hort for the
type of text that they regarded as the most nearly free from

later corruption and mixture, and as most closely approaching the wording of the autographs. The best representative of this text-type in their view is Codex Vaticanus (B), and the second best Codex Sinaiticus (ℵ). More recent textual scholars have dropped "Neutral" as a presumptive term, and are convinced also that Codex Vaticanus is not as pure as the Cambridge scholars believed it to be. Nor is there a clear-cut distinction between the "Neutral" and Alexandrian text-types. The two are generally combined today as the single Alexandrian text-type.

Old Latin Version(s) (Itala). One of the most interesting and important of the early versions of the NT. Although its precise history is obscure, it probably originated in North Africa before the end of the second century. It is an important witness to the "Western" form of the NT text. At least two forms of the version are recognized: (1) African, found in quotations of Cyprian (d. 258), and (2) European, found in the Latin writings of Irenaeus (end of second century). Some forty MSS of portions of the version are extant, which are officially designated by lower-case letters.

Papyri. The oldest existing witnesses for the NT text are written on papyrus, a form of paper manufactured from the stalks of the papyrus plant grown in Egypt. Some eighty papyrus manuscripts of portions of the NT are extant. They are designated by a capital "P" usually printed in Old English type, plus a small superlinear number. The two most important collections are the Chester Beatty Biblical Papyri (P^{45} of Gospels and Acts, third century; P^{46} of Paul's Letters, c. 200; and P^{47} of Revelation, third century) and the Bodmer Papyri (P^{66} of John, c. 200; P^{72} of Jude and 1 and 2 Peter; P^{74} of James, 1 and 2 Peter, 1, 2, 3 John, and Jude, seventh century; and P^{75} of Luke and John, c. 200). The earliest scrap of NT papyrus contains a small portion of John (P^{52}) from the first half of the second century.

Qumran, Khirbet. The site west of the Dead Sea about eight miles south of Jericho where the ruins of the Essene community that produced the Dead Sea Scrolls are located. Eleven caves in the surrounding hills contained MSS. The Hebrew scrolls of the OT there discovered have pushed back our knowledge of the Hebrew Bible by a thousand years.

Samaritan Pentateuch. A separate recension of the Hebrew text of the first five books of the Bible, written in a modified form of the Old Semitic alphabet, and transmitted independently from the Hebrew text that was standardized in the first century A.D. It is useful as a check on the transcriptional errors that have crept into the Hebrew text of the Pentateuch through its numerous copyings.

Septuagint. The Old Greek translation of the OT that is the oldest and most important of the ancient versions of the OT. The name is a transliteration of the Latin septuaginta ("seventy") shortened from *interpretatio septuaginta virorum,* "a translation of the seventy men." It is derived from the tradition set forth in the Letter of Aristeas that the version was produced by seventy or seventy-two Jewish translators in seventy-two days. Strictly, the name applies only to the Pentateuch produced in the third century B.C., to meet the religious needs of Greek-speaking Jews in Egypt. In the time of Origen (180–253) the name was used for the whole Greek OT that was completed about the second century B.C. Two facts make the version important for the textual study of the OT: (1) The translation was made before the Hebrew text was standardized about the first century A.D. Hence it is an aid in restoring a text before the Masoretes did their work. (2) Apart from the Dead Sea Scrolls, the extant MSS of the Septuagint (LXX) are substantially older than the Hebrew MSS on which the Hebrew Bible is based. Some of the Dead Sea Scrolls support the kind of Hebrew text underlying the LXX in some books.

Souter. In 1910 Alexander Souter reproduced the Greek text of the NT that Edwin Palmer had constructed inferentially as the text behind the Revised Version of 1881, to which he added a selected critical apparatus with valuable citation of evidence from the Fathers, especially those who wrote in Latin. This text was reproduced at Oxford in 1947 with the addition of newer evidence. Souter was used as the textual base for Helen Barrett Montgomery's Centenary Translation, The New Testament in Modern English, as well as the first edition of J. B. Phillips's The New Testament in Modern English.

Syriac Versions. Syriac is an eastern form of Aramaic. The chief center for early Syriac Christianity was Edessa, a town in northern Mesopotamia east of the Euphrates (modern Urfa in Turkey). The Diatessaron (c. 170) a fusion of the four Gospels into one continuous narrative, by Tatian, was probably the earliest form of the Syriac Gospels. The Old Syriac version of the "Separated Gospels" from about the end of the second century has been preserved in two manuscripts: (1) a fifth-century codex called the Curetonian, after its discoverer in Egypt in 1842, William Cureton, and (2) a fourth-century palimpsest MS known as the Sinaitic, because it was discovered at Mt. Sinai in 1892 by two English sisters, Mrs. A. C. Lewis and Mrs. A. D. Gibson. The standard Syriac version is the Peshitta ("simple") dating from the late fourth or early fifth century, which lacked 2 Peter, 2 and 3 John, Jude, and Revelation. The Philoxenian version, prepared for Philoxenus, Bishop of Maburg, in the early sixth century, had these books. The Harclean Syriac version prepared by Thomas (who calls himself "a poor sinner") of Harclea, dates from the seventh century. Finally another version, the Palestinian, known chiefly through lectionaries, uses a language similar to the Aramaic Targums of the OT.

Targums (pl. Targumin). Aramaic versions of portions of the Hebrew Bible, combining translation with paraphrase and interpretation. When Aramaic displaced Hebrew as the vernacular language of the Jews it became necessary to accompany the reading of the Hebrew text in the synagogue by an oral translation. These translations became stereotyped and were reduced to writing between the fifth and seventh centuries. Three Targums of the Pentateuch are extant, the best known is the so-called Onkelos. The official targum of the prophets is Jonathan. Targums of all the other books exist except Ezra, Nehemiah, and Daniel. Targums have a limited value for textual study, and are a rich source of Jewish religious thought and exegesis.

Text. A term meaning the body of words making up a document. Ideally, the text of a document is that contained in its autograph.

Textual Criticism. The philological discipline that examines the sources for the study of the text of the NT for the purpose of establishing the earliest attainable text of each book.

Textual Scholars. Usually called textual critics, are meticulous NT students of the Greek MSS, the early versions, and the quotations in early Christian writers for the purpose of restoring as far as possible the exact wording of the various documents as they came from the authors' hands.

Textus Receptus (Received Text). A late and corrupt form of the Byzantine text-type of the NT which dominated in the Western world for about three hundred years. The TR of England was the third edition of Robert Stephanus, which in turn was a slight revision of the third edition of Erasmus, the first publisher of the Greek NT in the age of printing. The TR of the continent was the 1624 edition of the Dutch Elzevir brothers. The name, however, is derived from the Latin words, *textum . . . receptum* in a sentence of the preface of their second edition of 1633, which translated asserts that in their edition the reader has "the text which is now received by all, in which we give nothing changed or corrupted." The Elzevir text was based on the editions of Stephanus and Beza, which are simply revisions of Erasmus. The KJV and all the chief Protestant versions before 1881 were based on this text. The NKJV continues to be based on this traditional text.

UBS Text. A critical edition of The Greek New Testament with an apparatus of exegetically significant variant readings prepared by an international committee under the sponsorship of the United Bible Societies and edited by Kurt Aland, Matthew Black, Bruce Metzger, and Allen Wikgren (plus Carlo M. Martini for the second and third editions), for the use of Bible translators (1st ed., 1966; 2nd ed., 1968; 3rd ed., 1975). The title page for the 3rd edition adds, "in cooperation with the Institute for New Testament Textual Research, Münster/Westphalia." This edition is identical in wording with the 26th edition of Nestle-Aland, but there are differences in paragraphing, orthography, and punctuation, as well as a completely different apparatus. The UBS text is the Greek base for the NT of the Good News Bible.

Uncials. From the Latin *uncia,* meaning "a twelfth part"—evidently of a line of writing. A formal style of handwritten letters used for literary documents until about the ninth century. These letters were adapted from the Greek capitals used in inscriptions, but more rounded rather than straight and angular. NT manuscripts written in this form of writing are also called uncials. The early uncials are the main source most textual scholars use for the reconstruction of the text of the NT.

Versions. A version (coming from a Latin verb meaning, to turn, or translate) is a translation, specifically of the Bible. Early versions give indirect evidence as to the wording of the Bible at an early date. The most important OT version is the Septuagint, or Old Greek. The three most important versions for the NT are the Syriac, Latin, and Coptic. The Old Syriac and the Old Latin translations were probably made in the second century, and are of great value.

Von Soden. A critical Greek text of the NT by Hermann Freiherr von Soden based on his textual theory with his division of MSS into three categories indicated by the Greek letters *Ēta* (Hesychius), *Iōta* (Jerusalem), and *Kappa* (*Koinē*, "common"), which are in turn divided into a bewildering number of sub-groups. His work, *Die Schriften des Neuen Testaments in ihrem ältesten erreichbaren Textgestalt,* published at Göttingen, also has a full but inaccurate apparatus using a new designation of MSS. The whole complicated scheme has been called "a magnificent failure." His text was, however, used as the basis for Moffatt's brilliant rendering of the NT and has influenced the work of other editors, e.g., the apparatus of Augustin Merk, S.J.

Vulgate. Latin—edito vulgata, common edition. The usual name since the end of the Middle Ages for the Latin translation of the Bible made by Jerome near the end of the fourth century, at the request of Pope Damasus. It became the official Bible of the Roman Catholic Church. More than 8000 MSS of the version are known. It was the basis for the first complete Bible in English by John Wycliffe. Its translation into English had a marked influence on the King James Version. The Ronald Knox version is based on it.

Westcott and Hort. A monumental critical Greek text of the NT, *The New Testament in the Original Greek,* published in 1881 by Brooke Foss Westcott and Fenton John Anthony Hort, after nearly thirty years of research on the textual problems of the NT. A second volume of *Introduction and Notes* by Hort sets forth the classical statement of the theory and method used in the production of this critical text. They begin by examining individual variant readings to determine the one that appears to be the most probable. In this process two kinds of evidence are examined: 1) *Intrinsic probability,* which looks at the variants and asks: In view of the author's style and habits of speech and thought, and in the light of the context, which one is the author most likely to have written? 2) *Transcriptional probability,* which asks: Knowing the proclivity of scribes, and the characteristic scribal errors that occur, which variant best explains the origin of the others, but cannot itself be accounted for by them? The second step is to apply these two evidences to a manuscript to determine the character and reliability of each. On this basis they concluded that Codex Vaticanus and Codex Sinaiticus are the best NT witnesses. The third step is to divide the MSS into four family groupings or text types: Syrian, Neutral, Alexandrian, and Western. Continuing studies since this theory and method were developed have modified these conclusions. A number of new MSS have been discovered, particularly papyri. The fourfold classification of MSS has been modified and clarified, and a new group, the Caesarean, has been discovered. More attention in recent years has been given to the ancient versions and the Fathers. Today it is doubtful that one text-type preserves all the original readings. Nevertheless, the Westcott and Hort text has had a marked impact on textual studies. It influenced the committee producing the RV and ASV, became the basis for the Twentieth Century New Testament, and Goodspeed's An American Translation, besides influencing such other Greek texts as Nestle and the UBS. It brought about the final dethronement of the TR in spite of its modern champions.

Western Text. An early form of the NT text characterized by freedom in making additions, great and small, striking omissions, substitutions, and frequent changes. This is especially true of the Book of Acts. It has been suggested that this text-type originated at a time when strict verbal accuracy was not demanded of a copyist. The Western text was early and widespread geographically. It can be traced as early as the second century, as may be seen by its use in the writings of Marcion, Tatian, Irenaeus, Tertullian, and Cyprian. It was used in Egypt, North Africa, Italy, and Gaul. The main witness to this text-type for the Gospels are Codex Bezae (D), a Greek and Latin bilingual MS of the fifth or sixth centuries, Mark 1:1 to 5:30 in the Washington Codex (W), and the Old Latin and Old Syriac Gospels. For Acts besides D, there are two papyri, P^{38} of c. 300, and P^{48}, from the end of the third century that have substantial parts of the text. For the Pauline Epistles there are three Greek/Latin bilingual codices: Claromontanus (D^{P}, sixth century), Augiensis (F^{P}, ninth century) and Boernerianus (G^{P}).

Bibliography

GENERAL

Beegle, Dewey M. *God's Word Into English*. Grand Rapids: Wm. B. Eerdmans Publishing Co., 1960.

Beekman, John, and Callow, John. *Translating the Word of God*. Grand Rapids: Zondervan Publishing House, 1974.

Branton, J. R. "Versions, English." *Interpreter's Dictionary of the Bible* 4:760–71.

Bratcher, Robert G. "One Bible in Many Translations." *Interpretation* 32 (1978): 115–29.

_____. "Englishing the Bible." *Review and Expositor* 70 (1979): 299–314.

Bridges, Ronald, and Weigle, Luther A. *The Bible Word Book, Concerning Obsolete or Archaic Words in the King James Version of the Bible*. New York: Thomas Nelson & Sons, 1960.

Bruce, F. F. *The Books and the Parchments: Some Chapters in the Transmission of the Bible*. 3rd rev. ed. Westwood, N.J.: Fleming H. Revell Co., 1963.

_____. *The English Bible: A History of Translations*. New rev. ed. New York: Oxford University Press, 1970.

Coggan, Frederick D. *Word and World*. London: Hodder & Stoughton, 1971.

Crim, Keith R. "Versions, English." *Interpreter's Dictionary of the Bible*, Supplementary Volume, pp. 933–38.

_____. "Old Testament Translations and Interpretation." *Interpretation* 32 (1978): 144–57.

Davies, Paul E. "A Descriptive List of Bible Translations Since 1901." *McCormick Quarterly* 19 (1966): 309–25.

Dennett, Herbert. *A Guide to Modern Versions of the New Testament: How to Understand and Use Them.* Chicago: Moody Press, 1965.

Elliott, Melvin E. *The Language of the King James Bible: A Glossary Explaining Its Words and Expressions.* Garden City, N.Y.: Doubleday & Co., Inc., 1967.

Grant, Frederick C. *Translating the Bible.* Greenwich, Conn.: Seabury Press, 1961.

Greenslade, S. L., ed. *The Cambridge History of the Bible: The West from the Reformation to the Present Day.* Cambridge: Cambridge University Press, 1963.

Kenyon, Frederic George *Our Bible and the Ancient Manuscripts.* Revised by A. W. Adams. New York: Harper & Brothers, 1958.

Levi, Peter. *The English Bible from Wycliff to William Barnes.* Grand Rapids: Wm. B. Eerdmans Publishing Co., 1974.

MacGregor, Geddes. *The Bible in the Making.* Philadelphia and New York: J. B. Lippincott Co., 1959.

_____. *A Literary History of the Bible: From the Middle Ages to the Present Day.* Nashville, Tenn.: Abingdon Press, 1968.

May, Herbert G. "Authorized Versions." *Interpreter's Dictionary of the Bible,* Supplementary Volume, p. 84.

_____. *Our English Bible in the Making: The Word of Life in Living Language.* Rev. ed. Philadelphia: Published for the Cooperative Publication Association by Westminster Press, 1965.

Nida, Eugene A., and Taber, Charles R. *The Theory and Practice of Translation.* Helps for Translators, 8. Leiden: Published for the United Bible Societies by E. J. Brill, 1969.

Partridge, A. C. *English Biblical Translation.* London: Andre Deutsch, 1973.

Pope, Hugh, O.P. *English Versions of the Bible.* Rev. and amplified by Sebastian Bullough, O.P. St. Louis: Herder, 1952.

Price, Ira M. *The Ancestry of the English Bible.* 3rd rev. ed by William A. Irwin and Allen P. Wikgren. New York: Harper & Brothers, 1956.

Reumann, John H. P. *Four Centuries of the English Bible.* Philadelphia: Muhlenberg Press, 1961.

_____. *The Romance of Bible Scripts and Scholars: Chapters in the History of Bible Transmission and Translation.* Englewood Cliffs, N.J.: Prentice-Hall, 1965.

Robertson, E. H. *The New Translations of the Bible*. Studies in Ministry and Worship. Naperville, Ill.: Alec R. Allenson, 1959.

Robinson, H. Wheeler, ed. *The Bible in Its Ancient and English Versions*. Rev. ed. Oxford: Clarendon Press, 1954.

Specht, Walter F. "The Use of Italics in English Versions of the New Testament." *Andrews University Seminary Studies* 6 (1968): 89–109.

Weigle, Luther A. *The English New Testament from Tyndale to the Revised Standard Edition*. New York: Abingdon-Cokesbury Press, 1949.

Williamson, Lamar, Jr. "Translation and Interpretation: New Testament." *Interpretation* 32 (1978): 158–70.

Wonderly, William L. *Bible Translations for Popular Use*. Helps for Translators, 7. Leiden: Published for the United Bible Societies by E. J. Brill, 1968.

CHAPTER 1. EARLY MODERN SPEECH VERSIONS

Clark, Kenneth W. "The Making of the Twentieth Century New Testament." *Bulletin of the John Rylands Library* 38 (1955): 58–81.

Goodspeed, Edgar Johnson. *As I Remember*. New York: Harper, 1953.

————. *New Chapters in New Testament Study*. New York: The Macmillan Co., 1937.

Reumann, John H. P. *The Romance of Bible Scripts and Scholars*. Englewood Cliffs, N.J.: Prentice-Hall, 1965.

Robertson, A. T. *Studies in the Text of the New Testament*. New York: George H. Doran Co., 1926.

Reviews

Bruce, F. F. *Evangelical Quarterly* 34 (1962): 43–44.

CHAPTER 2. THE REVISED STANDARD VERSION

Ackroyd, P. R. "An Authoritative Version of the Bible." *Expository Times* 85 (1974): 374–77.

Bender, Harold Stauffer, et al. *The Revised Standard Version: An Examination and Evaluation*. Scottsdale, Pa.: Herald Press, 1953.

Burrows, Millar. *Diligently Compared. The Revised Standard Version and the King James Version of the Old Testament*. New York: Thomas Nelson & Sons, 1964.

Feinberg, Charles Lee. *The Revised Standard Version: What Kind of Translation?* Los Angeles: Bible Institute of Los Angeles, 1953. (Pamphlet)

Huffman, Jaspar Abraham. *The Revised Standard Version, an Appraisal.* Winona Lake, Ind.: The Standard Press, 1953.

An Introduction to the Revised Standard Version of the Old Testament. By Members of the Revision Committee, Luther A. Weigle, Chairman. New York: Thomas Nelson & Sons, 1952.

An Introduction to the Revised Standard Version of the New Testament. By Members of the Revision Committee, Luther A. Weigle, Chairman. N.p.: International Council of Religious Education, 1946.

May, Herbert G. "The Revised Standard Version After Twenty Years." *McCormick Quarterly* 19 (1966): 301–8.

_____. "Revised Standard Version Bible." *Vetus Testamentum* 24 (1974): 238–40.

Metzger, B. M. "The Revised Standard Version." *Duke Divinity Review* 44 (1979): 70–87.

_____. "RSV: Ecumenical Edition." *Theology Today* 34 (1977): 315–17.

_____. "The Story Behind the Making of the Revised Standard Version of the Bible." *Princeton Seminary Bulletin,* n.s.1 (1978): 189–200.

An Open Letter Concerning the Revised Standard Version of the Bible. New York: Division of Christian Education, National Council of the Churches of Christ in the U.S.A., n.d. (Pamphlet)

Polhill, John. "The Revised Standard Version and the Oxford Annotated Bible." *Review and Expositor* 76 (1979): 315–24.

Swain, Joseph Carter. *New Insights into Scripture: Studying the Revised Standard Version.* Philadelphia: Cooperative Publication Assn. of the Westminster Press, 1962.

Thompson, Dorothy. "The Old Bible and the New." *Ladies' Home Journal,* March, 1953, pp. 11ff.

Reviews

Allis, Oswald T. *Christianity Today,* 8 July 1957, pp. 6, 7, 21–24.

Black, M. *Journal of Semitic Studies* 4 (1959): 395–97.

Bright, J. *Interpretation* 7 (1953): 338–44.

Burrows, M. *Supplements to Vetus Testamentum,* VII. Oxford: University Press, 1960, pp. 206–21.

Gilmour, S. MacLean. *Christianity Today,* 26 September 1960, pp. 6, 8, 10.

Higgins, A. J. B. *Congregation Quarterly* 31 (1953): 173–74.

Ladd, George Eldon. *Christianity Today,* 8 July 1957, pp. 7–11.

McKenzie, J. L. *Catholic Biblical Quarterly* 17 (1955): 88–90.

Major, H. D. A. *Modern Churchman* 44 (1954): 134–35.

Metzger, B. M. *Theology Today* 34 (1977): 315–17.

Myers, R. *Lutheran Quarterly* 4 (1952): 457–58.

Nesbitt, C. F. *Journal of Bible and Religion* 21 (1953): 33–34.

Peifer, C. *Worship* 47 (1973): 313–15.

Power, A. D. *Church Quarterly Review* 154 (1953): 122–27.

Reider, J. *Jewish Quarterly Review* 43 (1953): 381–84.

CHAPTER 3. THE KNOX TRANSLATION

Kleist, James A., S.J. "Monsignor R. A. Knox's New Rendering of the New Testament." *Catholic Biblical Quarterly* 5 (1943): 311–17.

Knox, Ronald A. *The Trials of a Translator.* New York: Sheed & Ward, 1949. Published in England under title *On Englishing the Bible.*

Reviews

Cooper, Charles M. *Lutheran Quarterly* 3 (1951): 366–82.

Ellard, Gerald, S.J. *Catholic Biblical Quarterly* 7 (1945): 120–21.

Hooke, S. H. Vol. I, *Church Quarterly Review* 149 (1949): 93–97; Vol. II, 152 (1951): 120–23.

Lussier, J. E., S.S.S. *Theological Studies* 11 (1950): 598–602.

Skehan, Patrick W. *Theological Studies* 10 (1949): 325–32.

CHAPTER 4. PHILLIPS'S TRANSLATION

Phillips, J.B. "The Problems of Making a Contemporary Translation." *Bible Translator* 16 (1965): 25–32.

————. "Some Personal Reflections on New Testament Translation." *Bible Translator* 4 (1953): 53–59.

Smalley, William A. "Phillips and the New English Bible: Some Comments on Style." *Bible Translator* 16 (1965): 165–70.

"Translating the Gospels: A Discussion Between Dr. E. V. Rieu and the Rev. J. B. Phillips." *Bible Translator* 6 (1955): 150–59.

Reviews

Andrews, Elias. *Canadian Journal of Theology* 6 (1960): 60–62.

Bratcher, Robert G. *Bible Translator* 10 (1959): 135–43.

Cartledge, Samuel A. *Interpretation* 7 (1953): 366–68.

Danker, Frederick W. *Concordia Theological Monthly* 30 (1959): 541–42.

Englert, D. M. C. *Theology and Life* 7 (1964): 245–46.

Habel, Norman C. *Concordia Theological Monthly* 37 (1966): 246–48.

Hammond, Philip C. *Interpretation* 18 (1964): 230–31.

Harrelson, Walter. *Journal of Biblical Literature* 83 (1964): 210.

Horton, D. *Harvard Divinity Bulletin* 24 (1960): 21–22.

Jones, G. H. *Religious Studies* 9 (1973): 367–68.

Kidner, D. *Churchman* 78 (1964): 63–64.

Maly, Eugene H. *Catholic Biblical Quarterly* 16 (1954): 112–14.

Mitton, C. L. *Expository Times* 84 (1973): 323–24.

Motyer, J. A. *Christianity Today*, 6 December 1963, pp. 38–39.

Petriburg, R. *Church Quarterly Review* 160 (1959): 373ff.

Price, B. F. *Bible Translator* 15 (1964): 98–100.

Robertson, E. H. *Frontier* 7 (1964): 70–71.

Schofield, J. N. *Modern Churchman* 7 (1964): 127–28.

Skilton, John. *Westminster Theological Journal* 21 (1959): 193–96.

Snape, H. C. *Modern Churchman* 5 (1962): 283–84.

Snyder, Russell. *Lutheran Quarterly* 6 (1954): 360.

CHAPTER 5. THE MODERN LANGUAGE BIBLE

Verkuyl, Gerrit. "The Berkeley Version of the New Testament." *Bible Translator* 2 (1951): 80–85.

Reviews

Anderson, R. A. *The Ministry* 35 (1962): 24–25.

Bratcher, Robert G. *Christianity Today*, 8 October 1971, pp. 16–19.

_____. *Bible Translator* 14 (1963): 140–43.

Danker, Frederick W. *Concordia Theological Monthly* 30 (1959): 951–52.

Hull, W. A. *Review and Expositor* 56 (1959): 423–24.

Kerr, David W. *Westminster Theological Journal* 23 (1960–61): 97–100.

Kuist, Howard Tillman. *Interpretation* 14 (1960): 85–86.

Surburg, Raymond F. *The Springfielder* 34 (1970–71): 151–52.

CHAPTER 6. THE NEW WORLD TRANSLATION AND THE BIBLE IN LIVING ENGLISH

Eddy, G. Norman. "The Jehovah's Witnesses: An Interpretation." *Journal of Bible and Religion* 26 (1958): 115–21.

"How Bible Translators Work: Behind the Scenes in the Preparation of a New Version of the New Testament." (Comments on Byington's Review of 1 November 1950 by New World Bible Translation Committee and Byington's Response to this) *Christian Century*, 9 May 1951, pp. 587–89.

Mattingly, John F. "Jehovah's Witnesses Translate the NT." *Catholic Biblical Quarterly* 13 (1951): 439–43.

Metzger, Bruce. "The Jehovah's Witnesses and Jesus Christ: A Biblical and Theological Appraisal." *Theology Today* 10 (1953): 65–85.

Stuermann, Walter E. "The Bible and Modern Religions. III. Jehovah's Witnesses." *Interpretation* 10 (1965): 323–46.

Reviews

Byington, Steven T. *Christian Century*, 1 November 1950, pp. 1295–96.

Haas, Samuel S. *Journal of Biblical Literature* 74 (1955): 282–83.

Metzger, Bruce. *Bible Translator* 15 (1964): 150–52.

Rowley, H. H. *Expository Times* 65 (1953–54): 41–42.

————. *Expository Times* 67 (1955–56): 107–8.

CHAPTER 7. THE NEW JEWISH VERSION

Borowitz, Eugene B. "Theological Issues in the New Torah Translation." *Judaism* 13 (1964): 335–45.

Crim, Keith R. "The New Jewish Version." *Duke Divinity Review* 44 (1979): 180–91.

————. "The New Jewish Version of the Scriptures." *Bible Translator* 26 (1975): 148–52.

Ginsberg, H. L. "The New Jewish Publication Society Translation of the Torah." *The Journal of Bible and Religion* 31 (July, 1963): 187–92.

————. "The Story of the Jewish Society's New Translation of the Torah." *Bible Translator* 14 (1963): 106–13.

Greenberg, Moshe. "The New Torah Translation." *Judaism* 12 (1963): 225–37.

Jocz, Jakob. "Rabbi, Why Torture the Pronoun?" *Christianity Today*, 12 April 1963, p. 44.

Meek, Theophile J. "A New Bible Translation." *Journal of Biblical Literature* 82 (1963): 265–71.

Orlinsky, Harry M. "The New Jewish Version of the Torah: Toward a New Philosophy of Bible Translation." *Journal of Biblical Literature* 82 (1963): 249–71.

_____. *Notes on the New Translation of the Torah*. Philadelphia: The Jewish Publication Society, 1969.

_____. "Some Recent Jewish Translations of the Bible." *McCormick Quarterly* 19 (1966): 293–300.

Sanders, James A. "Textual Criticism and the NJV Torah." *Journal of the American Academy of Religion* 39 (1971): 193–97.

Toombs, Lawrence E. "The Law in English." *Pulpit Digest*, March 1963, pp. 11–14.

Reviews

Beegle, D. M. *Catholic Biblical Quarterly* 42 (1980): 250–51.

Crim, Keith R. *Bible Translator* 26 (1975): 148–52.

Dahood, M. *Biblica* 45 (1964): 281–83.

Holladay, W. L. *Interpretation* 34 (1980): 964.

Johnstone, W. *Expository Times* 90 (1979): 212–16.

Stinespring, W. F. *Interpretation* 18 (1964): 88–90.

Wegner, Walter. *Concordia Theological Monthly* 44 (1973): 74.

CHAPTER 8. THE AMPLIFIED BIBLE

Reviews

Wegner, Walter, *Concordia Theological Monthly* 34 (1963): 53–54.

CHAPTER 9. THE JERUSALEM BIBLE

Benoit, Pierre. "The Jerusalem Bible." *Review and Expositor* 76 (1979): 341–49.

Brown, Raymond E. "Recent Roman Catholic Translations of the Bible." *McCormick Quarterly* 19 (1965–66): 283–92.

Danker, Frederick W. "The Jerusalem Bible: A Critical Examination." *Concordia Theological Monthly* 38 (1967): 168–80.

Rhodes, E. F. W. "Text of NT in Jerusalem and New English Bible." *Catholic Biblical Quarterly* 32 (1970): 41–57.

Scobie, Charles H. H. "Two Recent New Testament Texts and Translations." *Canadian Journal of Theology* 14 (1968): 54–63.

Vawter, Bruce. "The Jerusalem Bible." *Duke Divinity Review* 44 (1979): 88–103.

Reviews

Archer, Gleason L. *Westminster Theological Journal* 33 (1971): 191–94.

Child, R. L. *Baptist Quarterly* 22 (1967): 186–87.

Dewitz, L. R. M. *Christianity Today*, 16 January 1970, p. 131.

Di Lella, Alexander A., O.F.M. *Catholic Biblical Quarterly* 29 (1967): 148–51.

Fitzmyer, Joseph A., S.J. *Theological Studies* 28 (1967): 129–31.

Gold, V. R. *Lutheran World* 15 (1968): 354.

Grant, Frederick C. *Journal of Biblical Literature* 86 (1967)

Harrington, W. J., O.P. *Revue Biblique* 75 (1968): 450–52.

Herbert, Arthur S. *Bible Translator* 18 (1967): 95–97.

Hughes, P. E. *Churchman* 81 (1967): 134.

Kuyper, Lester J., and Oudersluys, Richard C. *Reformed Review* 21 (1967–68): 22–27.

Landes, George M. *Union Seminary Quarterly* 22 (1966–67): 280–83.

Metzger, Bruce M. *Princeton Seminary Bulletin* 60 (1967): 45–48.

Walker, L. L. *Southwestern Journal of Theology* 11 (1968): 120.

CHAPTER 10. BARCLAY'S NEW TESTAMENT

Reviews

Bratcher, R. G. *Bible Translator* 22 (1971): 47–48.

Duffield, Gervase E. *Churchman* 83 (1969): 251–54.

Harvey, A. E. *Theology* 72 (1969): 368–69.

Marshall, I. Howard. *Evangelical Quarterly* 41 (1969): 175–77.

————. *Evangelical Quarterly* 42 (1970): 114–15.

CHAPTER 11. THE GOOD NEWS BIBLE, TODAY'S ENGLISH VERSION

Bratcher, Robert G. "Good News for Modern Man." *Bible Translator* 17 (1966): 159–72.

————. "The Nature and Purpose of the New Testament in Today's English Version." *Bible Translator* 22 (1971): 97–107.

————. "The T.E.V. New Testament and the Greek Text." *Bible Translator* 18 (1967): 167–74.

Bullard, Roger A. "Sex-Oriented Language in TEV Proverbs." *Bible Translator* 28 (1977): 243–45.

Nida, Eugene A. *Good News For Everyone: How to Use the Good News Bible*. Waco, Tex.: Word Books, 1977.

Nixon, Robin. "Good News Bible." *Churchman* 91 (1977): 3–4.

Scobie, Charles H. H. "Two Recent New Testament Texts and Translations." *Canadian Journal of Theology* 14 (1968): 54–63.

Stinespring, W. F. "Today's English Version or The Good News Bible." *Duke Divinity Review* 44 (1979): 142–63.

Youngblood, Ronald. "Good News for Modern Man: Becoming a Bible." *Christianity Today*, 8 October 1976, pp. 16–19.

Reviews

Dahood, M. *Catholic Biblical Quarterly* 34 (1972): 240–42.

Danker, Frederick W. *Catholic Biblical Quarterly* 29 (1967): 257–58.

_____. *Concordia Theological Monthly* 39 (1968): 216.

Ebor, D. *Church Quarterly* 1 (1968): 66–67.

Hodges, Z. C. *Bibliotheca Sacra* 126 (1969): 86–87.

Jackson, J. J. *Interpretation* 26 (1972): 95–96.

McIntyre, J. A. *Scottish Journal of Theology* 31 (1978): 190–91.

May, Herbert. *Interpretation* 32 (1978): 187–90.

Metzger, Bruce M. *Princeton Seminary Bulletin* 60 (1966): 67–68.

Moody, Dale. *Review and Expositor* 76 (1979): 409–16.

Payne, D. F. *Evangelical Quarterly* 49 (1977): 180–83.

Prickett, S. *Theology* 80 (1977): 403–10.

Reumann, John. *Journal of Biblical Literature* 86 (1967): 234–36.

Rhys, J. *St. Luke's Journal* 23 (1979): 76–77.

Schliemann, D. *Concordia Theological Quarterly* 42 (1978): 167–71.

CHAPTER 12. THE NEW ENGLISH BIBLE

Barr, James. "After Five Years: A Retrospect on Two Major Translations of the Bible." *Heythrop Journal* 15 (1974): 381–405.

Brockington, Leonard Herbert, ed. *The Hebrew Text of the Old Testament: The Readings Adopted by the Translators of the New English Bible*. Oxford: Oxford University Press, 1973.

Bullard, Roger A. "The New English Bible." *Duke Divinity Review* 44 (1979): 104–23.

Dodd, C. H. *The New English Bible; A History of the Project*. Oxford: Oxford University Press. (Brochure)

Driver, G. R. "The New English Bible: The Old Testament." *Journal of Jewish Studies* 24 (1973): 1–7.

Hunt, Geoffrey. *About the New English Bible*. London: Oxford University Press, 1970.

Macintosh, A. A.; Stanton, G.; and Frost, D. L. "The 'New English Bible' Reviewed." *Theology* 74 (1971): 154–66.

Metzger, Bruce M. "Four English Translations of the New Testament." *Christianity Today*, 22 November 1963, pp. 6–10.

Nineham, Dennis Eric, ed. *The New English Bible Reviewed*. London: Epworth Press (c. 1965).

Pfeiffer, Charles F. "A Highly Readable Translation." *Christianity Today*, 27 March 1970, pp. 13–16.

Rice, G. "Isaiah 28:1–22 and the New English Bible." *Journal of Religious Thought* 30 (1973–74): 13–17.

Stinespring, William F. "Some Remarks on the New English Bible." *Understanding the Sacred Text*, ed. by John Reumann. Valley Forge, Pa.: Judson Press, 1972.

Tasker, R. V. G. *The Greek New Testament*. Oxford: University Press, 1964.

Tate, Marvin E. "The Oxford Study Edition of the New English Bible with Apocrypha." *Review and Expositor* 76 (1979): 325–39.

Terrien, Samuel. "The New English Bible with the Apocrypha." *Union Seminary Quarterly Review* 25 (1969): 549–55.

Reviews

Allis, Oswald T. *Westminster Theological Journal* 33 (1970): 81–93.

Bartels, R. A. *Lutheran Quarterly* 13 (1961): 269–71.

Beare, F. W. *New Testament Studies* 8 (1961): 80–92.

Benoit, P. *Revue Biblique* 69 (1962): 147–49.

Boling, R. G. *McCormick Quarterly* 23 (1970): 277–83.

Bratcher, Robert. *Bible Translator* 12 (1961): 97–106.

Brown, Raymond E. *Catholic Biblical Quarterly* 23 (1961): 321–24.

Bruce, F. F. *Christianity Today*, 13 March 1961, pp. 5–8.

———. *Christianity Today*, 30 January 1970, pp. 8–11.

———. *Scottish Journal of Theology* 14 (1961): 194–96.

Burrows, M. *Journal of Biblical Literature* 89 (1970): 220–22.

Cadbury, H. J. *Theology Today* 18 (1961): 188–200.

Child, R. L. *Baptist Quarterly* 19 (1961): 52–58.

———. *Baptist Quarterly* 23 (1970): 330–31.

———. *Christianity Today*, 30 January 1961, pp. 25–26.

Clements, R. E. *Church Quarterly* 2 (1970): 335–38.

Clines, D. J. A. *Evangelical Quarterly* 42 (1970): 168–75.

Dahood, M. *Biblica* 52 (1971): 117–23.

Dalches, D. *Commentary*, May 1970, pp. 59–68.

Davidson, R. *Scottish Journal of Theology* 23 (1970): 231–36.

Davies, P. E. *Interpretation* 15 (1961): 339–44.

———. *Evangelical Quarterly* 33 (1961): 112–16.

Goetchius, E. V. N. *Anglican Theological Review* 52 (1970): 167–76.

Gordon, Cyrus H. *Christianity Today*, 27 March 1970, pp. 6–8.
Grant, F. C. *Journal of Biblical Literature* 80 (1961): 173–76.
Hibbitts, J. B. *Canadian Journal of Theology* 7 (1961): 286–90.
Hobbs, E. C. *Anglican Theological Journal* 43 (1961): 413–15.
Howes, J. *Frontier* 5 (1962): 429–33.
Kraus, C. N. *Mennonite Quarterly Review* 45 (1971): 390–91.
Lloyd, G. *Japan Christian Quarterly* 27 (1961): 269–71.
Metzger, Bruce M. *Interpretation* 24 (1970): 375–78.
_____. *Princeton Seminary Bulletin* 55 (1961): 56–63.
Meyer, W. F. *Springfielder* 34 (1970): 51–55.
Mitton, C. L. *Expository Times* 72 (1961): 206–7.
Murphy, R. E. *Theological Studies* 31 (1970): 320–21.
Petersen, L. M. *Springfielder* 25 (1961):65–67.
Petrie, C. S. *Reformed Theological Review* 20 (1961): 57–58.
Rhodes, E. F. *Catholic Biblical Quarterly* 32 (1970): 41–57.
Robertson, E. H. *Expository Times* 81 (1970): 203–4.
Sanders, J. A. *Christian Century*, 18 March 1970, pp. 326–28.
Skilton, J. H. *Westminster Theological Journal* 24 (1961): 70–79.
Stendahl, K. *Harvard Divinity Bulletin* 27 (1962): 25–30.
Summers, R. *Review and Expositor* 58 (1961): 233–37.
Swain, J. C. *Journal of Ecumenical Studies* 7 (1970): 823–24.
Tait, R. C. *Modern Churchman* 14 (1971): 169–70.
Throckmorton, B. H., Jr. *Journal of Bible and Religion* 29 (1961): 193–203.
Vawter, B. *Catholic Biblical Quarterly* 32 (1970): 426–28.

CHAPTER 13. THE NEW AMERICAN BIBLE

Barr, James. "After Five Years: A Retrospect on Two Major Translations of the Bible." *Heythrop Journal* 15 (1974): 381–405.
Harrleson, Walter. "The New American Bible," *Duke Divinity Review* 44 (1979): 124–36.

Reviews

Arbez, Edward P. *Catholic Biblical Quarterly* 14 (1952): 237–54.
Crim, Keith. *Interpretation* 26 (1972): 77–80
Danker, Frederick W. *Catholic Biblical Quarterly* 33 (1971): 405–9.
Expository Times 82 (1970–71): 381.
Metzger, Bruce M. *Princeton Seminary Bulletin* 54 (1971): 90–99.
Peifer, Claude J. *Worship* 45 (1972): 381.
Reumann, John. *Journal of Biblical Literature* 92 (1973): 275–78.

Sabourin, L. *Biblical Theology Bulletin* 2 (1972): 206–8.
Stagg, Frank. *Review and Expositor* 68 (1971): 400–402.

CHAPTER 14. THE NEW AMERICAN STANDARD BIBLE

Reviews

Alden, R. L. *Westminster Theological Journal* 34 (1972): 217–23.
Bratcher, Robert G. *Bible Translator* 13 (1962): 234–36.
Culpepper, R. Alan. "The New American Standard Bible." *Review and Expositor* 76 (1976): 351–61.
Hodges, Z. C. *Bibliotheca Sacra* 121 (1964): 267–68.
Pfeifer, C. J. *Worship* 45 (1971): 102–13.

CHAPTER 15. THE LIVING BIBLE

Bowman, R. C. "The Living Bible: A Critique." *Brethren Life and Thought* 18 (1973): 137–44.
Garland, David E. "The Living Bible." *Review and Expositor* 76 (1979): 387–408.
Neufeld, Don F. "Will the New Bibles Let You Down?" *Insight*, 29 February 1972, pp. 14–18.
Smart, James D. "The Living Bible." *Duke Divinity Review* 44 (1979): 137–41.
"The Story of the Living Bible." *Eternity*, April 1973, pp. 64–65, 74–75.

Reviews

Bratcher, Robert G. *Bible Translator* 20, no. 3 (1969): 36–39.
Crim, Keith R. *Bible Translator* 22 (1972): 340–44.
Douglas, J. D. "The Living Bible." *Christianity Today*, 5 October 1979, p. 78.
Ellington, John. *Presbyterian Survey*, October 1978, pp. 9–11.
Houston, Jack. *Moody Monthly*, November 1971, pp. 28, 68, 69.
Kerr, William. "Living Bible: Not Just Another Version." *Christianity Today*, 23 May 1975, pp. 29–40.
Leaney, R. *Church Quarterly Review* 167 (1966): 255–56.
Smart, James D. *Presbyterian Record*, July-August.
Waltke, B. K. *Bibliotheca Sacra* 125 (1968): 73–74.

CHAPTER 16. THE NEW INTERNATIONAL VERSION

All About the NIV (Brochure) Grand Rapids: Zondervan Publishing House.
Bratcher, Robert G. "The New International Version." *Duke Divinity Review* 44 (1979): 164–79.

Harris, R. Laird, and Hardwick, Stanley E. "Do Evangelicals Need a New Bible Translation?" *Christianity Today*, 27 September 1968, pp. 10–15.

Linton, Calvin D. "NIV Style." *Christianity Today*, 28 September 1973, p. 41.

Miller, E. L. "The New International Version of the Prologue of John." *Harvard Theological Review*, 72 (1979): 307–11.

Paine, Stephen W. "Why We Need Another Translation." *United Evangelical Action*, October 1967.

Stagg, Frank. "The New International Version: New Testament." *Review and Expositor* 76 (1979): 377–85.

Tate, Marvin E. "The New International Version: The Old Testament." *Review and Expositor* 76 (1979): 363–75.

_____. *The Story of The New International Verson* (Pamphlet) New York International Bible Society, 1978.

Youngblood, Carolyn Johnson. "The New International Version Translation Project: Its Conception and Implementation." *Journal of the Evangelical Theological Society* 21 (1978): 239–49.

Reviews

Bruce, F. F. *Christianity Today* 17 (1973): 25–31.

_____. *Eternity* 70 (1979): 46–47.

Craigie, P. C. *Journal of the Evangelical Theological Society* 21 (1978): 251–54.

De Boer, W. P. *Calvin Theological Journal* 10 (1975): 66–78.

Doyle, B. R. *Australian Biblical Review* 23 (1975): 37–38.

Lasor, W. S. *Christianity Today*, 20 October 1978, pp. 78–80.

Ludlow, William L. *Church Management: The Clergy Review*, January 1974, pp. 23–25.

MacRae, George W. *America*, 23 November 1974, p. 330.

Miller, Donald G. *Eternity*, March 1974, pp. 46–47, 50, 52.

Moody, Dale. *Review and Expositor* 71 (1974): 397–98.

Payne, D. F. *Evangelical Quarterly* 51 (1979): 235–38.

Ryken, Leland. *Christianity Today*, 20 October 1978, pp. 76–77.

Scaer, David P. "The New International Version—Nothing New." *Concordia Theological Quarterly* 43 (1979): 242–45.

Scholer, David M. *Journal of Biblical Literature* 93 (1974): 591–94.

Skilton, J. H. *Westminster Theological Journal* 37 (1975): 256–65.

CHAPTER 17. THE NEW KING JAMES VERSION

Carson, D. A. *The King James Version Debate.* Grand Rapids: Baker Book House, 1979.

"Making the King James Even Better" (Brochure) Nashville: Thomas Nelson & Sons.

"The New King James Bible New Testament: Monograph 1" and "Monograph 2" (Pamphlets). Nashville: Thomas Nelson & Sons, 1979.

Reviews

Elwell, W. A. *Christianity Today,* 1 November 1979, pp. 44f.

Mooday, D. *Review and Expositor* 77 (1980): 110–13.

Studer, Gerald C. *Eternity* 30 (1979): 44–45.

The Debate: The Textus Receptus Vs. A Critical Greek Text

Carson, D. A. *The King James Version Debate.* Grand Rapids: Baker Book House, 1979.

Fee, Gordon D. "Modern Textual Criticism and the Revival of the Textus Receptus." *Journal of the Evangelical Theological Society* 21:1 (March 1978): 19–33.

_____. "Modern Textual Criticism and the Majority Text: A Rejoinder." *Journal of the Evangelical Theological Society* 21:2 (June 1978): 157–60.

_____. "The Textual Criticism of the New Testament." *Biblical Criticism—Historical, Literary and Textual,* by Harrison, Waltke, Guthrie, and Fee. Grand Rapids: Zondervan, 1978.

Fuller, David Otis, ed. *Which Bible?* 3rd ed., Revised and Enlarged. Grand Rapids: International Publications, 1972.

Hodges, Zane C. "Modern Textual Criticism and the Majority Text: A Response." *Journal of the Evangelical Theological Society* 21:2 (June 1978): 143–55.

Hodges, Zane C., and Farstad, Arthur L., eds. *The Greek New Testament According to the Majority Text.* Nashville, Camden, New York: Thomas Nelson & Sons, 1982.

Kenyon, Sir Frederic. *Our Bible and the Ancient Manuscripts.* Revised by A. W. Adams. New York: Harper & Brothers, 1958, pp. 154–78.

Pickering, Wilbur N. "'Queen Anne . . .' and All That: A Response." *Journal of the Evangelical Theological Society* 21:2 (June 1978): 165–67.

Pickering, Wilbur N. *The Identity of the New Testament Text.* Nashville and New York: Thomas Nelson & Sons, 1977.

Robertson, A. T. *An Introduction to the Textual Criticism of the New Testament.* New York: George H. Doran, 1925, pp. 17–40.

Taylor, Richard A. "'Queen Anne' Revisited: A Rejoinder." *Journal of the Evangelical Theological Society* 21:2 (June 1978): 169–71.

CHAPTER 20. GUIDELINES

Fee, Gordon D. "The Text of the New Testament and Modern Translations." *Christianity Today*, 22 June 1973, pp. 6–11.

Hawthorne, Gerald F. "After the King James Version, What?" *Eternity*, September 1973, pp. 29–33.

Kubo, Sakae. "What Should I Look for in Choosing a Bible Version?" *These Times*, Special Issue, June 1974, pp. 30–33.

Kubo, Sakae and Specht, Walter F. *Which Version Today?* Washington, D.C.: Biblical Research Committee, 1976.

Pilch, John J. "Selecting a Bible Translation." *Biblical Theology Bulletin* 10 (1980): 71–77.

Specht, Walter F. "Which Bible Today?" *Loma Linda University Scope*, July-September, 1980, pp. 25–33.

_____. "Which Bible Is Best for You?" *Eternity*, April 1974, pp. 27–31.